WITHDRAWN

Crisis and Conversion
in Apuleius' *Metamorphoses*

Crisis and Conversion
in Apuleius' *Metamorphoses*

Nancy Shumate

Ann Arbor

THE UNIVERSITY OF MICHIGAN PRESS

1999   1998   1997   1996   4   3   2   1

A CIP catalog record for this book is available from the British Library

Library of Congress Cataloging-in-Publication Data

Shumate, Nancy.
    Crisis and conversion in Apuleius' Metamorphoses / Nancy Shumate.
        p.   cm.
    Includes bibliographical references and index.
    ISBN 0-472-10599-X (alk. paper)
    1. Apuleius. Metamorphoses. 2. Latin fiction—History and
criticism. 3. Mythology, Classical, in literature.
4. Metamorphosis in literature.   I. Title.
PA6217.S48   1995
873'.01—dc20   95-25607
                                                                      CIP

illis qui mihi novos mundos aperuerunt,
in primis illi quae nuperrime

Acknowledgments

I would like to thank Ellen Bauerle of the University of Michigan Press for her expert guidance both in editorial and more substantive matters at all stages of the manuscript's preparation. The anonymous readers for the University of Michigan Press provided useful commentary and constructive criticism at various points in the book's development. My colleague Ann Rosalind Jones read the entire draft with her keen comparatist's eye and offered many helpful insights and suggestions. A special thanks is due to Zeph Stewart for supporting the project at its inception and for continuing to do so over the years as it lurched sporadically toward its present form. Any errors or omissions remaining in spite of the efforts of those mentioned are of course my own.

Gathering together the large collection of sometimes obscure secondary literature would not have been possible without the unfailingly efficient and cheerful services of the Interlibrary Loan department of Neilson Library at Smith College. I am also grateful to Smith College for granting me a sabbatical and leave in 1990–91, and for awarding me a Jean Picker Fellowship in 1992–93, both of which gave me much needed time for uninterrupted work.

Substantial portions of chapter 4 originally appeared in "The Augustinian Pursuit of False Values as a Conversion Motif in Apuleius' *Metamorphoses*," *Phoenix* 42 (1988): 35–60. I am grateful to the editors of that journal for permission to reproduce those portions here.

Contents

Introduction. Apuleius' *Metamorphoses:*
    Critical History, Cultural Context   1

Part 1: Things Fall Apart
Chapter 1. Books 1–4.27: The Material World   43
Chapter 2. Books 6.25–10: The Social World   91

Part 2: The "Sick Soul"
Chapter 3. The Role of Disintegration in Crisis
    and Conversion: Classic and Modern Views   137
Chapter 4. Autobiographical Representation   201
Chapter 5. Poetic and Fictional Representation   251

Part 3: The New World
Chapter 6. Book 11: Conversion as Integration   285

References   329
Index   339

Introduction

Apuleius' *Metamorphoses:* **Critical History, Cultural Context**

This book represents a new reading of the *Metamorphoses* of Apuleius as a narrative of religious experience and specifically as a narrative of conversion. As such, it is, I think, quite different from any of the range of religious readings produced in the past. Of course, in the era after John Winkler's landmark study *Auctor and Actor,* any approach to this complex piece of Latin prose fiction that gives even the appearance of claiming to be definitive is bound to be greeted with skepticism.[1] It is fair to say that Winkler rewrote the rules of Apuleian criticism, squarely confronting the central fact about the *Metamorphoses* that generations of critics perhaps uncomfortably suspected but nevertheless managed to suppress: that no totalizing scheme can account for all the novel's disparate and in some respects apparently contradictory elements. According to Winkler, the problem with Apuleian studies has been that the novel's critics, almost exclusively classicists, have labored under "the conventional premises of modern historical and literary studies, that the reader qua reader is an opaque, characterless, subservient receptor of the author's message and that the scholar too is a self-effacing servant of the fetishized text" (1985, 187). In Winkler's critical universe this is a dubious way to read any text, but in the case of the *Metamorphoses* it is particularly distorting because of the novel's character as an "open-ended problem text" whose "revisionary interplay of shifting meanings" encourages the reader's participation and in fact requires the reader's active intervention in order for any sense to be made of it at all (241, 187).

---

1. For those unfamiliar with them, an easily accessible account of the life and works of Apuleius against a background of the major literary and intellectual currents of the second century A.D. can be found in Walsh 1982, 774–86. On the work's two traditional titles, *Metamorphoses* and *Asinus Aureus* (The Golden Ass), see chapter 1, n. 9.

Rather than encoding the novel with a monolithic "message" of his own to be extracted by subsequent generations of readers, the author has, in Winkler's view, "invested the reader with the opportunity, the materials, and the necessity for interpreting Lucius's narrative one way or another." Apuleius has given us a kind of toolbox full of parts that we can reassemble in any number of different ways (222). Thus the *Metamorphoses* is a sort of do-it-yourself novel, a prototypical polysemic text. It is "dialogic," as Winkler says, from beginning to end, and its often vilified failure to tie up loose ends by the time the Isisbook comes to a close, and to fill in the "flexible space in which the [*Metamorphoses* has] been continually playing," is the result of a deliberate choice on the author's part. Apuleius meant to create a silence that would encourage writing by the reader, a "gap" that "no spark can cross . . . but what the reader supplies" (195, 224). The *Metamorphoses,* Winkler argues, is a "deliberately unauthorized, self-questioning performance" characterized by the multiplication of perspectives and a ringing refusal to be univocal. We get no "clear and final authorization" of one meaning from either the narrator or the author (126, 131). I accept the premises put forward in Winkler's *prolegomenon,* as he himself calls it; what follows is *a* reading of the *Metamorphoses,* not *the* reading. Furthermore, in the course of the argument it will become clear that Winkler's approach and mine complement each other in unexpected ways. This is because the strains of contemporary literary theory that inform his reading and the ideas from the social psychology of religion on which I will be drawing ultimately intersect in issues of cognition and epistemology. The instability of knowledge, whose expressions in the *Metamorphoses* Winkler explicates with poststructuralist glee, turns out to have the potential for playing a major role in certain kinds of religious experience.

Before Winkler the world of Apuleian criticism was fairly clearly mapped.[2] On the one hand, there has always been a "bawdy" school whose adherents have taken the work as an uncomplicated comic romance, a source of pleasant diversion and lascivious entertainment for the reader. On the other hand, there have been those who take the *Metamorphoses* seriously, so to speak, by building their reading of it

---

2. Winkler (1985, 5–6) offers his own summary of the "five major critical readings of [the *Metamorphoses*] that are now current."

around the perception of some unifying philosophical, religious, or moral scheme. The first group of critics has tended to deny the Isis-book any real status as a document of religious experience; instead they have explained it away as simply the last and most spectacular of Lucius' many cheap thrills. When they could not quite persuade themselves that Book 11 lacks any trace of convincing religious solemnity and awe, they have been puzzled by the apparent tonal disjunction between the final book and the preceding ten. It is fair to say that B.E. Perry is the uncontested patriarch of this school of Apuleian studies, and he expressed its views as succinctly as anyone. Perry concedes that Book 11 has a certain power as an invocation of religious experience, but argues that it was tacked on "in a very perfunctory and superficial fashion" in order to get the whole book past the censors, so to speak. By trotting out Isis at the end, Apuleius accomplished his two main objectives:

> [T]he author will have delivered . . . the kind of entertainment with which he knew that his readers would be charmed, in spite of its disrespectability as literature; and . . . his book . . . will have been redeemed . . . from the appearance of complete frivolity and from the scorn of his learned contemporaries. (1967, 244–45)

Perry's assumption that prose fiction was universally viewed as a literary form that precluded the possibility of serious intellectual content is problematic; I will return to this question momentarily. In his view, Book 11 of the *Metamorphoses* was added as the arbitrary conclusion in a "mechanical way" that dooms all efforts to see in the earlier parts of the novel any preparation for the events of the finale (234). Perry's conclusion is that the "real nature and *raison d'être* of the *Metamorphoses* [is to be] primarily a series of mundane stories exploited on their own account as such for the reader's entertainment." He furthermore locates the novel's roots—or some of them—in paradoxography, when he says that one of its main concerns is simply to move "from the contemplation of one wonderful thing to another" (242–43).[3]

---

3. In *The Ancient Romances* (1967), Perry reiterates positions that he began to develop much earlier in a series of articles (e.g., 1925, 1929). For a similar view of the *Metamorphoses*, see, e.g., Helm 1961.

To a great extent, readings such as that of Perry were informed by the assumption that something like the *Metamorphoses* could only have been frivolous, that this was all that lay within the "horizons of expectation" of ancient readers when they picked up such a text. Perry says as much: the romance or novel was a "despised form" in antiquity, one that was never even considered to merit discussion or classification by the ancient critics. Romances were cranked out "in defiance of the intellectual fashion" to satisfy popular taste, but those desiring respectability as writers and a solid literary reputation avoided contamination through contact with the genre. This, according to Perry, is why Apuleius felt the need to graft the disjunctive religious resolution onto his work: to prevent the *Metamorphoses* from being taken as trash in toto (1967, 245–47). Few critics today take such a dismissive view of the potential of ancient prose fiction to be a site of intellectual discourse or of ideological engagement, whether these took the form of ideas incorporated consciously by the author or of cultural values inextricably tied up with the genesis and continued production of the form.

Still, the scanty evidence pertaining to the reception of the *Metamorphoses* in antiquity suggests some ancient readings of the work not far from Perry's, except that they apparently fail to take even the conclusion "seriously." In the late collection of lives of the Roman emperors known as the *Historia Augusta*, the biographer Julius Capitolinus includes in his life of Clodius Albinus a letter of Clodius' enemy Septimius Severus in which Severus attacks the former's character on the grounds that he has a taste for the frivolous stories and Milesian tales of Apuleius (*Vita Clodii Albini* 12). In the prologue to the *Metamorphoses*, Apuleius himself appears to invite the identification of his work with the tradition of often pornographic short stories known as Milesian tales when he announces his plan to weave together stories "in the Milesian style" [*sermone isto Milesio*] (1.1). It is far from certain which aspect of his work Apuleius means to designate by this phrase, but there is little doubt that its appearance would invoke this "low" tradition and its connotations in broad terms, at least. This is reflected in the *HA* passage, which seems to express the general repute in antiquity of both the Milesian tale and the self-incriminating *Metamorphoses*. A second pejorative reference to the novel of Apuleius comes in the commentary on Cicero's *Somnium Scipionis* by the fourth-century Platonist

Macrobius. Macrobius is discussing the validity of using myths and fictions for didactic purposes. He decides that this strategy is acceptable because it can beguile people into virtue just as comedies and erotic tales *(argumenta fictis casibus amatorum referta)* can beguile them, presumably into other things (1.2.8). In connection with the latter type of fiction, he mentions Apuleius, in a tone of shock and disappointment *(quibus . . . Apuleium nonnumquam lusisse miramur).* Although there is nothing in Macrobius of the Milesian connection, the spirit of his comment is clear enough, and it is clear as well that he specifically excludes the *Metamorphoses* from the realm of therapeutic fictions. As Tatum puts it, "it is difficult to avoid the conclusion that Apuleius described his novel in such a way as virtually to guarantee its being taken for a piece of triviality."[4]

But Apuleius is a master of irony, and his self-presentation often plays off other truths in complex parodic ways. Furthermore, here we have out of any number of possible citations of the *Metamorphoses* from antiquity itself only two that happen to be condemnations of sorts, preserved like all other ancient evidence by sheer accident. As it happens, both surviving pagan references indicate a tendency to see only the scabrous aspects of the *Metamorphoses* and to be blind to its considerable nonscabrous content, much of which is scarcely obscure (the Platonic overtones of the tale of Cupid and Psyche, for example). In spite of the absence of specific testimony to the effect that the novel received serious readings in its own cultural setting, there are reasons to believe that the contemporary horizons of expectation for a work of its kind would have allowed for such a reading. Indeed, this is the assumption behind virtually all Apuleian criticism in the era after Perry, even if the exact character of the novel's seri-

---

4. 1979, 101. See Tatum 1979, 92–104 on the Milesian tale, its repute in antiquity, and the implication of the *Metamorphoses* in that tradition. See also Perry 1967, 372 n. 11 on the assessments of the novel implied in Julius Capitolinus and Macrobius ("the fellow countrymen of Apuleius in Africa had no difficulty in seeing through his disguise, and were shocked by the triviality of his performance"). The other surviving citation of the *Metamorphoses* from antiquity is in Augustine, but it is not relevant to the question of whether the novel, or its genre, was read as "serious" or "frivolous." At *de Civitate Dei* 18.18, Augustine uses the *Metamorphoses* as source material in his discussion of the plausibility of magical transformations.

ous content is still very much a matter of dispute.[5] Before we consider these reasons, however, let us examine more closely what I mean when I say "a work such as the *Metamorphoses*." What *is* the *Metamorphoses* generically? What literary strains and traditions feed into it? The work appears to have as hybrid a pedigree as a literary text could have in antiquity, drawing not only on several established genres for general models, but also on a specific Greek predecessor in the form of an existing ass narrative.

The evidence suggests that there were three such literary narratives circulating in antiquity, and efforts to sort out their relationship have a long and tortured history. The two pieces of evidence other than the *Metamorphoses* itself are, first, a short ass narrative in Greek that in its general outline as well as in many details parallels the Apuleian version, entitled *Lucius or the Ass* (hereafter the *Onos*) and transmitted in the corpus of the satirist Lucian; and second, a discussion in the ninth-century Byzantine scholar and patriarch Photius of two ass narratives recently encountered by him in his voracious reading. One is apparently the clearly satiric (Photius recognizes this) *Onos*. The other is a lost work called *Metamorphoses*, written in Greek by one Lucius of Patrae in an uncritical and credulous spirit, according to Photius (*Bibliotheca*, cod. 129). Photius is unsure which of these two patently related Greek works came first, but current scholarly consensus holds that "Lucius of Patrae" preceded both the *Onos* and the *Metamorphoses* of Apuleius, the former being an abridgement of "Lucius," the latter an expansion, although the problem of the exact degree and nature of that expansion will remain intractable. Photius was probably wrong in his reading of the tone of "Lucius," conflating the credulous narrator "Lucius" and the skeptical author, who is now generally agreed to have

---

5. Reviewing P. James 1987 and Gianotti 1986, the latter of which itself represents current critics' lack of hesitation to connect the *Metamorphoses* with "ideology," Elsom (1988, 248–49) writes: "After a long tradition of evaluative readings, dating at least from Macrobius, Apuleius' *Golden Ass* has at last found scholarly readers prepared to take on its epistemological and encyclopaedic challenge." Her comment reflects the assumption of most modern critics that some sort of treatment of epistemological questions was within the capacities of ancient prose fiction, even if these subtleties were lost on the two surviving ancient commentators.

been none other than Lucian himself. The *Onos*, then, would be an epitome of a Lucianic work done by another hand.[6]

At this juncture the point of all this for our purposes is to determine
whether Apuleius' particular model was bound by the constraints of its
genre to be read entirely for delectation. If, as most now agree, the
Greek *Metamorphoses* was by the satirist Lucian, then in a general sense
Apuleius was operating within the realm of the "serious" (for want of
a better term) in drawing on it, since in spite of its often uproarious
comic strategies, satirical writing in antiquity was always ultimately
critical and didactic. But Apuleius' performance is more complex than
the simple reproduction of a Lucianic satire whose object of ridicule
was a common type of quest narrative found in the paradoxographic
tradition, a type in which the protagonist or narrator searches for wonders or secret knowledge. What the Latin author has done is preserve
much of the satiric tone, but subvert it by adding (among other things)
the vividly and in many ways sympathetically depicted religious resolution, so that what we end up with is simultaneously a satire of
credulity and a seductive evocation of religious belief. He has sabo-
taged the parodic tone of the Lucianic original while keeping it very
much in play; he has taken inherited materials and established generic
conventions and forged, as Winkler puts it, a "vehicle for both belief
and ridicule of belief."[7] It is characteristically Apuleian to wreak havoc
on traditional definitions of genre by transgressing generic boundaries
and combining generic values in this way, and this originality greatly
vexes the question of what the ancient horizons of expectation for the
Metamorphoses would have been.

---

6. Photius' probable slip in confusing author and narrator should not
cause us to smirk at his critical naïveté; until relatively recently just such a conflation characterized much criticism of the Latin *Metamorphoses*. It was Perry
who originally developed the thesis that Photius' author "Lucius of Patrae"
was actually Lucian (1920). For brief accounts of the history of the problem of
the three asses, see Mason 1978 and Winkler 1985, 252–56; also Schlam 1992,
18–28; and P. James 1987, 7–24. All of these provide bibliography for those
inclined to follow this detective story in more detail.

7. 1985, 256. See also 256–75 for more on the thesis of "parody lost" (in
Winkler's words), which Winkler develops from Perry's (1920) conclusion that
the lost Greek *Metamorphoses* was a satire of a paradoxographical narrative
much as was Lucian's *True History*. In the course of his discussion Winkler
examines various exemplars of this type of narrative. On parodoxographical
elements in the Latin *Metamorphoses* in general, see Scobie 1969, 30–54.

In addition to its twisted roots in satire and paradoxography, the *Metamorphoses* owes something to at least two other ancient genres. We have already mentioned its association with the Milesian tale, which both ancient and modern critics agree was a form concerned primarily with delectation and titillation. The *Metamorphoses* also has many formal and thematic affinities with the body of surviving fictional narratives in prose known collectively as the Greek novel or romance. These terms are used by modern critics to designate the broad and variegated genre encompassing the five extant "ideal" romances (young lovers separated and reunited after a series of implausible adventures) as well as numerous related prose narratives. The surviving exemplars of this type of literature have been thought to span as many as five centuries (first B.C. to fourth A.D.) in their dates of composition, depending on who is doing the reckoning.[8] Clearly, much in the *Metamorphoses* is novelistic, from broad themes and patterns down to details of motif: the structuring of the narrative around travels; the prominence of Fortuna-*Tuche* and other types of divine intervention; the operation of Eros; stock characters such as robbers and beautiful and virtuous damsels in distress; and elaborate digressive descriptions of art and nature, to name but a few examples of common ground, even if that ground shifts through parody in the *Metamorphoses*.

Perry's views notwithstanding, the Greek novels were ideological texts par excellence. This is especially evident in connection with what we might now call bourgeois values, which the ideal romance inscribed and promoted in countless ways. If indeed the novels were read primarily as entertainment, then they provide a perfect illustration of the principle that the masks of ideology are more dangerous than ideology itself. The form's prescriptive potential can be seen even more clearly in its Jewish and Christian incarnations. The Jewish romance of *Joseph and Aseneth* and the romance of St. Clement or the *Acts of Paul and Thecla* typify the directed adaptation of the novelistic adventure-story frame

---

8. See Bowie 1985 for a brief introductory discussion of the genre and some of the problems that it has presented to scholars; for a survey of recent work on the ancient novel, see Bowie and Harrison 1993. The Greek novels and related works are now conveniently available in modern English translations in Reardon 1989. General studies of the novel in antiquity include Anderson 1982 and 1984; Hägg 1983; Heiserman 1977; Kuch 1985 and 1992; and Reardon 1991; see also Tatum 1994. On the novel's intended audience, see Levin 1977 and Wesseling 1988.

by Jewish and Christian writers for religious purposes. In the Christian era there seems to have been a very large body of this type of literature in circulation.[9] Religion can figure prominently in the pagan novels as well, although there is a difference between the critically timed and often melodramatic divine interventions that abound in the Greek narratives and the personal conversion of the narrator that distinguishes the *Metamorphoses.* Isis is also the saving divinity in, for example, the *Ephesian Tale* of Xenophon of Ephesus, but there she presides over a restoration of the civic and moral status quo rather than the rupture of the status quo that Lucius' conversion represents. In any case, the Greek novelistic tradition in general shows a clear enough pattern of imbrication between narrative form and ideological content—religious or social, masked or naked—that it is unlikely that all readers or all authors would have been unaware of the possibilities.

Apart from the "serious" potential inherent in any of the genres or permutations of genre upon which he drew, Apuleius had behind him the much larger tradition of *spoudaiogeloion,* or the interpenetration of the comic and the serious, which can be traced over a long period of time in many different branches of Greek and Latin literature. Horace left us one of the best known and most succinct expressions of the principle of *spoudaiogeloion* in *Satire* 1.1.24–25: "What prevents me from telling the truth laughing?" [*ridentem dicere verum / quid vetat?*], he asks. The tradition of combining instruction and entertainment was alive and well in the literary milieu of Apuleius, as we can see from the observation of his contemporary Aulus Gellius that the best way to make sure an audience will grasp a salutary truth is to put it in the form of an entertaining story (*Attic Nights* 2.29). In this context a rigid dichotomy between "seriousness" and "frivolity"—the "time-honored antipodes of Apuleian criticism," as Tatum puts it (1979, 103)—begins to seem misplaced as we consider the *Metamorphoses.*[10] The evidence

---

9. On Christian fiction in general, see Koester 1982; also (e.g.) Gallagher 1990, 121–23 on Joseph, and Misch 1951, 492–93 on the *Clementina.* Braun 1938 remains a useful treatment of what he calls Jewish-Hellenistic or Greco-Oriental novelistic literature.

10. On *spoudaiogeloion* in Greek and Latin literature in general, see Giangrande 1972. Studies of the *Metamorphoses* that focus on its techniques of *spoudaiogeloion* include those of Beaujeu 1975 and Schlam 1992. Of course, this is precisely Winkler's ultimate concern as well, and his study remains by far the most sophisticated treatment of the novel's seriocomic character to date.

suggests that ancient readers would have been conditioned to negotiate undismayed the coexistence of comic and serious modes in the same text, and that that text could belong formally to any one of several genres, or to a combination thereof. It will become clear that my approach simply expands the range of possible readings of the novel's serious content beyond those that are already reasonably well established. But the expansion is significant, because it moves from a more or less accepted notion of ancient prose fiction as a potential medium for the discussion of philosophical issues or the prescription of cultural values to one that grants this ancient form the very modern ability to represent the (imagined) subjective experience of a fictional narrator-protagonist.

We can see, then, that the inclination of recent critics to take the *Metamorphoses* in some sense seriously is justified, even if the form that their serious reading takes is a view of the novel as engaging in some kind of serious play; Winkler represents the most elaborate working out of such a view. More conventionally, "serious" readings have tended to focus on identifying the work's philosophical or religious content. The most common of the philosophical readings treats the *Metamorphoses* as a sort of fictionalized Platonic treatise. It is an allegory representing the ascent of the soul in stages from its limited existence in this world of transience and illusion to participation in the true reality of the ideal world. Plato had first articulated this vision of spiritual ascent in the *Phaedrus* and the *Symposium*. Commentators and critics with this orientation have concentrated in particular on the apparently allegorizing features of the tale of Cupid and Psyche (Books 4.28–6.24). Platonism offers a plausible framework upon which to construct a signification for the *Metamorphoses*, not only because of the suggestions of the text itself, but also because we know that the author was a prominent figure in Middle Platonism whose *oeuvre* included rather derivative Platonic treatises as well as this comic novel. Furthermore, the well-documented syncretistic tendencies of the age make a fusion of Platonic philosophy and Isiac religion not at all strange in a text from the imperial period; Plutarch's treatise *On Isis and Osiris* makes this very clear. There is no question that the *Metamorphoses* has Platonic features. But rather than replicate the work already done in this connection or continue in this vein, I propose to approach the *Metamorphoses* from another angle and in the process situate earlier Platonically oriented studies of the novel in a larger context. By identifying the generic features that make the novel a prototypical narrative of conversion, we may learn something new about what conversion meant in Platonism.[11]

Religious (as opposed to philosophical) readings of the *Metamorphoses* have taken essentially two forms. One concentrates heavily on the aspects of the novel that allegedly represent Isiac myth and actual cult practice. According to this view, a system of allusions to Isiac *arcana* pervades the text and anticipates its culmination in Lucius' initiation into the cult of Isis in the final book. The most extreme example of this approach is the work of Merkelbach (1962), who argued essentially that the novel was an elaborately encoded mystery text fully intelligible only to initiates. I do not claim that all such cult-centered readings of the novel lack validity, but when they are carried to the extreme of obscure detail invoked by Merkelbach, they begin to seem implausible in the extreme, if not fantastic. Furthermore these readings tend to reproduce a blind spot that characterizes the study of Greco-Roman paganism in general: they focus entirely on the externalized manifestations and the narratives of religion—rituals, actions, myths—while avoiding the question of what emotional and cognitive content such actions and myths, and indeed cult membership and a relationship with the divine in general, had for the religious individual. Finally, approaches to the novel based on locating Isiac symbolism in it inevitably privilege Book 11 as an almost independently standing episode, without explaining what the previous ten-elevenths of the novel have to do with it. The last problem is not, however, limited to cultic readings. General discussions of personal religious experience in antiquity that draw on the "experience" of Lucius have also tended to sound as if the Isisbook were the *Metamorphoses* in its entirety. Thus Nock, in his chapter on the conversion of Lucius, barely mentions Books 1 through 10, making no attempt to find there (and where else could it be found?) what it is that brings Lucius to Isis (1933, 138–55).[12]

---

11. For further discussion, with relevant bibliography, of Platonism in the *Metamorphoses* and especially in the tale of Cupid and Psyche, see chapter 5, section 1 and notes.

12. The chapter of Festugière 1954, 68–84 is similar in this regard. The thesis of Merkelbach 1962 was greeted with general skepticism; see, e.g., the review of Turcan 1963. Other examples of readings that foreground cult *arcana* are those of Derchain and Hubaux 1958 and Griffiths 1978. Burkert 1987 uses the *Metamorphoses* as a source for the historical cult of Isis and the "ancient mystery cults" in general.

The other type of religious reading is built around a more general moral scheme involving ideas of sin, punishment, and redemption. The tradition of reading the *Metamorphoses* as a moral allegory goes back at least as far as the Renaissance. In the introduction to his Elizabethan translation, Adlington offers this view of the significance of the story for the conduct of its readers' lives: "Verily under the wrap of this transformation is taxed the life of mortal man, when as we suffer our minds to be so drowned in the sensual lusts of the flesh and the beastly pleasure thereof . . . we lose wholly the use of reason and virtue . . . which . . . by mediation of prayer we may assuredly attain" (in Gaselee 1977, xvi–xvii). Four centuries later, Festugière (1954, 77) and Vallette (1972, xxxiv), among others, still tread this path, the one deeming the *Metamorphoses* "the story of a soul which fell, and which suffered by reason of that fall, and which the merciful hand of Isis raised up and saved"; the other seeing in Lucius "a creature who fell into perdition" on account of his "fatal curiosity." In the same spirit, Walsh speaks of the hero as traveling along "a course of slavish sensuality . . . [in which] a connection is implied between his sexual obsession . . . and his obsession with magic." Walsh concludes that "Lucius' sufferings as an ass are a punishment for involving himself in base sensuality and magic" (1970, 177).

I agree that sex and magic are to be connected as representing destructive impulses in the text but not in the sense that Walsh suggests, as we will see; and I will argue that any cause-and-effect idea of punishment meted out specifically for transgressions in those areas is wholly inappropriate. A variation of the moralistic approach to the novel's religious content identifies the many inserted tales as negative moral *exempla* that mirror and implicitly condemn Lucius' own sexual self-indulgence and his curiosity about magic. Here also, it is these two vices of Lucius that make him culpable for his own misfortunes prior to his rescue by Isis. As Tatum puts it straightforwardly, "Lucius is transformed into an ass as a punishment for his lust and *curiositas*. . . . [I]t is . . . weakness of the flesh which [the] narrator Lucius finally rejects altogether" (1972, 308, 312; see also 1969). It is true that Lucius' life with Isis appears to involve certain concessions to religious asceticism. Still, in my mind, more vaguely Christian erotophobia informs these readings than is appropriate as we grapple with a pagan text that in fact appears actually to celebrate sex in certain circumstances, even cross-species sex, as we will see. I will argue that sex per se is not presented as being morally problematic in the *Metamorphoses* and that the hero's tendency to allow himself to be pulled off course to pursue sexual and magical adventures is symptomatic of a much more general failure. His "sin"— his *hamartia*, his missing the mark—and the substance of his preconversion crisis are not what we might call moral, but rather epistemological.

In a sense, Winkler can oddly enough be viewed as working within the tradition of religious readings of the *Metamorphoses*. There is, however, a fundamental difference that sets him distinctly apart from the others: whereas they want to make the novel a statement of some kind of religious belief, Winkler argues that ultimately it is a statement of religious skepticism. If the author has an overarching "message," it is about the arbitrary nature of religious knowledge and the highly subjective character of religious experience; the open text itself serves as a kind of illustration of this principle. As Winkler explains:

> The [*Metamorphoses*] insistently raises and evades the question of its own authoritative meaning as a way of illustrating and actually reproducing the state of aporia toward the cosmos that can only be resolved by a radically individual and unsharable leap of faith. Apuleius does not recommend that leap, he does not discourage that leap, he only signifies that it is there for some to make. (1985, 125)

Thus the "exquisite ambiguity" of the text has been purposefully contrived by the author to allow the reader to "rewrite" the text according to whether he or she has the temperament of a religious believer or a religious skeptic. Apuleius has incorporated both positions while endorsing neither, according to Winkler; he has "made both responses possible as a lesson about the nature of religious conviction" (226). Neither the book nor life can be unified except through an individual "reader's" perhaps informed, but ultimately arbitrary, decision to see it in a certain way (131–32). Even as Lucius must simply decide whether to accept an integrating structure that makes sense of his fragmented experience, so we as readers must arbitrarily "supply [the] missing rule" that gives the text a meaning and brings it to closure. "The essential experience of reading the [*Metamorphoses*]," writes Winkler, "is that we watch from the ground while Lucius ascends into some realm of light above the clouds and that we cannot follow" (317).[13]

Winkler's view of the *Metamorphoses* as a statement about the arbitrary nature of religious (and by extension, all) knowledge depends on his now well-established distinction between the *auctor* and the *actor*, or more precisely, between (or among) Apuleius the (skeptical) author, Lucius the author-narrator, and Lucius the (credulous) *actor* or experiencing ego moving through the past (re)constructed by the narrative. Winkler's focus on the *auctor* Apuleius and his tricks led him, I think, to ignore the "credulous" track or voice in the text, with its rich evocation of the religious experience of Lucius the *actor*. It may be true that the overarching lesson of the *Metamorphoses* is that all structures, including religious systems, are arbitrary; that formulating and accepting one interpretation of any text, including the text of the world, is, like religious belief, an act of faith; and that all closure is the product of an act of will on the part of the reader rather than a feature of objective reality. But in the midst of all this premodern poststructuralism, and interacting with it in complex ways, is the compelling picture of the crisis and conversion of Lucius the *actor*, and I do not think that it has been adequately understood as such. This will be the focus of my reading.

I will argue that the experience of Lucius as it is represented in the *Metamorphoses* exemplifies a type of conversion that operates within a cognitive framework rather than a moral one. According to this pattern of crisis and conversion, a perception of the collapse of familiar cognitive constructs precedes the convert's reconstruction of a new world and world view along religious lines. The process of conversion is a kind of shift in cognitive paradigms, and the period of crisis before conversion is an unsettling sojourn in paradigm limbo, so to speak, during which habituated structures of meaning and systems for organizing

---

13. Winkler further explains: "[The *Metamorphoses*] presents a value-free description of what a conversion with cosmic, life-reorienting consequences would be like. 'Value-free' corresponds to what I have been calling non-endorsement and non-authorization, and here I would endorse the remark of Ninian Smart: 'This should not blind us to the fact that such [value-free] descriptions also must be in a certain way value-rich, for they need to be evocative rather than flat, though the evocations themselves are of course bracketed.' The [novel] is an evocation of religious experience bracketed in such a way that the reader must . . . decide on the question of its truth" (179). Winkler quotes from Smart 1973, 21.

reality disintegrate. It is a period of gradual but irremediable alienation from the old "structures of understanding that enable us to locate ourselves in the universe and therefore to function" (Ebel 1970, 161). Religious discourse offers a means of restructuring the preconvert's broken world and of reestablishing a foundation upon which to build a reliable system of knowledge. In this strain of religious experience divinity is not an agent of moral redemption but rather an epistemological anchor and a transcendent source of meaning and order—in poststructuralist terms, a transcendental signified. Religious discourse represents a fixed, grounded, and noncontingent structure of meaning to replace one that was not cosmically rooted and that has been swept away for any of a variety of possible reasons. The process of conversion with which we will be concerned, then, involves nothing less than the collapse of an entire system of premises and assumptions about how the world works and its replacement by one radically different, or at least so it seems to the convert.

The sources upon which I will draw to establish this as a generic model of conversion are eclectic. I will select and synthesize from two apparently very different classes of comparative material: first, modern studies of the psychology and the social psychology of conversion and related phenomena, beginning with the classic work of William James, and then a range of autobiographical, poetic, and fictional first-person narratives of conversion. Texts about conversion generated within modern analytical frameworks and literary representations of conversion as a real or imagined experience of the narrator both yield up the pattern outlined above over and over again. If, as I argue, the pattern is present in the *Metamorphoses* as well, the implications for the novel would seem to depend on which class of *comparanda* is being invoked. In the first case the obvious implication is that there is a certain psychological verisimilitude in the representation of Lucius' religious experience; in the second it is that there are good reasons to expand the generic classification of the *Metamorphoses* beyond the formal boundaries of comic romance or wonder-tale within which it has traditionally been confined. The novel can be resituated very comfortably in the genre "narrative of conversion" and in fact could be said to stand at the head of that tradition.

Of course, no one would argue that the work is *not* a conversion story in its basic outline; its resolution hinges, after all, on its protagonist turning to Isis. Furthermore, it is not the only account of conversion to have been produced in pagan antiquity. On the contrary, in spite of the paucity of surviving exemplars, the evidence suggests that the production of conversion stories was something of an industry in the philosophical schools. But these seem to have been extremely formulaic and superficial in their representation of the preconvert's experience. They typically involve little more than an obligatory tour through the various schools of philosophy by a questing narrator or protagonist in search of an agreeable ethical system. Certainly the *Metamorphoses* shows traces of some of the formulas found in this narrative tradition. But in arguing that the *Metamorphoses* should be reconceptualized as a narrative of conversion, and moreover as a (or even the) prototypical one, I mean that its sophistication as a narrative of subjective experience and its grasp and representation of the complex issues of world building that are often at the center of conversion make it unique in pagan antiquity. In these respects it anticipates a highly developed and clearly identifiable type of conversion narrative ordinarily associated only with later eras.

But to return to the two possible conclusions to be drawn from any demonstration of affinities between the *Metamorphoses* and, on the one hand, theoretical or even clinical descriptions of conversion and, on the other, literary narratives of conversion from later periods, ultimately we will find, I think, that the conclusions suggested above are inadequate, whether taken separately or together. They are too simplistic and too little integrated with each other. What makes them inadequate is the complex relationship between the two types of comparative material—between reality and representation—which colors the meaning of the parallels asserting themselves when the *Metamorphoses* is read against the background of both of them. In order to explain what I mean by this, I need to address a question that in all likelihood has already formulated itself in the reader's mind: are my *comparanda* really comparable? By invoking social scientific texts on the one hand and literary texts on the other, am I not committing the basic methodological error of confusing experience with narrative, reality with representation? What do these two types of artifact have to do with one another? Their relationship is a complicated one. My contention is not simply that there is such a thing as pure, original, and unmediated experience that social science accurately locates and describes and literary narrative faithfully represents, and that the *Metamorphoses* is one of those faithful representations. Rather, reality and representation, experience and narrative reinforce each other in a kind of discursive loop. Narrative is never a transparent mirror of reality; instead, it is inevitably shaped by previous narratives, be they literary or cultural, that is, the larger system of discourses within which the narrative is produced.

Furthermore, these same factors shape experience itself, insofar as we have no choice but to resort to established conceptual systems in order to interpret and describe our experience. Raw experience occurs within particular attributional systems that give it particular and culturally contingent meanings. Literary narratives certainly have a place in such systems, but overarching them are the larger and more thoroughly naturalized master narratives of the culture, which in turn shape subsequent narratives of all kinds as well as experience itself, and on and on. One could say that for all intents and purposes there is no such thing as experience per se or, to put it more precisely, there may be experience but it is not possible for it to have any meaning outside of an attributional system. This is because from the moment subjectivity begins, it enters a discursive system already saturated with interpretations and reports of experience, that is, with the preexisting scripts that we use to make sense of reality. Even areas commonly regarded as bastions of objectivity—notably those of scientific and social scientific inquiry—are not immune. As Thomas Kuhn argued thirty years ago, scientists too work within culturally defined paradigms that inform and limit the way they think about problems. Any "scientific revolution" is defined by a shift in these cognitive paradigms more than by any positivistic advance toward true and objective knowledge.[14]

---

14. Kuhn 1962, about whose theory we will be hearing more in chapter 3. In connection with the question of reality versus representation, I should make it clear that it is not my purpose to conduct original research on religious experience, but rather to synthesize previous studies into a background for reading the *Metamorphoses*. Furthermore, because I regard these studies primarily as components in a system of discourse about conversion, my purpose does not require that I critique either the methodology or the results of the ones I invoke in the sense of attempting to determine how close they come to reconstructing the actual conversion experiences of real people. Finally, this book makes no

None of these qualifications will be new to anyone familiar with the poststructuralist critique of the Aristotelian understanding of representation that has formed the foundation of humanistic criticism. Interestingly enough, intimations of this critique found their way into the psychology of religion very early on. Although on the whole William James was a staunch believer in the premise that there could be "original and unborrowed" experience (1958, 186), he also seemed to appreciate that at least in some cases or to some degree culturally produced models could play a role in culturally producing and defining experience. "The particular form which [converts] affect," he writes, "is the result of suggestion and imitation. If they went through their growth-crisis in other faiths and other countries, although the essence of the change would be the same, the accidents would be different." Quoting from Jonathan Edwards, James notes that even the Puritan firebrand understood that "'what [converts] have experienced is insensibly strained, so as to bring it to an exact conformity to the scheme already established in their minds'" (164–65, n. 5). Elsewhere James suggests that the type of conversion common during the great Protestant revivals in Britain and America in the nineteenth century was a "codified and stereotyped procedure" (184). It is no surprise, given contem-

---

claims to be an exhaustive survey of studies or narratives of conversion. Indeed, such a project would be virtually impossible. By necessity and by design the comparative material that I invoke represents a selection, and a directed one at that. The potential pool of conversion narratives is vast, as is the range of potentially relevant scholarship, which would include "many areas of scholarly work . . . including sociology of religion . . . but also the broad areas of social movements and collective behavior, socialization (and resocialization), deviancy, attitude change (broadly defined to include such phenomena as 'thought reform', and belief and value change), and some other areas of social psychology" (Richardson et al. 1979, 232). To Richardson's list I would add certain branches of philosophy, notably epistemology, and much recent work in literary theory and cultural studies. All of this is potentially relevant to the study of conversion, and much of it would no doubt suggest models of conversion other than the one that I argue is exemplified in the *Metamorphoses*. Like Richardson, I limit myself to the "definable literature of conversion that is generally social psychological in nature." Because of this necessity to select, my book could be viewed as a *prolegomenon*, even as Winkler viewed his as one.

porary intellectual currents, that recent scholars are all the more emphatic in stating the case for the mediated character of religious—and all—experience. Proudfoot, for example, forcefully denies that religious experience is or can be immediate, autonomous, and independent of preexisting theoretical frameworks. He instead claims that:

> Our experience is already informed and constituted by our conceptions and tacit theories about ourselves and the world. All observation is theory-laden. . . . [A]ny perception or experience is already shaped by the concepts and implicit judgments we bring to it. . . . [Religious] experience is shaped by a complex pattern of concepts, commitments, and expectations which [the subject] brings to it. These beliefs and attitudes are formative of, rather than consequent upon, the experience. They define in advance what experiences are possible. (1985, 43, 121)

In other words, cultural discourse (or ideology or doctrine or theory) precedes and informs experience itself.[15]

By the same token, cultural discourse informs any narrative construct imposed upon experience, and moreover, such narratives inform each other across the boundaries of genre. The question of whether autobiographical, fictional, and poetic accounts of conversion can be legitimately compared is another one that will have occurred to the reader, and indeed this question represents a sort of ancillary issue within the more general one of whether the classes of material that I compare are really comparable. Can boundaries of genre be ignored with impunity? Not always; but here, I think that they can. Each of the three types of narrative is a form of mimesis positing the same referent in the real world; each of them is a literary representation of conversion. There is no reason to privilege autobiography as a truer mirror of

---

15. For other discussions of the nexus of ideology, experience, and narrative as it is relevant to religious conversion, see, e.g., Beckford 1978; Hawkins 1985, 22–23, 28, 92–95, 106; Spilka, Hood, and Gorsuch 1985, 187, passim; Fredriksen 1986; and Gallagher 1990.

reality than fiction or poetry or to distinguish it sharply from those more openly fabricating forms. Autobiography is not an accurate record of what "really" happened, but rather another interpretive scheme, a consciously or unconsciously selective and creative rewriting of history according to the present purposes and the current paradigmatic orientation of the narrator. It is productive of reality as much as it is reflective of it, and its truth-value is not necessarily significantly greater than that of the other two genres. More important for us, all three types of narrative operate within the same self-perpetuating system of discourse about conversion, whose components are mutually informing and which also includes the narratives of the social sciences and the experience itself. It is this closed system that will ultimately concern us more than unmediated reality, which is an elusive thing indeed.

Obviously, I am touching on extremely complex issues that could be pursued at great length, but I think that enough groundwork has been laid to return to the original question: by invoking in the same breath, so to speak, *comparanda* from worlds so apparently disparate as that of the social sciences and that of literary mimesis, am I not conflating reality and representation? My answer is that reality and representation are already hopelessly intertwined. To the extent that any "scientific" analysis can uncover and faithfully describe actual religious (or other) experience (and this proposition is in itself problematic because of the inevitable presence of controlling cognitive paradigms in the analyzers), it is experience that is already heavily mediated by previous narratives and by the all-embracing penumbra of cultural discourse. Thus, whenever I use the terms *reality* or *experience* in what follows, it is always with this qualification understood. A straightforward humanistic statement of my project might run thus: modern studies analyze the social-psychological dynamics of conversion, and literary narrative in turn has the capacity to represent this experience; the *Metamorphoses* belongs to this tradition of narratives and represents under its own particular guises a generic process of actual conversion experience. I would not go so far as to say that this is wrong; in fact, it is right, insofar as social theory can reliably describe reality, especially the highly subjective reality of religious experience, and insofar as narrative can accurately represent it. But this book is not primarily concerned to demonstrate that the *Metamorphoses* is an "authentic" reflection or representation of actual religious experience.[16] It may well be; but at another level and more precisely what I will do is reposition this ancient novel within a system of talk—of discourse—about conversion, which in a real sense is all there is, or at any rate, is all that is accessible to us. If this system of talk overlaps with experience, as in fact it must; in other words, if in the end I demonstrate something about experience as well as about narrative, then so much the better.

As it happens, such a system can be assembled only by drawing on modern analyses of (on the whole) modern conversions and on narratives produced later than the *Metamorphoses* itself because antiquity (and in fact most of human history) lacked the analytical frameworks devised by the social sciences to account for human experience, and because no narratives of conversion comparable to the *Metamorphoses* have survived from pagan antiquity. The fact that no such frameworks for analyzing certain experiences existed in antiquity does not, however, mean that these experiences could not occur or that the discourses that made them possible were not operative. By reading the *Metamorphoses* in the context of later explanations and subsequent narratives of conversion, I hope to show that the novel exemplifies a recurrent pattern of conversion experience/narrative. This pattern appears in its essentials to be generic, at least in a qualified sense, and has never been identified in the *Metamorphoses* qua narrative of conversion. One must, of course, proceed with caution when making the claim that any phenomenon is transcultural, that its persistence in different cultural settings militates against viewing it as the unique product of a particular set of historical circumstances. Yet we will see that, in a wide range of studies of conversion and related phenomena with very different orientations, methodologies, and aims, the generic character of the basic operations involved in attitude change (of which religious conversion is one type) is stressed over and over again. Furthermore, these basic

16. I should, however, remind the reader that there is a highly respectable tradition of using the *Metamorphoses* as a source for reconstructing pagan religious belief and practice. This tradition includes the work of Merkelbach (1962), Festugière (1954), and Burkert (1987), all titans in the scholarship in ancient religion. More recently, in an approach different from these in its particulars but similar in its assumption that literature can reflect social reality, Habinek (1990) has read parts of the novel in the light of anthropological theory about the identity and cohesion of communities.

operations in turn find expression in a variety of literary representations of conversion. In both cases they persist underneath, or at least alongside, the most salient of the culturally and ideologically determined particulars of the conversion in question and to a great extent function independently of the culturally scripted interpretation imposed by the convert on his or her experience.

I do think it likely that if one were to probe further, one would find that the basic operations themselves are also culturally scripted, and this is the basis of my qualifying the claim that the pattern is generic in any essentialist sense. Although the cultures that produced the literary narratives enlisted here and the ones that produced the theoretical narratives and their subjects of study are indeed quite different in significant ways, I suspect that they have something very basic in common that serves as the condition of possibility for the shared features of the narratives. I am inclined to think that this fundamental community has something to do with, in general terms, the discourse of dualism and with dualistic cosmic and cognitive structures; in spite of their differences, these cultures can be gathered together under this very large discursive umbrella. But pursuing this line of thought would lead us very far afield indeed. It will suffice for my current purpose to note that, even if we "distill [the] most value-neutral definition" of conversion (Segal 1990, 285), we are still unlikely to be left with a truly universal phenomenon that is not at some level shaped by its cultural environment. As long as we read "generic" to mean "common to a very wide, but not exhaustive, range of expressions of conversion which share a cultural foundation of dualism," rather than "universal," we can say that conversion experiences and narratives can have generic features, even if they are the products of very different systems of discourse in other respects.

The persistence of these common features undergirds my premise that modern scholarship's theories and findings about conversions occurring in contemporary settings are applicable to conversion in pagan antiquity and that there is a fundamental community between later narratives of conversion and one generated in the world of Greco-Roman paganism, in this case, the *Metamorphoses*.[17] This proposition

---

17. Segal's (1990) area of investigation is the nature of conversion in Hellenistic Judaism, and a premise that runs through his work too is that modern

has considerable implications for our understanding of the conversion experience of individuals within that world, an experience about whose inner workings we know next to nothing. Whether one takes the *Metamorphoses* as an account of a Platonically colored Isiac conversion with one or the other element foregrounded, or as a more general composite picture of conversion (the latter being my own inclination), my comparison will suggest that it is valid to read back into the silence surrounding personal religious experience in antiquity the patterns that assert themselves so persistently in later, and I believe comparable, sources. Ultimately, my argument will suggest the need to expand our notions of the cognitive and emotional content of pagan religious experience. In the end, in contrast to past approaches, I will use the *Metamorphoses* as much to interrogate established views about conversion in pagan antiquity and about the constraints of ancient genre as vice versa.

That I look to modern theoretical formulations and to postpagan narratives of conversion for material from which to construct a context for the *Metamorphoses* should not be taken by the reader to mean that I must resort to these sources because no work has been done on conversion in antiquity or no other narratives of pagan conversion from that period are extant. It is true that the only first-person narrative of *religious* conversion surviving from Greco-Roman paganism is a fictional

---

studies of the basic mechanics of modern conversions can elucidate the problem. See especially chapter 3, "Conversion in Paul's Society" (72–114) and the appendix "Paul's Conversion: Psychological Study" (285–300). In the latter he writes, "the analogies between Paul's experience and modern day conversion are striking. By tracing its history within the social sciences, trying to distill its most value-neutral definition, we can apply insights gained in the modern period to the ancient data [and] transport some successfully tested empirical data back to the time of Paul" (285). Fisher (1973) likewise proceeds on the assumption that the character of conversion as a generic phenomenon in religion makes it legitimate to compare the growth of Christianity in late antiquity to the expansion of Islam in sub-Saharan Africa. For the application of modern theory to ancient experience, see also, e.g., Remus 1984. Much earlier, Nock's study of conversion in antiquity had been thoroughly informed by the theories of William James, published some thirty years earlier. In my view Nock's error was not in drawing on James but in stressing the moral strain in James' analysis at the expense of the epistemological or the cognitive.

one and that it is the *Metamorphoses*. We do, however, have two narratives of conversion to philosophy: Dio Chrysostom's *Thirteenth Discourse* and Lucian's *Nigrinus,* the former serious in some sense but perhaps a politically motivated fiction; the latter, clearly parodic. But these brief and extremely formulaic narratives are in no way comparable in psychological depth and complexity to the sort of conversion narrative that I will argue that the *Metamorphoses* is. It may well be the result of the accidents of transmission, but for real parallels we have to go to later accounts. As far as scholarship is concerned, significant studies of different aspects of conversion in antiquity do in fact exist. The problem with these studies is that their focus and methodology, and on some points their prejudices, are such that they are not very useful for reconstructing the subjective experience of individuals and for understanding the relationship of narrative to that experience, both of which are central to my project. Perhaps two of the best-known students of conversion in antiquity are Arthur Darby Nock and Ramsay MacMullen. Their work illustrates how two very different scholars from different generations, with different theoretical and methodological orientations, can still produce studies that are similarly limited in their possible application to the question of the dynamics of personal religious experience in pagan antiquity.

Nock (1933) states that the guiding purpose of his study is to "understand the success of Christianity outside Judaea." He proposes to do this by examining "the forms of worship to which men turned although they had not been reared in them . . . the ways in which these spread, [and] the psychological factors making them attractive" (10). In his attempt to reconstruct these "psychological factors," Nock relies heavily on individual case histories in one form or another, records of which inevitably tend to come from a highly literate elite. He thus demonstrates his debt to William James and replicates the latter's concern with extraordinary individuals and religious pioneers as opposed to ordinary people and their allegedly unreflective piety (so James). As many, including MacMullen, have pointed out, the problem with Nock's approach is that it tries to explain a broad historical movement, namely the growth of Christianity in later antiquity, as the result of a conjunction of many individual psychologies implausibly experiencing the same "spiritual needs" roughly simultaneously, while ignoring larger social, economic, and political factors. The inappropriateness of some of Nock's material to the task of answering the basic question he poses does not, however, mean that his discussion of it is not valuable in other ways, or that the material itself is not useful for other purposes.

Two well-known and related distinctions lie at the heart of Nock's study. Nock insists first of all on a sharp contrast between what he calls primitive, or traditional, religion (that is, paganism) on the one hand and prophetic religion on the other.[18] What drives traditional religion is not belief or "faith" or ideas of any kind, but rather an apparently unthinking observance of ritual. "[I]n religions of tradition," he writes, "the essential element is the practice and there is no underlying idea other than the sanctity of custom" (3). It is fair to say, I think, that this notion of paganism as psychologically and emotionally sterile continues to inform discussions of Greco-Roman religion to a great extent, whether it is implied or explicitly stated. Nock goes on to maintain that in primitive religions "there is no religious frontier to cross, no difficult decision to make between two views of life" or two sharply contrasted "world-orders"; in prophetic religions, on the other hand, "the individual stands before a choice" (5, 13). This claim is the basis of his second distinction, that between the soft and nonexclusive adhesion of paganism and true conversion. In a clear invocation of William James, Nock defines the latter as "the reorientation of the soul of an individual . . . a turning which implies a consciousness that a great change is involved, that the old was wrong and the new right" (7). According to Nock, this sort of radical change in attitude, and the exclusiveness of allegiance that generally goes with it, was altogether alien to paganism because of its externalizing and infinitely accommodating features and the monistic character of the pagan universe. "True" conversion in antiquity was possible only when it was a conversion to Christianity or Judaism. The only comparable phenomenon within paganism, Nock maintains, was conversion to philosophy, which "held a clear concept of two types of life, a higher and a lower" (14).

---

18. Nock's distinction corresponds to that of Bellah 1964. The latter distinguishes between "primitive" or "archaic" religion, which conceptualizes the cosmos as a continuum with no sharp break between the divine and the natural worlds, and "historic" religion with its notions of a transcendent god (or gods) and a dualistic universe. Clearly the paganism represented in *Metamorphoses* 11 is edging into the latter. See chapter 6, n. 22.

Given the rigidity of the scheme that Nock sets up, it is no surprise that he appears to be at something of a loss when it comes to explaining where a pagan narrative of conversion like the *Metamorphoses* fits into it. I have already noted in my survey of previous religious readings of the novel that Nock's discussion of it shows two related deficiencies: he ignores all but Book 11 (a mere one-eleventh of the whole), and he makes no effort to understand the psychological dynamics behind the conversion of Lucius as it is represented by Apuleius. We can now see that these failings are at least in part governed by Nock's presuppositions about the limitations of pagan religious experience in general. For him the *Metamorphoses* is a problem text because it violates the rules that Nock himself constructs. He does not deny the richness and intensity of the picture of religious devotion in Book 11; on the contrary, he acknowledges and discusses it at some length. But he persists in viewing that devotion as a kind of fluke, an anomaly within paganism:

> Our survey of paganism has given us little reason to expect that the adhesion of any individual to a cult would involve any marked spiritual reorientation, any recoil from his moral and religious past, any idea of starting a new life. . . . It cannot be supposed that [Lucius'] is a normal level of pagan religious emotion. (138, 155)

But why not? No one needs to be reminded that the sources, literary and other, that managed to survive from antiquity represent only the tiniest fraction of all the artifacts produced by the Greeks and the Romans. In view of this, my own inclination would be to assume that if we have one testimonial of a pagan conversion to rival Augustine's, there probably were others. Nock does admit that the experience represented in the *Metamorphoses* seems to meet his criteria for real conversion—a special attachment to the deity in question and deep emotion, gratitude, self-surrender, and moral reform on the part of the convert (14). It thus represents the "high-water mark of the piety which grew out of the mystery religions" (138). But I will argue that the conversion of Lucius involves far more than just emotional attachment and "moral" reform. Its central event is in fact precisely the sort of radical cognitive reorientation that Nock claims characterized conversions to

Judaism and Christianity (and possibly philosophy) exclusively. The conversion of Lucius *does* involve the adoption of a "world-order sharply contrasted with [that] in which the neophyte had previously moved" (13).[19]

Some fifty years after the publication of Nock's *Conversion,* Mac-Mullen began a series of studies in which he approached the problem of conversion in antiquity in a manner altogether different from that of Nock. He maintains that it is a distorting practice to rely on the auto-biographical narratives of elite intellectuals when attempting to reconstruct the nature of religious experience in the Roman period: "Marcus Aurelius in our minds stands too easily for 'religion in the Roman Empire'" (1981, 94). MacMullen allows for the possibility that a tortured route of self-scrutiny, all duly recorded in writing, might have led to conversion in some cases. But he is interested primarily in the religious experience of the masses and so rejects the methodology of Nock and James before him, both of whom relied heavily on written "confessions" in which individuals had chronicled their psychological and spiritual development. The vast majority of conversions, and certainly the tide of conversions to Christianity that transformed the empire, were in MacMullen's view much less psychologically complex. Citing numerous brief and anecdotal third-person accounts describing the "moments of conversion" of assembled groups of people either within paganism or to Christianity, he surmises that what produced conversions in most cases was simply a convincing demonstration of divine power. Miracles were the key: "*That* was what produced converts. Nothing else is attested" (1981, 95–96). Having established this model, MacMullen goes on to assert that what he identifies as the two surviving extended first-person accounts of the conversion of individuals within paganism—the *Metamorphoses* and the *Sacred Tales* of Aelius Aristides—"only confirm in greater psychological depth the outline of cause and effect that can be traced in scenes involving hundreds or thousands" (1981, 97). Certainly, Isis demonstrates that she wields supernatural powers when she orchestrates Lucius' deliverance from bestiality. But I will argue that he turns to her out of more than awe and

---

19. See also Nock 1986a for further enumeration of descriptions of conversion events in the classical period.

gratitude, and that she comes to represent deliverance to him in a vastly broader sense.[20]

In *Christianizing the Roman Empire*, MacMullen brings his orientation toward conversion to bear on the question of "how the whole empire was converted." His goal is to explain the success of Christianity or, as he puts it, "the slow but gigantic growth of a community of believers" (1984, 3). This is, of course, the same question that Nock had set for himself. But MacMullen explicitly rejects Nock's methodology, claiming that by considering as evidence only the "more richly intellectual and dramatically interesting conversions," Nock had ignored "the overwhelming bulk of the Christian population." This is simply inadequate if one is attempting to explain a mass historical movement (4). Underlying Nock's approach, MacMullen infers, is "the fundamental assumption that religious belief does not deserve the name unless it is intense and consuming." But as MacMullen correctly notes, people can adopt a new religion for all sorts of reasons other than doctrinal or deeply personal ones; these can include the most pragmatic of considerations:

---

20. I would not call the *Sacred Tales* a narrative of conversion, although it certainly is a narrative of religious experience. To be sure, Aristides' account of how Asclepius showed him the way to relief from his countless medical complaints expresses a gradually growing devotion to one god, but it does not reflect the sort of fundamental shift in world view that characterizes the type of narrative of conversion with which I am concerned. In spite of his developing relationship with the god, there is a continuity between Aristides' former life and his current one, whereas Lucius' encounter with Isis marks a rupture between the old and the new. Obviously, I am betraying my own loyalty to Jamesian definitions here. According to a broader view of conversion, the *Sacred Tales* might be considered a conversion narrative. Definitions of conversion are expandable and contractable, and I have chosen to focus on a particularly radical and intellectually complex type, partly in response to widespread claims that such a type could not occur in Greco-Roman paganism.

On the question of the utility of accounts of individual experience for piecing together the broader historical picture: among modern scholars Segal, for one, endorses such an approach. He remarks, for example, that we would need more "individual case histories" (1990, 109) to understand fully the various motives for conversion—a type of source more or less dismissed by MacMullen. Elsewhere (87) Segal suggests that something more complicated than naked awe at supernatural powers could be responsible for interactive chains of conversions in communities ("most conversions took place on a person-to-person level"). The difference in Segal's and MacMullen's aims accounts to some extent for their different methodologies.

[W]e who observe long-distant periods on their own terms, free-
ing ourselves of theological presuppositions, must be ready to
recognize and to treat as religious history an almost unmanageably broad range of psychological phenomena, of which the most
historically significant need not have been at all intense or complicated intellectually. (4–5)

I am struck here by his inclusion of an "unmanageably broad range of
psychological phenomena" under the rubric of conversion. The range
of experience that MacMullen counts as conversion may serve his own
agenda well, but it expands the definition of conversion to include so
many forms of religious experience that the definition becomes almost
meaningless for any other purpose. At any rate, I am not claiming that
any of the "psychological phenomena" encompassed in MacMullen's
definition were not religious experience, nor am I adjudicating (as
Nock and some of the church fathers might) between genuine and deficient conversions. MacMullen is justified in defining conversion in his
simultaneously broad and reductive way, if that way is most suited to
answering his particular historical question, and I think that it is obvious that his approach is, in fact, far more appropriate to answering that
question than Nock's. My own purpose, however, leads us back to
Nock's focus on the "body and soul" experiences (MacMullen 1984, 4)
of individuals, without in any way proposing to use accounts of them
to explain a large historical movement.

   The crucial thing for us to notice is that, in spite of the radical differences in methodology and orientation that separate Nock and Mac-
Mullen, each of them in his own way takes the position that pagan religious experience, and in particular the experience of conversion, had a
very circumscribed potential for involving any real psychological
depth or complexity. This premise grounds most of the major studies of
Greco-Roman paganism. Burkert, for example, similarly maintains that
the "ancient mystery cults" could provide practical but not metaphysical benefits to their adherents. Nock states this principle explicitly in his
preliminary definitions; MacMullen implies it in the course of his discussion, as when he dismisses everything in the *Metamorphoses* but the
thaumata. MacMullen's prejudices emerge again, it seems to me, in his
discussion of "Conversion" in *Paganism in the Roman Empire* (1981,
94–112). Here he concludes in essence that there was no conversion in
paganism because there is no evidence for any kind of evangelizing or

proselytizing, that is, for any active efforts of cult adherents to win new members. Such a limited view of conversion leaves entirely out of the picture the possibility that individuals might have their own sponta- neous experiences of ethical or epistemological crisis and conversion without falling into the hands of recruiters. Nock's and MacMullen's assumptions about the nature of paganism, the idiosyncrasies in their definitions of conversion, and the ultimate interest of both scholars in the historical problem of the Christianization of the empire, all seri- ously limit the relevance of their work to any consideration of the psy- chosocial dynamics of personal conversion in paganism or of how these dynamics might be represented in a literary text. Psychological and sociological studies of the conversion of individuals drawing on evi- dence from more recent history all the way up to the present day are much better suited to this task.[21]

Having located in both Nock and MacMullen a tendency to under- estimate or to be indifferent to the psychological capacities of pagan- ism, I would hasten to add that "paganism" takes in a great deal of ter- ritory and that the *Metamorphoses* as a religious text is informed by more than the traditions of Greco-Roman paganism, as broad as they themselves were. Being a work whose savior god is at least ostensibly Isis, it additionally reflects various aspects of Egyptian religion with its established dualistic structures. The novel furthermore participates in the philosophical discourses of the second century, especially that of Middle Platonism, and thus in its intellectual and religious content emerges as a sort of international pagan and philosophical crossover text. Its fusion of Egyptian and Greco-Roman religious elements, how- ever, makes it more pagan than the purely philosophical testimony that Nock opposed to pagan religion. On the other hand, the simultaneous presence of philosophical currents in the novel reminds us that the very idea of conversion was born in the philosophical schools and had a

---

21. On the meaning of conversion in the Greco-Roman world, see also Hadot 1981; MacMullen's articles (1983; 1985–86, the latter with responses by Babcock and Jordan); and Gallagher's chapter "Understanding Conversion in Late Antiquity" (1990, 109–33). Aubin (1963) offers an exhaustive study of the term *epistrophe* as it was used in the philosophical schools and in early Chris- tianity. He does not, however, involve himself in the kind of analysis that char- acterizes work on conversion in sociology and psychology and thus makes it far more relevant to my purposes.

long philosophical tradition. In fact, the only ego-narratives of conversion apart from the *Metamorphoses* to survive from pagan antiquity describe, with greater or lesser degrees of seriousness, conversion to the philosophical life. It was Plato who invented, so to speak, the very concept of conversion when he described the reorientation of the psyche from the world of transience to the world of essence as a philosophical ideal and the purpose of education in *Republic* 518c–d; and it was Cicero qua eclectic interpreter of earlier philosophy who first translated the originally Platonic and later Christian term *epistrophe* with *conversio* (*De Natura Deorum* 1.77). It is an open question whether the figures of the Second Sophistic were philosophers in any ordinary sense of the word at all. Still, many of them were certainly at pains to style themselves as such, and among them the idea of a de rigueur experience of conversion, which they inherited from the philosophical tradition, was very much alive. Tatum notes this when he says "[c]onversion to belief in some kind of transcendent authority was a familiar occurrence in the lives of sophists in the Roman Empire" (1979, 127); he gives as examples Aelius Aristides, Dio Chrysostom, and Apuleius.

There is a wealth of anecdotal literary material describing in very dramatic terms the moments of conversion allegedly experienced by various ancient philosophical figures. According to the conventions of the genre, such moments often came quite unexpectedly and occurred as the result of the future philosopher's hearing a persuasive speech delivered by an inspiring sage. These accounts are highly formulaic representations of a stereotyped experience and are frequently incorporated as a kind of obligatory set piece into biographies of philosophers written by such purveyors of pagan hagiography as the third-century compiler Diogenes Laertius.[22] The central stress of accounts in this tradition is ethical, that is, the focus is on the movement of the individual from vice to virtue. This is true also in the two first-person narratives of philosophical conversion to survive from pagan antiquity, the *Thirteenth Discourse* of Dio Chrysostom, a self-described rhetorician-turned-philosopher of the late first century A.D., and a piece

---

22. See Malherbe on "The Philosophers' Call to Conversion" (1987, 21–28) for an overview of the topos of philosophical conversion as it developed in the Hellenistic world, with many citations of examples.

entitled *Nigrinus,* by Apuleius' contemporary the satirist Lucian. Dio dates his change of heart from the time he was sent into exile by the emperor Domitian in 82. He begins his narrative by musing on the possibility that exile may be a blessing in disguise, in spite of the common view that it is among the worst of calamities. In recounting his adoption of the philosophical life, Dio very self-consciously casts himself in a Socratic mold. Like Socrates, he receives encouragement in his mission from an oracle (9–10; cf. *Apology* 20). Furthermore, a large segment of the narrative (16–28) is occupied by a hortatory speech of unclear derivation, which Dio attributes to Socrates, upon whose ideas he claims he drew as he addressed the ethical questions of those he encountered in the course of his wanderings.

We learn as much about the conventions of this type of narrative from parodies of it as we do from earnest versions such as that of Dio. The *Nigrinus* is an epistolary piece in which Lucian (the name of both author and narrator) writes to the Platonic philosopher Nigrinus, reproducing a dialogue that he alleges occurred between himself and another man. In this conversation Lucian enthusiastically explains to his interlocutor how hearing Nigrinus speak completely changed his life. With the true zeal of a convert, Lucian effuses, "I have come back to you transformed . . . into a happy and a blissful man . . . once a slave, I am now free . . . once witless and befogged, now saner." He describes his moment of conversion as one of confusion and internal struggle, then surrender; and remembers the narcotic effect of Nigrinus' speech, which left him spellbound, giddy, confounded, speechless, and in tears (we think of Alcibiades' description of the effect of Socrates' words on him, at the end of Plato's *Symposium*). No doubt this satirical treatment reflects the hackneyed formulas current in both autobiographical narratives and third-person accounts of conversion to philosophy. As a result of his encounter with Nigrinus, Lucian the narrator is moved entirely to forsake his old way of life and to devote himself to the pursuit of virtue, justice, and truth. Thus we see here and throughout the work the Socratic ethical strain, albeit in parody, which also runs through the *Thirteenth Discourse.*[23]

---

23. The works of both Dio and Lucian are readily available in the Loeb Classical Library (I quote here from the Loeb translation of Lucian by Harmon

Many of the topoi and patterns that I will invoke to identify the *Metamorphoses* as a narrative of conversion on the same footing with those of Augustine and Dante, among others, were already in their basic outline well established in the Hellenistic type of conversion narrative that Dio and Lucian, in their different ways, represent, and indeed in the mainstream philosophical tradition as a whole. In addition, they appear with some regularity in the amorphous collection of roughly contemporary religio-philosophical treatises known as the *Hermetic Corpus* and in other Gnostic and quasi-Gnostic writings and became standard in Christian texts as well.[24] Among these topoi are the expression of scorn for conventional values, and the claim that the unenlightened are deceived by these "false" values and led astray by the lure of "false" desires and pleasures. True knowledge is regularly set against mere opinion, and being in the grip of the latter is often described in medical terms, that is, as suffering from a disease of the soul (one wonders whether William James knew how far back his language resonated when he coined the term *soul-sickness* for his Gifford lectures in 1902). The apprehension of truth furthermore is conventionally represented as a transformation and as a movement from blindness to sight, darkness to light, slavery to freedom, drunkenness to sobriety, sleep to waking—in a word, as Nock puts it, from the old to the new. Finally, there is a tendency, surely deriving originally from Plato, to eroticize the quest for wisdom: we need to "fall in love" with justice,

---

[1927, 101]). For the cultural and literary background of both writers, see C.P. Jones (1978; 1986). See also Moles (1978) for a critical look at the "authenticity" of Dio's conversion. On "The Hellenistic Type of Stories of Conversion," to which both these accounts owe a debt, see Misch 1951, 2:487–95. Nock (1933, 164–86) has a chapter on conversion to philosophy, which it will be remembered was in his view as close to real conversion as one could come in paganism. Both evangelizing speeches and stereotyped conversion narratives were adopted from the philosophical tradition into Christianity. One of the earliest examples of the form's Christian incarnation is Justin Martyr's *Dialogue with Trypho*, with its obligatory account of Justin's search for answers in different schools of philosophy. See, e.g., MacMullen 1984, 68–73, "The Conversion of Intellectuals."

24. For an overview of Hermetic and Gnostic writings and their preoccupations, see Dodds (1965), especially chapter 1; and Nock (1986b). For the text of the *Hermetic Corpus*, see Nock and Festugière 1945–54; tractates 1 and 7 show the topoi in question with particular clarity.

says Dio (33; for all these topoi, see the *Thirteenth Discourse* and *Nigrinus*, passim).

I will argue that while the *Metamorphoses* incorporates many of these conventional elements, its parts add up to a great deal more than a compendium of conversion clichés. These conventional images qua signifiers of the benighted and the enlightened states are a function of the philosophical tradition's much larger contribution to the making of the *Metamorphoses*: after Plato it was a tradition shot through with a discourse of dualism, which was and remains the sine qua non that allows conversion to be experienced, conceptualized, and described in the first place. Religious conversion, at least in the admittedly Jamesian sense in which I use the term, is not possible in a monistic universe. The *Metamorphoses* represents a particular way in which a subject whose consciousness is structured by the discourse of dualism can experience the movement from the "old" to the "new." It is the novel's vivid representation of this subjective experience that distinguishes it from other pagan texts that treat conversion in some form. As a narrative, the *Metamorphoses* is much more highly developed and represents a much greater degree of psychological complexity than the extremely stereotyped and ethically centered narratives of conversion to philosophy that constitute the only roughly contemporary comparative material. The axis upon which the conversion of Lucius turns is one of epistemological rupture rather than moral reform, and the representation of this rupture is accomplished in the novel on many levels and in many ways. In order to provide an adequate context in which to reposition the *Metamorphoses* as a particular type of narrative of conversion, it is necessary to look to later narratives for parallels and read their features back into ancient religious experience and modes of literary representation. The justification for assimilating ancient and modern in this way lies, as I have suggested, in the generic patterns discernible in the basic dynamics of conversion and in its representation, patterns that assert themselves across significant temporal and cultural gaps.

Certainly, I do not contend that the *Metamorphoses* was entirely unique in antiquity. Everything is, after all, always already written, and Apuleius necessarily tapped into a preexisting network of literary, religious, and philosophical ideas. By the same token, I am not suggesting that the more clearly formulaic character of other pagan conversion narratives precludes their carrying any real meaning in terms of human experience. But I do think that the novel distinguishes itself in the way it represents a type of conversion experience not found in other ancient pagan accounts, at least not in any extant ones. By dislodging the *Metamorphoses* from its second-century context and resituating it among other, later representatives of what I argue is its genre, which in turn are read for generic features more than as artifacts of particular historical circumstances, I know that I run the risk of appearing to produce an ahistorical reading that takes the convergence of particular cultural discourses within which the *Metamorphoses* was generated too little into account. But many have labored to show how the novel "entered the complex cultural discourse of the second century," as Winkler (1985, 251) puts it. My point, in fact, hinges precisely on eschewing that approach in favor of taking a much longer view, in full awareness of the difficulties associated with arguing, even implicitly, for the transcultural assertion of psychological and narrative phenomena.

This book, I know, seems to put out its tentacles in many different directions, and I hope it will have value for those interested less in the *Metamorphoses* in itself than they are in conversion, or conversion narratives, or Augustine, or any number of other topics upon which those tentacles light. In spite of this range, however, I view it primarily as a study of the novel of Apuleius, and that is where I will begin. Chapters 1 and 2 set forth my reading of the text of the *Metamorphoses* itself, concentrating in particular on the nature of the reality—the *actor*'s reality—represented in Books 1 through 10 of the novel. What is the world of the *Metamorphoses* like and, more specifically, the world as Lucius the preconvert perceives it? I argue that it is a world characterized by a gradual disintegration of the categories devised to organize its parts into a tidy and meaningful whole. Lucius' environment is one that is radically defamiliarized by changes that rupture its previous unity; it is marked by every kind of instability. His world is one where matter itself is unstable and where familiar ontological and cultural categories—death and life, animal and human, male and female, for example—merge unpredictably into one another. In this world, once predictable sequences of cause and effect have broken down, and the conventions that are supposed to regulate human society have lost their force, leaving characters stumbling about, acting on misconstructions of fact and mistaken inferences rather than on "solid" knowledge, if indeed such a thing exists and is accessible. The fundamental and persistent fact about Lucius the *actor*'s world in both its material and its social aspects is that it is gradually being stripped of all its familiar orienting signposts. Ultimately, my point will be that these features of the novel's reality can be read as representing the breakdown of familiar structures of meaning and the loosening grasp of the subject on habituated ways of ordering experience that are often central to the process of conversion and to narratives about it.

Earlier critics have remarked in passing on the aporetic quality in the fictional reality of the novel, for example, van Thiel's comment that much of the action in the novel is characterized by a "departure from the conception of a rationally ordered world, whose connections can be understood and depicted according to the laws of causality" (1971, 157), and Solmsen's that in Lucius' world "you do not know whom to trust, what to believe—surely not your eyes." He continues that the story takes place in:

> an uncanny condition halfway between substantial reality and a mere façade that may dissolve any moment and reveal horrors undreamt of and indeed impossible as long as normal causality and the laws of nature remain in force. (1979, 97–98)

It is true that Solmsen is speaking primarily about the first three books of the novel, where the menacing specter of magic is always looming. But others have sensed a strong element of the irrational and the unintelligible in the novel as a whole.[25] What I do in chapters 1 and 2 is systematically flesh out the undeveloped suggestions of these earlier critics, giving more attention to the disorder of Lucius' world than to the idea of lurking evil that some of their readings seem to imply. In my discussion of the preconversion books of the *Metamorphoses*, I postpone considering the tale of Cupid and Psyche (Books 4.28–6.24) until a later point in the argument rather than including it in the first two chapters. I have done so because it seems to me to be qualitatively different in tone and type from the rest of *Metamorphoses* Books 1–10. It is distinguished both from the other tales and from the main action by its remote fairy-tale atmosphere, its divine characters, and its happy ending. These features put it outside the scope of chapters 1 and 2, which

---

25. See also, e.g., Auerbach 1959, 55, 58, 62; Rüdiger 1960, 544–46; Johnson 1976, 144; and Tatum 1979, 72.

are concerned with the new impression of his world that Lucius the *actor* is forming as the result either of his own experience or of others' reports of "actual" events. Cupid and Psyche are not part of that world; rather, their tale is an interlude that stops the action and transports the ass momentarily out of his current reality. The tale is important, however, for the representation of another aspect of Lucius' preconversion experience, and I return to it and its place in my overall scheme in chapter 5.

Chapter 3 draws on modern studies of conversion and related phenomena from William James to the present to explain how the picture of reality constructed in *Metamorphoses* 1–10 is consistent with the representation of subjective preconversion experience. In particular, I will argue that it is consistent with the representation of a cognitively or epistemologically rooted conversion whose central event is a sort of Kuhnian shift in the paradigms used to organize and understand the world. Outlines of this as a generic model of conversion emerge from the early work on the psychology of religion exemplified by James and from the work of later theorists who are more sociological or social-psychological in their orientation. The model is, moreover, supported by studies of processes that are analogous to conversion: the creative process, coerced attitude change (as in, for example, what are popularly known as "brainwashing" and "deprogramming"), and therapeutically directed psychological change all seem to involve the same or similar cognitive dynamics as conversion does or, more precisely, can. It is important to note that I say *cognitive dynamics*, since it is my insistence that problems of knowledge rather than of morality are to be understood as forming the crux of Lucius' preconversion crisis that most fundamentally distinguishes mine from other religious readings of the *Metamorphoses*. From the work on conversion that makes reference to analogous processes, it is clear that attitude change can be spontaneous or coerced. In both cases, however, what is involved is a rupture in the subject's old structure of values and knowledge, and in the smooth working of all the formerly integrated parts of his or her old world view.

The conversion of individuals, as I have suggested, can occur as the result of pressure exerted by outside forces to achieve a desired result. The same sort of shift in cognitive paradigms can also unfold more or less spontaneously. In cases of the second type, the precipitating challenge to the subject's naturalized structure of meaning often consists of a creeping disillusionment with the conventional system of goals and rewards that had long formed the basis of that structure. Frequently the impetus behind this disillusionment is existential; it materializes when the preconvert, for whatever reasons, begins to reevaluate his or her activities in the context of a heightened awareness of mortality. This is a common motivating pattern; there can be others. In any case, the ground for conversion is laid when old cognitive structures become inadequate to the task of explaining empirical reality. These structures strain and break as new and heretofore unaccommodated realities put pressure on them. Once the initial cracks appear in the foundation upon which the entire world view of the preconvert had been based, there can be a kind of domino effect, leading to an epistemological (and secondarily moral) crisis working on many levels, in which the truth-value of virtually everything formerly taken as knowledge comes into question. The preconvert's entire world can quite literally begin to look different as the result of this rupture. It "falls apart," its components drifting undifferentiated in a vacuum devoid of order and meaning. These are the cognitive dynamics of preconversion experience as they are documented in a range of studies and theoretical works, and this is the world represented in the first ten books of the *Metamorphoses*, before Isis resolves its instability. Earlier critics have been struck by some of the features that contribute to this quality in the *actor's* reality, but they have not offered any comprehensive account of that quality. Having closely scrutinized the world of *Metamorphoses* 1 through 10 in chapters 1 and 2, I provide such an account in the theoretical framework that I assemble in chapter 3.

Chapters 4 and 5 examine how the pattern of preconversion experience outlined above expresses itself in selected autobiographical, poetic, and fictional narratives of conversion, and in the process demonstrate that the scheme persists across a range of narrative types. These chapters focus in particular on a refinement or specialized manifestation of paradigm shift that is typical of religious discourse or, to put it another way, of crisis and conversion when they are experienced and interpreted within the sort of dualistic framework that characterizes many religious world views. When conversion takes place within such a system, the convert-narrator regularly testifies that his or her former life was driven by "false" values and displaced desires and that the new religious self has found the true object of its desire and has discovered the realm of "true" value. This is certainly the basic pattern in

Augustine and Dante; it can be detected in Sartre too, although his pre-convert Roquentin comes close to being left in the lurch because the religious solutions of earlier ages are no longer available to him. I argue that this scheme finds expression in the *Metamorphoses* also. In chapter 6, I consider conversion proper, so to speak, as opposed to the crisis leading up to it. How does anchoring one's self and one's reality in a transcendent system solve the problem of the unpredictable slippage in world and world view under which all of our preconverts have seemed to chafe? To answer this question I move from scholarly comments on the function of divinity as an epistemological or metaphysical center to expressions of this idea in other narratives and, then, in the Isis book of the *Metamorphoses* itself. In chapter 6 I also return to the question of the novel's two voices and whether and in what sense we are meant to take the conversion of Lucius, and in fact the entire book, seriously. It is, after all, a comic novel—a basic fact that any "serious" reading risks obfuscating. The ultimate answer to the question of whether Apuleius is serious is quintessentially Apuleian: yes and no. But for now we need to focus on the yes, as we begin our scrutiny of Lucius' journey toward Isis.

Part 1
Things Fall Apart

Books 1–4.27: The Material World

1

Questions of epistemology lie at the heart of the *Metamorphoses*. The text illustrates in countless ways the difficulties involved in correctly interpreting evidence and the traps lying in wait for anyone attempting to sort out true knowledge from false opinion. But underneath the conflict between knowledge and opinion lurks an even more intractable problem: when knowledge is as unstable as it appears to be in this novel, the reader inevitably begins to ask whether the common conviction that objective fact exists and can be recovered is anything more than a fond hope born of the human need for certainty. The world of the *Metamorphoses* is one where questions long thought settled and assumptions long unexamined assert their need for reassessment, and where characters are repeatedly required to weigh and reweigh evidence in their efforts to get at the facts. Yet, in spite of the often muddleheaded commitment of Apuleian characters to some idea of truth, the skeptical voice of the author persistently asserts itself to ask whether all efforts to arrive at it are not bound to be futile. These aspects of the *Metamorphoses* are in large measure the substance of Winkler's *Auctor and Actor*. Winkler's primary concern, however, was with the *auctor*'s point of view. His focus was on the strategies devised by Apuleius to create an open text through an ongoing series of "hermeneutic games" that anticipate the ultimate refusal of the author to endorse any totalizing interpretation of the whole.[1]

---

1. In Winkler's view, furthermore, the novel's many inserted tales are its main medium for exploring these issues. The tales provide "hermeneutic entertainment," at once amusing and philosophically sophisticated, by raising questions about the truth-value of stories (and by extension of any text), and by

But what about the perspective of the *actor*, what about Lucius? How are we to understand *his* experience of the world that Apuleius creates? The author may be playing epistemological games, but at the same time he traps his protagonist in a world that is rapidly coming epistemologically unglued, and in spite of the sensational and comic features operating at other levels of the novel, the "game" from Lucius' perspective stops being amusing early on in his adventures. Apuleius offers an aporetic epistemology, but Lucius is represented as experiencing the trauma of spontaneous and unmediated epistemic breakdown. With a routine business trip to Hypata, Lucius steps into a sort of twilight zone, where a whole range of "knowledge" commonly considered firm is thrown into doubt; where cherished premises and assumptions are overturned; where fiction and truth are indistinguishable; where, in short, his acquired epistemological apparatus is no longer adequate to interpret the text of the world. Seen not from the detached philosophical perspective of the author, but through the eyes of the experiencing *actor*, the instability that defines the novel's world is not a component in a scholarly meditation on the elusiveness of truth but rather a feature in the initial

---

exploring the endless ways in which texts can be misread and evidence misinterpreted (1985, 11–13, passim). Through the "epistemological exercises" of the tales, Apuleius expresses his interest "in distinctions of faith from fact and truth from conjecture" and pays "constant attention to the phenomenon that what seems for the moment to be a true interpretation (of narrative or personal experience) is later shown to depend on the perspective of the interpreter" (96, 21, 319). Winkler further argues that the episodes constructed around issues of interpretation in Books 1 through 10 are designed to train the reader in the hermeneutic method required for negotiating the narratological minefield of Book 11, which represents an "extreme case of the narrative game played throughout 1–10." Apuleius' method is to present various interpretive possibilities in the tales, then to invite the reader to bring these possibilities to bear as he or she constructs a reading of the novel as a whole and, by implication, of any text, including ultimately all the material of our experience (21, 76, 100, passim). Even as the *Metamorphoses* is an open text, suggesting many interpretations but resisting any definitive one, so also the amorphous matter of human experience "can only be unified by the reader's decision to see it in a certain way." All answers, to literary and to cosmic questions, are nonauthorized (131–32, passim).

phase—the crisis phase—of Lucius' religious experience. For him, the text is open only temporarily, and this is not a game but a disorienting and ultimately intolerable state of affairs.

The epistemological concerns central to the work receive a clear programmatic statement at its very outset, in the discussion between the ever credulous Lucius and the skeptical unnamed traveler that frames Aristophanes' tale in Book 1 (2–20). This discussion escalates into a veritable *agon* weighing the relative merits of credulity and skepticism as critical attitudes. It raises for the first time the questions that will reverberate in various guises throughout the novel: How can we know what to believe? Is it possible to discriminate between truth and its imitations, and does this distinction have any real meaning in the first place? What does it mean when our customary knowledge-gathering apparatus encounters evidence belonging to categories outside the preprogrammed ones? The subject of Lucius' and the skeptic's exchange is the plausibility of the supernatural events described in the narrative of Aristomenes. When Lucius encounters Aristomenes and his companion, the latter is scoffing in rationalistic disbelief at the tale he has just heard: "With a loud guffaw he said, 'Knock it off! Stop telling such absurd and outrageous lies!'" [*exerto cacchino, 'parce' inquit, 'in verba ista haec tam absurda tamque immania mentiendo'*] (1.2).[2] When Lucius expresses interest in hearing the story, the skeptic persists in his belligerent incredulity: "Ha! That lie has about as much truth to it as if someone were to say . . ." ['*ne,' inquit, 'istud mendacium tam verum est quam siqui velit dicere . . .'*] (1.3); he then produces a conventional catalogue of "impossible" violations of the natural order, most of which Aristomenes vouches for as entirely possible in his narrative. Far from being undermined by these protests, Lucius' wide-eyed *fides* is strengthened. His exhortation to Aristomenes to continue with the story includes a swipe at the other's intractable skepticism:

At that point, growing more confident by the minute, I said to him, "You there with the plugged-up ears and the stubborn mind, you're rejecting a story that might well be true. You're not being

2. The text of the *Metamorphoses* is that of Helm (1992); translations are my own.

very smart, by God, if your wrong-headed opinions lead you to label things lies just because they seem new to the ear or strange to the eye or high above the grasp of reason; for if you look a little more closely, you will find them not only accessible to understanding, but even easy to reproduce."

[Tunc ego in verba fidentior: . . . "tu vero crassis auribus et obstinato corde respuis quae forsitan vere perhibeantur. minus hercule calles pravissimis opinionibus ea putari mendacia, quae vel auditu nova vel visu rudia vel certe supra captum cogitationis ardua videantur; quae si paulo accuratius exploraris, non modo compertu evidentia, verum etiam factu facilia senties."] (1.3)

To support this expression of his willingness to consider the truth of the implausible, Lucius offers a detailed description of an unlikely event that he nevertheless saw with his own eyes: the fantastic feat of an itinerant sword-swallower (1.4).

At Lucius' prodding, Aristomenes then proceeds to tell of his experience with Socrates and the witches. His narrative recapitulates in microcosm the problems of belief and disbelief introduced by his two traveling companions: at one point, when recalling his fear that he would be linked to Socrates' (apparent) murder, he remembers that it had caused him to cry out in despair, "Who will ever believe me even though I'm telling the truth?" [cui videbor veri similia dicere proferens vera?] (1.14). When Aristomenes finishes his story, Lucius and the skeptic go another round of their debate. The anonymous traveler remains unpersuaded:

But Aristomenes' companion, who from the beginning had rejected his account with a stubborn incredulity, still maintained that nothing was more fabulous than that fable, nothing more ridiculous than that lie.

[at ille comes eius, qui statim initio obstinata incredulitate sermonem eius respuebat: "nihil," inquit, "hac fabula fabulosius, nihil isto mendacio absurdius."] (1.20)

To this Lucius responds by emphatically reiterating his open-minded approach to problems of belief:

"Well," I said, "I don't think that anything is impossible . . . after all, you and I and all human beings have had wondrous and seemingly impossible experiences, which don't mean anything to someone who's never had them when we try to explain."

["Ego vero," inquam, "nihil impossibile arbitror . . . nam et mihi et tibi et cunctis hominibus multa usu venire mira et paene infecta, quae tamen ignaro relata fidem perdant."] (1.20)

Lucius' suggestion here, that the final arbiter of truth is individual experience, is one that will reappear in different forms as the narrative progresses, until it undergoes its ultimate metamorphosis in the sphere of religious knowledge in Book 11.

Commentators have tended to view the issues raised in the debate between Lucius and the skeptic as being applicable only to the question of whether people should believe in magic, which is the ostensible subject of Aristomenes' tale and indeed of the first three books of the novel.[3] And in fact, the opening debate's immediate relevance clearly is to the plausibility of Aristomenes' claims, and this exchange and the preliminary wonders clearly do foreshadow subsequent magical events in the narrative. But in this work both the idea of magic and the debate about belief have a relevance far beyond the scope of events immediately at hand in the plot. It will become clear, I think, that in this book magic is ultimately the chief symbol of the epistemologically slippery nature of the world as a whole. The question of whether to exercise credulity or skepticism needs to be asked not only when one deals with the realm of black magic but more generally as one negotiates every sphere of experience, since they all are equally unstable and treacherous. To complicate matters further, neither sense perception nor intellect, those two traditionally competing or complementary epistemological organs, appears to be consistently reliable for hermeneutic purposes.

With this opening sequence—the tale of Aristomenes and the ongoing debate between Lucius and the traveler—the reader is made to experience for the first time the maddening suspension between conflicting versions of truth and different orders of explanation that he or she will encounter many times before facing the ultimate suspension of

3. So, e.g., Scobie 1975, 86, 120.

judgment in Book 11. The program is restated several times later in the narrative, as if for the benefit of the reader who might have missed the point of the initial version. This happens in contexts where it is no longer the plausibility of magical events that is formally at issue. Milo's tale of the astrologer Diophanes (2.11–15) and the discussion of its meaning between Lucius and his host provide a case in point. The epistemological challenge presented by the existence of multiple perspectives is demonstrated in the tale itself, where Diophanes' long-lost friend, the merchant seeking advice, and the crowd of bystanders all put different constructions on the same sequence of events. Furthermore, after the tale is told, Lucius again assumes the role of antiskeptic, this time against Milo's skeptic, in a discussion of the plausibility of divine intervention and the existence of extranormal powers and a higher order of knowledge.[4]

The problem of belief continues to assert itself after the old woman narrates the tale of Cupid and Psyche to Charite (4.28–6.24), and it is often worked out in a dialogue between representatives of different ways of approaching it. For example, the conflicting responses of Charite and Lucius to the tale of "Haemus" the bandit (7.5–8), actually Charite's betrothed Tlepolemus in disguise, show Charite as the obligatory skeptic, exercising her critical powers to discriminate the truth underneath the pretense, and Lucius as ever as the *credulus*, accepting everything at face value. In earlier treatments neither approach seemed to be unambiguously condemned or recommended, although the balance is tipped in favor of Lucius' credulity by the striking pattern of the "confirmation of the unbelievable" (Scobie 1973, 35) that tends to vindicate Lucius' attitude and mock the skeptics, and ultimately by the necessity that the reader practice a kindred resistance to dogmatism in order to make sense of the end of the novel. But here, when as a result of his utter misconstruction of the events and the text (i.e., "Haemus'"

---

4. See Winkler 1985, 27–32, 81–86 on Aristomenes' tale and its framing debate. Winkler too thinks that this sequence articulates a "discussion of the possible truth of fictions," which is "programmatic . . . for the hermeneutic game of 'What is true?'" as it is played *throughout* the novel (117). He notes the thematic importance of the skeptic and Lucius the antiskeptic as exemplifications of two ways of perceiving a tale, neither of which is necessarily right or wrong. On Diophanes, see Winkler 1985, 39–42; here too his reading of the tale's programmatic function is similar to mine. See also Penwill 1990 on the tension between skepticism and belief in the novel.

tale) before him he reaches a seriously mistaken judgment about the virtuous Charite's character, Lucius looks like an ass. The highly ironic coda with which Apuleius has the narrator cap his subsequent tirade against all of womankind makes the backfiring potential of Lucius' approach humorously clear: "At that moment the character of the entire female race depended on the judgment of an ass" [et tunc quidem totarum mulierum secta moresque de asini pendebant iudicio] (7.10). The tale of the wicked stepmother in Book 10 reiterates these issues by similarly "play[ing] games with our system of judgment," as Winkler put it.[5] It is clear that the question of how to nail down true knowledge (and indeed whether this is possible) is central to the novel.

Since I have touched on the potential of credulity to lead the *credulus* astray as well as to open him up to valuable insights "beyond the grasp of reason," it is appropriate at this juncture to consider how Apuleius characterizes Lucius in these programmatic passages and, in particular, how Lucius' *credulitas* displays a double-edged quality that will be important to keep in mind as we proceed. Certainly, we get an impression of Lucius as someone who is, to use Winkler's words, in the habit of "bracketing and suspending prejudgment" of any text and who understands that "the requirements for acquiring new knowledge . . . are suspended judgment, an open mind, and an acknowledgement of the limitations of individual experience" (1985, 29, 31). Furthermore, Lucius' self-proclaimed lack of dogmatism seems to make him an especially suitable candidate for conversion because it makes it easier for him to loosen his grip on habituated cognitive constructs, a process integral to the experience of conversion. Lucius' preconversion disengagement from conventional definitions of reality occurs in stages: at first he actually pursues it in the realm of magic, to give himself a wondrous break from the monotony of his conventional life. His attitude of excitement is, however, confined to the period of anticipation; once things start falling apart in earnest, watching the face of his world disintegrate stops being a thrill and begins to be deeply unsettling, as I will argue in these first two chapters. Finally, with his prejudgments *truly* stripped away, Lucius is tabula rasa and free to integrate into his conception of reality in a comprehensive and not just a casual, diversionary way something that would appear implausible to most observers: a

---

5. Winkler 1985, 80; Apuleius actually uses this phrase: *ludificato nostro iudicio,* 10.11. See Winkler 1985, 46–50 on "Haemus"; 77–80 on the stepmother.

divinity who not only is beyond the grasp of a detached reason (*supra captum cogitationis,* 1.3), but who also gives the lie (or so it appears to the convert) to the whole complex of his former values and assumptions.

Thus, in my reading of the novel, Lucius begins with his world view bounded by conventional structures of meaning and is thrown off balance when these structures collapse. For this reason it is in the end the structuring function of Isis, that is, divinity qua ordering principle, to which he is especially attracted. But can a character who proclaims *nihil impossibile arbitror* be read as a prisoner of conventional structures of meaning? We have only to recall his barely contained excitement on his first morning in Hypata, as he eagerly anticipates delving into forbidden realms and feels thrills of excitement when the town's topography seems to swim before his eyes (2.1), to conjure up a picture of a young man who appears to thrive on being a cognitive outlaw. But is he really? In spite of his rhetoric, in important ways he is not. All his talk about breaking down boundaries is precisely that; it is a form of wishful thinking, conceived within such limits as to ensure that nothing in his life will really change; it is a longing for something out of the ordinary entirely consistent with the character of a bored, curious, but ultimately conventional young aristocrat. The realm of magic and his openness toward it are quite circumscribed when considered alongside the truly comprehensive chaos that he ultimately must confront and the adjustments he must make in his thinking as the result of that confrontation. Lucius craves a change, but the changes that come are far more radical than he has bargained for. He tries a little diversionary fine tuning (his feathered existence was supposed to be brief) but soon finds himself on a different wavelength altogether, and after his harrowing season on the ontological edge, with the tenuousness of the structures that conventionally delineate reality exposed, he welcomes the order that Isis brings back to his world.

The Lucius of the novel's early books is nowhere near the free spirit that he thinks he is. His tolerance of ambiguity and his willingness to let go of normative models have strict limits, and when he articulates these limits he throws *all* his expressions of open-mindedness into doubt. He is ready, for example, to censure Charite (whose imputed infatuation with the bandit violates taboos of both gender and class: a well-bred young lady should not lust after anyone, least of all a criminal) and other allegedly or actually "misbehaving" women (for example, the baker's adulterous wife, whose lover's hiding place Lucius indignantly exposes to her husband, 9.26–27), while granting himself virtually unrestrained sexual license. His inculcated prejudices masquerade as moral principles, but like many tenets of conventional sexual morality, these "principles" betray anxiety about the dangers presented by transgressions of these rules to the conventional structures of order and power that he cherishes in spite of being a self-styled freethinker. It is easy to imagine Lucius disapproving of a liaison such as that between himself and Fotis if the genders were reversed, that is, between an aristocratic young woman and a slave boy. The very pride Lucius seems to take in his lack of dogmatism in the beginning should alert us to its limitations. As the novel progresses, he will be revealed as its main champion of conventional values and its central exemplum of intellectual complacency, both of which his new ass-body symbolizes and satirizes. The Lucius who arrives fresh in Hypata may think that he is open-minded, and in regard to his attitude toward the supernatural realm his claim appears to have a limited validity. But the vision that unfolds for him after his arrival there and that continues until his moment of truth outside the Corinthian arena in Book 10 will expose the complacency with which he adheres to unexamined assumptions in other spheres.

In this connection a closer examination of the characterization of Lucius' *credulitas* in the "Haemus" episode is revealing. When we compare the conclusions to which his disposition toward belief leads him here with those to which he comes in the earlier episodes where magic is the issue, we can see that credulity itself is a slippery thing, in that exercising it has the potential for producing two rather opposite effects. It is true that taking such an attitude can afford access to important but marginalized or discredited aspects of experience and to insights not grasped by reason. But the very fact that *credulitas* blocks the critical apparatus can sometimes turn the often commendable open-mindedness of the *credulus* into a passive complacency toward appearances when they are false, as they are in the case of "Haemus." Rarified insights can follow from *credulitas*, but so can "asinine judgments." In some spheres, Lucius' *credulitas* can cause him precisely *not* to suspend judgment, as he does when he hears Aristomenes' tale, but rather to make instantaneous uncritical judgments shaped by other prescribed modes of thinking and by dogmatism of another stripe, in this case, his assumptions about female lasciviousness and his uncharitable *opinio* of all women's ethical character. Here, it is Charite qua *skeptic* who suspends judgment, and she is rewarded by perceiving the truth. Credulity takes on a dogmatic cast, and skepticism is an unprejudiced openness toward all the evidence rather than the unnamed traveler's obstinate narrow-mindedness.

This capacity of *credulitas* to play an integral role in the perpetuation of conventional beliefs and constructions of reality is a critical component in the preconversion cognitive structure implied for Lucius by the text. Furthermore, his attitude *after* his conversion is not simply the mature expression of the openness toward extraintellectual realms and experiences that he has professed all along (as opposed to the more skeptical assessment of the author-*auctor*). It is rather a sort of hybrid between belief and disbelief, credulity and critical acumen: he displays openness toward divine solutions, but a corresponding new-found skepticism toward the values assigned by convention to phenomena in the empirical world. Likewise the attitude recommended in the end by the author-*auctor* is not a pure skepticism that manages to provide an unmistakable critique of the *actor*'s acceptance of unverified belief in the midst of an oddly compelling picture of it (after all, Lucius' unverified beliefs tend to be vindicated in the earlier parts of the work). It is instead a skepticism that includes elements of credulity in the sense that it admits *all* possibilities in the face of uncertainty about any *one*.[6] Thus the conflation of the formerly competing approaches that is first suggested in the "Haemus" episode is reprised in the novel's final book. In the course of the narrative these apparent binary opposites of intellectual attitude collapse together as surely as the ontological opposites that fuse before Lucius' eyes in the physical world.

To return to the notion of "bad" *credulitas*, that is, credulity that dulls our powers of discrimination and allows us to be duped by the false impressions collected by the senses: this notion has a clear and consistent relevance to narratives of religious awakening as a genre. In narra-

---

6. This is not exactly how Winkler formulates Apuleius' attitude, but it is implicit at, e.g., 1985, 124: "The effect of [the novel's] hermeneutic playfulness, including the final book, is to raise the question whether there is a higher order that can integrate conflicting individual judgments. . . . Such a posing of the question without giving an answer (a posing that includes Lucius's curiously unendorsed finding of *an* answer) amounts to a limited skepticism. The implicit argument of the novel is that belief in Isis or in any integrating cosmic hypothesis is a radically individual act that cannot be shared."

tives of this type, the awakened regularly comes to believe, gradually or suddenly, that the sensible world and all its values, once accepted by the benighted preconvert as self-evidently true, is in fact a realm of falseness and illusion, whereas the invisible realm of the divine is the enduring source of true knowledge. This commonplace paradox of religious discourse will prove no less true for Lucius the *actor*. Read in this context, the recurrent assimilation of the novel's action to the fictions of literature and drama serves as a reminder of the possible fictiveness of everything in our experience. The theatrical allusions and self-conscious fictionality that appear throughout the work constitute a warning to guard against seduction by appearance, while the floating about between truth and imitation that these allusions often suggest underscores the difficulty, if not the impossibility, of telling the difference. Thus, for example, the theatrical description of the ruse-unto-death of Thrasyleon the bandit in his bear disguise, under attack by ravenous dogs, is a conventional way of reinforcing the theme of the potential duplicity of all experience ("To his dying breath he persisted in the role that he had volunteered to assume" [*scaenam denique, quam sponte sumpserat, cum anima retinens*] [4.20]). In a different vein, Charite, who perceives her own kidnapping and captivity as a tragedy and offers a melodramatic commentary on it, extends the confusion between the real and the fictional to the deluded minds of the characters themselves (4.26).

The most complex and sustained piece of theatricality occurs in connection with the reluctant performance of Lucius at the Risus festival in Book 3. His sensation that life has suddenly acquired an unreal and stagey quality is exacerbated by the physical setting of the trial: because of its larger capacity, the crowd demands that the proceedings be conducted in the theater, and Lucius is led across the stage and placed in the middle of the orchestra to hear the charges (*cuncti . . . flagitant . . . iudicium tantum theatro redderetur. . . . me per proscaenium medium . . . et orchestrae mediae sistunt,* (3.2). After the charade has been played out, Lucius is, to his dismay, treated as "an actor who is congratulated on his performance" by the townspeople, as van der Paardt notes (1971, 83). The citizens' attitude is depicted as that of satisfied theatergoers who have gotten their money's worth. Later, in their attempt to be conciliatory, the magistrates unintentionally corroborate Lucius' unpleasant feeling of having been put on display against his will when they refer to him as the *auctor et actor* of their little play (3.11). In this episode,

Lucius abruptly finds that his life has become a dramatic production; the play's producers willfully manipulate a recalcitrant performer, and only in the end do the actor and the reader become aware of the totality of the illusion that has been perpetrated. Such an interplay between fact and fiction, and in particular the way in which the degree of factuality or fictionality in an event or experience shifts according to the perspectives of different observers or participants, reiterates the novel's central concern with the elusiveness of true knowledge.

The narrative's coy self-referentiality further tangles the web of fact and fiction. In Book 2, Lucius reports to Milo what Diophanes had prognosticated about Lucius' future: "He foretold that I would become a long story, an incredible tale, and a book in many volumes" [*respondit . . . historiam magnam et incredundam fabulam et libros me futurum*] (2.12). The book's reference to itself as a book abruptly breaks the dramatic illusion and forces on the reader an active awareness that he or she is being seduced by the calculated fabrications of an author. But here this device also contains another, less conventional suggestion. Scobie notes that "Apuleius uses the word *historia,* the term usually applied only to a factual account, in the *Metamorphoses* to designate a fictional narrative."[7] In view of this, it seems that events in the novel are legitimated by being accorded the same status as historical fact even as their fictionality is ironically exposed. The fictional construct is undermined by the intrusion of comments that abruptly create an awareness of its artifice, even as it is elevated to the respectable, credible genre of history. This tendency of the Apuleian text to slide unpredictably back and forth between claims of faithful mimesis and the sabotaging of those claims works on two levels. On the one hand, it is a way of formulating the central problem posed by the skeptical author, that of the ultimate elusiveness of all knowledge. At the same time it reflects Lucius the *actor*'s own growing doubts about the reliability of the knowledge that he has taken for granted, doubts that unlike the author's will ultimately have a resolution. As such it represents the choice between "true" and

---

7. 1975, 76. He compares two passages for their similarly double-edged use of *historia:* 6.29 (Charite imagining how her trials with the ass will be commemorated: *visetur et in fabulis audietur doctorumque stilis rudis perpetuabitur historia*) and 8.1 (a messenger brings the news of her demise: *referam vobis a capite, quae gesta sunt quaeque possint merito doctiores, quibus stilos fortuna subministrat, in historiae specimen chartis involvere*).

"imitation" knowledge that is characteristic of dualistic religious traditions.

An unresolved authorial aporia does indeed hang over the *Metamorphoses* from beginning to end, but my concern is to scrutinize the more circumscribed perspective of the *actor* Lucius as he moves through the *terra infirma* that constitutes the world of the *Metamorphoses*.[8] From this point of view, the narrative represents the experience of a subject dogged by the perception that virtually all the structures—physical, ontological, cognitive, logical, social—upon which he has come to rely to make sense of experience are breaking down. For Lucius, this uncertainty eventually becomes so intolerable that in the end he makes the leap of faith to a world of absolutes. As far as Lucius the convert is concerned, in the end the text *is* closed, and the choice between truth and falsehood is real and resolvable. The ongoing dialogue about belief and disbelief that Apuleius has threaded through the text forms a kind of intellectual frame for the representation of the *actor*'s view of the world and of the experiences leading to his conversion. For him, the instability of knowledge is not merely the subject of detached philosophical speculation; it characterizes his immediate world all the way down to its most basic physical levels.

2

As any reader of the *Metamorphoses* knows, magic is a primary engine of its plot. Witches ply their trade, and transformations and other magically induced disruptions of the natural order abound, especially in

---

8. Authorial aporia is, again, Winkler's focus. It seems to me that he himself waffles a bit on the question of whether truth can be recovered from "text" or, more precisely, of whether truth and text are to be distinguished in the first place: e.g., "Apuleius is extraordinarily sensitive to distinctions of faith from fact and truth from conjecture" (21) vs., e.g., "Apuleius's hermeneutic entertainment continuously alludes to the gap between seeing a possible meaning and accepting it as uniquely true" (318). I take this apparent vacillation as testimony to the persistence of the idea of truth even in the mind of a poststructuralist. In this connection I should point out that wherever I speak in terms of appearance, falsehood, form, surface, etc., as opposed to reality, truth, substance, depth, etc., I am not myself endorsing them as categories. I do, however, think that they would have been meaningful as categories to a second-century amateur Platonist such as Apuleius, and that they are standard as categories in narratives of conversion, as we will see.

the first three books. But I think that these features of the plot have a significance beyond their status as standard subjects of paradoxography, related for their value as entertainment. I will argue that in the *Metamorphoses* magic functions ultimately as a metaphor for the shifting nature of all matter, of all states of being, and even of social structures, and for the tenuousness of the lines along which these are conventionally organized. This much has been suggested before by others but never systematically developed. Ebel, for example, held the view that the thematic core of the novel is "the universal fact (of which 'magic' is as much an expression as a cause) that all appearances are unreliable and all 'realities' transient" (1970, 163). By incorporating two voices, a credulous one (the *actor*'s) and a skeptical one (the author's), into the whole of the text and especially into its (ir)resolution, Apuleius explores how different temperaments might respond to this "universal fact" once it is grasped.

Let us begin by considering the metaphorical potential in the idea of metamorphosis. In the past critics have pointed out that proponents of *Metamorphoses* as the Apuleian title of the work must explain why the author would name his book so as to create the expectation of an orgy of transformation when only two (Pamphile's and Lucius') actually figure in the main plot, and when long stretches of narrative proceed with no transformations at all.[9] But from the very beginning Apuleius hints that he has more than physical transformations in mind. He states in the preface (1.1) his intention to "weave together diverse tales" [*varias fabulas conseram*] in order to present the reader with "the transformation of human figures and fortunes into alien forms and back into themselves by a reciprocal spell" [*figuras fortunasque hominum in alias imagines conversas et in se rursum mutuo nexu refectas*]. The linking of *fortuna* with *figura* at the outset vastly broadens the definition of transformation to include changes in the fortune, fate, and condition of human beings, as well as in their physical form. This surpasses what is promised in the prefatory remarks of Ovid in *his Metamorphoses:* "I am

---

9. On the debate over the relative authenticity of the two transmitted titles, *Metamorphoses* and *Asinus Aureus* (The Golden Ass), see Tatum 1972, 306–7 and n. 8 for references. For a summary of the arguments for one title or the other, see most recently Winkler 1985, 292–98. I am satisfied with his conclusion that "Apuleius's original title was double—like those of Varro's *Menippean Satires* or Plato's dialogues as known in Apuleius's day—*Asinus Aureus, peri metamorphoseon (The Golden Ass, Concerning Metamorphoses)*" (294–95).

moved to tell of shapes changed into new bodies" [*in nova fert animus mutatas dicere formas / corpora*] (1.1–2), although of course what the ever coy Augustan promises and what he delivers are two different things.

The proem also offers a subtle demonstration of the range of manifestations that transformation will have in the Latin *Metamorphoses*. In asking indulgence as a native Greek speaker for the quirkiness of his Latin, the prologue speaker explains why the switch is appropriate to the endeavor: "In fact this very change of language corresponds to the type of writing I have in mind, which involves jumping from subject to subject as a circus rider jumps from horse to horse" [*iam haec equidem ipsa vocis immutatio desultoriae scientiae stilo quem accessimus respondet*] (1.1). With the phrase *immutatio vocis* Apuleius suggests that "a metamorphosis of language is the first change of shape which appropriately ushers in a series of tales the subject of which is metamorphosis."[10] This play at the linguistic level with the motif of transformation reflects the breadth of Apuleius' definition of the term. As Tatum has shown, this definition can "range from true changes in form, to religious conversion, to nothing more than a clever play on words which exploits the work's theme of metamorphoses"; it includes, moreover, the psychological transformations that dominate Books 7 through 10 (1972, 308–9, 311 n. 35). All these types of metamorphosis taken together are more than enough to satisfy the implications of the title *Metamorphoses*.

Such a broad interpretation of the word appears to have had no counterpart in the lost Greek ass story that served as Apuleius' model. According to the Byzantine scholar Photius' summary of this work, its author, whom he calls "Lucius of Patrae," recounted in a credulous spirit tales of "the transformations of human beings into other human beings and of mute beasts into humans and vice versa" (*Bibliotheca*, cod. 129). Photius' reading of "Lucius'" tone may well have missed the mark, but his account of the content is straightforward enough and suggests that its metamorphoses were limited to the physical variety. A comparison of the Latin version with the extant Greek *Onos*, apparently epitomized from the lost work and transmitted in the corpus of Lucian, reveals that while metamorphosis is present as a motif and as an engine

---

10. Scobie 1975, 76; also 75–76 on the phrase *desultoria scientia*, obscure even for Apuleius. On the preface in general, especially the question of its speaker's identity, see Wright 1963; Dowden 1982, 427–28; Winkler 1985, 180–203; P. James 1987, 25–41; and Harrison 1990.

of the plot in the epitome, the episodes apparently added by Apuleius make it much more pervasive and complex. Furthermore, not only does the Apuleian conception of metamorphosis move well beyond that of his particular Greek model; such a conception is also alien to the Greek literary tradition as a whole.[11] It is reasonably clear that in the range of uses to which he puts metamorphosis, Apuleius lies squarely in the Latin tradition, a tradition that can be summarized in one word: Ovid. When he carried out the vast project of tracing the whole of human history in terms of metamorphosis from the primal slime to the Age of Augustus, Ovid set a standard for the chronological and conceptual scope of metamorphosis that has never been surpassed, and this in spite of the modesty of the proposal appearing in his proem (see Tatum 1972, 310–13 and references). It is the identically titled Latin poem, rather than any Greek model, that the Apuleian *Metamorphoses* most closely approximates in the imaginative range of applications that it gives to the idea.

In order to pursue the suggestion that Apuleius was a direct heir of Ovid in the ways he exploited the traditional motif of metamorphosis to express larger philosophical concerns, we need briefly to consider Ovidian metamorphosis and what it is generally thought to represent. What is in many ways a typical modern discussion of the significance of metamorphosis in Ovid is at hand in Skulsky's study of metamorphosis as a literary motif from Homer to Virginia Woolf. Skulsky agrees that "the central theme in Apuleius' romance of transformations has the same generous range" as it does in Ovid's poem (1981, 62), but in his opinion the function of the motif in the two works is quite different: whereas Apuleius connects it primarily with the idea of the transformative powers unleashed by mystical initiation ("Metamorphosis as Satire and Mystery," 62–106), in Ovid it is a means of expressing the poet's conviction that confronting "metaphysical doubt" is as close as we can come to true knowledge ("Metamorphosis as Metaphysical

---

11. "Such latitude as we seek in the meaning of this word is not to be found in any Greek author. Wherever the word appears, it means a 'change in form' or 'transformation,' and nothing more complicated can be inferred. . . . The word enjoyed some currency in writers of the first and second centuries, but it seems to have been used only in a literal sense; for example, we never read of a *metamorphosis* of *tuche* [fortune]" (Tatum 1972, 310). See Junghanns 1932, 161 on the question of which episodes concerned with metamorphosis were added by Apuleius to the original ass story.

Doubt," 24–61). It seems to me, on the contrary, that the Apuleian conception of metamorphosis is closer to what Skulsky attributes to Ovid than is generally recognized.

In Ovid's vision of the cosmos, according to Skulsky, all matter constantly struggles to assert its integrity and its differentiated form against a powerful "reductionist impulse"; the pull of primal chaos could cause the discrete phenomena of reality as we know it to disintegrate at any moment into a throbbing amorphous mass. The "vision of the original chaos" that occupies the bulk of Book 1 exposes the "incoherence and caprice" lurking behind all apparently discrete phenomena, including the *corpora* whose permutations are the official subject of Ovid's poem. What characterizes all matter is "absurd flux" and "continual and unresting change" (1981, 24–26). Ovid's metaphysical doubt has an "epic sweep": "[T]he endless rarefaction and condensation of matter, the foreseeable succession of unforeseeable shapes, the variety that gives no spice to life—these are the materials with which the poet has built an edifice not of faith" (which one might expect of a less subversive Augustan writer) "but of doubt" (46, 55–56). In such a universe, "stripped of the least suggestion of causal order," it is a mistake to assume that experience is regulated by any reliable physical, or moral, laws; it consists instead of a series of physically and morally random, and intrinsically meaningless, events (51, 59). Those struggling to make their way in the Ovidian universe must face, usually unsuccessfully, a relentless onslaught of forces tending toward the annihilation of any conception of a unified, autonomous self. As Skulsky puts it, "the fantasy of transformation, in Ovid's treatment, is the story of the self as it endures a catastrophic physical change, a change sometimes attended by a loss of awareness . . . sometimes by the persistence of a mind alienated from all selves including the self it belongs to" (29–30, 35–36).

In the Ovidian world, physical fluidity has social and moral correlates: moral "facts," slippery under any circumstances, are going to be all the more so where solid physical ground itself is always treacherous. Social convention is meant to regulate human behavior and human society, but it is entirely arbitrary and therefore an extremely precarious ordering device (Skulsky 1981, 40–41). Human knowledge and character alike are marked by indeterminacy rather than clarity. People stumble about, blindly basing their decisions and actions on the "mingling of truths and fabrications . . . [and a] confusion of true and false opinion . . . matched by the confusion of perception and misperception" (46). Character in Ovid is as unstable as knowledge: his people are subject to radical transformations of personality and are often reduced to the abstraction of their ruling passions (35–37). And finally justice, which ordinarily relies on rules of cause and effect for its operation, in a world devoid of these principles is a joke, as capricious as everything else (52). In Ovid's world, and in that of the later *Metamorphoses* as well, *all* laws—physical, social, moral—simply break down. Few critics would argue with the essential features of Skulsky's account of the Ovidian universe; the world of Apuleius' novel has been described in these terms less often. And so, let us follow Lucius on his journey "down a road through a wilderness, past the uncanny, toward the unforeseeable" (Stephenson 1964, 90), as things fall apart.

On his first morning in Hypata, Lucius explores the city with an overwhelming sensation of the volatility of his new surroundings:

> There was nothing in that city that I believed to be what it was as I looked at it, but everything seemed to have been transformed into another shape by some deadly incantation: I thought that the stones I was treading upon had been hardened from human beings, that the birds I heard had once been human but now sported feathers, that the trees surrounding the city were likewise humans with leaves, and that the running water in the fountains had its source in human bodies; it seemed to me that any minute the statues and the pictures would walk, the walls talk.

> [nec fuit in illa civitate quod aspiciens id esse crederem, quod esset, sed omnia prorsus ferali murmure in aliam effigiem translata, ut et lapides, quos offenderem, de homine duratos et aves, quas audirem, indidem plumatas et arbores, quae pomerium ambirent, similiter foliatas et fontanos latices de corporibus humanis fluxos crederem; iam statuas et imagines incessuras, parietes locuturos.] (2.1)

Here Lucius is shown groping tentatively and yet with great excitement along shifting ground where nothing is in reality what it appears to be. It is true that his eager anticipation of getting involved in magical activities has caused his imagination to run away with him, and on that level the picture of the city's face transformed in Lucius' eyes by the very thought of magic aids in creating an atmosphere that signals the inexorable approach and arrival of real magical events. But on another level, the one at which the novel ultimately works, Lucius' altered perception represents the first instance of the blurring of familiar boundaries that will come to characterize his world in *all* its spheres, long after his rash naïveté has ceased to will a new and (so he thinks at this point) more exciting reality into being, and long after magic has ceased to play a central role in the plot. Here Lucius' vision is marked by the collapsing together of categories ordinarily thought to exist in opposition to one another: the animal and the human, the animate and the inanimate, art and life.

This apparent transgression of material boundaries continues when Lucius arrives at the house of his Aunt Byrrhena to attend a sumptuous banquet given by her in celebration of the Risus festival (2.19). As soon as he steps into the foyer, the guest of honor finds himself in the midst of a riot of shimmering sensual opulence. The aura of unreality is general—"Whatever could not be, was there" [*quicquid fieri non potest ibi est*], recalls Lucius—but many details of the description heighten the impression of the instability of the physical world. Tables "gleam with citron wood and ivory" [*mensae . . . citro et ebore nitentes*], silver shines, gold glistens (*argentum alibi clarum et aurum fulgurans*); the entire scene pulsates with an unusually vivid sensory quality. Labored references to the genesis of certain implements are another way of alluding to the shifting identity of matter: Byrrhena serves drinks in "hollowed out amber and stones carved to drink from" [*sucinum . . . cavatum et lapides ut bibas*], and slave boys offer wine in "precious gems formed into cups" [*gemmae formatae in pocula*]. It is doubly significant that Apuleius endows Byrrhena's *riches* with a chimerical character when we read the novel as a fictional spiritual autobiography and remember that the transience of material wealth and the pleasures it brings is a religious and philosophical commonplace. But matter ebbs and flows in subtler realms as well. The instability of the human ego, for example, is suggested in apparently incidental phrases long before it is fully developed in the episodes of psychological transformation that dominate Books 7 through 10. Socrates' poverty causes him to appear to be "almost someone else" [*paene alius lurore*] (1.5). Likewise, Lucius recalls that in his ecstasy at witnessing Pamphile's transformation he seemed to himself to be "anything other than Lucius" [*quidvis aliud magis videbar esse quam Lucius*] (3.22). Figurative expressions such as these serve as reminders that the ego-self is as tenuous as the coarser matter of Byrrhena's banquet hall.[12]

A consistent feature of Lucius' unfolding preconversion world view is the disintegration of the ontological and conventional categories that would have been the mainstays of his quotidian thinking and organization of reality. Common oppositions that structure thought and whose axiomatic status is rarely questioned—those between death and life, sleep and waking, animal and human, art and life, animate and inanimate—begin to collapse.[13] In the world of the *Metamorphoses*, the dead cannot be relied upon to remain in that state, nor can the apparently living to be so in reality. In Book 2, the witches' pillaging of the resting places of the dead for body parts to be used in their sinister spells gives the dead an inappropriate force among the living, when the two realms ought to be safely and reliably discrete. Beyond this indirect form of resurrection, it is not uncommon for the dead to come back to life intact through feats of necromancy. The most spectacular instance of this is the reanimation of the murdered groom by Zatchlas the Egyptian prophet in Thelyphron's story (2.28–29). Interestingly

12. Surely more tenuous, we would say. Lucius' curious habit of referring to his former human self in the third person and by his proper name ("Rather insistently, Lucius is used as the name not of the I whose thinking persisted, but as the name of the visible human body that the ego has lost") is discussed in its function as a "teasing reference to the ultimately unfixed and unlocatable authority of the text itself" by Winkler (1985, 149–53).

13. Auerbach, in enumerating the ways in which a "spectral, dreadful distortion of reality" is expressed in the history of Ammianus Marcellinus, cites the "many comparisons of human beings with animals or of events in real life with those of the theater or the world of the dead" (1959, 60, 63; translations mine). Auerbach identifies Apuleius as the precursor of Ammianus in the representation of a "spectrally distorted reality." Looking at Apuleius from another angle, Johnson (1976, 144) observes in connection with the irrational tone of much of the *Aeneid* that "we are passing from the world of Graeco-Roman rationalism into the worlds of Seneca's tragedies, of Lucan, of Apuleius, and of barbaric Christianity"—and of Ammianus, Auerbach would add. The concept of a unifying zeitgeist is implied by both critics to explain the tonal community that links the authors they cite. In contrast, my reading of the *Metamorphoses* stresses the way the text limits this world view to the experience of one individual, Lucius, and presents its disorienting features as the impetus behind one particular religious conversion. What happens to Lucius' perception and what motivates Apuleius' representation of it have no necessary relationship to any larger zeitgeist in which they might be situated, if indeed that concept has any validity.

enough, the corpse itself has a strong sense of proper ontological boundaries: "Why are you calling me back to the duties of mortal life when I had already drunk the waters of Lethe and was making my way swimming through the Stygian marshes? Cease and desist, I beg you, and let go back to my rest," he complains [quid, oro, me post Lethaea pocula iam Stygiis paludibus innatantem ad momentariae vitae reducitis officia? desine iam, precor, desine ac me in meam quietem permitte]. It is worth noting the disparagement of mortal life implied in the phrase momentaria vita, with its two possible meanings: "momentary restoration to life," or "fleeting mortal life." The devaluation of mortal life implied in the second reading of the phrase is standard in narratives of religious conversion. Incidents such as the resurrection of the murdered husband render Thelyphron's skeptical query, "Are the dead in the habit of getting up and running away here?" [hicine mortui solent aufugere?] (2.21), highly ironic.[14]

Not only do the dead come to life, but those who appear to be living might in fact be well on their way past the Stygian swamps. Socrates walks the earth for a time after his heart is extracted by witches, but that time is brief. Far from being the healthy companion (integer, sanus, incolumis) that he appears to be to Aristomenes, after a gradual and ghastly weakening he pitches into a stream from which he has been drinking, now fully the lifeless corpse (corpus exanimatum) he has in fact been since the previous night (2.13, 18–19). "A spurious life is brought to a close by a spurious death," as Skulsky puts it (1981, 80). Death can masquerade as life; sleep can masquerade as death: the sleep that enabled the witches to trick Thelyphron is described by both the storyteller himself and by the revived corpse as rendering the hapless guard essentially dead ("A profound sleep submerged me suddenly in a deep

---

14. Two important considerations qualify my inclusion of the Zatchlas scene as one of Apuleius' sites for representing a world coming ontologically unglued. First, this resurrection is sought in the interests of justice and is orchestrated by an Egyptian priest who is said to be an implement of divine providence. Second, necromantic activity, or reports of it, were not strange in antiquity; a certain amount of commerce between the living and the dead was taken for granted. I think, however, that in a text where the conflation of death and life, along with other collapsing oppositions, is repeatedly refined and elaborated in nonmagical and non-necromantic settings, arguably for the purpose of making a statement about the unsettling instability of reality in general, polysemy allows all instances of the motif to be taken as components in the overarching scheme.

abyss, so that not even Apollo himself would have easily been able to determine which one of us was more dead, the corpse or me" [*me somnus profundus in imum barathrum repente demergit, ut ne deus quidem Delficus ipse facile discerneret duobus nobis iacentibus, quis esset magis mortuus*] [2.25; cf. 30]). Moreover, figurative deaths abound and add to the impression of ontological instability.[15]

Confusion between the waking and the sleeping or dreaming states blurs the picture even further. Aristomenes half convinces himself that the gruesome events of the previous night were all a bad dream. "Because I was immoderate in my drinking yesterday evening, a bad night brought grim and dreadful visions to me, so that even now I think that I am spattered and polluted with human blood" [*mihi denique, quod poculis vesperi minus temperavi, nox acerba diras et truces imagines optulit, ut adhuc me credam cruore humano aspersum atque impiatum*] (1.18). This is the rationalization that he offers to Socrates, but of course the *imagines* were not a dream at all. The tone is different but the problem the same when Lucius, stupefied with incredulity at Pamphile's metamorphosis, wonders whether it is not all just a dream: "Although awake, I was dreaming; I rubbed my eyes over and over again and tried to figure out whether I was really awake" [*vigilians somniabar; defrictis adeo diu pupulis, an vigilarem, scire quaerebam*] (3.22). Lucius and Aristomenes, observing "real" events, believe that they are dreaming. Later, Charite has a dream about her newlywed husband's murder so real in its horror that she abruptly awakens: "Terrified by the monstrousness of such a vision, I was shaken trembling from my deathly sleep" [*talis aspectus atrocitate perterrita somno funesto pavens excussa sum*] (4.27). Whereas Aristomenes and Lucius take reality for a dream, Charite is convinced that a nightmare vision is reality. This inversion is accompanied by the old woman's folk commentary about the unreality of the *imagines falsae* seen during sleep (4.27). Her assertion complements the suspicion of Lucius and Aristomenes that *imagines* witnessed while waking can be just as

---

15. E.g., Aristomenes' fear of the witches nearly kills him (1.14); Lucius is mortified by his experience at the Risus festival (3.9, 10); his suffering as a beast of burden leaves him and his less fortunate ass companion metaphorically dead (3.29; 4.5).

deceptive.[16] In Lucius' world reality itself is assuming the puzzling nonlinear quality ordinarily associated exclusively with the "empty fictions of dreams" [*vana somniorum figmenta*] (4.27).

The permeability of the line separating the animal realm from the human is illustrated in the most concrete of ways when Lucius the young Corinthian aristocrat is transformed into an ass. The complexity of Lucius' new condition offers material for further commentary on the inadequacy of conventional categories for organizing and describing experience. His curious half-man, half-beast state is the subject of frequent ruminations and disclaimers on the part of the narrator Lucius, who repeatedly reminds the reader that he was an ass in form alone, having retained his human intellect. "Although now a perfect ass and a beast of burden instead of Lucius, I nevertheless still had human perception" [*quamquam perfectus asinus et pro Lucio iumentum sensum tamen retinebam humanum*] (3.26), he informs us soon after recounting his transformation; his "insides were not completely animal" [*non usquequaque ferina praecordia*] (4.2). Lucius the narrator seems anxious to anticipate and defend himself against charges of complete asininity. He offers his photographic recollection of the robbers' cave as evidence that his *mens* and *sensus* remained intact throughout his ordeal (4.6). Thus it is not simply a case of a man becoming an animal. Lucius is stuck somewhere between the two; he does not belong unambiguously to one category or the other. In view of his predicament, the categories themselves begin to seem quite inadequate. Instead of being mutually exclusive, the two identities shade into one another on a continuum, and Lucius is suspended somewhere in the overlapping space.

Of course on one level, Lucius' retention of human intellect is a narrative necessity, for had he lost it he never would have been able to register his experiences as an ass in a way that would allow him to tell his tale later. But one mention of the persistence of his human faculties ought to have sufficed to explain how he was later able to produce a memoir of the events, and one mention is all it is accorded in the parallel Greek epitome (*Onos* 15). Seen from another angle, Lucius' double identity could be read as simply a conventional feature of tales of transformation. Observations about human attributes retained after physical transformation occur in Homer (*Od.* 10.239, Circe's new pigs) and in

---

16. For relevant ancient dream theories, see, e.g., Hijmans et al. 1977, 205–6.

Ovid (*Met.* 3.203, Actaeon).[17] But in the later *Metamorphoses,* Lucius' almost obsessive awareness of the untenability of his position in onto-logical limbo is repeatedly foregrounded. The extreme care with which the narrator chooses words to designate his problematic status points to its central thematic importance. As Winkler (1985, 151–52) observes, "if the speaker enjoys saying that he is not Lucius, he takes equal care not to identify himself with the ass. He finds himself 'in the appearance of an ass' (3.29); Fortuna has brought him 'into a beast' (7.2); 'I confess myself gratefully grateful to my ass that, while hidden under its hide . . .' (9.13)." Here, the human animal epitomizes the breakdown of the natural order or, more precisely, of human structures for ordering a resistant reality, that is everywhere in evidence in the *Metamorphoses*. Skulsky describes Ovid's Actaeon, similarly stuck between the two realms and unable fully to materialize in either, as a "metaphysical castaway in a class by itself" who like Lucius "has lost his passport in the realm of matter" (1981, 29, 72). We will soon see that Apuleius also chooses Actaeon as a leading emblem of "metaphysical doubt," and specifically as a point where the manifestations of metaphysical doubt developed in the novel converge.

An instance of breached boundaries between animal and human one level removed from that of Lucius is the metamorphosis in Book 4 (14–21) of Thrasyleon the bandit into a bear, as part of a scheme to infil-trate a rich man's house. So true is Thrasyleon to his assumed *persona* that he deceives all and inspires admiration in his comrades. The ban-dit narrator begins his account of Thrasyleon's change by describing it as a "cleverly contrived appearance" [*sollers species*] (15) and a "decep-tive ruse" [*fallacia*] (16). Yet in spite of this initial acknowledgment of the element of calculation, the tale comes to stress the totality of the transformation and the way in which Thrasyleon's ursine *persona,* at the outset a self-conscious fabrication, gradually takes on a life of its

---

17. As Winkler puts it, "the folk metaphysics of transformation tales requires that the person before and the animal after have a common core of identity. The same thinking *ego* is transferred to a new body, there to discover new physical sensations . . . but with memory, language, values, and personal-ity intact" (1985, 151). In the Homeric and Ovidian passages, incidentally, the third-person narration rules out the explanation that the device is required to account for the production of a first-person narrative. Hijmans et al. 1977, 30 note the persistence of "the motif of the ass who is not quite an ass" in Apuleius.

own. The narrator consistently refers to Thrasyleon as "the beast" (*bestia*), not "our friend in his bear costume": "We put our heroic comrade, now altogether turned beast, into a cage" [*fortissimum socium nostrum prorsus bestiam factum inmittimus caveae*] (15). Thereafter an unqualified *bestia* designates Thrasyleon six times (16, 19, and 21). Slowly but surely, the bandit to all intents and purposes becomes a bear. Whereas the original plan had called for one of the bandits to "assume the *likeness* of a bear" [*ursae subiret effigiem*] (14), in the end Thrasyleon dies a bear pure and simple: "A strong fellow hurled a spear right into the midsection of the bear" [*validus . . . lanceam mediis iniecit ursae praecordiis*] (21). In his death throes Thrasyleon emits not human cries but "animal bellows and growls" [*mugitus et ferinos fremitus*] (21).[18] The entire episode, for all its comic and mock-heroic tone, is constructed in such a way as to encourage the reader to reflect not only on the persuasiveness of illusion, but even on whether illusion is a valid category in view of the truth-value that it frequently acquires.

The fusion of the animal and the human that Thrasyleon's exploits represent makes its first sustained appearance in a lengthy *ecphrasis* at the beginning of Book 2. This passage describes a sculpture of Actaeon being transformed into a stag in consequence of his unauthorized spying on the goddess Diana as she bathed (2.4). The group of statues in Byrrhena's atrium that the *ecphrasis* depicts has an obvious foreshadowing function and constitutes an unheeded admonition to Lucius about the dangers of prying into the forbidden: "Everything you see is yours" [*tua sunt cuncta quae vides*], his aunt comments, perhaps too enigmatically for Lucius to appreciate the warning even if he had been inclined to prudence. But the statues and in particular the details of Apuleius' description of them also constitute a programmatic statement about the instability of supposedly fixed ontological categories. Not only is the subject of the work a man-to-beast metamorphosis, but the stress of the *ecphrasis* falls on the artificiality of the dichotomies that would oppose art and life and the animate and the inanimate. The volatility of these oppositions is expressed in similar terms elsewhere in the text. At 3.10, Lucius recalls his reaction to the discovery that he has been the butt of Hypata's elaborate practical joke. It contrasts starkly with the mirthful belly laughs of the spectators: "As soon as I

18. Hijmans et al. (1977, 122–23) and Tatum (1969, 135) have pointed out how complete a metamorphosis the language of 4.15 and 21 suggests.

had pulled back that cloth [covering the wineskins], I stood there
frozen, fixed in stone, in no way different from the other statues or
columns of the theater" [*ut primum illam laciniam prenderam, fixus in lapi-
dem steti gelidus nihil secus quam una de ceteris theatri statuis vel columnis*].
Here, having figuratively traded his flesh and blood for stone, Lucius
feels himself merging imperceptibly into the artwork. The image is
given a final twist in the next chapter when the magistrates report that
the city has proposed to erect a *real* statue of its guest to reward him for
his troubles (3.11).[19]

Displaying all the hallmarks of a favorite Apuleian device, inversion, this sequence represents a reversal of the central movement of the
earlier Actaeon scene. Whereas in Book 3 Lucius seems to stiffen into a
piece of stone statuary, at 2.4 a group of stone statues is so lifelike that
it all but seduces the viewer into believing in the reality of the world it
represents. The impression of art coming to life that is created by the
Actaeon group recalls the sensation reported by Lucius just a little earlier when, dazzled by magical possibilities, he had fully expected "the
statues and images to get up and walk" [*crederem . . . statuas et imagines
incessuras*] (2.1). The *ecphrasis* moreover anticipates features of the Thrasyleon episode in the way it alternates foregrounding the power of illusion and the role of artifice. In spite of its length, the passage is enough
of a tour de force to warrant quotation in its entirety:

> And then there was a chunk of Parian marble fashioned into
> Diana, occupying the exact center of the scene. It was a perfectly
> brilliant statue, with its garment blowing in the wind, lively in
> step, going to meet those who entered the room, awesome with
> the majesty of divinity. Dogs protected both sides of the goddess,
> and the dogs were stone also. Their eyes were threatening, their
> ears stood up stiff, their nostrils flared, their mouths gaped
> fiercely, in such a way that if the sound of barking had broken in
> from nearby, you would have thought that it came from those
> stone jaws. But that marvelous sculptor offered the greatest proof

---

19. As van der Paardt remarks on 3.10, "*ceteris* . . . stresses the idea that
Lucius is one of the statues (or columns) himself" (1971, 84). Actually the final
twist may be the self-conscious allusion to events in the author's own life: twice
in *Florida* 16, Apuleius mentions that in Carthage statues of him were erected
during his lifetime; see also Augustine *Epistle* 138.19.

of his craftsmanship by making the dogs rear up on their hind legs with their breasts held high, their forefeet running while their hind feet were rooted in the ground. Behind the goddess a rock rose up in the manner of a cave, with moss and grass and leaves and twigs and here tendrils of vines and there shrubs flowering out of stone; the shining stone inside the cave reflected the statue outside. Under the very edge of the rock there hung apples and very skillfully polished grapes, which art the rival of nature displayed, looking just like real fruit. You would think that some of them could be picked to eat, when autumn abounding in new wine breathes new color on them; and if you were to look into the stream running along near the goddess' feet and rustling into a gentle wave, you would believe that the clusters of grapes hanging there as if in the countryside were actually able to move, as a culmination of their other lifelike qualities. In the middle of the stone foliage you could see a marble likeness of Actaeon, reflected in both the rock and the water, leaning toward the goddess with a curious gaze, waiting for her to bathe and already changing into a stag.

[ecce lapis Parius in Dianam factus tenet libratam totius loci medietatem, signum perfecte luculentum, veste reflatum, procursu vegetum, introeuntibus obvium et maiestate numinis venerabile; canes utrumquesecus deae latera muniunt, qui canes et ipsi lapis erant; his oculi minantur, aures rigent, nares hiant, ora saeviunt et sicunde de proximo latratus ingruerit, eum putabis de faucibus lapidis exire et, in quo summum specimen operae fabrilis egregius ille signifex prodidit, sublatis canibus in pectus arduis pedes imi resistunt, currunt priores. pone tergum deae saxum insurgit in speluncae modum muscis et herbis et foliis et virgulis et alicubi pampinis et arbusculis alibi de lapide florentibus. splendet intus umbra signi de nitore lapidis. sub extrema saxi margine poma et uvae faberrime politae dependent, quas ars aemula naturae veritati similes explicuit. putes ad cibum inde quaedam, cum mustulentus autumnus maturum colorem adflaverit, posse decerpi et, si fontem, qui deae vestigio discurrens in lenem vibratur undam, pronus aspexeris, credes illos ut rure pendentes racemos inter cetera veritatis nec agitationis officio carere. inter medias frondes lapidis Actaeon simulacrum curioso optutu in deam proiectus, iam in cervum ferinus et in saxo simul et in fonte loturam Dianam opperiens visitur.] (2.4)

The central focus of this description is clearly on how true to life the sculptures are: they have the ability to seduce the viewer into believing that they are what they are not, that a representation is the real thing. But a persistent undercurrent of details pulls simultaneously against that impression to make the reader aware of the images' constructedness. The illusion is repeatedly broken up by strategically placed references to the operation of artifice and the counterfeiting activity of artificers: we are reminded that behind it all is a skilled artisan (*egregius ille signifex*) practicing his craft, which is to imitate "nature" and "truth" as completely as possible (*ars aemula naturae veritati similes [uvas] explicuit*). The gleam of these grapes is not natural but the result of much craftsmanlike polishing, and it is not really Actaeon we see, but a stone simulacrum of him. Furthermore, the almost badgering recurrence of *lapis* forces the reader to remember that in spite of their apparent animation the substance of the statues is inanimate matter. Finally, their membership in an endlessly refracted world of illusion is signaled by the construction of an otherwise puzzling system of multiple reflections. Not only are Actaeon and Diana apparently reflected in both the cavelike rock *(saxum)* and the water (which seems to be a real fountain, but is not unambiguously so), but the viewer can perceive the apparent motion of the grapes, and thus their verisimilitude, only by examining their reflection in the moving stream (or the apparently moving sculpted stream). This is a strangely indirect and convoluted way of saying the clusters looked real. Yet it is one entirely consistent with the passage's function as a statement about the unstable and mediated character of "reality," which upon closer examination could prove to be a complex system of interdependent illusions—a text, in other words.

Winkler reads the statue of Actaeon as an illustration of the most extreme degree of stability and unity possible in a narrative; it represents "a frozen tale," a "story that is fixed in place." The point of having this "very solid model of stability, of narrative that does not move" appear so volatile is to show that "it is a triumph of unity . . . to emerge against the centrifugal forces of disunity." In Winkler's view, stability is winning out here; the statues are primarily a symbol of hyperdelineation or hyper-unity to the point of rigidity. As such they function only by implication as a warning against the dangers of a contrived superstability; the description's suggestions of the potential "breakup of or resistance to . . . unity" are strictly secondary.[20] In my view, on the other hand, it is fluidity more than rigidity that is foregrounded in the manner of the statues' representation; furthermore they epitomize the fluidity of Lucius' world (as text) as much as the fluidity of Apuleius' text itself. Clearly the passage includes ideas about the rigidity of "petrified" ontological and conceptual categories. But this reading is consistently undermined by the counterimpression of blurring lines. There is a vestigial presence of familiar distinctions (art/life, animate/inanimate, animal/human), but the way these distinctions bleed in the total picture makes it in the end not so much an image of hyperorganization as a statement that *any* organization of reality is provisional and contingent.

The Actaeon passage is an emblem of the liquescent quality that marks the physical world of the *Metamorphoses* as a whole, or more precisely the physical world as Lucius perceives it. But his world and its organization are coming unhinged in less concrete areas as well, and perhaps because of their intangibility these disruptions of the usual order can have an even more disturbing effect.

3

B.E. Perry devoted part of his career to scrutinizing the alleged logical lapses in the *Metamorphoses* in order to demonstrate that the narrative is a sloppily assembled patchwork of swatches from disparate sources. Perry argued that the author was indifferent to the seams glaringly evident in his composite narrative as long as each piece was engaging on its own merits and served his guiding purpose, which was simply to entertain. In recent years, virtually all critics have abandoned the

---

20. Winkler further argues that for Actaeon, and for Lucius in his moments of paralysis and stupefaction, to become a piece of sculpture either literally or metaphorically is to lose the dynamism that defines real experience. It is to be turned by "psychological immobility" into a "frozen, immobile self"—in other words, into a closed text. Winkler writes, "[t]he statue represents a fixed narrative unity (Actaeon's story, the Risus-festival story). . . . Lucius resists the attempt to unify and finish him by setting up a statue; Actaeon's statue tells the story of his own dismemberment and loss of self." These images together function as a "symbolic reflection of the [text's] fluctuating unity/disunity or stability/mobility" (1985, 168–73).

patchwork theory of Apuleian composition and now take for granted that the novel is very carefully crafted. Still, it will be useful to resurrect a sampling of Perry's critiques insofar as they will in their own way help us to get at another important aspect of Lucius' disintegrating world. Let us begin with Perry's analysis of the episode involving Aristomenes' attempted suicide in Book 1.14–17 (1967, 262–64 = 1929, 394–400). He argues that it is filled with logical contradictions that result from the slipshod interpolation of a lover's melodramatic suicide attempt into the basic story of the supernatural. Perry's critique centers around what he calls Apuleius' "interpolated *ianitor*" (doorman). Fear of this doorman's suspicion drives Aristomenes to attempt the suicide that was not a part of the basic story from which the author was working, but that he nevertheless wanted to introduce in order to compound the drama and suspense. The careless attribution (so Perry) to this *ianitor* of lines that would only make sense coming from Socrates in Perry's reconstructed version of the original story of the supernatural renders most of the dialogue between Aristomenes and the *ianitor* "completely unintelligible."

The primary *ianitor*-related problems, as enumerated by Perry, are as follows. When Aristomenes, anticipating a murder charge, makes his initial attempt to escape, he demands to be let out of the inn by the *ianitor*, who replies:

> Are you crazy? Do you want to set out this time of night when the roads are infested with bandits? Even if you are eager to die because you have a guilty conscience, I'm not such a pumpkin-head that I would die for you.

> [quid? tu . . . ignoras latronibus infestari vias, qui hoc noctis iter incipis? nam etsi tu alicuius facinoris tibi conscius scilicet mori cupis, nos cucurbitae caput non habemus, ut pro te moriamur.] (1.15)

The insinuation that Aristomenes has been involved in wrongdoing is jarring coming from the doorman, as it would also be in the mouth of Socrates, since it is completely unclear on what grounds either of them would make such a suggestion. Perry theorizes that the insinuation was inserted quite without motivation by Apuleius to drive Aristomenes, convinced that his account would not be believed, to the botched comic suicide that Apuleius was determined to include. The rest would be logical coming from Socrates, resisting the attempts of Aristomenes to rouse him so that they could depart together during the night. But for the doorman to insist that he would risk dying for Aristomenes should he let the latter out is puzzling indeed.

Another problem arises in the Apuleian version when the rope breaks and sends Aristomenes tumbling down on the sleeping Socrates, and both of them to the floor. At that point, the doorman enters and demands, "Where are you, who rashly tried to hurry off in the middle of the night, and now are snoring there rolled up in the covers?" [ubi es tu, qui alta nocte immodice festinabas et nunc stertis involutus?] (17). Since the clamor should have suggested to the doorman that both lodgers are wide awake, the whole question and especially stertis involutus are inscrutable unless originally posed by Socrates in his efforts to get his sleeping companion on the road the next morning. Furthermore, the mention of a window (16) through which it oddly does not occur to this potential fugitive from justice to escape, but through which a distraught lover bent on suicide would have no desire to escape, as well as Aristomenes' stylized lover's invocation to his bed (16), which produces a strange disjunction of tone on top of the logical problems, are cited by Perry as marking the incompetently interpolated character of the narrative.

Various rationalizing explanations have been put forward to vindicate the integrity of the entire episode as received and, in particular, to explain the doorman's mystifying words.[21] But I share Perry's response to the doorman; there is no escaping the absurdity of the dialogue between him and Aristomenes. It seems to me, however, that Perry, in spite of himself, provides a clue to a way of understanding this and similar passages that spares our writing them off as clumsy splicing on the one hand or propping them up with extratextual rationalizing on the other. In writing about the effects of allegedly careless interpolation in the Metamorphoses, he says:

> The strange conflicts in motivation, and the absence of natural sequence, which we find in these composite narratives . . . go far to explain the dreamland atmosphere of mystery and unreality which pervades much of the Metamorphoses in the first four books

---

21. E.g., Molt 1938, 83–86; Scobie 1975, 112–14.

. . . . No folktales . . . relating supernatural events, however para-
tactic or agglutinative their structure may be, have this puzzling
contradictory quality . . . [this] unique atmosphere of mystery and
surrealism . . . [and this] mysterious, unworldly effect. (1967, 258,
281)

Because of his insistence that this effect is entirely accidental, Perry dis-
counts even the obvious explanation that it is consistent with the representation of an enchanted place where a whole range of conditioned
expectations about how the world works must be suspended (1967,
258). Such an atmosphere clearly does provide an appropriate backdrop for the narration of tales involving magic. But beyond this local
function, the "atmosphere of surrealism" has a much larger significance, and in this respect it is comparable to the motif of metamorphosis. For when we step into the world of the *Metamorphoses*, we find that
our assumption that events will be logically connected is repeatedly
challenged. This is true not only of scenes where magic could be the
culprit, but also where magic is only peripherally a factor, or not at all.
The impression that the laws of cause and effect have gone haywire
may begin with magic, but it is soon generalized. Much of the action of
the novel as a whole is characterized by a "departure from the conception of a rationally ordered world whose connections can be grasped
and represented according to the laws of causality."[22] The incoherence
of the doorman can be read as part of this pattern or, more precisely, as
part of this breakdown of patterns.

A similarly baffling episode occurs shortly after the Aristomenes
sequence in Book 1. Because in this case there has never been any suspicion of textual contamination, this passage better lends itself to testing the proposition that violations of cause and effect are built into the
plot, as crucial elements in the representation of a world that is gradually being stripped of all familiar points of reference. At 1.24–25, Lucius
purchases a fish for his supper at the local market. On his way back to
Milo's house he meets his old friend Pythias, who is now the aedile in
charge of the provisions market in Hypata. Upon learning the exorbi-
tant price paid by Lucius for the fish, the outraged magistrate storms
back to the market and upbraids the fishmonger for his cupidity.
Pythias orders his attendant to stomp the fish to bits, apparently to

22. Van Thiel 1971, 1:157; (my translation).

show the merchant that his style of business will not be tolerated. "I'll show you how price-gougers will be dealt with while I'm in office!" [iam enim faxo scias, quem ad modum sub meo magisterio mali debeant coherceri], shouts Pythias to the merchant. He then turns and assures Lucius, "I think that's enough abuse of the old man to do the trick" [sufficit mihi . . . seniculi tanta haec contumelia]. At that point Pythias, presumably quite pleased with himself, appears to stalk off, as no more is heard from him. The absurdity of his actions is manifest, as the only one to be punished is Lucius himself, "deprived of both his money and his dinner" [nummis simul privatus et cena]. The scene has left commentators and readers as "disturbed and dumbfounded" as the victimized protagonist (his actis consternatus ac prorsus obstupidus).[23] But the impression created by this episode, with its lapses in logic and unsettling non sequiturs, is absolutely central to the way reality is represented in Metamorphoses 1–10. It is true that we as readers often find ourselves looking "instinctively but in vain for organic connections between things which the author has not given" us (Perry 1967, 281), but it is precisely the assumption that things are organically connected that the text means to confound.

Perry identified and dissected many sequences in the Metamorphoses that he alleged to be egregiously illogical as the result of careless composition.[24] The major ones in Books 1 through 4 are as follows:

---

23. Scobie tries to explain the episode by situating it in the "Roman satirical tradition in which the exposure of the pretentious airs and graces of municipal magistrates is a topos" (1975, 127). But the Latin Metamorphoses is not on the whole a satirical work. A more arcane approach is to take the fish-stomping as a cryptic allusion to an Egyptian rite and thus an intimation of Lucius' ultimate salvation by an Egyptian goddess (e.g., Derchain and Hubaux 1958). Winkler at one point accepts the business with the fish as a "veiled Isiac allusion" (1985, 317–18), but elsewhere judges it a "rather pointless" incident prompting "a desire simply to escape"; a vestige of slapstick stage business; and a trace of Apuleius' debt to the Aesopic tradition (122 n. 47; 163; 284). I think that Auerbach comes closest to the real spirit of the episode when he remarks that it conveys a "half absurd, half eerie distortion of the usual and normal incidents of life" (1959, 65; translation mine).

24. This is not the place to catalogue exhaustively all of Perry's attacks on the integrity of the text, with their naïve assumption that literature is (or should be) a faithful mirror of an intelligible and autonomous reality. Readers are referred to his chapter on the Metamorphoses in The Ancient Romances (1967), which recapitulates the essential points of his earlier articles.

(1) 3.12 (Perry 1967, 255). Here, the ability of Lucius to respond coherently to a straightforward question appears more than a little shaky when he is made to reply to his aunt's invitation to dinner, delivered by her messenger, as if he were addressing Byrrhena herself. The slave enters and announces: "Your Aunt Byrrhena extends her invitation and reminds you that the banquet you promised late last night to attend will soon begin" [*rogat te tua parens Byrrhena et convivii, cui te sero desponderas, iam appropinquantis admonet*]. Lucius, drained by his experience at the Risus festival, turns down her invitation with these inappropriately addressed words: "How I wish, aunt, that I could comply with your wishes. . . ." [*quam vellem, parens, iussis tuis obsequium commodare. . . .*].

(2) 2.31–3.20, the Risus festival sequence (Lucius' murder of the "bandits," his trial and its aftermath, and Fotis' account of the animation of the wineskins). The logical problems presented by this episode are essentially two, according to Perry (1967, 273–82 = 1925). First, Fotis inexplicably postpones revealing the events leading up to Lucius' battle with the wineskins and her own role in them. Perry theorizes that the Latin author interpolated the trial, and another full day, between the utricide and the slave girl's account of the wineskins' accidental animation, which he found in the Greek original, but that he failed on several counts to make the necessary adjustments. Thus, Fotis recalls seeing her mistress casting her ill-fated aphrodisiac spell *vesperi* (3.16), which Perry insists must be translated "this evening." This would have made sense if she were speaking with Lucius immediately upon his entering the house after doing battle, as she must have done in the original. But it is unintelligible if she is speaking twenty-four hours later when Pamphile's actions occurred "yesterday evening." Once again (so Perry) Apuleius' inept methods of combining material introduce glaring violations of any realistic sequence of events. His methods are responsible for Fotis' improbable failure to explain immediately to Lucius the true nature of the "men" he has slain, and also for the implication that Lucius goes straight to bed after being admitted, as if nothing out of the ordinary has happened. But of course, if she had explained immediately, as was natural, there would have

been no motivation for the mock trial that Apuleius was determined to have intervene. He thoughtlessly leaves in the mouth of the slave girl a speech of explanation that is in his version anticlimactic and oddly lacking in any mention of the trial or festival.

The interpolated Risus episode is incompatible with the wineskin sequence in another way, according to Perry. It violates plausibility that the elaborate planning for the mock trial could have occurred between midnight (when the "slaying" occurred) and sunrise (when the magistrates appear at Lucius' door to indict him for the crime). Yet this is what we must infer, since the "killing" could not have been predicted, and the plans necessarily would have been made after the event, which was clearly accidental. But accepting the instantaneous mobilization of Hypata, as difficult as it is, still is preferable (in Perry's view) to the explanation offered by others, that Byrrhena and her friends somehow were responsible for entangling Lucius in the apparent murder as their contribution to the rites of Risus. Because the event could not have been foreseen, and because other aspects of Byrrhena's characterization would seem to preclude her being involved in any way with Pamphile (for example, her apparently genuine concern to warn Lucius about his host's wife, 2.5), Perry labels this scenario "simply not possible." Furthermore, Apuleius' inability to tell a story coherently is further demonstrated by his hints at Byrrhena's involvement in the face of its impossibility.[25] Perry blames these "puzzling contradictions in motivation" as well on the intrusion of the Risus episode (3.1–12) into the wineskin saga of the Greek model (2.32 and 3.13–20 in Apuleius) without the Latin author's having bothered to make the adjustments necessary to produce an intelligible narrative.

(3) 2.21–30, Thelyphron's tale (Perry 1967, 264–73 = 1929, 231–38). This sequence, according to Perry, presents one logical prob-

---

25. Hints at 2.31, where Byrrhena tells Lucius, "By your presence you will make this day more pleasing to us" [*hunc tua praesentia nobis efficies gratiorem*]; and 3.12, his trepidation at the thought of going back to her house after the trial.

lem after another. He begins with minor objections: do not the genuinely grieving widow of the story's beginning and the murderess she is revealed to be seem to be two different women (from two distinct original stories)? Also, why didn't Thelyphron's substitute nose and ears fall off in the course of his beating by the widow's slaves? And if they were durable enough to survive this assault, why didn't he keep them instead of resorting to covering his scars with his hair and a cloth plaster, which is how he appears at the banquet?

From these details, Perry moves on to more basic problems. First, the conclusion initially indicated—that the watchman must replace any parts stolen from the corpse with parts from his own body—is entirely forgotten in the unexpected and chaotic dénouement that we actually get. Thelyphron's exit "black and blue" [*laceratus atque discerptus*] (26) from his beating by the superstitious slaves was a remnant from an earlier version in which he was mutilated to satisfy the requirements of the agreement that he pay in kind for his failure as a guard. In the Apuleian reworking, Thelyphron's dog-eared exit is poorly motivated, since it seems unlikely that the widow would allow her slaves to punish him for so slight a *faux pas* (his unintentionally ill-omened words, "If you ever need my services, don't hesitate to call" [*quotiens operam nostram desiderabis, fidenter impera*] (26), and that they would beat him without her permission. Second, the "clear proofs of truth" [*veritatis documenta perlucida*] (30) offered by the corpse to establish his credibility in no way demonstrate his veracity with regard to the question at hand, that is, whether or not the widow murdered him. The sudden introduction of irrelevant evidence is Apuleius' awkward transition to his own conclusion for a preexisting episode involving allegations of murder and the resurrection of the chief witness. But the murder plot is abandoned unresolved for an anticlimactic reversion to witch stories.

Finally, there are puzzling inconsistencies between the version of Thelyphron's mutilation that he himself implies and the corpse's version. According to Thelyphron, a weasel (a witch in disguise) entered the room and unnerved him as he kept vigil. The witches therefore were able to enter the room easily and had access to the corpse. There was no need for them to summon the dead man and, having animated him (or, as happened by mistake, Thelyphron), to remove his members through a chink in the door. Yet this is what they do in the husband's version of the story because of their apparent inability to come inside. Why didn't the witch, having entered as a weasel, help herself to the corpse while Thelyphron slept, as we are led to expect? Perry sees the entire disjointed episode as resulting from the inept combination of three independent tales: that of a brash young man hired as a guard against spoil-seeking witches and paying with his own nose and ears when the corpse is discovered mutilated in the morning (2.21–26); a sensational tale of murder and necromancy (27–29); and one involving a disastrous case of mistaken identity, the fashioning of surrogate members (itself unexplained), and the subject's humiliation and exile (29–30). But Apuleius' "sutures" are so "conspicuously disruptive" that readers "cannot understand just what goes on in [the Apuleian version], and are . . . mystified by its atmosphere of surrealism" (1967, 265).

Critics responding to these charges in the past have commonly fallen into the trap of engaging with Perry on his own terms, which are problematic. Any quibbling about the logic of events in a literary text is undergirded by the assumption that literature faithfully and realistically represents life, and that life is straightforward and makes sense. The standard of logic to which Perry held the narrative is almost comically inappropriate, and his implied views about mimesis and the relationship between representation and a reality that is in this instance fictional to begin with are bound to seem quaint to us now. To the extent that some of these episodes do have a vaguely unsettling, if not downright bizarre, quality, I think that instead of being evidence of mimetic failure, this quality is a function of the character of the *Metamorphoses* as a narrative about perception and the workings of structuring mechanisms.

Let us look again at the Risus episode. Even by the conventional standards of literary realism, Perry's fussing over detail is unwarranted.[26] And yet there *is* something tenuous about the coherence of

---

26. There is no reason why Fotis should have revealed the "bandits'" true identity to Lucius as he stumbled in from the fray; little did she know the use

the basic sequence of events that does leave both Lucius and the reader unsettled. The implication that Lucius and Fotis did not even mention the wild nocturnal brawl, but instead immediately carried on as if nothing out of the ordinary had happened ("After Fotis opened the doors, I went straight to bed and dropped right off to sleep" [*patefactis aedibus me statim fatigatum lecto simul et somno tradidi*] [2.32]), is typical of the loose connections running through the episode. This sequence creates the jarring impression of an unusual event's sudden and violent intrusion into everyday life, followed instantaneously by the resumption of business as usual. Indeed, something is wrong with this entire picture, and it is rooted to a great extent in the thoroughness with which Lucius is deceived and in his mistaken belief in his own guilt while both Fotis and the citizens knew the truth and withheld it for different reasons. The uncanny speed with which Hypata is mobilized adds to his sense of vulnerability and paranoia, and his vaguely formulated suspicion of Byrrhena is testimony to it (he receives the slave's message "shuddering and terrified from a distance even at the thought of her house" [*formidans et procul perhorrescens etiam ipsam domum eius*] [3.12]). She need not have taken part in the preparations for the trial to inspire this intensity of feeling. In his mind she is understandably guilty by association. Her banquet of the previous evening, where Lucius is introduced to the god Risus and hears the oddly relished tale of a fellow victim, seems after all to mark the beginning of his troubles. Lucius' jumbled response to his aunt's vicariously delivered invitation needs to be read in the context of the paranoia that runs through the entire Risus episode—at least from the *actor's* point of view. The confused reply reflects the disruption of his mental equi-

---

her fellow citizens would make of the incident. The men he supposedly slew were hoodlums, after all, and at least that evening Lucius does not seem to be worried about being charged with their murder. As for Fotis' alleged failure the next night to mention Lucius' intervening experiences, the "trouble" and "anguish" (*molestia* and *angor*, 3.13) that she speaks of as having herself precipitated for him would seem to describe the mock trial far better than it does a brief, victorious skirmish with criminal-wineskins. Finally, *vesperi* is well attested as meaning an uncommitted "in the evening"; thus Fotis' words do not sabotage the temporal sequence. For an alternative explanation of *vesperi*, see P. James 1987, 87 n. 3.

librium and the disorientation and emotional exhaustion brought on by the mock trial.[27]

The narrative's irrational (and sometimes sinister) undercurrents are equally undeniable in the tale of Thelyphron. Again, some of Perry's objections can easily be dismissed. The simulated grief of the widow is one; Thelyphron's thrashing at the hands of the slaves is another, when we remember the seriousness with which ill-omened words were taken and the scope of Thelyphron's insinuation. Still, all is not well; upon finishing the story the reader is haunted by a lingering sense that he or she must have missed some critical connections. It *is* strange, when so much is made of the substitute features, that Thelyphron inexplicably appears at Byrrhena's with makeshift coverings over his scars. And it *is* odd that the witches would have provided the parts at all, when the widow's fear that her husband's corpse will be vandalized indicates a long tradition of mutilation without compensation. Moreover, the body's gratuitous introduction of irrelevant *documenta veritatis*, which in no way prove what we are led to expect them to prove, is strongly reminiscent of the scene with Pythias in its confident assertion of rational connection when in fact none exists. The reader is likewise left at a loss by the witches' unexplained change of strategy in removing the members of the animated "corpse" through a chink in the door when their preliminary forays have established the expectation of a more direct method. The narrative as a whole lurches repeatedly off course. We keep ending up precisely where we could have least predicted we would be and wondering how we got there. Events seem to unfold in a sort of logical void, and the length of time it takes the reader to grasp its dimensions, lulled as he or she is by the superficial appearance of normal sequence, adds to the sense of insidiousness.

---

27. On this point so also Riefstahl 1938, 25. P. James 1987, 90 suggests that Lucius' dread of his aunt's house is fueled in part by his understanding that he has replaced Thelyphron as "court jester" and will be forced, as Thelyphron was, to relive his humiliation by telling the tale of the trial if he joins her for dinner. Far from being accidental, the fact that Byrrhena's role in the proceedings remains unclear is, I think, quintessentially Apuleian. There is something vaguely hostile about her, but we can never quite put our finger on it; that we never know for sure whether she is friend or foe makes her all the more sinister. Milo has the same unsettling ambiguity: see the next section.

4

The laws of cause and effect are not the only ones to collapse in the tale of Thelyphron and Lucius' narrative of his experience at the Risus festival. The gleeful *Schadenfreude* with which the townspeople greet the sufferings first of Thelyphron and then of Lucius signals that regulators of social behavior are breaking down as well. At Byrrhena's banquet, a guest responds to Lucius' queries about the rumors that witches regularly mutilate the dead in Thessaly, by coyly pointing out that sometimes even the living bear such scars. "But here not even the living are spared; a certain man suffered the same misfortune and had his face completely mutilated" [*immo vero istic nec viventibus quidem ullis parcitur. et nescio qui simile passus ore undique omnifariam deformato truncatus est*] (2.20). The other guests understand him to mean Thelyphron, and contrary to expectation, they immediately burst into raucous guffaws: "At his words everyone present broke into licentious laughter" [*inter haec convivium totum in licentiosos cachinnos effunditur*]. Thelyphron tells his tale of woe under protest and concludes by describing his lonely exile and his pathetic efforts to conceal his wounds. On this sad note, the diners again burst inexplicably into gales of laughter: "As soon as Thelyphron finished his story, the banqueters, by now saturated with wine, began to laugh all over again" [*cum primum Thelyphron hanc fabulam posuit, compotores vino madidi rursum cachinnum integrant*] (31).

Lucius does not fare any better as the object of the townspeople's strange sense of humor. As he is led away to be tried for murder, he is astonished at the jovial mood of his persecutors: "Out of the corner of my eye I caught a truly mystifying sight: of all those people surrounding me there was not one who was not beside himself with laughter" [*obliquato . . . aspectu rem admirationis maximae conspicio: nam inter tot milia populi circumsecus vadentis nemo prorsum, qui non risu dirumperetur, aderat*] (3.2). His pain is exacerbated by a feeling of betrayal when he sees that his host, Milo, whom the bonds of hospitality ought to have made a reliable ally, is the most amused of all: "I saw the entire population broken up with raucous laughter, and my good host and intimate, Milo, having the loudest laugh of all" [*conspicio prorsus totum populum—risu cachinnabili diffluebant—nec secus illum bonum hospitem parentemque meum Milonem risu maximo dissolutum*] (7). When Lucius uncovers the "bodies" and the joke is at last exposed to him, he himself is mortified, but the incongruous laughter with which he is assaulted now borders on hysteria: "At that point the laughter, which some had managed to stifle, spread wildly through the entire mob. Some hooted with unrestrained mirth, others pressed their aching sides with their hands" [*tunc ille quorundam astu paulisper cohibitus risus libere iam exarsit in plebem. hi gaudii nimietate graculari, illi dolorem ventris manuum compressione sedare*] (10). That the crowd should be rendered helpless with laughter at the sight of Lucius' *dolor* is baffling to both victim and reader. Why are these people laughing?

Others have noticed the cruel and unsettling quality of the laughter in the *Metamorphoses*. Indeed its consistent designation in the Risus episode as *cachinnus*, in spite of the god's name, underscores its derisive edge. Efforts to explain its tone have attempted to connect it and the Risus festival in general with the historical tradition of community rituals involving scapegoats, which often include apotropaic laughter.[28] But if time-honored ritual is to explain and excuse the laughter in these episodes, why is Apuleius so careful to stress its shrill, sadistic quality by calling it *cachinnus*, and moreover to suggest that *Schadenfreude* is a universal impulse and not just a ritual obligation? Thelyphron is of course derided by the Risus revelers to whom he tells his tale. But within the tale itself is his recollection of how his misfortune provoked a similar reaction *in the initial incident:*

> I raised my hand and pulled at my nose: it fell off; I touched my ears: they came off too. Everyone pointed their fingers and twisted their heads round to look at me, and burst into laughter. Soaked with a cold sweat, I escaped through their legs. Nor have I been able to return to my ancestral home in this mutilated and absurd condition.

> [iniecta manu nasum prehendo: sequiter; aures pertracto: deruunt. ac dum directis digitis et detortis nutibus praesentium denotor, dum risus ebullit, inter pedes circumstantium frigido sudore

---

28. See Skulsky 1981, 103 on the derisive character of the laughter in the *Metamorphoses* as a whole. For *cachinnus* vs. *risus*, see Heine 1962, 290 ("*Cachinnus* is a shrill, malevolent, cruel kind of laughter" [my translation]); and van der Paardt 1971, 67, where he marshals testimony, e.g., Jerome *Epistle* 60.10.6, *gaudium risu, non cachinno intellegeres*. For explanations drawing on civic/religious ritual, see, e.g., Robertson 1919; Grimal 1972; P. James 1987, 78–79, 87; and Bartalucci 1988.

defluens evado. nec postea debilis ac sic riduculus Lari me patrio
reddere potui.] (2.30)

The humiliation and alienation of the object of laughter is excruciat-
ingly clear here, but there is no festival to sanction it. People stare and
point at Thelyphron even as they will at Lucius, but here their cruelty is
clearly gratuitous. In the context of the complete collapse of protocol-
based civil behavior that will occur in Books 7 through 10, the Apuleian
Risus festival appears to function as a highly stylized preview of this
later development.

The feature of these scenes that fatally disrupts reading them as
simply a fictional version of an established religious tradition is the
consistent focus on what Winkler calls the "anesthesia and alienation"
of the victims.[29] Indeed, the Risus episode is a masterpiece in the representation of subjective perspective, and this is the lens through which
the reader sees the proceedings. Regardless of any extenuating circumstances, the laughter that reaches the ears of Thelyphron and Lucius
resounds loudly and clearly as *cachinnus* and not *risus*. We can feel Thelyphron's acute discomfort when he is conscripted into entertaining
and when "all faces and eyes are turned toward one man sitting alone
in the corner" [*ora et optutus in unum quempiam angulo secubantem confe-
runtur*] (2.20). He is so upset at what is *to him* the *insolentia* of the other
guests and so embarrassed at the unwanted attention that he attempts
to leave: "Upset by their intolerable persistence he mumbled to himself
as he tried to leave" [*qui cunctorum obstinatione confusus indigna mur-
murabundus cum vellet exsurgere*]. In the end, he complies unwillingly
and only at his hostess' insistence ("she compelled him to speak against
his will" [*ingratis cogebat effari*], striking an exaggerated orator's pose to
salvage what little dignity he has left [*contra* Winkler] (1985, 111)], who
interprets Thelyphron's pose as an indication that he really wants to tell
the tale). Thelyphron's obvious suffering at being forced to relive his
harrowing experience and the fact that all present, except for Lucius,
already know what the story entails make Byrrhena's exhortation that

29. "Lucius' resistance to this religion, to this community laughter . . . spoils
the reader's easy enjoyment of the Risus festival as a carefully designed scenario whose revelation of the corpses and the truth is meant to be the commonly shared climax and peripety of the plot. . . . Lucius' frigid, statuelike presence at those events . . . dissipates and alienates for us that moment of
celebration, of unity, of shared laughter at things falling into place" (1985, 172).

Thelyphron tell it so that her nephew can "share in the charm of your pleasant conversation" [ut et filius meus iste Lucius lepidi sermonis tui perfruatur comitate] (2.20) all the more dissonant, and as disconnected from actual events as her guests' intrusive laughter.

Likewise the reader sees the contrived murder trial through the defendant's eyes, and from this perspective the humor is elusive indeed. Surely Lucius' vivid sense of being a sacrificial victim (3.2) has more than a ritual significance. We empathize with him as he is helplessly and miserably (maestus) swept along by the crowd (3.2), and as his desperate pleas for his life fall, as it seems to him, on the deaf ears of the inscrutable arbiters of his fate (3.7). Lucius' sense of persecution rankles long after the joke is revealed and the citizens try to make amends. As the gathering breaks up he is so disoriented that he has to be guided forcibly home by Milo, but he cannot trust his host's words of comfort because of his apparent complicity in the affair. Lucius' chief emotion is not relief but indelible bitterness:

> Milo grabbed my hand and led me along with merciful force, although my tears were welling up again and I was sobbing uncontrollably. He attempted to comfort me with various remarks but I was upset and still shaking. He was in no way able to sooth my indignation at the injustice done to me, which rankled deep in my breast.

> [Milon . . . iniecta manu me renitentem lacrimisque rursum promicantibus crebra singultientem clementi violentia secum adtraxit . . . maestumque me atque etiam tunc trepidum variis solatur affatibus. nec tamen indignationem iniuriae, quae inhaeserat altius meo pectori, ullo modo permulcere quivit.] (3.10)

Only a heroic feat of dissimulation allows Lucius to appear civil to the curiously insensitive magistrates when they later pay him a visit as if all were well: "Cracking a little smile I pretended to be more cheerful to the extent that I was able and pleasantly bade farewell to the officials as they departed" [paulisper hilaro vultu renidens quantumque poteram laetiorem me refingens comiter abeuntes magistratus appello] (3.12). His shame and resentment cannot, however, be eradicated by forced cordialities. He shrinks from public appearances in the painful belief that everyone is snickering at him. Yet Milo insists on their going out to the baths:

I avoided the eyes of all and turned away from the laughter of those we met, which I myself had fabricated; I walked along plastered to Milo's side, trying to conceal myself. I was blinded by shame and cannot remember how I washed, how I dried, how I got home: that is how insanely stupefied I was by the staring eyes, the knowing nods, and the pointing fingers of all.

[ego vitans oculos omnium et, quem ipse fabricaveram, risum obviorum declinans lateri eius adambulabam obtectus. nec qui laverim, qui terserim, qui domum rursum reverterim, prae rubore memini; sic omnium oculis, nutibus ac denique manibus denotatus inpos animi stupebam.] (3.12)

Even when Lucius has escaped from the stares and pointing fingers into the safety of his own room, the obsessive memory of his experience keeps his humiliation alive: "I threw myself down on the bed and unhappily retraced what had happened to me blow by blow" [abiectus in lectulo meo, quae gesta fuerant, singula maestus recordabar] (3.13).

Even if actual ritual practice does inform these scenes, what comes across much more clearly than the reaffirmation of a community's cohesion through collective ritual is Lucius' and Thelyphron's isolation from that entire structure of meaning. The *Metamorphoses* is a prototype in a long line of representations of what Smith (1989) has called the "perspective of the victimized narrator." He elaborates on this aspect of the Latin novel in the context of suggesting a comparison between it and the stories of Kafka, specifically (and all the more significantly, given Lucius' experiences) *The Trial (Das Urteil)* and *The Metamorphosis (Die Verwandlung)*. Recalling Auerbach, Smith sees in Apuleius a "dreamlike, even nightmarish quality . . . in Kafka's manner." The experiences of Aristomenes, Thelyphron, and finally Lucius are bound together in a "Kafkaesque pattern" that hinges on the "narrator's sense of guilt, which distorts his perception of reality, causing him to veer between protestations of his own innocence and despair as he sinks into shame." Thus "in Apuleius we find a new kind of protagonist, not just in the sense that he is racked by self-doubt . . . but that due to his supposed inadequacy, he constantly dreads imminent condemnation by a hostile environment" (1, 7–8). The atmosphere in these three episodes, and indeed often in the subsequent narrative, is darkened by a "sense of helplessness, [of] the impossibility of finding a dependable ally." Aristomenes and Lucius, and to a lesser extent Thelyphron, like the narrator Joseph K. in *The Trial*, "struggle . . . to attain some sort of definite support, reassurance that someone is on [their] side—a struggle in which [they] find only ambiguity and doubt" (10, 12). In Lucius' case, the sense of abandonment is later compounded as he gradually grasps how thoroughly he was deceived. He was completely taken in by the trick; his fear had been absolutely real. This experience understandably throws him off balance and implants in him a nagging suspicion of everyone and everything he encounters.

An inscrutable and "strangely enigmatic" quality surrounding major and minor characters is also, according to Smith, quintessential Kafka. But Apuleius before him had put the reader in the position of "view[ing] his characters from a distance, guessing at their inner selves. In the *Metamorphoses* too, even the most minor figures may leave us with a sense of dread." In this group Smith includes the innkeeper from the tale of Aristomenes, "who seems to have an uncanny knowledge of Socrates' death," and Pythias the aedile, whose motives, words, and actions are equally difficult to read. Both exchanges—between Aristomenes and the innkeeper, and between Lucius and his old friend—are "conversations at cross purposes," in which ordinary channels of communication seem to have broken down (6, 11, 12). A more prominent character who projects the same aura of unresolved ambiguity is Milo. He seems, as Smith notes, "vaguely hostile . . . but the nature of his malice is never clearly defined." He betrays the bonds of hospitality by exposing his guest to ridicule, only to resume quite abruptly the role of kind protector. The reader is suspended between Milo the "malicious trickster who has framed Lucius and made him a spectacle in order to raise a laugh" and the Milo who is "Lucius' protector, his only friend in the crowd, consoling him as, like a father, he leads him home" (5, 8–9). Byrrhena too, it seems to me, as the enigmatic and vaguely sinister mother figure of Lucius' Thessalian sojourn, has exactly the same unsettling effect. The Risus episode as a whole serves as a transition to the idea that human behavior is as inscrutable and unreliable as the phenomena of the material world.

One of the reasons for this unreliability is that the laws that conventionally regulate behavior and make it predictable are breaking down. This problem is the main focus of the later books of the *Metamorphoses*, but a pillar of social law that begins to crumble early in Lucius' adventures is *fides*, the principle of trust or loyalty that guarantees the authenticity of human actions and words. Lucius expresses his newfound doubts about the inviolability of this trust when Milo's enthusiastic participation in the trial leads Lucius to lament that if a host cannot be trusted, then no one can:

> Alas for trust and any moral sense! Here I am a homicide and on trial for my life for protecting *his* home, and he not only refuses to assist in my defense but goes on to cackle at my ruin.
>
> [en fides . . . en conscientia; ego quidem pro hospitis salute et homicida sum et reus capitis inducor, at ille non contentus, quod mihi nec adsistendi solacium perhibuit, insuper exitium meum cachinnat.] (3.7)

The dictates of *fides* are transgressed even by mute beasts. Newly transformed, Lucius assumes that he will be a welcome guest in the stable where Milo's ass and his own trusty steed are quartered, but the horse disappoints him with its *perfidia* when it conspires with the real donkey to exclude the newcomer from their fodder and shelter. Lucius is rudely disabused of his expectation that the "unspoken and natural bond" [*tacitum et naturale sacramentum*] among beasts would cause them to receive him not only with hospitality *(hospitium)* but by offering him the best spot in the house *(loca lautia)*. He responds with indignation at the offense to "Jupiter the god of hospitality and the remote deities of Trust" [*Iuppiter hospitalis et Fidei secreta numina*] (3.26). This is not the last time that a naïve but intrepid Lucius will appear to be the last bastion of conventional morality in the novel. There is, of course, a heavy element of comedy and just plain silliness in his assumption that social laws will obtain in the animal world. Yet his miscalculation highlights the artificiality of these precepts and the narrowness of the province in which they operate, and for all the comic tone we are with Lucius as he realizes twice in rapid succession that he can no longer rely on the regulatory nexus of trust and hospitality.

Indeed, *fides* would appear to reside only among thieves and the dead. In the cave of the robbers in Book 4, a bandit recalls the strategy that he and his comrades hit upon for concealing their loot on their last raid: they break into some tombs and hide it in the "homes of the dead, the most faithful of all" [*in illis aedibus fidelissimorum mortuorum*]. He refers again to the "faithful dead" [*fideles mortui*] when he recalls how the bandits collected the goods they had stashed in the graveyard and how they made their escape, musing among themselves that "it is no wonder that no trust can be found in our lives, since it has fled out of disgust at our perfidy and is in exile among the dead" [*reputabamus merito nullam fidem in vita nostra repperiri, quod ad manis iam et mortuos odio perfidiae nostrae demigrarit*] (4.18, 21). The persistence of the *fides* motif in this sequence is very striking. Again there is humor, this time in the bombastic moralizing of a band of cutthroats in the very act of violating the social contract whose demise they lament. The dead furthermore earn their odd sobriquet merely by agreeably ignoring the robbers' activities. Yet the bandit has struck a nerve. When he laments that *fides* has disappeared from "our lives" out of anger at "our faithlessness," he is speaking generically ("the lives and the faithlessness of the whole human race"). In doing so he alludes to the tradition that the cardinal virtues evacuated the earth along with the gods shortly after the Golden Age, when the incorrigibly degenerate tendencies of man became clear. And in fact *fides* (among other virtues) *is* nowhere to be found in the world of the *Metamorphoses*—except, ironically, in the society of outlaws.

When the injured Lamachus begs his comrades "by the loyalty we swore to" [*per fidem sacramenti*] (4.11) to finish him off rather than preserve him to be a one-armed bandit, he invokes an agreement among the robbers that they consider sacrosanct.[30] In this episode, they manage to inspire more sympathy than the miser Chryseros, whose grotesque mutilation of Lamachus foils their attempted burglary. In spite of, or perhaps in part because of, their bumbling criminality, these outlaws are oddly appealing, and one of the reasons for this is that, unlike others, they seem to take their oaths seriously. Of their number it is Thrasyleon who endures the most extreme challenges to the oath, yet even when beset by men with lances and ferocious dogs, he does not give away the stratagem of his comrades by revealing his true identity: "Neither with shouting nor wailing did he betray his loyalty to the

---

30. Hildebrand used his understanding of this ethic to defend the older MS reading *trepidi religionis* against the *trepidi regionis* of the *recentiores*. Here, the robber-narrator describes the desperation of the raiding party as they try to escape with the "rest of Lamachus": *ceterum Lamachum raptim reportamus. ac dum trepidi religionis urguemur gravi tumultu . . .* (4.11). Hildebrand ad loc.: "*Trepidi religionis* optime dicuntur latrones, qui de sacramenti fide solliciti, deserere vulneratum Lamachum nolunt." Helm, however, reads *regionis*.

oath" [*neque clamore ac ne ululatu quidem fidem sacramenti prodidit*] (4.21).
It is only in these sections of the novel that any kind of *fides* is consistently in evidence. Thus the society of the outlaws has more structure
than society at large, and the conspicuous absence of any reliable ethical framework in respectable society makes this all the more glaring.
Furthermore, the cultivation of a traditional mainstream virtue like
fides by marginalized members of society is in itself another manifestation of the disturbance of the established order that Lucius encounters
everywhere he turns. The obsolescence of *fides* is one corollary in
human society to the disappearance of boundaries in the physical
world and its resulting treacherousness: people are not to be trusted
any more than matter. The text shifts to this aspect of the disintegration
of Lucius' world in Books 7 through 10, when after the action-stopping
interlude of the tale of Cupid and Psyche his troubles resume.[31]

---

31. See chapter 5, section 1 on the tale of Cupid and Psyche.

Books 6.25–10: The Social World

1

In chapter 1, I read the first four books of the *Metamorphoses* as a representation of Lucius the preconvert's new and deepening perception that the phenomena of the material world are straining against their familiar boundaries. Fluidity increasingly characterizes forms of knowledge ordinarily regarded as fixed. The features of Books 1 through 4 that combine to create this impression persist in the later books; often, however, their tone is altered, darker. The idea of the instability of matter and the unreliability of appearance, for example, dominates the description of the *pestilens regio* through which Lucius and his shepherd owners journey in Book 8, encountering one visual trap after another (8.15–21). The travelers find themselves in a region disengaged from normal space and time, where strange and inexplicable things occur as a matter of course. The sinister undercurrents in this episode are in sharp contrast to Lucius' initial naïve anticipation of the joys of transgressing ontological boundaries. On the whole, however, the volatility of the material world recedes into the background in Books 7 through 10, as the main locus of the text's basic issues shifts to their manifestations in the social world of the novel. Now the countless false opinions and mistaken hypotheses developed and held by the characters illustrate how the rules governing human relations, like narratives and indeed like any structuring system, can be a tissue of fictions whose basis in some solid realm of objective fact is elusive indeed. Whereas earlier in the work ontological fluidity and transformation characterized the physical world, in the later books these concepts are reworked to apply to the social and psychological spheres. The vagaries of human thought and behavior become the latest expressions of a ubiquitous instability. For this reason the human characters of the novel often seem to be no more than extensions of their unstable environment.[1]

Skulsky (1981, 94–95) has observed that a "running theme of the romance [is] the ubiquitous danger of unfair or corrupted judgment." He locates the culmination of this theme in the masque that Lucius observes in the Corinthian amphitheater in Book 10. Its subject is the bought judgment of Paris. The tableau inspires the indignant ass to reel off a list of historical and mythological worthies ruined by false judgments against themselves (10.30–33). Here it is important to remember, as Skulsky does, that although the focus of Lucius' tirade in Book 10 is the venality of judges, in the *Metamorphoses* "one need not be bribed to arrive at unfair judgments of one's fellows." Such judgments, on the contrary, are often spontaneously formulated and sincerely held as truth. Indeed, most of the frenetic activity in the last third of the novel can be traced to some original false opinion that has set off a chain reaction of derivative false opinions. Apuleius' depiction of all this deluded bumbling about is a natural continuation of his interrogation of the stability of knowledge in the earlier books. But the texts that resist being fixed in Books 7 through 10 are characters and situations more than the inscrutable physical phenomena and the tales about their unpredictable behavior that dominate Books 1 through 4. In both the main narrative and in the tales told within it, Apuleius repeatedly demonstrates how virtually any collection of facts has the potential to generate multiple constructions whose character depends on the preconceptions of the observer. In these books, it is the situations, events, and characters of the plot that generate fictions and perpetrate illusions.[2]

---

1. Ebel (1970, 164) seems to share my view that the locus of the novel's central problem shifts from the physical to the social worlds: "[The theme of] the complete unreliability of appearances, and the resulting ease of transformation of one deceptive solid into another . . . applies not only to those magical episodes in which a woman becomes a bird or an old man a dragon, but to those moments when a solid and well-founded opinion about another human being—that he is a friend, or hospitable, or selfless, or an enemy—turns out to be the diametrical opposite of the truth." See also 163 on the *pestilens regio* as the "ultimate concentrated negation of all appearances."

2. It is important to note that in these later books Apuleius seems to be moving away from the epistemological open-endedness that characterizes the ear-

Characters arrive at mistaken beliefs about reality by a number of routes in the *Metamorphoses*. Frequently they are represented as simply drawing the wrong conclusion from a given collection of objective facts. They have all the information they need to construct an accurate assessment of the situation at hand, but they fail to do so because they rely too heavily on prejudices and allow conditioned expectations to restrict the possibilities that they consider. Because of their intellectual complacency, they tend to accept uncritically the aggregate appearance created by a conjunction of indifferent facts. These habits of mind are the culprit in their chronic failure to apprehend what is really going on. To make matters worse, once an inference is rashly drawn, it can become the first link in a long chain of dependent beliefs and actions, each further from the truth than the previous one, and all deriving ultimately from one tenuous hypothesis that takes on a life of its own as soon as it is accepted as fact.

We have already seen how Lucius, in a demonstration of the negative potential of credulity and the danger of preconceptions, arrives at a seriously flawed assessment of Charite's character in Book 7. Although the lesson is as usual lost on Lucius, he himself has been the loser in a similarly wrongheaded evaluation of the facts conducted after the robbery of Milo's house earlier in the same book. Milo's neighbors have decided that all appearances point to Lucius as the guilty party, and they do not probe beyond this easy—too easy—inference. A bandit spy reports to his comrades what the people in town are saying about Lucius:

> The entire crowd at the scene was in unanimous agreement, and their conclusion (they said) was based on probability and not unfounded conjecture. As a result somebody named Lucius

---

lier books. Implicit in this flurry of episodes in which characters repeatedly use the evidence to hypothesize incorrectly is the premise that in the midst of conflicting versions of truth there is a correct version to be recovered. The slippage of the text on this issue is, I think, a function of its operation on two levels: that of the skeptical author who resists final answers and the idea of authorization, and that of the *actor*-convert who endorses the discourse of truth and falsehood by opting for a resolution to his crisis in dualistic, transcendental religion.

was being sought as the clear perpetrator of the crime. In recent days he had insinuated himself into Milo's favor by means of fabricated letters of recommendation which falsely claimed that he was a good man. The ruse worked, and this Lucius was received into the family's bosom as a guest. He waited a few more days, and after creeping into the affections of Milo's slave girl with false claims of love, he had carefully investigated the locks.

[nec argumentis dubiis, sed rationibus probabilibus congruo cunctae multitudinis consensu nescio qui Lucius auctor manifestus facinoris postulabatur, qui proximis diebus fictis commendaticiis litteris Miloni sese virum commentitus bonum artius conciliaverat, ut etiam hospitio susceptus inter familiaris intimos haberetur plusculisque ibidem diebus demoratus falsis amoribus ancillae Milonis animum inrepens ianuae claustra sedulo exploraverat.] (7.1)

Determined to bolster and legitimate the narrative that they have decided to adopt as truth, the townspeople construct an elaborate and completely false account of Lucius and his carefully premeditated crime on the basis of a few scraps of circumstantial evidence.

With characteristic sophistication, Apuleius here weaves together a complex of alleged and "actual" illusions: the citizens mistakenly impute willful deception to Lucius even as they themselves are being deceived by the appearance created by the collection of facts that presents itself to them for interpretation. Lucius' authentic letters and genuine affection for Fotis are dismissed as lies, while a fictional account of his activities, generated by his uncle's neighbors to explain something that needs explaining, is elevated to the status of proven fact: true things are called false and false true. The narrative that grows out of the "hermeneutic *hamartia* of the Hypatan investigators" (Winkler 1985, 107), itself based on a misconstruction of random facts, is then, significantly, given a somewhat different reading by each of the three parties who come into contact with it: depending on whether the interpreter is Lucius, the robbers, or the citizens themselves, the account has varying degrees of value as truth, because each reader's perspective brings with it a different set of premises and different pieces of information (see Winkler, 105–8). Thus even into the briefest of episodes Apuleius manages to weave his guiding concern with multiple perspectives and the arbitrary roots of what we call knowledge. All this unnecessary but perhaps inevitable confusion is the result of the Hypatans' need for a "simple, satisfying reading of events" (Winkler, 107). This is a dangerous, if compelling, need that causes them to take the easy way out and not to consider less obvious possibilities.[3]

Sometimes Apuleius' treatment of the workings of false opinion can be unambiguously comic. The household of the rich patron of the Syrian goddess is led by an accidental conjunction of unrelated events—the sight of Lucius the ass racing through the house to an upstairs chamber to escape the knife of the cook, who is about to make imitation venison of him; the nearly simultaneous announcement by a neighbor that a mad dog is on a rampage in the vicinity—to conclude that the ass is rabid. This false inference (Lucius calls it a "crazy presumption": *vesana praesumptio*) is responsible for a sustained stretch of slapstick confusion (9.2–4). On the other hand, the problem of false opinion might be incorporated into one of the novel's many episodes of gratuitous sadism, such as the account of the ass's unhappy sojourn with the cruel boy *(puer nequissimus)* in Book 7 (17–28). Winkler (1985, 104–5) offers a summary of this sequence that is useful for our purposes:

> The wicked boy who mistreats the ass in Book 7 commits a crime: he sells the wood he has gathered to another farmhouse but blames the ass, accusing him of tossing the load off in order to knock a woman down and mount her. He elaborates a lie about the ass's history of lustful attempts on pretty women, marriageable maidens, and tender boys.
>
> The other shepherds, taking this lie for true and knowing that they would be subject to capital punishment for their animal's crimes, decide to kill the ass and cover his death with a lie to their master: "It will be easy for us to lie and say he was killed by a wolf." But while the boy and the ass are gathering wood again, an

---

3. Winkler rightly maintains that this desire for a "simple, satisfying reading of events" is precisely what must be resisted when we grapple with the complexities and ambiguities of the novel's ending. On a minor point, the same critic seems to suggest that we are to take Lucius' affection for Fotis as feigned in the service of his ulterior motive: to be privy to the forbidden activities of her mistress (1985, 106–7). But it seems to me that Lucius' interest in Fotis and her status as an avenue to magic were for him a happy coincidence.

enormous bear appears, and the ass breaks his tether and runs away. The boy, guilty of a lie (that the ass almost killed a woman) that produced another lie (that a wolf killed the ass), is killed in a manner that mirrors those two lies (torn apart by the bear). Both lies were devised to cover human crimes by blaming an animal; the boy's miserable death, though due to an animal, is falsely regarded as a human crime. For a wayfarer who finds the ass is apprehended by the farm hands—the discovery of the boy's dismembered body creates a circumstantial case of homicide against the wayfarer.

Here we have a typical Apuleian nexus of lies, counterlies, and false inferences, all spinning out of control. Not only does the poor wayfarer find himself falsely accused of a crime as a result of his being in the wrong place at the wrong time, much like Lucius at the beginning of the book, but by the book's end Lucius' own experience of unfair judgment is repeated when the boy's mother holds the ass responsible for her son's death because he did not intervene. This episode is notable for the way it combines the two possible sources of false opinion in the novel: characters may put the wrong construction on an intrinsically innocent situation or conjunction of facts, but more often their intellectual complacency allows them to be seduced by a deliberately constructed illusion or system of illusions. Mendacity is an engine of the action to a very striking degree in the later books of the *Metamorphoses*, and a systematically deployed vocabulary of deceit unifies the episodes in question.[4]

Lying, deception, and betrayal lie at the heart of all the major sequences in Books 7 through 10; the accelerating destruction in these episodes is almost always the result of the exponential growth of an initial lie. The tragic demise of Charite and Tlepolemus (8.1–14) is rooted in deceit in one of its most insidious forms: the exploitation of trust in the bonds of friendship, which also involves the episode in the theme of

---

4. This consists of: verbs (*mentiri, fingere, simulare, dissimulare, occultare, fallere*: to lie, to fabricate, to simulate, to dissimulate, to conceal, to deceive); nouns (*mendacium, simulatio/similitudo, imago, fraus, fallacia, persona*: lie, simulation, false image, deception, treachery, mask or appearance); adjectives (*mendosus, fictus, fallax/fallaciosus, deceptus, personatus*: lying, fictitious, fallacious, deceived, impersonating). These are, of course, simplified translations; the reader will be alert to nuance in what follows.

the transgression of social codes and institutions. Thrasyllus' strategy is calculated from the beginning to take advantage of the newlyweds' well-founded belief that he is a faithful friend and a man of good will. He initially insinuates himself into the couple's household at their wedding reception, where he conceals his true design—to seduce the bride—under a charade of devoted friendship: "Hiding his evil plan, he deceitfully played the role of the most faithful of friends" [occultato consilio sceleris, amici fidelissimi personam mentiebatur] (8.2). After he takes the opportunity presented by a boar hunt to trick Tlepolemus, murder him, and blame the death on accident, Thrasyllus grows bolder in his histrionics. He now becomes so thoroughly involved in the performance that he seems to convince himself of its truth:

> Although Thrasyllus was overjoyed now that his wish was fulfilled and his rival done away with, nevertheless he covered up his happiness with a feigned expression, and wrinkled his brow and simulated grief and passionately embraced the corpse, which he himself had made so, and in general carefully acted out all the duties of a mourner; only the tears were missing. Thus he fashioned his appearance to a likeness of ours, who were truly grieving, and blamed the beast for the deed of his own hand.

> [at ille quanquam perfecto voto, prostrato inimico laetus ageret, vultu tamen gaudium tegit et frontem adseverat et dolorem simulat et cadaver, quod ipse fecerat, avide circumplexus omnia quidem lugentium officia sollerter adfinxit, sed solae lacrimae procedere noluerunt. sic ad nostri similitudinem, qui vere lamentabamur, conformatus manus suae culpam bestiae dabat.] (8.6)

Thrasyllus persists in his role as chief mourner for quite some time, hoping to win the confidence of the vulnerable Charite by becoming a source of comfort and strength in her time of need. The "pretend piety" [mentita pietas] (8.7) and the "treacherous roundabout ways" [fraudulentes ambages] (8.12) of the murderer thoroughly deceive not only Charite and her household, but Truth itself (Veritatem ipsam fallere, 8.7). She suspects nothing sinister until she is informed of the plot by her murdered husband in a dream.

At this point the narrative becomes a study in the tendency of fictions to generate more fictions as any "truth" recedes further and further from view. Once Charite discovers that she has been misled, she bases her strategy of vengeance on turning Thrasyllus' own weapons against him. Feigning naïveté and the trust that he has already violated, she lulls him into complacency just as he had her; he, of course, is too preoccupied with his own charade and too excited at the prospect of its successful outcome to suspect that he too is being deceived. The description of Charite's countermeasures is laced with the vocabulary of deceit that is establishing itself as a major unifying device in the later books of the *Metamorphoses*. After her husband's nocturnal epiphany, she continues to behave as she had before and pretends to have no knowledge of the crime (*indicio facinoris prorsus dissimulato*). When Thrasyllus pesters her with eager proposals of marriage, she puts him off by insisting that he must allow her a respectable period of mourning, "gently spurning his chatter and playing her part with wondrous skill" [*clementer aspernata sermonem Thrasylli astuque miro personata*] (8.9). Finally she pretends to yield (*simulanter revicta*), but only on the condition that he agree to keep their union secret for a year, offering him a "treacherous promise" [*promissio fallaciosa*], to which her suitor readily agrees (8.10). Even Charite's nurse is pulled into the web of deception. When she is charged by her mistress to affect an anxious watch for his nocturnal arrival at Charite's chamber, he is duly taken in by this little piece of theater as well (*nutricis captiosa vigilia deceptus*). As she plies Thrasyllus with drugged wine, the nurse further lies about the reasons for Charite's lateness, saying that she is tending her father who is ill (*mentita dominae tarditatem quasi parentem assideret aegrotum*, 8.11). In the end Thrasyllus lies drugged, cursed, and gruesomely blinded on his beloved's bedroom floor, and Charite herself, after a mad dash through town, takes her own life at her husband's tomb. It is a typically Apuleian paroxysm of violence, whose spectacular features come close to obscuring the crucial fact that at its heart lie the distorting powers of a self-replicating mendacity. When we consider that in the *Onos* (34) Charite and Tlepolemus suffer a briefly reported accidental death by drowning, it is not only clear that Apuleius has gone to some length to make his version more dramatic and pessimistic, but just as importantly that he has forged it into a study of the workings of pretense, betrayal, and false belief.

The ripple effect of mendacity is illustrated even more clearly in the two tales of evil women in Book 10. In the tale of the wicked stepmother

(10.2–12), the lying begins when the smitten Phaedra figure lures her stepson into her bedroom by pretending that she is ill ("feigning sickness, she lied about her wounded heart" [*languore simulato vulnus animi mentitur*] [10.2]). Its seeds thus sown, deception is the catalyst for all the action that follows, as the characters grope about, either lying or reacting to lies, deceiving or being deceived. The woman resolves to prevent her stepson from revealing her attempted seduction of him, but his unsuspecting half brother (he is described as "ignorant of hidden treachery" [*nescius fraudis occultae*] [10.5]), in search of an after-school snack, drinks the cup of poison intended for the older boy, and dies. The stepmother immediately seizes the opportunity to fabricate an accusation designed to serve her thwarted purpose of eliminating the surviving boy:

> Playing her part with extreme boldness, she pretended that her own son had been done in by her stepson with poison. And in fact this was not exactly a lie, since the younger boy had anticipated the death planned for the youth. In any case, she fashioned a story about how the older boy had murdered his little brother, her son, to get even with her for refusing to succumb to the shameful lust with which he himself had tried to seduce her. She was not content with these monstrous lies, but added that the stepson had also threatened her with a sword for revealing his crime. . . . And so the husband was driven to extreme hatred of his own son by the lying lamentations of the wife he loved too much.

> [personata nimia temeritate insimulat privigni veneno filium suum interceptum. et hoc quidem non adeo mentiebatur, quod iam destinatam iuveni mortem praevenisset puer, sed fratrem iuniorem fingebat ideo privigni scelere peremptum, quod eius probrosae libidini, qua se comprimere temptaverat, noluisset succumbere. nec tam inmanibus contenta mendacis addebat sibi quoque ob detectum flagitium eundem illum gladium comminari. . . . uxoris dilectae nimium mentitis lamentationibus ad extremum subolis impellebatur [maritus] odium.] (10.5)

This passage is notable for more than its reliance on the now familiar thematic vocabulary of deceit. First, there is the impression that the woman is beginning to heap up and embellish her lies to a degree above and beyond what is strictly necessary to accomplish her purpose. Her lies are not exactly gratuitous, but the ease with which they come once she adopts a course of deceit illustrates the general principle that initial lies tend to spawn more complex and subdivided lies. The more an individual lies, the easier lying becomes, even as a fundamental lie in one's construction of reality can expand into a complete and self-per-petuating edifice of progressively refined fictions. Second, it is significant that the husband is lulled into complacency by an excessive love for his wife, which obstructs any objective evaluation of the facts. He is seduced by the preconceptions to which he is "wedded" into accepting the account that is less disagreeable to him. Like the younger brother, the husband is "ignorant of deceit" [*nescius fraudium*] (10.6). This pointedly repeated epithet carries a warning that everyone, but especially innocents such as these, must be vigilant in a world where mendacity is pervasive. The father verges on ruining his entire household when he acts on the basis of one uncritically formed and utterly false *opinio*. He does not step back to analyze or investigate. Instead he himself leads the townspeople in their demands for the summary punishment of his son.

The case does go to trial, where a chief witness for the prosecution is one of the stepmother's loyal slaves. This minion convincingly renders what is false true as he corroborates the fictions of his mistress:

> He began to affirm and to declare as true those things that he himself had fabricated. . . . The trial was adjourned after that scoundrel, with shudders of imitation fear, had very skillfully put these things forward in the likeness of truth.

> [quae ipse finxerat, quasi vera adseverare atque adserere incipit. . . . haec eximie ac nimis ad veritatis imaginem verberone illo simulata cum trepidatione proferente finitum est iudicium.] (10.7)[5]

---

5. The text is unsound. I find Blümner's conjecture of *eximie mentita* more attractive than the commonly accepted reading of *eximie ac nimis* (Leo/Helm) for the *eximia enim* of the MSS, for two reasons: (1) *eximie ac nimis* is a strange and redundant expression, and exactly what it modifies adverbially is unclear: *proferente* is difficult; and (2) *haec eximie mentita* (as the object of *proferente*) rings true in view of the frequency with which Apuleius employs *mentior* and its derivatives to bind together this and thematically similar episodes. It is one of his favorite words.

Dark as things look for truth at this moment, it does triumph in the end after an observant doctor exposes the fabrications. This happens, however, only after a protracted period of danger that the lie will prevail. The doctor's devotion to "naked truth" itself [nuda veritas] (10.12) rather than to dogmatic and arbitrary prejudices that obstruct access to the truth, along with his probing, inductive method of uncovering it, makes him unique in the *Metamorphoses*. Further, his ability to evaluate evidence impartially is directly responsible for one of the novel's few happy endings. Yet the reader should know better than to grow sanguine at the "all's right in the world" note on which this episode ends. Its conclusion is not part of any accelerating pattern of satisfying resolutions but rather leaps out of the text for its singularity. Mendacity (and the injustice that often accompanies its acceptance) prevails in the novel far more often than truth, however it is defined. Furthermore, whether truth or lies win out in the end is always a matter of caprice and is no more subject to any laws of causality than physical matter or human behavior.

Deception also underlies the series of crimes committed by the condemned woman with whom Lucius is to perform in the Corinthian amphitheater. The crescendo of criminal activity for which she is responsible (10.23–28) provides a suitable backdrop for the ass's fateful decision to make his final escape at the end of Book 10. The woman's initial victim is her husband's sister. Rashly jumping to conclusions from the incomplete and ambiguous evidence of his kindness toward the girl, the deluded wife thinks that she is her husband's mistress. The innocent girl, clearly of the type *nescia fraudis*, although Apuleius does not say so explicitly, trusts in a fictitious message allegedly sent by her brother and is lured to an isolated spot. There she falls into the clutches of his jealous wife ("she slipped in a trap of very skillful deceit and fell into the snares of treachery" [*fraudis extremae lapsa decipulo laqueos insidiarum accessit*] [10.24]). When the doomed sister tries to reveal her true identity, the wife assumes that she is lying and kills her anyway ("she did her in as if she were lying and fabricating the whole thing" [*velut mentitam atque cuncta fingentem . . . necavit*]). Attempting to tell the truth in a world saturated with lies appears more and more to be a futile endeavor.

The woman's behavior at this point becomes increasingly irrational. Whereas she did have a motive for snuffing out her purported rival, the murder of her husband, whose relationship with herself she was presumably trying to save by killing his "lover," is completely unexpected. Likewise the fatal blows she deals the doctor and his wife are murkily motivated at best. Thus again we see a kind of domino effect, as her crimes and the mendacity upon which they are built feed on themselves long after their initial purpose has been served. The husband dies "amid the feigned and fabricated tears of his wife" [*inter fictas mentitasque lacrimas uxoris*] (10.27), but not until after she has tricked the hypocritical doctor into drinking the same poison. The doctor's wife is the next to fall into the trap (she is "led into the snares of the worst sort of treachery" [*laqueis fraudium pessimarum uxor inducta medici*] [10.27]), when she obligingly procures more poison to aid and abet the woman's criminal designs. The readiness with which people let themselves be duped is epitomized by the doctor's wife's eager participation in the plans of her husband's murderer, her judgment confounded by the false blandishments of the *vilis*, who "suppresses the true face of trust, and offers a false likeness of it" [*fidei supprimens faciem, praetendens imaginem*] (10.27). The fact that the doctor's wife has every reason *not* to trust the woman, knowing as she does from her husband's deathbed revelation that at least two people have already been deceived and poisoned by her, somehow does not register as evidence that she should reconsider her cooperation. Some powerful force is blocking her ability to see the situation clearly, just as it blocks that of countless others in the novel. They routinely see what they want to see and believe what they want to believe, adjusting the evidence in their minds to fit a conclusion already determined.

It would be foolish to claim that moral concerns are absent in these passages. The characters here as elsewhere exhibit extreme passions—jealousy, lust, greed, sadism—which are clearly meant to be seen as destructive when allowed to range unconstrained. Apuleian people on the whole are not pretty. Nevertheless, the repetition of thematic words and images leaves no doubt that the focus is at least equally, and I would argue primarily, on the dissemination and wide acceptance of lies as truth in these books. Mendacity accommodates evil by providing the modus operandi through which it works. Apuleius suggests that destructive passions would triumph less frequently if people's *epistemological* apparatus were more discriminating. Thus again we see at issue a kind of epistemological breakdown, which occurs when truth and fiction become indistinguishable, and opinion is elevated to the status of knowledge. In the above cases the results are disastrous.

Apuleius again raises the question of whether habituated modes of interpreting the world's text are adequate if characters employing these modes so often find themselves seriously derailed.[6]

Recognizing the importance of mendacity and false opinion in the last third of the novel gives us good reason to shine our interpretive light from a new angle on the account of Lucius' sojourn with the eunuch priests (8.24–9.10). This episode is especially instructive with regard to Apuleius' use of inherited material. It stands out from the other inserted tales by virtue of its unambiguously satiric (one might say Lucianic) spirit, which it shares with its parallel in the *Onos* (35–41). Insofar as in both Apuleius and the Greek version the priests are presented as charlatans, it is not surprising that the themes of clerical fraud and popular gullibility would loom large in these accounts. In Apuleius, however, the sequence is nested among several other episodes in which mendacity is a central concern; these episodes and their controlling theme have no parallel in the extant Greek version of the story. Thus, even while apparently preserving the essential tone and sequence of the Greek original (in contrast to his treatment of the story of Charite, whose denouement he appears to have changed considerably), Apuleius manages to bend the material to conform to his own scheme. In the Latin version the eunuch priests are demoted to being merely one party among many responsible for the dissemination of false opinion. Diversity of setting, subject, and tone is one of the Latin text's devices for illustrating the ubiquity of this problem. In spite of this diversity, however, the established vocabulary of deceit that links the episode of the eunuchs with the others ensures that it will be read in the context of the text's more general concerns.

So, for example, the priests extort a farmer's prize ram for a sacrifice (and their own supper) by terrorizing the rustic with the "lie of a ficti-

---

6. The concern with mendacity and deception and with the intellectual complacency on which they depend for success is kept in play in comic and/or minor episodes. See, for example, the adultery tales in Book 9 (22–31), especially the description of the cuckolded Barbarus: "Barbarus was taken in by the timely deception of the quick-witted youth, in fact he was overjoyed and slipped readily into credulity" [*hac opportuna fallacia vigorati iuvenis inductus immo sublatus et ad credulitatem delapsus*] (9.21). Barbarus has heard what he wanted to hear.

tious prophecy" [*fictae vaticinationis mendacio*] (8.29), in which (they claim) the Syrian goddess orders the farmer to provide it. They are able to make a comfortable living peddling similar false prophecies to the credulous masses: "In this way they had managed to rake together a fair amount of cash with the captious cunning of their divination" [*ad istum modum divinationis astu captioso conraserant non parvas pecunias*] (9.8). *Astus*, cunning, was what Charite had exercised in her performance (*astuque miro personata*, 8.9), and the watch feigned by her nurse was, like the cunning of the priests, *captiosa* (8.11). The most spectacular piece of theater orchestrated by the priests is their orgiastic demonstration of religious frenzy at 8.27–28. The performance of the most histrionic celebrant is a lie on two levels: not only is his initial ecstatic raving a pose, but the "sin against the law of sacred religion" that he cites as the reason for his bloody atonement is a lie as well: "Producing rapid panting from the depths of his chest, he simulated a fit of wounded madness as if he were filled up with the divine spirit . . . and began to attack and accuse himself with an altogether fabricated lie" [*de imis praecordiis anhelitus crebros referens velut numinis divino spiritu repletus simulabat sauciam vecordiam . . . infit . . . conficto mendacio semet ipsum incessere atque criminari*]. The townspeople, finally realizing that they have been the victims of an "imitation of divine rites" [*simulatio solemnium*] (9.9), demand the return of a golden vessel that the rogues have looted from a local temple. True to form, like Thrasyleon qua bear beset by vicious dogs, the intrepid clerics persist in the masquerade up to the bitter end, maintaining their innocence and "making light of the charge with false laughter" [*mendoso risu cavillantes*] (9.10). When we scrutinize the details, we can see that although the Latin text is true to the basic spirit and sequence of the Greek version of this episode, the context into which the episode is placed and the diction that elaborates it transform the received material from an isolated episode of systematic duplicity to one illustration among many others of the ubiquitous problem of false opinion.[7]

In Books 7 through 10, it becomes clear that Lucius the *actor*'s episte-

---

7. The possibility that this episode is suggesting that false religion is a category of false opinion is exceedingly remote. It is clear that the spurious priests are the focus of critical scrutiny here; there is no trace of vilification of the Syrian goddess herself. The idea of "true" and "false" religions is alien to pagan-

mological moorings in human society are cut as surely as are those in the physical world. He discovers that any knowledge about the "true" nature of both the material and now the social worlds is provisional and inherently unstable. As trust in the transparent and straightforward workings of matter in both spheres is eroded, we share the *actor's* sense of drifting without familiar bearings, of traveling without the benefit of signposts that can be reliably read. Thus, although the primary impression created in the later books is one of destructively flaring passions, closer scrutiny reveals that the problem of knowledge is fundamental here also. The breakdown of morality in Books 7 through 10 is facilitated by a breakdown in the ability to determine the epistemological status of people's words and actions. Characters fail to get closer to the "truth" because truth is a fluid and highly mediated object and because they are hemmed in by their own preconceptions and habits of thought. This tendency to continue operating within one paradigm when another might better accommodate empirical reality is, like the breakdown of cognitive paradigms itself, a common feature in the crisis phase of conversion experience and in narrative representations of it.

2

Another important aspect of the wholesale collapse of the social world's regulating structures that occurs in these books is the increasingly frequent violation of social and religious institutions whose col-

---

ism: witness the attack on monotheism at 9.14, where one of the baker's wife's vices is her belief in *deus unicus.* (Whether she is a Jew or a Christian is unclear, but Pliny [*Epistle* 10.96] lists several irritating Christian personality traits [for example, *pertinacia,* obstinacy] that seem to match those of this woman.) In fact, the warm hospitality with which the rich man greets the goddess (and her priests) at 8.30 is refreshing in the midst of the general disregard for *religio* and *fides.* The suggestion is that people need to be vigilant about whom they trust as divinity's representatives.

Winkler notes in another connection that the "plainest feature of [the episode of the eunuch priests] is the emphasis on lying and dissimulation" (1985, 110), but does not pursue this feature as a thematic link with other episodes.

lective acceptance and observation is a condition of the social contract. The abandonment of these values begins early on, but it accelerates wildly as Lucius moves closer to the saving goddess. The whole idea of fictions moreover receives its ultimate refinement here, insofar as conventions are social fictions that share with other kinds of fictions the paradoxically coexistent qualities of precariousness on the one hand and seductive persuasiveness on the other. This subtle variation on the theme of fictionality is a culmination of its earlier manifestations in the question of whether incredible tales are credible and later in the implication that all human action can have its basis in fictions. The disintegration of the institution of *fides* in particular is lamented by the bandits in Book 4, but in the course of the later books it becomes clear that *religio* and *pietas* have lost their constraining force as well.

We have noted that it was by means of his pose as the "most trusted friend" [*fidelissimus amicus*] (8.2) of Tlepolemus that Thrasyllus was able to deceive and murder him. His plot hinged also on the persuasiveness of his "posed piety" [*mentita pietas*] (8.7) toward the murdered man's household. Charite specifies the law that has been violated when she begins the ironic imprecation over her drugged suitor at 8.12: "Behold my husband's faithful friend" [*en fidus coniugis mei comes*]. That traditional social values have lost their regulating power is further clarified when people express the conviction that these rules can be disregarded at will and with impunity. The wicked stepmother, for example, betrays her assumption that time-honored deterrent forces are not to be taken seriously, when she attempts to persuade the object of her desire that if a behavioral injunction is inconvenient, it can simply be ignored: "Don't let any pangs of conscience about your father bother you one bit," she encourages the boy [*nec te religio patris omnino deterreat*] (10.3). *Fides* has as little force as *religio*, as far as she is concerned: when she initially fails in her objective, she quickly and unreflectively hatches her "faithless plans" [*perfidiae suae consilia*] (10.4).

As we move toward the end of Book 10, we find that a complete disregard for *fides* consistently characterizes the accomplices of the murderess there. The slave whom she charges to report the fictitious instructions to her husband's sister is described as "faithful to his mistress, but having no conception of true Faith" [*sibi (i.e., dominae) quidem fidelis, sed de ipsa Fide pessime merens*] (10.24). Another character who aids and abets the condemned woman in her crimes is a physician of proven faithlessness (*medicus notae perfidiae*, 10.25). He is rewarded for his services by being tricked into quaffing the poison that he himself has concocted for the woman's husband. Intent on the destruction of both husband and chief witness, she insists that the doctor first test the "medicine" supposedly meant to cure the young man's depression about his sister's death. The words she uses to force the doctor to drink or risk exposing his own role in the husband's death show that, to her, *religio* and *pietas* are merely words with no real referent, to be exploited for sinister purposes: by asking the doctor to test the beverage, she says, she is simply "exercising the obligatory piety that any religious wife would exercise if she were troubled about the safety of her husband" [*religiosa uxor circa salutem mariti sollicita necessariam adfero pietatem*] (10.26). The invocation of these values by the likes of the condemned woman and Thrasyllus serves as a warning to the complacent and the credulous that they should resist taking for granted the continuing operation of these behavioral constraints. The doctor's wife falls victim to the same pretense when she does not stop to probe the false *imago fidei* (10.27) that the murderess presents to her. The breakdown of social institutions such as *fides, religio,* and *pietas* renders oaths and prayers delivered in their name by those naïve enough still to believe in them empty and ironic: the innocent traveler who is falsely accused of killing the sadistic boy and stealing his ass invokes the "trust of men and gods" [*fides hominum deumque*] (7.25), but to no avail.[8]

The obsolescence of social regulators is dramatized in Books 7 through 10 in a way that reworks and refines two of the main motifs used to express the fluidity of the material world in Books 1 through 4: the transgression of ontological boundaries and the idea of metamorphosis. Now, social constraints are regularly violated by perpetrators who are represented as having *metaphorically* become beasts, as having *psychologically* undergone a transformation. The assumption of feral traits by character after character in these books is always implicit in their acts and in glimpses we are afforded into their state of mind. But as usual it is the precisely constructed patterns of diction that leave no room for doubt about the connection. The fact that terms ordinarily designating animal activity are regularly employed here to denote

---

8. Like the problem of false opinion, that of disintegrating social institutions asserts itself in ostensibly comic episodes as well, especially in the tales of adultery. Consider, e.g., the stress laid on the famous but ultimately corruptible *fides* of the slave Myrmex in Book 9 (17, 18, 19).

human activity makes it clear that these human beings are to be seen as beasts in all but form as surely as Lucius, the closer he gets to Isis, is a man in all but form. We get a preview of this device in Book 4, in the description of the response of the gardener and his allies when Lucius eats the gardener's vegetables. The incensed villagers—or is it their dogs?—chase the ass off, "agitated by their rabid anger" [*rabie perciti*] (4.3). "Rabies" is a quintessentially animal affliction, but the syntax here allows for ambiguity as to whether it is the canines or their masters who are rabid.[9] It seems unlikely that this preliminary ambiguity is insignificant in view of the systematic attribution of animal wildness to human beings later on throughout Books 7 through 10.

In order to appreciate fully how carefully worked out this transfer of attributes is, we must first examine in some detail how the steady parade of genuine wild beasts engaged in a full range of beastly activities is represented in these books. What follows is a catalogue of programmatic passages with special attention to critical diction:

> Book 7.16. The jealous stallions that suspect the ass of having designs on their mares: "Raging with extreme hatred they attacked their rival" [*rivalem summo furentes persecuntur odio*].
>
> Book 8.4 and 5. The wild boar being pursued in the hunting expedition during which Thrasyllus eliminates his rival: "A boar . . . with flaming eyes and threatening look; the savage attack of his roaring mouth made him one big lightning bolt" [*aper . . . oculis aspectu minaci flammeus, impetu saevo frementis oris totus fulmineus*]; a beast "burning with the fire of its wildness" [*incendio feritatis ardescens*]; a "raging boar" [*furens aper*].
>
> Book 8.15. The wolves threatening the village through which Lucius and his companions must pass: the villagers explain that the countryside around their town is infested with "many wolves . . . savage and extremely ferocious . . . rabid with mad hunger" [*lupos enim numerosos . . . et nimia ferocitate saevientes . . . vaesana fame rabidos*].

---

9. The sentence reads: *cuncti enim pagani fletibus eius exciti statim conclamant canes atque, ad me laniandum rabie perciti ferrent impetum, passim cohortantur.* This is Helm's punctuation, which attempts to clear matters up a bit; but I think that it is unnecessary and misses the point of the conflation.

Book 8.17. The dogs called out by a group of farmers to drive
away the party with which Lucius is traveling and which the
farmers have mistakenly identified as bandits: "Rabid dogs . . .
more savage than any wolves or bears . . . which were provoked
beyond their ordinary level of native ferocity by the confusion
of their owners, and rushed against us . . . with burning hearts"
[canes rabidos . . . et quibusvis lupis et ursis saeviores . . . qui praeter
genuinam ferocitatem tumultu suorum exasperati contra nos ruunt
. . . ardentibus animis].

Book 9.36 and 37. The attack dogs of the ruthless landlord: this
final set of dogs is described as "wild and enormous" [feros
atque immanes]; "agitated with raging rabies" [furiosa rabie
conciti]; and "savage and extremely ferocious" [saevisque illis et
ferocissimis canibus].

It is easy to see that the text's vocabulary of beastliness is as systematic as its vocabulary of deception. Wild animals are characterized with
a limited and recurring set of adjectives meaning "ferocious, wild, raging, savage, rabid, mad, roaring, and burning or flashing" [ferox; ferus;
furens/furiosus; saevus/saeviens; rabidus; vaesanus; fremens; ardens/ardes-
cens/flammeus/fulmineus]. Their defining attributes are "ferocity, wildness, and rabid madness" [ferocitas, feritas, rabies], and their typical
actions are attacking (impetus) and rushing about (ruere).

It is precisely this vocabulary and these images that are repeatedly
and pointedly associated also with human activities and states of mind
as the novel careens toward its final book. The equation of animals and
human beings begins in small ways. The behavior of the wicked boy in
Book 7 is so bestial that the ass views with equal disfavor the prospects
of remaining in the boy's clutches and of being torn apart by a ravenous
bear. Lucius describes himself fleeing both boy and bear as "escaping
from the enormous bear and the boy who was worse than a bear"
[fugiens immanem ursam ursaque peiorem illum puerum] (7.24). From such
a fleeting suggestion the device is developed into one of the unifying
features of the major episodes in these books. Obsessed with Charite,
Thrasyllus displays all the qualities of Apuleian animals. The narrator
of the tale recounts Thrasyllus' symptoms in this way: "What else could
you expect, since the flame of savage love when it is small delights us
with its first warmth, but when kindled with the nourishment of habit
burns us up altogether with its excessive heat. . . . Listen to what hap-

pened when those attacks of raging lust burst forth" [*quidni, cum flamma saevi amoris parva quidem primo vapore delectet, sed fomentis consuetudinis exaestuans inmodicis ardoribus totos amburat homines. . . . intendite, quorsum furiosae libidinis proruperint impetus*] (8.2–3). The passage teems with all the images of raging, seething, burning, and frenzied impulse that the reader is being conditioned to associate with wild beasts. The appearance of the wild boar in the very next chapters (8.4–5), described in the same terms, fixes the connection.

Like mendacity, bestiality is contagious. Upon learning of the death of her husband in a hunting accident (for so it was reported to her), the well-bred young lady who was the companion of Lucius' captivity among the bandits is reduced by grief to ranging blindly through the city like a rabid animal: "[When she heard the news] Charite went out of her mind. Stirred up into madness, she ran raving with a furious gait through the crowded streets and the country fields, lamenting the fate of her husband in a deranged voice" [*amens et vecordia percita cursuque bacchata furibundo per plateas populosas et arva rurestria fertur, insana voce casum mariti quiritans*] (8.6). Charite's madness and raging fury recall that of the wild boar falsely blamed for the death of Tlepolemus. The animal connection is even clearer when Thrasyllus' persistent proposals of marriage jolt her into suddenly understanding what the situation truly is. Charite responds to this revelation by "bellowing repeatedly like an animal" [*ferinos mugitus iterans*] (8.8). The disintegration of her personality accelerates when the ghost of her husband appears in a dream and confirms what she suspects. Now a passionate desire for vengeance consumes the once blushing bride, who madly beats her arms "with savage hands" [*saevientibus palmulis*] (8.9). After the nurse drugs Thrasyllus, Charite moves in for the kill: "Raging in her dire attack she rushed in and stood over the assassin" [*impetu diro fremens invadit ac supersistit sicariam*] (8.11). Finally, with Thrasyllus blinded, Charite makes her way, "running furiously" [*cursu furioso*] (8.13), to the tomb of Tlepolemus, where she has resolved to commit suicide. Because she begins life in the novel as such a paragon of conventional femininity, Charite's metamorphosis is all the more dramatic and her degeneration into raging bestiality all the more radical a transformation.[10]

---

10. For much of the tone and many of the details in this episode, Apuleius is heavily indebted to Latin love elegy (Propertius, Tibullus, Ovid, and before

The circle of animalistic violence continues to expand in Book 9 with the provocations of the insolent young landlord. This episode (9.35–38) explicitly connects animal imagery with the disintegration of social mandates. The initial picture of this man is that of someone who engages in antisocial behavior by arbitrarily exempting himself from the dictates of law and social custom. His arrogant overreaching leads him to torment his poor but honest neighbor in an effort to drive the latter off his small plot and to take possession of the land himself. The rich youth harasses the farmer with raids during which he steals or kills the farmer's animals and vandalizes his crops (9.35). The three noble sons of Lucius' current host come to the defense of the poor man, invoking the impartial protection of the law. The haughty and tyrannical threats of the rich will be in vain, they confidently say, "since . . . even the poor

---

them Catullus) and to Book 4 of Virgil's *Aeneid*. Drawing on conventions going back as far as Sappho, the elegists depicted love, which to them was always erotic compulsion, in pathological terms, as a kind of madness accompanied by symptoms of physical disease. Love is cruel *(saevus)*, the lover burns. These conventions inform Virgil's representation of the fall of Dido, and Apuleius' of the smitten Thrasyllus. Although Charite is reduced by anger and hatred rather than love, the picture of her raging through the streets like a maenad *(bacchata)* unmistakably recalls the Carthaginian queen's demented behavior in *Aeneid* 4 (300–303; see Forbes 1943–44). Virgil relies on the Bacchic image again in describing the war fever of Amata and the Latin women at the beginning of Book 7 (385–405). Thus in the *Aeneid* such madness is not associated exclusively with Eros. In fact, *Aeneid* 7 through 12 is an orgy of largely martial *furor*, which eventually infects even the levelheaded Aeneas and (in the reading of many critics) casts a pall over his final victory. The essential community in the epic of martial *furor* and the erotically inspired *furor* of Dido is made clear through linking systems of vocabulary very much like those of Apuleius. Like that of Virgil, the Apuleian conception encompasses a range of motivations for such behavior, so described. Although the erotic voice is clearly present in the tale of Charite, the impulse behind the raving of Charite herself is not erotic, and neither is that of the young landlord in Book 9. In the novel, as in the epic, Eros is only one of several instigators of *furor*, and in the novel such behavior is furthermore connected to beastliness through diction that links together descriptions of wild animals and the major episodes concerned with the infiltration of *furor* into human society. This is another case of Apuleius' opening up the signification of inherited, in this case elegiac, material, taking his cue from the earlier innovations of Virgil.

have customarily been protected against the insolence of rich men by the liberal bulwark of the law" [cum . . . pauperes etiam liberali legum praesidio de insolentia locupletium consueverint vindicari] (9.36).

The landlord, who has already been called a "madman" [vaesanus] (9.36), only becomes more frenzied and unreasonable in response to these protests against his injustice. He utterly loses control of himself:

> As oil to flame, as sulphur to fire, as the whip to a Fury, so these words of theirs simply fed his savagery. Mad to the point of total insanity, he shouted that he would order both them and the laws themselves to be hanged.

> [quod oleum flammae, quod sulpur incendio, quod flagellum Furiae, hoc et iste sermo truculentiae hominis nutrimento fuit. iamque ad extremam insaniam vecors, suspendium sese et totis illis et ipsis legibus mandare proclamans.] (9.36)

Lest the bestiality of his behavior be lost on the reader, a description of the savage mastiffs that he turns on the brothers and the farmer follows immediately (9.36–37). Like their master, they are characterized in terms of fire and fury: "Ignited and inflamed, stirred up with raging rabid madness" [incensi atque inflammati . . . furiosa rabie conciti], "savage and extremely ferocious" [saevisque illis et ferocissimis canibus], they rush against (aggressi) the helpless defenders of justice. Thus, as in the case of Thrasyllus and the boar, a pointed juxtaposition aids in foregrounding the growing indistinction between human and animal behavior.[11] The rich youth's willful proclamation of his own abrogation of the law is crucial, coming as it does at the height of his animal fury. That he can dismiss the rule of law and, for all intents and purposes, get away with it (he is finally killed, but so are the good brothers) exposes the social contract and specifically the idea of law as another fragile organizational framework imposed upon a resistant reality. Significantly, the youth is described as a "raging bandit" [furiosus latro] at 9.38. We are reminded of the "real" bandits who held Charite and Lucius captive in

---

11. The idea of bestial *rabies* as a contagion is present here too. Spurred on by the death of one of their number, the remaining brothers attack "in a mad rush, with burning hearts" [ardentibus animis impetuque vaesano] (9.37).

the cave. In their own way they were gentlemen who tried to adhere faithfully to a quasi-religious code of conduct. It is this rich young landowner who is the *real* outlaw. The transfer of aristocratic values to the bandits and criminal values to the aristocrat exemplifies the sort of inversion through which the text undermines established assumptions about social order.

In the world of the *Metamorphoses*, a variety of destructive passions strains the boundaries set by social conventions and institutions. The desire for power and wealth cause the young landowner's transgressions; the desire for vengeance, Charite's; sadism, that of the *puer nequissimus*. In the two tales of lawless women in Book 10, the initial impulse is either sexual desire, as in the case of Thrasyllus, or wild jealousy. It is therefore to be expected that the immediately discernible voice in the descriptions of the women's motivating impulses is the voice of erotic poetry, with its burning, mad lust, and physical debility (e.g., 10.2–4, 10.24; see note 10 above). This is the primary intertextual echo, but the intratextual resonance is richer. It embraces a wide range of antinomian qualities and behaviors, many of which are not erotically driven and all of which are united in the *Metamorphoses* by a system of images and diction consistently associated with a force classically antithetical to ordered society, namely, beasts in the wild. The word *efferata*, "made wild like a wild beast," which describes the effect of desire on the condemned woman, marks the animal subtext of her narrative in spite of its erotic overtones. The irrational quality of the accelerating violence in which each woman engages cannot but recall the destruction wrought by the landlord. His bestiality is made clear by the association between him and his dogs, but Eros plays no part in his actions. In all three of these episodes the momentum of the violence carries it far beyond the bounds of its original purpose. It may have been "savage jealousy" [*saeva Rivalitas*] (10.24) that impelled the condemned woman to a consuming hatred of her husband's sister and finally to her murder (which is carried out with gratuitous sadism, 10.24), but her decision to kill her partner in the marriage she was supposedly trying to preserve by eliminating an imputed rival serves no apparent purpose. Significantly, this ordinarily self-possessed young man does not die before being reduced to the same animal affects that mark all of the lawless activity in Books 7 through 10: "Moved by grief [at his sister's death] in his very marrow and overcome by the destructive fury of very bitter bile, he burned from that time on with the hottest of fevers" [*medullitus dolore commotus acerrimaeque bilis noxio furore perfusus exin flagrantissimis febribus ardebat]* (10.25). Although in this case the fever is physical, the general associations are unmistakable. The husband, like Charite, is pulled into the antinomian force field in spite of his own virtues.

Although the condemned woman has reasons for widening her net to encompass her own daughter and the doctor and his wife, the general impression created by this episode as it unfolds is that matters are getting more and more out of hand. The woman seems to be almost randomly casting about for victims: "Once she had obtained the wherewithal for committing crimes [that is, the poison supplied by the doctor's wife], she stretched her bloody hands far and wide" *[grandem scelerum nancta materiam longe lateque cruentas suas manus porrigit]* (10.27). Likewise, earlier on, the stepmother, frustrated in her effort to obtain the object of her desire, had blazed up into a sweeping vindictiveness that involved nothing less than the destruction of the entire family:

> That dreadful woman, a singular example of stepmotherly wickedness, disturbed neither by the bitter death of her son, nor by guilt for her part in it, nor by the misfortune of the house, nor by the grief of her husband, nor by the calamity of death, dragged the whole family down to serve her own sense of vengeance.

> [dira illa femina et malitiae novercalis exemplar unicum non acerba filii morte, non parricidii conscientia, non infortunio domus, non luctu mariti vel aerumna funeris commota cladem familiae in vindictae compendium traxit.] (10.5)

By the time the reader reaches the point of Lucius' escape toward the end of Book 10, the cumulative force of these tales has created an overwhelming sense that social law has entirely broken down. There is a cataclysmic movement of the action toward a total dissolution of the social fabric, and the characters who contribute to this movement increasingly lack even sinister rationales for doing so.[12]

---

12. As usual, the motif has comic manifestations. In pursuit of his wife's lover, Barbarus "hastens off bellowing silently to himself" *[tacitos secum mugi-*

Another image linking the stages of this dissolution is that of the Furies, those mythical overseers of vengeance. They are invoked in the novel chiefly through the use of the adjective *dirus-a-um*, "dire or dreadful," the usual Latin epithet of the infernal sisters. The presence of these disseminators of chaotic violence is first felt in connection with Charite's relentless pursuit of Thrasyllus. Resolved to avenge her husband, she storms into the room where his killer lies drugged, "roaring with manly courage and dire force" [*masculis animis impetuque diro fremens*] (8.11). The use of *diro* in the context of seeking vengeance strongly suggests that Charite is to be seen as acting the part of a Fury here. The association is strengthened by the clear debt that the description of Charite's demise owes to Virgil's picture of the jilted Dido's ravings in *Aeneid* 4, where the queen is explicitly connected with the Furies several times (4.376, 473, 610, 625). The initial appearance of a Fury in the novel, then, occurs in connection with revenge, the sisters' traditional province. In subsequent appearances, however, the avenging function of the Fury is extremely vague or does not figure at all. *Dira* is applied to the wicked stepmother, as we have seen above, in the passage where she hardens her heart to the impending ruin of her family (*dira illa femina et malitiae novercalis exemplar unicum*, 10.5). Yet in spite of the fact that her actions are said to satisfy her need for vengeance (*cladem familiae in vindictae compendium traxit*), it is vengeance in the loosest sense of the word, an indiscriminate lashing out after the failure of her plans rather than a particular act done in repayment for any injustice perpetrated against herself.

Other invocations of the Furies in the novel see them even further removed from their traditional circumscribed function. As we saw above, the landlord is explicitly likened to a Fury goaded by the "whip" of the noble youth's protests (*quod oleum flammae, quod sulpur incendio, quod flagellum Furiae*, 9.36). But the landlord's seething wrath and destructive actions have nothing to do with a desire for vengeance, just or unjust. Likewise, the condemned woman is goaded by a Fury, but it is a "fury of lust" [*libidinosae furiae stimulis efferata*] (10.24), not one of

---

tus iterans rapidum dirigit gressum] (9.21); and the fuller, his heart "seething" (*fervens*) with *rabies* at the disclosure of his wife's infidelity, attempts to mount a "furious attack" (*impetus furiosus*) against his rival (9.25).

vengeance. Although the Furies begin their career in the *Metamorphoses* doing their narrow inherited duty, they ultimately are made to preside over violence that is gratuitous and irrational (for whatever one may think of revenge, it has a rationale). In this expansion of the Furies' province Apuleius is drawing here, as he often does, on Virgil, for these are Virgil's Furies. W.R. Johnson (1976, 144) describes them:

> These figures, Allecto and the Dira, frame the action of the second half of the *Aeneid*; both are creatures of darkness that are connected with irrational and utterly incomprehensible works of destruction, and both are, whatever their specific models might be, Vergil's reimaginings of nightmarish beings that Greek rationalism had utterly excluded from its normal modes of conceiving the human world. Both are Furies, but in their behavior they show not only the dark violence of hellish powers but also the gratuitous sadism that marks a special kind of hell.

Both *Aeneid* 7 through 12 and *Metamorphoses* 7 through 10 blaze toward their cataclysmic conclusions driven by *furor* and by the Furies, and in both the movement is represented in the same terms and with the same images. Apuleius does homage to Virgil here while, as usual, reserving the right to give the material his own final stamp. The important difference is that the epic ends with Aeneas, the Pyrrhic victor, himself conquered by *furor*, standing anticlimactically amidst the ruins wrought by it. Although the Augustan state lurks in the background as the sole bulwark against future incursions of the Furies, we have a sinking sense that it is always going to be an uphill battle. Two centuries later there will be another way out.

The orgy of bestial human activity in Books 7 through 10 is a comment on the tenuousness of the social constraints that are supposed to prevent destructive passions from irrupting into the social order. This is Apuleius' concern as much as the passions themselves. Repeatedly, the failure of some set of social laws to perform its assigned task is made the crux of an episode, be those laws grouped under *fides, religio, pietas,* or another rubric. In view of this, we can only read ironically any appeals made to the common laws of humanity. The leader of the peripatetic shepherds who have been mistaken for bandits in Book 8 pleads in these words with the farmers to cease their attack: "Surely you do not inhabit the caves of wild beasts or the rocky crags of savages, that you enjoy shedding human blood" [*at non speluncas ferarum vel cautes incolitis barbarorum, ut humano sanguine profuso gaudeatis*] (8.18). Likewise, the magistrates attempting to dissuade a mob from lynching the unjustly accused stepson argue that the people must not allow "someone to be condemned unheard in the manner of barbarians, who are no better than wild animals, or of unchecked tyrants" [*ad instar barbaricae feritatis vel tyrannicae impotentiae damnaretur aliquis inauditus*] (10.6) (there is a link here to the landlord in Book 9, who is likened to a tyrant as well as to a raging animal when he is described as "trusting in his tyrant's arrogance" [*confisus tyrannica superbia*] at 9.36). Of course the joke, so to speak, is that characters *routinely* behave like wild animals in Books 7 through 10, thus rendering all such pleas meaningless. Interestingly enough, Lucius the ass clings to the social code abandoned by humanity, and in fact his *fides* is cited, although perhaps with some authorial irony, as a reason for his deserving salvation in Book 11 (16). But although *fides*, for example, persists out of habit as a prop in his ethical system, there are other conventional values that have given his life cohesion that *do* finally fail him, as we will see.

The bestial humans fulminating their way through Books 7 through 10 represent another of the many collapses of fixed categories and distinctions that characterize the drifting world of Lucius the preconvert. The animal motif has other relevant significations as well. Questions of form and substance and the issue of whether the relationship between the two is defined more by disjunction or by continuum are, I think, central to the text. The apparent absence of correspondence in these cases between form and substance, at least if one accepts the traditional delineation of human and animal attributes, is one half of another Apuleian inversion that is balanced by the simultaneous presence of Lucius, an animal whose comportment and sensibilities become progressively more human. Apuleius constructs an inverted parallel of movement in which the degeneration and feralization of human beings unfolds alongside the graduation of the ass (back) into humanity. In its early stages his reentry is marked by the adoption of some of the more superficial social conventions (sleeping in a bed and eating at table, for example). We will see, however, that in the later stages of this pilgrim's progress Lucius is depicted as moving beyond the unthinking adherence to social forms posited by Apuleius as constituting the minimum requirement for membership in humanity without being proof of it, to something more "substantially" human than any of the human beings in these books of the novel achieves.[13]

I noted in chapter 1 some features in Apuleius' representation of the ass that make him an emblem of the fluidity that seems to characterize all of the novel's reality. There I discussed the narrator's habit of constantly drawing attention to his former suspension in a state of ontological limbo; this habit continues in Books 7 through 10. Thus, for example, when he explains how he learned of the machinations of the baker's wife, he does not neglect to include a reference to his dual identity: "See how I, a curious man sustaining the form of a beast of burden, learned all the things that were done to ruin my master the baker" [*accipe . . . quem ad modum homo curiosus iumenti faciem sustinens cuncta, quae in perniciem pistoris mei gesta sunt, cognovi*] (9.30). The reader's awareness of Lucius' predicament is ironically kept alive in the observations of others. Charite seems to sense that there is something unusual about this ass when she praises him after he rescues her from the bandits: "But if Jupiter truly bellowed in the form of a bull [when he ferried Europa across the sea], some face of a man or likeness of the gods might lie hidden in my ass" [*quodsi vere Iuppiter mugivit in bove, potest in asino meo latere aliqui vultus hominis vel facies deorum*] (6.29). In a more caustic spirit, the auctioneer who eventually sells Lucius to the eunuch priests also inadvertently hits upon the truth: "You see here a wether, not an ass, gentle for any use you put him to, not a biter nor

---

13. "In Apuleius the transformed hero's parallel claim to a measure of humanity is ironically subverted by his estimate of humanity itself; . . . the ass . . . marks a stage in the hero's progress toward a *humanitas* that, as far as the romance lets us judge, is neither peculiar nor habitual to the species of the featherless biped" (Skulsky 1981, 70, 73).

Here and throughout this discussion, I use the categories of substance and form, and the premise that intrinsic or essential and definitive human qualities exist underneath a patina of social convention, very advisedly and in full knowledge of the problems raised by these propositions in the postmodern world, where "social forms" are all there is, and networks of social discourse, rather than any innate qualities, constitute human identity. But certainly the humanist paradigm was well established in the world of Apuleius, even if he plays with and pokes at it a bit, and it is fundamental to the type of conversion narrative that I will ultimately be arguing the *Metamorphoses* is. The point is that the paradigms of Lucius the preconvert are disrupted, and in this case the disruption consists in the revelation that form and substance do not correspond in ways he has come to expect, rather than that they are the same thing. Apuleius was advanced, but he was not that advanced.

even a kicker: really, you would think that a mild-mannered human being were living inside this ass's hide" [*vervecem, non asinum vides, ad usus omnes quietum, non mordacem nec calcitronem quidem, sed prorsus ut in asini corio modestum hominem inhabitare credas*] (8.25). The presence of a paradox on four hooves is also signaled by the continuing reference to Lucius' retention of his rational faculties, sometimes with subtle ironic twists. Finding himself thinking stupid thoughts, he berates them as "inept and completely asinine cogitations" [*inepta et prorsus asinina cogitatio*] (6.26). But just what does he think he is if he is not an ass?

Another hallmark of Lucius the man that survives his transformation is his dogged sense of conventional morality. The result is the pointed seriocomic juxtaposition of an ass intrepidly clinging to learned notions of how civilized people should behave, alongside human beings to whom these precepts seem to mean less and less. But at the same time, the context in which his often misplaced moral pronouncements are made; their smugness and hypocrisy; their dogmatism, which can lead Lucius into egregious errors of judgment; and finally the simple ludicrousness of an ass who casts himself in the role of moral arbiter, all have the effect of satirizing the morality that Lucius professes. Lucius proves that it is possible to subscribe out of habit to a code of conventional morality and still be morally derailed. His "sin," however, is not to be defined legalistically as the transgression of specific clauses of this code (for example, indulging in "carnal lust"), as some critics would have it. It consists rather in his missing the mark in a much larger sense, as I will argue in chapter 4. By juxtaposing the widespread breakdown of social prescripts among humans with their dubiously motivated and often just plain silly defense by an ass, the text seems to present us with a choice between the chaos resulting from a complete disregard for these prescripts and an order regulated by prescripts that are in some sense hollow, not to say asinine. But in the course of Book 10, and in the unlikeliest of circumstances—the sexual union of the ass and the Corinthian matron—we will be presented with a third possibility. For it is at this critical point that Lucius is represented as moving beyond a morality of form to a morality of substance, as we will see momentarily.

It is when the ass witnesses his idea of sexual morality being violated that he is most likely to take up a self-righteous moralizing stance. When the eunuch priests begin to take advantage of an unsuspecting dinner guest, his reaction is indignant but ultimately mute: he tries to call for help, but can only manage a loud, braying "O!" (8.29). He equates the priests' lascivious behavior with that of the baker's adulterous wife in Book 9 by describing their actions as "crimes" *(facinora)* in both cases. In the second he is inspired to contrive ways of exposing the woman's philanderings by his deeply offended sense of propriety: "My heart was disturbed deep down inside as I considered the past crime and the present inconstancy of that dreadful woman" [*mihi penita carpebantur praecordia et praecedens facinus et praesentem deterrimae feminae constantiam cogitanti*] (9.26). All this *saeva indignatio* is a little hard to take seriously, coming as it does from an ass, and one whose own record of self-restraint, sexual or otherwise, is hardly beyond reproach. And while in the first case it is true that the youth is being handled against his will, the second involves the double standard for masculine and feminine virtue that is implicitly satirized in Book 7 when with an "ass's judgment" Lucius sweepingly convicts the entire female sex of infidelity (7.10). It is worth remembering that in that episode, where Lucius delivers one of his most impassioned laments for lost virtue, he is dead wrong in what he surmises about Charite. The pompous declamatory rhetoric with which he scolds her makes his indignation all the more ridiculous (7.11).

Another important precept in Lucius' code is regard for the laws of hospitality. He is shocked when his host, Milo, appears to betray these laws during the Risus festival while Lucius is still a man (3.7). His transformation does not change his expectation that his fellows, now beasts, will respect the dictates of hospitality invented by human society. Lucius is disappointed in this expectation when his own horse boots him out of the barn shortly after the fiasco with the ointments (3.26). His trust in this institution is assaulted all over again when he is put to pasture with a group of stallions who regard him as a rival for the affections of some eligible mares: "Raging with extreme hatred, they pursued me as a usurper, completely disregarding the bonds of Jupiter, the god of hospitality" [*nec hospitalis Iovis servato foedere rivalem summo furentes persecuntur odio*] (7.16). Indeed it is his horror at the possibility that he himself might be considered a transgressor of these laws that exposes a third important component in his system of values: an abiding concern for his own reputation, which in his world can be secured only through moral and social conformity. This is why the ass is so upset when he discovers that it is commonly believed back in

Hypata that Lucius was the one who sacked Milo's house. He desperately wants to clear his name by pronouncing "I did not do it" [non feci] but is frustrated, as he often is, in his attempts to speak and can only manage a hee-haw version of the first syllable (7.3). He is equally disturbed by his inability to defend himself against the charges of making lascivious advances against women and youths, trumped up by the evil boy in Book 7 (21). It is Lucius' dogged and increasingly besieged belief in a reliable system of social imperatives and constraints that creates the jarring impression of a successfully socialized human being inhabiting a beast's body, surrounded by others whom the terms of the social contract do not control in spite of their having the appearance of human beings.

Yet at the same time, the treatment of Lucius' morality has a satirical strain. For as much of an improvement as there might have been in the course of the novel's events if the criminals of Books 7 through 10 had shared Lucius' values, these are at bottom complacent and superficial. Their only basis is an unreflective adherence to an externally imposed moral and social code. His superiority to his feral human counterparts is the result of the successful inculcation of the values of his class rather than any ongoing Socratic process of scrutinizing and reformulating his views. In fact, from the beginning Lucius shows little inclination to engage in conscious or systematic ethical thought. His virtues as well as his vices are practiced out of habit. He has occasional flashes of insight into the limitations of his approach to life, as at 9.13, where he seems fleetingly to understand that the pleasures of *curiositas* are merely diversionary. These flashes are never long sustained, however, and the force of complacency always causes him to revert to his old ways of thinking and acting instead of using the insights that assert themselves in his more lucid moments and the lessons of experience as a foundation for examining and reforming his life. He remains essentially incapable of doing so, fettered by habit and short-range vision. Thus the *Metamorphoses* is not a *Bildungsroman* in any ordinary sense. There is no evidence in the text that Lucius is to be seen as growing in conscious moral awareness as the plot unfolds, in spite of a tradition among Apuleian critics of sifting the text for signs of such growth. The way to Lucius' conversion is not prepared by any conscious Platonic spiritual striving. In terms of Jamesian psychology, it is the last stage in the maturation of unconscious motives; in theological terms, Lucius is saved by grace alone. Whichever way one chooses to look at it, the preparation for conversion operates on an almost entirely passive subject, and it is the fictional representation of this process with which I am concerned.

As an ass Lucius may retain his powers of cogitation and his conventional sense of morality, but a human capacity that he sorely lacks and whose absence he laments as often as he notes his retention of intellect is the ability to speak. Lucius draws attention to his muteness immediately after his transformation (he is "deprived of a voice," *voce privatus*, he says), when he describes his frustration at not being able to reproach Fotis for mixing up the ointments (3.25). From this beginning his muteness comes up over and over again. Three references to it, occurring in close succession in Book 7, illustrate the stress laid on Lucius' vocal limitations. The traveler unjustly accused by the unsavory shepherds of stealing the ass and killing the boy wishes that Lucius, the only witness, could come to his defense: "I wish that this ass were able to speak like a human being and give testimony to my innocence" [*utinam ipse asinus . . . vocem quiret humanam dare meaeque testimonium innocentiae perhibere posset*] (7.25). For his part, Lucius is acutely aware of his own powerlessness to help: "By Hercules, I would have said what I knew, if only I had had the ability to speak" [*dicerem quod sciebam, si loquendi copia suppeditaret*] (7.26). Finally, the dismembered boy's mother, who holds the ass responsible for her son's death because he did not hurry to the rescue, insists that the ass would not be able to offer a persuasive defense even if he were to acquire the power of speech (*licet precariam vocis usuram sumeres*, 7.27). Why the persistence of this motif?

One could speculate in several directions, but in the context of my reading it is important to remember that language is the ordering mechanism that permeates all others. The loss of its use is therefore a perfect metaphor for Lucius' weakening grip on the entire range of his world's ordering mechanisms. A clear statement of this principle comes from the sociologist of religion and knowledge, Peter Berger:

> The fact of language . . . can readily be seen as the imposition of order upon experience. Language nomizes [i.e., creates a socially constructed framework of meaning] by imposing differentiation and structure upon the ongoing flux of experience. As an item of experience is named, it is *ipso facto* taken out of this flux and given stability *as* the entity so named. Language further provides a fun-

damental order of relationships by the addition of syntax and grammar to vocabulary. It is impossible to use language without participating in its order. Every empirical language may be said to constitute a nomos in the making, or, with equal validity, be seen as the historical consequence of the nomizing activity of generations of men. The original nomizing act is to say that an item is *this,* and thus *not that.* As this original incorporation of the item into an order that includes other items is followed by sharper linguistic designations (the item is male and not female, singular and not plural, a noun and not a verb, and so forth), the nomizing act intends a comprehensive order of *all* items that may be linguistically objectivated, that is, intends a totalizing nomos.

On the foundation of language, and by means of it, is built up the cognitive and normative edifice that passes for "knowledge" in a society. (1967, 20–21)

Thus it makes sense that in Book 11, when with his conversion Lucius constructs a new "cognitive and normative edifice" to take the place of the old one that has shattered, his voice, which marks his participation in some "nomizing" system, will be "reborn." Before that, the connection between language qua ordering structure and the social conventions that order experience is dramatized by the fact that Lucius never feels his muteness more intensely than when he is filled with moral outrage at assaults on conventional morality and attempts to speak up in its defense.

And so this walking paradox, this ass with human sensibilities, serves as a kind of foil to all the *homines sapientes* raging with animal passions through the penultimate books of the *Metamorphoses*. The reader's sense that form and substance are out of their usual alignment and that two normally distinct categories—animal and human—have become hopelessly entangled is heightened by the picture that we are given of Lucius' "education," drawn against the background of social disintegration. Although the ass does not seem consciously to reformulate his moral and epistemological premises, his graduation to progressively more complex forms of human behavior provides a symbolic preparation for his conversion and readmission into humanity. Lucius' first symbolically human act occurs when several members of his current household, who are mistakenly convinced that he is rabid, drive him to seek refuge in a locked bedroom. Finding himself with some time on his hands, Lucius decides to take a nap: "I threw myself onto the made-up bed and slept like a human being for the first time in a long while" [*super constratum lectum abiectus, post multum equidem temporis somnum humanum quievi*] (9.2). In the next book he graduates from this human-style nap to a demonstration of gustatory sophistication made possible by his residence with two brothers whose occupations are cooking and baking. Lucius helps himself to their creations when his keepers are not looking and grows accustomed to feeling "stuffed to satiety with human food" [*humanis adfatim cibis saginatus*] (10.15). As a result, he shudders at the prospect of returning to coarser fare: "I was not so stupid nor so much of a real ass that I would dine on the roughest hay when I could have those sweet leftovers" [*nec enim tam stultus eram tamque vere asinus, ut dulcissimis illis relictis cibis cenarem asperrimum faenum*] (10.13). The finishing touches are put on Lucius' formal education by his trainer in Book 10, who treats him "as if he were a civilized human being" [*satis humane satisque comiter*] (10.17) and elicits from him further displays of gentility: dining at table, sitting up, dancing, and "speaking" by means of signals (10.16–18). The animal's attainments are perfected to the point that his master, Thiasos, considers him not just a means of transportation but his true companion (10.18).

I say that this is the ultimate stage in Lucius' *formal* education because up to now that is exactly what it has been: the acquisition of the most mechanical social skills. At this point, however, the content of his progress becomes more complicated. It shifts from formally to substantively human behavior in unexpected ways. What is more, the setting in which this change occurs involves an apparent disjunction of form and substance or, more precisely, a disruption of conditioned notions of what content is to be associated with particular forms. Lucius' more substantive human qualities emerge in circumstances where the form is all "wrong": during his sexual liaison with the aristocratic Corinthian lady in Book 10. The standard view of this episode is that it represents the nadir in the moral lives of both parties and the ultimate depth of Lucius' humiliation as an ass before being cleansed by Isis. And indeed several factors conspire to seduce the reader into this view. Among them is the diction applied to the *matrona*'s infatuation with the ass and to her enjoyment of the experience with him. At points these are described in terms elsewhere reserved for destructive animal and/or erotic passions or for the meaningless ephemeral pleasures of the secular world, whose emptiness will be exposed by devotion to the goddess. So, for example, the lady's lust is "insane" [*vaesana*], she waits for her lover "ardently" [*ardenter*], and her movements during sex are "rabid" [*rabidus*] (10.19, 22). It is furthermore her overwhelming desire (*cupido, libido*) that drives her to seek this unorthodox pleasure (*voluptas*) (10.19, 20, 22). If there were nothing to undermine the effect of these details, critics would perhaps be justified in considering the episode a negative representation of "perverse and uncontrolled sexuality" at its worst.[14]

But to do so is to fall into Apuleius' trap. That indeed is the programmed reading, the conventional response; but convention is rapidly receding as a standard of truth in this text. Here the reader is set up to fall into a certain conditioned reaction based on a widely accepted system of prejudices and associations but is suddenly caught off guard by the intrusion of details about the *substance* of the exchange that unexpectedly alter the tone of the passage and render it strangely touching. We become aware in spite of ourselves that this beauty and her beast share a spirit of mutual caring that is virtually unknown elsewhere in the world of the novel. Their improbable union represents a case of successful human contact in a world where countless forces conspire to block it. The ass's sexuality is far from "uncontrolled" here. On the contrary, his concern for the woman's safety causes him to take exceptional care not to hurt her (10.22). It is consistent with the clear pattern of Lucius' progressively more human behavior in these books to give his assumption of the role of a cultivated lady's paramour its rightful place in his expanding repertoire of human activities, in spite of prejudices that resist this reading. This time, however, in contrast to the mechanical quality of his earlier accomplishments, the subtleties of the exchange complicate the definition of what it is to be human. Here is how the Corinthian lady's reception of her hero is described:

---

14. This is the phrase of Mason (1971, 162). See more recently Schlam (1992, 37), who also equates the scene with the worst sort of "perversion and bestiality": "The encounter of the Ass with a wealthy woman of rank . . . is a macabre replay of the scenes of Lucius and Fotis." Schlam also has a discussion of "Animal and Human" (chap. 9, 99–112) but does not situate this theme in the larger context of the disintegration of categories in the *Metamorphoses* as a whole. The novel's vocabulary of desire and pleasure and its significance will be studied fully in chapter 4.

Then she kissed me intimately, not the sort of kisses that are tossed about in whorehouses, the mercenary kisses of the prostitutes or the niggardly kisses of the customers, but pure and sincere little kisses; and she addressed very tender words to me.

[tunc exosculata pressule, non qualia in lupinari solent basiola iactari vel meretricum poscinummia vel adventorum negantinummia, sed pura atque sincera instruit et blandissimos adfatus.] (10.21)

This is the only instance of any form of *sincerus* anywhere in the *Metamorphoses*. Of the other six occurrences of forms of *purus*, four (11.10, 16, 21, 23) are used in connection with Isis, who definitively ensures Lucius' humanity, while the remaining two (8.29, 9.8) are applied with unambiguous irony to the hypocritical eunuch priests of the Syrian goddess. But the unmistakably jeering satirical spirit that characterizes the Syrian sequence is entirely absent from the episode of the Corinthian *matrona*.[15]

This episode exemplifies a narrative strategy deployed throughout the *Metamorphoses*, one that hinges on twists designed to undermine the assumptions and confound the expectations of the reader. The assumption here is that the sexual union of an ass and a woman will be grotesque and "unnatural" at worst and pornographically titillating at best. Things are progressing according to the received script when suddenly the reader's complacency is given a jolt by the unexpected tenderness of the scene. As one critic put it, "This bizarre union, long turned to the titillation of the prurient . . . is a pivotal juncture in [Lucius'] transformation back into a man. . . . His spirit has been purified. And nothing focuses this alteration better than such a night of odd, but perfect, love."[16] With the *matrona* Lucius the ass achieves

---

15. So also Skulsky 1981, 74: "[The matron's] fascination with the animal's cleverness has grown somehow into authentic passion. . . . Apuleius' insistence on the *sinceritas* of the lady's passion is, I think, worth emphasizing; it does not appear in the cognate Greek story, which has a gratuitously cynical denouement in which the lady rebuffs the hero, who has returned in human form to renew acquaintances: 'You come to me after having been transformed from that noble and useful animal into a monkey?'"

16. Nethercut 1969, 124–25. For a similar assessment, see Journoud 1965. Her comments come in a discussion of the so-called *spurcum additamentum*, a

something like real human connection. This encounter is a crucial step in his progress toward Isis. It provides a final test of *puritas* before his conversion, and marks the greatest degree of human potential that he is able to attain without the intervention of the goddess. With this experience he moves beyond the superficiality of his previous advances out of the animal kingdom. He had been a master of the forms in his previous life, after all; now, as an ass, he is more of a "real" man than he had been when he looked the part. Lucius' engagement with the matron marks the beginning of his transition to a new life. The *voluptas* that he experiences here is a harbinger of the pure and lasting pleasure that he will derive from communion with the goddess. If Lucius makes any moral or epistemological progress in the course of his journey toward Isis, its pinnacle is reflected in this episode. As perverse as this claim may seem to some readers, I think that it will be vindicated in chapter 4 when we consider just what constitutes "sin" or moral transgression in this novel, and find that sexual activity per se does not figure in the definition.[17]

A final important point: the episode of the Corinthian lady marks the first time the novel presents a disruption of the usual order in a positive light. Here, an event that cannot be computed according to accepted formulas begins to acquire a sense and integrity of its own. Thus the reader is given a hint that the anarchy into which Lucius has

---

piece of obscene marginalia found in certain manuscripts and believed by some to be a fragment of Sisenna, by others to be a later forgery. In refuting the contention of Hermann (1951) that the addition is integral to the episode of the Corinthian matron and therefore authentic, Journoud argues that the pornographic tone of the fragment is incompatible with the Apuleian narrative.

17. Winkler comments on this episode: "The ass finds [the Corinthian matron] endearing, sentimental, and in no way like the usual picture of a lewd woman. . . . [T]here are Catonian contexts in real life in which one might feel called on to disapprove . . . the Corinthian lady's desire for the ass, but such a perspective does not enter the [novel]. . . . Neither Photis nor the Corinthian lady are condemned for their desire or their readiness to share it mutually. Quite the contrary, Lucius makes rather a point of the rich lady's sincerity and tenderness, her non-whorish kisses, her affectionate language of love. . . . Readers who recoil from this episode tend to interpret [it] in a way wholly unjustified by anything Lucius says. They supplement the sense of the text to fit an imposed moral pattern" (1985, 177, 193).

fallen will not be resolved by retrenchment into old categories and definitions; resolution can occur only when these are abandoned for a new order constructed on new premises and centering on the goddess. Conversion would not be a true "turning," after all, if it involved only a restoration of the status quo. This is what routinely happens to the lovers in Greek romance, who at the end of their trials are restored to their rightful place in society, or before that to the soul-searching Achilles of the *Iliad*, who engages in a mighty struggle with the values of his culture only to resubscribe to them in the end, albeit with a deeper understanding of their function and limitations.[18] In contrast, Lucius' movement is not circular but linear, and far from reaffirming the order upon which he had always relied, his conversion sweeps it away and substitutes a "higher" order that cannot take root until Lucius' old way of seeing the world has been radically shaken up and the clutter cleared away.

3

In these first two chapters, I have argued that the reality of the principal *actor* as it is represented in the *Metamorphoses* is one that is characterized by instability and indeterminacy on virtually every front and at virtually every level of his existence. In the course of this argument, I elaborated on various features of the narrative that contribute to the radically off-balance character of Lucius' world. But the *Metamorphoses* was not created *ex nihilo*. Apuleius shaped his product from a store of inherited material, and some of the devices that I invoke as helping to convey a decentered world view occur in these sources and models without necessarily carrying the same charge. The Latin novel shares, for example, certain motifs and episodes with the Lucianic *Onos*, which is all that remains of Apuleius' specific Greek source.[19] Some of these common features are generic and reflect the paradoxographic nature of the source or, more precisely, the probable character of the source as a satire of the quest strain of paradoxographic narrative. Magic and metamorphosis are in the air in the *Onos* too; there, as in the Apuleian

---

18. See (e.g.) Haight 1943, 186–201 for general points of contrast between the *Metamorphoses* and the Greek romances.

19. For an overview of the three ass narratives, two extant and one lost, and their relationship, see the introduction.

narrative, it is a desire to see or experience "something wondrous" [*ti paradoxon*] (4) that gets the protagonist into trouble and results in his transformation. Traces of other kinds of ontological boundary crossing are in evidence in the Greek epitome as well (sleeping and waking, living flesh and stone: 13 and 19), and the narrator "Lucius of Patrae" several times comments on his voicelessness as an ass (13, 15, 16, 38). Furthermore, Apuleius seems to have taken whole episodes from the lost *Metamorphoses,* insofar as we can judge from the epitome. The eunuch priests and the sadistic boy are there in the *Onos* (35–41, 29–33), as is the incremental education of Lucius the ass in the accomplishments of civilized life (47–50). As in Apuleius, the end point of this trajectory is a liaison with an aristocratic lady (50–52), although whether this can be read as the culmination of Lucius' training in "real" humanity as I argue it can in the Latin work is open to question.

Even where there is no evidence that the roots of the devices elaborated in the Apuleian text appeared in the lost Greek source, it is obvious that in some cases more general models for these devices existed in the form of conventions well established in the other genres feeding into the *Metamorphoses.* Apart from being a staple of paradoxography, magical and necromantic themes are not uncommon in the Greek novels, along with the *Scheintode* that they often bring in their wake. Furthermore, the prominence of disguise in these works represents the transgression of another set of boundaries—those of gender—which Apuleius also exploits. Finally, play with issues of fact and fiction, needless to say, does not appear for the first (or the last) time in the *Metamorphoses.* In this connection the Greek novels show a similar tendency to assimilate their action to high literary or dramatic forms. Theatrical imagery and metaphors from the stage appear in the novels regularly, as does the melodrama that represents the "theatricalization of experience" (to borrow a phrase from Susan Sontag) in its most extreme form. Obligatory *ecphraseis,* or extended descriptions of works of art, add to the conflation of art and life that marks this genre, as does the frequent self-consciousness of the narrative. Indeed it is safe to say that various forms of play with appearance and reality constitute a generic feature of the Greek novel.[20]

---

20. For examples of all these features in the Greek novels, see Reardon 1989 passim. For other novelistic themes and motifs in the *Metamorphoses,* see the introduction.

In view of the derivative character of much of the Apuleian vocabulary, what are my grounds for claiming that elements of this vocabulary
have a special signification in the Latin *Metamorphoses*? First, the substance of my discussion in these chapters has not been built primarily
on Apuleian instances of the clearly conventional motifs enumerated
above; where it does, as in the case of magic, I have made an effort to
show that there is something unique or refined about the Apuleian
treatment. Furthermore, the major sites in the Latin text for the exposition of what are, in my view, crucial and characteristically Apuleian
issues are entirely missing from the *Onos*. There is no question that we
are on infirm ground here, since it is at least theoretically possible that
all of these episodes appeared in some form in the lost Greek ass story.
But in the final analysis the fact remains that the *Onos* is all we have to
go on, and to attempt (as many have done) to reconstruct a work that
has disappeared virtually without a trace can only lead to entrapment
in the quagmire of "unanswerable questions" and to the "receding vis-
tas of fruitless speculation" wisely avoided by Winkler in favor of a
more manageable agenda.[21] But even where the Latin text and the *Onos*
do share features, there is usually evidence that Apuleius has put his
own stamp on the inherited material.

It is true that the Greek narrator recalls his asinine muteness, but that
muteness is not consistently aligned with the growing normlessness of

---

21. 1985, 256. To the perennial question, "How many books long was the
[Greek] *Metamorphoses*?" Winkler's simple, and realistic, response is: "No
telling." Ultimately, Mason takes a less dismissive but equally conservative
view: "For incidents where we do not have a Greek text, it is impossible for us
to tell if Apuleius is making major changes . . . or keeping closer to the original. . . . It seems to me, under the circumstances, methodologically unsound to
ascribe to the [Greek] *Metamorphoses* anything more than what we can prove
with reasonable certainty; this produces a *Metamorphoses* much closer in content and dimensions to the *Onos* than to the *Golden Ass*" (1978, 4). The major
Apuleian episodes entirely absent from the epitome are: Aristomene's tale and
the framing debate, Pythias and the fish (Book 1); the Actaeon *ecphrasis*,
Byrrhena's banquet, the tale of Thelyphron, Milo's tale of Diophanes (2); the
Risus episode (2–3); the bandits' tales (Thrasyleon) (4); the "Haemus" episode
(7); the story of Thrasyllus and Charite (8); the adultery tales (9); the two
wicked women, Lucius' reflections on corrupted judgment (10); as well as, in
the view of virtually all scholars, the story of Cupid and Psyche and the Isisbook.

Lucius' world as it is in the Latin narrative, where his frustration at being unable to speak is regularly correlated with his indignant observation of the transgression of social or moral codes. Lucius' horse and a real ass fail to make the newly transformed protagonist feel welcome in the stable in both versions, but only in the Apuleian narrative does this incident inspire a lament for lost *fides* (3.26), which in turn connects the episode thematically with the many others hinging on the disintegration of this and related mechanisms of social regulation. In general it would appear that the Latin author has taken great pains to shape inherited episodes in such a way as to put them in the service of his own overarching themes. So, for example, the demise of Charite is completely reworked from what the brief note in the *Onos* suggests (34) into a major episode involving deception, the breakdown of social codes, and a descent into bestiality—and all the epistemological questions that those raise (8.1–14). Likewise, the sequences involving the sadistic boy and the eunuch priests, although present in the *Onos,* are given an entirely new cast in the Latin narrative when Apuleius uses a linking network of diction and imagery to appropriate them as illustrations in the ongoing discussion of how deception, mendacity, and false accusation present serious challenges to epistemological certainty. Finally, the education of Lucius and his affair with the *matrona* are similarly recontextualized. In the *Onos* there is no highly elaborated negative corollary depicting the transformation of humans into wild beasts and their ruinous transgression of established boundaries. This corollary supports the reading of Lucius' experience, including its culmination with the lady, as progress, and suggests some vexed questions about established form-substance correspondences that are entirely alien to the spirit of the *Onos* and presumably to that of the common Greek source as well.

Thus it is not so much a matter of calculating which Greek episodes are or are not in the Latin *Metamorphoses* as it is of scrutinizing how Apuleius redirects and links the episodes that he includes, whatever their source.[22] It is reasonably clear, I think, that the tale of Aris-

---

22. Schlam puts it this way: "Apuleius' originality does not consist in creating stories. Rather he has shaped and ordered material drawn from various

tomenes, with its framing discussion of belief and disbelief, credulous and critical intellectual dispositions, and, in a word, the arbitrary and subjective character of knowledge, has all the trappings of a programmatic sequence. This reading is strengthened by the unmistakable reiteration of the same issues in several different settings as the narrative progresses (Milo's tale of Diophanes, Lucius and Charite read "Haemus"). These statements of the issue in turn branch out into its ever more complex elaboration in Books 7 through 10, where the crux of the action in virtually all the tales and episodes is some false inference, mistaken judgment, or misconstruction of evidence. There, the layers of lies are so thick and polysemic facts so ubiquitous that the question of what "reality" is begins to look intractable, especially when truth is evidently a function of perspective, and when preconceived ideas limit the range of possibilities that characters admit as they grapple with a problem. This metamorphosing restatement of the proposition that systems of knowledge are local, contingent, and precarious is one of the main features of the Latin text that both characterizes material apparently original with Apuleius and breathes new life into episodes inherited and rewritten by him.

Much of the aporetic spirit of the Latin narrative has been misunderstood or missed altogether, it seems to me, because the relentless scrutiny of Greek sources that has tended to occupy practitioners of Apuleian *Quellenforschung* has also led them virtually to ignore Apuleius' debt to his Latin literary antecedents, in which it is clear he was equally well versed.[23] The extent to which Apuleius drew on Ovid as a model for expanding the range and symbolic significance of transformation well beyond those found in any Greek source has never been fully appreciated. The extension of the motif from the physical realm into the social and psychological worlds, as a metaphor for the breakdown of social laws and institutions, as well as for radical psychologi-

---

sources to achieve literary effects and to express meanings of his own. . . . Whatever sources he drew upon, he stamps upon the material his own style and intent" (1968a, 8–9, 12). I note that when one engages with the questions of tradition and originality that have in many ways lain at the heart of the study of Latin literature, one inevitably begins speaking the language of authorial intent called into question by some strains of contemporary literary theory.

23. See Finkelpearl 1986.

cal change, is particularly Ovidian. Similarly, significant Virgilian patterns in the prose *Metamorphoses* have gone unnoticed. It is obvious
enough that Dido is the source for many aspects of the depiction of
Charite in her final days. But those making this observation have failed
to see that the Charite episode, like Book 4 of the *Aeneid*, is merely the
first in a series of related episodes and the point from which emanates
circle after circle of *furor*, driven initially by Eros but ultimately by a
wide range of misguided attitudes, until it brings about a complete
unraveling of the social fabric. This is a movement, I think, that
Apuleius identified in the second half of the epic poem and incorporated into his own narrative, along with much of Virgil's diction and
imagery. The Ovidian and Virgilian perspectives together are well
suited to adaptation by a philosophically inclined later provincial, concerned as they were with the fragility of structures in all spheres. Add
to this directed reappropriation of the Latin classics the apparently
quite unique features of the prose *Metamorphoses*—the disorienting
breakdown of predictable sequences of cause and effect and the related
representation of the *actor*'s alienated perspective, which makes the
Risus episode something more than the obligatory courtroom scene
common in the Greek novels; the religious resolution, which causes the
reader to reconsider the signification of any preceding conventional
material—and the result is a narrative very different in tone and preoccupation from those in the Greek ass tradition.[24]

No writer has ever had any choice but to use the tools already at his
or her disposal in the form of an established vocabulary of conventions,
no choice but to rewrite what has already been written. This was no less
true for the author of the Latin *Metamorphoses*. Still, by recontextualiz-
ing the conventional material at his disposal, he effected another kind
of transformation; this material was indeed rewritten, to be read in a
new way. Another way of stating how I think that the lens through
which the novel has generally been viewed could be profitably refo-
cused is this: traditionally, readings of the *Metamorphoses* have relied on

---

24. The complex character of Apuleius' originality, consisting as it does for
the most part in recasting existing material, is well stated in Winkler's comment
on the elements converging in the Apuleian denouement: "Apuleius has translated the parody [of the lost Greek version], with all its ridicule of the quester
intact, but has added at the end the very sort of epiphany and revelation that
the parodied works contained" (1985, 273).

situating it in its ancient generic context: Greek novel or romance, para-doxography, satire, and so on—a perfectly reasonable approach. But I am suggesting that we resituate it in an apparently very different generic context, one represented (as far as we can tell) solely by later exemplars, in order to gain a new appreciation of the place of the novel in literary and cultural history. When viewed from this perspective, the *Metamorphoses* becomes a prototype of another genre, a transitional or bridge text with one foot in one generic world and one in another; much of the conventional material in it then begins to look as if it is sus-pended in a kind of limbo between serving the old genre(s) and serving the new.[25] The possibility that the *Metamorphoses* is a forward-looking, polysemic prototype rather than merely a site for the mechanical repli-cation of literary conventions has gone as undeveloped as the indica-tions of how perceptively Apuleius read his Latin predecessors. In the next chapters I will put the novel through a new grid, looking at it from a new angle oriented toward narratives of conversion as a genre and toward what we know about how conversion works in "reality," the assumption being that there is some kind of commerce between the two.

---

25. I would argue that the *Metamorphoses* is prototypical of later literary developments, not only at the level of genre, but also at the level of more cir-cumscribed techniques of representation. I am thinking in particular of what Smith (1989) regarded, legitimately in my view, as Apuleius' proto-Kafkaesque representation of the subjective perspective of the victimized narrator (or *actor*). In connection with the Apuleian recontextualization of conventional motifs, Winkler remarks that the Latin author's repeated use of familiar "ploys" from popular fiction "raises no suspicion of larger hermeneutic design in the first-reader" (1985, 72 n. 24).

Part 2
The "Sick Soul"

The Role of Disintegration in Crisis and Conversion: Classic and Modern Views

1

In my introduction I alluded to the number of times modern critics, independent of each other and often in a connection incidental to their main purpose, have remarked upon the fragmented, shifting nature of the reality represented in the *Metamorphoses*. Apuleius, these critics maintain, has shaped his conventional material to situate Lucius in a world that is, in Tatum's words, "disorienting and disoriented" (1979, 72). This reading of Apuleian reality is also suggested by Winkler, who calls Lucius' wanderings "a brutal odyssey through alien terrain" and a quest with "ever-changing matrices" that is marked by an "undertow of irrationality amidst the semblance of order" (1985, 59, 95, 36). My first two chapters were devoted to fleshing out earlier scattered comments to this effect. I argued there that Lucius' environment in both its physical and social aspects suffers a gradual and systematic loss of virtually all the signposts and points of reference whose function had been to orient him in experience and to form a foundation for the construction of a system of knowledge. Lucius finds himself epistemologically adrift, with his moorings to familiar structures of meaning and ways of ordering reality irremediably cut.

The claim that an ancient text has represented reality in a way that is usually identified exclusively with the modern and the postmodern worlds will give pause to some. But part of my point is that it may be time to rethink some of the restrictions placed on the experience of the ancients, and literary representations of it, by modern prejudice. Indeed the focus of Winkler's study is just this aporetic quality in the *Metamorphoses*, although he discusses it primarily in connection with the author's failure to authorize a meaning for the work as a whole, rather than with the reality that the novel represents and the problems of meaning encountered by the experiencing Lucius within that reality.

The important thing for the current argument about precisely these features of the text is that, in spite of their postmodern ring, they can readily serve as the basis of a new religious reading of the novel. This is because Books 1 through 10 of the work (excluding the tale of Cupid and Psyche) present us with a picture of reality strikingly evocative of the ways in which reality is often perceived during the crisis phase of conversion experience as it is represented in other narratives and described in theory.[1] In the course of the following discussion, it will become clear that an approach to the *Metamorphoses* such as that of Winkler, based on the methods of modern literary theory, and an approach utilizing work in the social psychology of religious conversion are mutually informing in unexpected ways because, in spite of their apparent lack of relation, both are ultimately grounded in questions of epistemology and cognition.

Briefly, the type of conversion experience with which we will be concerned begins with some kind of challenge to the values held, in most cases unthinkingly, by the preconvert. This challenge often takes the form of a creeping disillusionment with the conventional system of goals and rewards that has constituted the core of the preconvert's habituated structure of meaning. For a variety of possible reasons, these values can begin to seem arbitrary and therefore intrinsically meaningless after years of their seeming self-evidently worth achieving. Obviously, there are some assumptions lurking in the association of contingency and ephemerality with meaninglessness in this model of religious experience. In a postmodern world view, after all, the contingency of all meaning is cause for rejoicing rather than despair. But it is safe to say that through a substantial portion of human history people have felt the need to ground their values in a metaphysical source. Any suggestion that no such authority stands behind meaning

---

1. I will discuss the place of the tale of Cupid and Psyche in my reading in chapter 5. It should be stressed here that my argument involves applying to the novel only one of many possible models of conversion. These can also include, for example, forced conversion (such as the "brainwashing" of individuals and the forced conversion of whole cultures) and the sort of conscious and deliberate change of religious allegiance that comes at the end of a period of study and is motivated by shifts in social affiliation, such as interfaith marriage. My purpose is not to generalize or universalize all conversion experience but rather to isolate one strain or pattern of it and its corollaries in narrative and then to use that pattern as a framework for reading the *Metamorphoses*. It will become clear that even this one pattern is open to variations and complications.

has been met with dismay and resistance. The impetus behind the sudden change in outlook critical to conversion is often existential, that is, the change is the result of the preconvert's reevaluation of his or her activities in the context of a heightened awareness of mortality. The collapse of the epistemic and moral foundations upon which the preconvert's world view has been based can lead to a fundamental shift in individual perspective and a defamiliarization or estrangement of the entire face of the subject's world. Without the glue of collectively accepted valorizations to hold the disparate parts of the preconvert's world in a unified and coherent whole, it becomes a sort of vacuum devoid of meaning and structure. Conversion to a religious system as a resolution to this type of crisis is essentially a measure to restore structures of meaning to the individual's world, where old ones have failed. Thus crisis and conversion involves a comprehensive and radical shift from one paradigm of interpreting and constructing reality to another. In spite of its having secondary moral components, this model of conversion is primarily a cognitive one. The preconvert's problem is experienced as a problem of knowledge, of having basic misconceptions about how reality "really" works and about how phenomena are to be ordered and valorized.

There is considerable variation within the parameters of this model, but this is its essential outline. In this chapter, I will discuss classic and modern analyses of conversion that imply or explicitly delineate this particular pattern, and I will provide a running commentary on the relevance of this material to my reading of the conversion experience of Lucius as it is represented in the *Metamorphoses*. In chapters 4 and 5 I will examine how this pattern asserts itself in autobiographical, poetic, and fictional narratives of crisis and conversion, again with the ultimate aim of showing how the same patterns appear in the *Metamorphoses*. My primary purpose is to produce a new reading of the *Metamorphoses* as a narrative of religious experience by situating it in a larger system of theoretical studies and narratives of conversion. Secondarily, my discussion will implicitly interrogate commonly held views of pagan conversion in the Greco-Roman world by stressing the recurrent claim in the secondary literature on conversion that there are generic features in the process, regardless of the particular religious or ideological system involved. These features allow us to read the features and patterns of later accounts back into a narrative of pagan conversion and thus perhaps into the experience itself. The assumption that pagan conversion was a qualitatively different phenomenon from later and, in particular, Christian conversion—an assumption that one often encounters in studies of pagan religious experience—is thus called into question.

William James is the most prominent of the early pioneers in the field of religious psychology, which from the beginning was an American movement.[2] His classic work *The Varieties of Religious Experience* was first published in 1902. It is obvious that in the ninety-two years intervening between then and now, methodologies in the academic study of religious psychology will have changed enormously. Yet for my purposes the work of William James is hardly obsolete; on the contrary, I think that it warrants a central place in my discussion, for two reasons. First, I have attempted to make clear from the beginning that my goal is not to determine how faithfully the representation of Lucius' conversion reflects the workings of conversion in reality but rather to situate the *Metamorphoses* within a circular system of discourse about conversion, a system whose major components include the narratives

---

2. The study of the psychology of religion, which has always given a central place to the phenomenon of conversion, falls into roughly three periods: the early or classic period from the 1890s to around 1930; a lull when the subject fell out of favor from the 1940s through the 1960s; and a revival and reorientation of the field beginning in the 1970s and resulting in no small part from the burgeoning of religious cults among young people in the United States during that period. In its later incarnation the psychology of religion has become less purely psychological and more sociological and social psychological in orientation, with studies concentrating on conversion as a matter of the individual's constructing a new world of meaning to accommodate a change in group allegiance and identification. This model has superseded the paradigm of solitary internal struggle favored by the early researchers. Methodology has also undergone radical changes, toward the sort of quantification in the service of scientific objectivity (or at least the appearance of it) that characterizes the social sciences as a whole, although there is still a great range in the methodological orientation and testability of studies and their results. For surveys of the history of the field and critical commentary on its various phases, see Spilka, Hood, and Gorsuch 1985, especially chapter 9 on conversion; Wulff 1991; Beit-Hallahmi 1974 on the early decades of the movement; and Flakoll 1976 on methodology. Wulff's is an especially rich and comprehensive survey that incorporates work from many related areas. See also Snow and Machalek 1984 for trends in the sociological study of conversion, and Rambo 1982 for a useful annotated bibliography of research on conversion. A very brief and selective summary can be found in Hawkins 1985, 20 n. 18; and a somewhat fuller one in the appendix (285–300) of Segal 1990.

of the social sciences as well as literary narratives of conversion. From this perspective, James' work remains an extremely prominent and formative link in the system, not to be taken as necessarily having any less truth-value than, for example, the hyperquantifying sociological studies of the 1970s. Second, as we will see, the model of conversion worked out by James and those induced much more recently by sociologists and social psychologists share a significant structural community in spite of the differences in rhetoric and other trappings between the generations.

James' famous discussion of conversion appears in a central section of *The Varieties of Religious Experience* and is organized under the rubrics "The Sick Soul," "The Divided Self, and the Process of Its Unification," and "Conversion." These chapter titles encapsulate a pattern that he discerned in the records of many and disparate converts. It is a pattern involving a progression from disillusionment with conventional systems of goals and rewards and the larger consequences of that disillusionment to a resolution of the crisis through the acquisition of a religious world view. In this and the next two chapters I will argue that the *Metamorphoses* is a fictional representation of this movement. But in order to understand the "twice-born," as James calls those who experience such a dramatic shift in world view, it is important to note that he sets his entire discussion of conversion against what he calls "the religion of healthy-mindedness." The healthy-minded, according to James' taxonomy of human temperament, are those in whom "the tendency to see things optimistically is like a water of crystallization in which the individual's character is set" (1958, 112). "The sanguine and healthy-minded," he continues, "live habitually on the sunny side of their misery line"; they are people "who seem to have started in life with a bottle or two of champagne to their credit" (117). Their temperamental indisposition toward existential *angst* rings in their rallying cry, " 'Hurrah for the Universe! God's in his Heaven, all's right with the world' " (118).

In contrast with the healthy-minded, or the "once-born," as James also calls them, there are those who naturally have a "more morbid way of looking at the situation," who "seem to have been born close to the pain-threshold, which the slightest irritants fatally send them over" (114, 117). These are the "twice-born," whose path to the divine is circuitous and tortured. Their problems begin with a pessimistic disposition that leads them to be preoccupied with the question, "How *can* things so insecure as the successful experiences of this world afford a stable anchorage?" This question reverberates through their consciousness and leaves them "with an irremediable sense of precariousness." For them life is a "bell with a crack; it draws its breath on sufferance and by an accident" (118). These and related sentiments characterize the period of "soul-sickness" or "melancholy," which builds to a crisis and is dissipated only through some kind of death and rebirth, through conversion and a radical reorientation of the psyche. James describes the gulf between the world views of the "healthy-minded" and the melancholy in the following way:

> [W]e can see how great an antagonism may naturally arise between the healthy-minded way of viewing life and the way that takes all this experience of evil as something essential. To this latter way, the morbid-minded way, as we might call it, healthy-mindedness pure and simple seems unspeakably blind and shallow. To the healthy-minded way, on the other hand, the way of the sick soul seems unmanly and diseased. With their grubbing in rat-holes instead of living in the light; with their manufacture of fears, and preoccupation with every unwholesome kind of misery, there is something almost obscene about these children of wrath and cravers of a second birth. (137)

It is these temperamentally predetermined (so James) "cravers of a second birth" who are the focus of James' chapters on religious conversion. In connection with them he declares, "Here is the real core of the religious problem: Help! Help!" (137). With this assertion James anticipates in his own overwrought Victorian way the categorical statement of two very recent students of the social psychology of religion: "Religious experience is rooted in dissatisfaction at an existential level" (Batson and Ventis 1982, 82). These excerpts also show clearly that although James the empiricist was in general very much in sympathy with the religious experience of others, his discussion of conversion has a strong pathologizing tendency to treat what we might call existential crisis as a form of the melancholy so prevalent in nineteenth-century medical thought.

James' predilection for diagnosing the crisis that can lead to religious conversion in psychopathological (with a trace of moral) terms is even more pronounced in chapter 8, entitled "The Divided Self, and the

Process of Its Unification." Here he elaborates further on the difference between the once-born and the twice-born:

> The psychological basis of the twice-born character seems to be a certain discordancy or heterogeneity in the native temperament of the subject. . . . Some persons are born with an inner constitution which is harmonious and well balanced from the outset. Their impulses are consistent with one another, their will follows without trouble the guidance of their intellect, their passions are not excessive, and their lives are little haunted by regrets. Others are oppositely constituted; and are so in degrees which may vary from something so slight as to result in a merely odd or whimsical inconsistency, to a discordancy of which the consequences may be inconvenient in the extreme. . . . [Their] existence is little more than a series of zigzags, as now one tendency and now another gets the upper hand. Their spirit wars with their flesh, they wish for incompatibles, wayward impulses interrupt their most deliberate plans. (141–42)

An "existence [that] is little more than a series of zigzags, as now one tendency and now another gets the upper hand," seems to be a fair description of Lucius' approach to life, and one we will want to keep in mind when we come in the next chapter to how the novel represents *his* precipitating crisis or "soul-sickness." But my main concern here is with James' tendency to pathologize the conversion experience. This tendency, it is important to note for our purposes, is not consistently in evidence in his analysis. For in spite of strong statements of it such as the one above, when James comes to discussing one of his central case histories, that of Tolstoy, the crisis begins to sound like an honest philosophical struggle over values, a struggle involving a search for psychic integrity as much as confused psychic impulses:

> [Tolstoy's melancholy] was logically called for by the clash between his inner character and his outer activities and aims. Although a literary artist, Tolstoy was one of those primitive oaks of men to whom the superfluities and insincerities, the cupidities, complications, and cruelties of our polite civilization are profoundly unsatisfying, and for whom the eternal veracities lie with more natural and animal things. His crisis was the getting of his

soul in order, the discovery of its genuine habitat and vocation, the escape from falsehoods into what for him were ways of truth. It was a case of heterogeneous personality tardily and slowly finding its unity and level. (154)

This passage is noteworthy incidentally for the way it demonstrates James' unquestioned acceptance of the idea that there are "eternal veracities" as well as a "true" self lying under cultural trivia. The first of these propositions at least had a long history before the second century A.D. and would have been, I think, as unremarkable to Apuleius as it was to James.

The philosophical note struck in the previous passage is sounded in another summary of the differences between the once-born and the twice-born. These two types, James says, represent

two different conceptions of the universe of our experience. In the religion of the once-born the world is a sort of rectilinear or one-storied affair, whose accounts are kept in one denomination, whose parts have just the values which naturally they appear to have. . . . In the religion of the twice-born, on the other hand, the world is a double-storied mystery. . . . Natural good is not simply insufficient in amount and transient, there lurks a falsity in its very being. Cancelled as it all is by death, . . . it . . . can never be the thing intended for our lasting worship. It keeps us from our real good, rather; and renunciation and despair of it are our first step in the direction of truth. There are two lives, the natural and the spiritual, and we must lose the one before we can participate in the other. (140)

Here James correlates the psychology and the world view of the twice-born with a kind of generic philosophical dualism without addressing the question of whether this view of reality is somehow spontaneously generated in certain kinds of naturally occurring temperaments, or whether it is suggested by preexisting and socially constructed frameworks that then inform and constitute the temperament, perception, and cognitive structure of the subject. The general tendency and the context of James' discussion make it seem as if he is promoting the former view, but there are times when it is clear that he understands the interdependency of established, internalized discursive frameworks and individuals' accounts of their experience as well as any modern social psychologist or cultural theorist. The dualistic penchants of James' twice-born souls reflect an attitude and an operation of cultural discourse that would have been completely at home in the religious and philosophical world of the second century. We will see in the next chapter how a dualistic idea of the "inversion of natural appearances" (James 1958, 141) and of the "falseness" of this world and the reality of one unseen is a key to understanding the religious content of the novel and, more specifically, the nature of the religious experience represented in it. For now it is enough to note that in spite of prominent pathologizing tendencies in James' analysis, there is room in it also for interpreting preconversion crisis as a longing and a quest for stable values. This is the model that will be most relevant to our reading.

After arguing for the division of human temperaments into the "healthy-minded" and the "twice-born," James goes on to propose that the twice-born themselves fall into two categories according to the nature of their crisis. He fails to assign these categories convenient labels, but the features of each are clear from his discussion and the documents that he offers in support of it. Invoking Tolstoy again as an exemplum, James describes the first type of crisis as one in which a growing sense of the "vanity of mortal things" and nagging questions about the "purpose and meaning of life in general" in view of this new sense are what trouble those suffering from it. The source of their melancholy is external to themselves, and their "preoccupations [are] largely objective"; it is "the lack of rational meaning of the universe . . . [that] is the burden that weighs upon" them (133, 136, 167, and n. 9). In "intellectual and general metaphysical" cases such as this, preconverts are moved to engage actively in a search for alternatives to the structure of meaning that has failed them. James dramatizes their response to that failure:

> The strangeness is wrong. The unreality cannot be. A mystery is concealed, and a metaphysical solution must exist. If the natural world is so double-faced and unhomelike, what world, what thing is real? An urgent wondering and questioning is set up, a poring theoretic activity, and in the desperate effort to get into right relations with the matter, the sufferer is often led to what becomes for him a satisfying religious resolution. (130)

Again I note what James does not (and this applies to my entire discussion of James): that these ruminations could not take the shape they do (or are imagined as taking) if a cultural discourse of dualism did not already structure the subject's consciousness. James opposes this type of crisis and conversion to another model, of which he offers John Bunyan as the chief exemplar. In contrast to Tolstoy's, "Bunyan's troubles," writes James, "were over the condition of his own personal self." Bunyan's crisis (which he recounted in his autobiography *Grace Abounding to the Chief of Sinners*) was marked by contempt for himself and an obsession with his own supposed wickedness and unworthiness, along with an oppressive sense of inherited personal sin that he himself was helpless to remedy in the absence of God's grace (James 1958, 133–35). James, as usual, does not elaborate on this point, but Bunyan's case is clearly one in which the shape of the account and probably of the experience itself was determined by the available cultural framework, namely Puritan theology. The crisis that Bunyan describes so vividly is the only kind a Puritan was allowed to have.

In her recent study of narratives of conversion, Anne Hawkins offers a typology of conversion experience and narrative that echoes the earlier work of James. Two of her paradigms are of immediate concern to us: the "heroic paradigm" of intellectual or spiritual quest and the "conflictive paradigm," which is characterized by "psychomachia" or inner psychic turmoil (1985: 16–17, passim). These correspond exactly to James' "Tolstoy" and "Bunyan" models, and in fact Hawkins chooses Bunyan to exemplify the conflictive paradigm, as did James; her exemplary searcher is, however, Augustine. In summarizing the differences between the two paradigms, Hawkins writes:

> The differences . . . point toward two alternative modes whereby the soul comes to God—modes that I will refer to as *eros* and *logos*. The spiritual dynamic of *eros* is the yearning for God and the archetype of pilgrimage that embodies that yearning; that of *logos* is guilt before God and the archetype of *psychomachia*, or conflict, embodying the inner tension between good and evil impulses which produces those feelings of guilt. . . . The difference between the Augustinian *eros* and the Bunyanesque *logos* is that of the incomplete self, longing for completion in the divine embrace, and the wrong self, whose sinfulness requires that it be punished and disciplined. . . . In a religiosity governed by *eros*, the experi-

ential reality will be a deep and unappeasable yearning, with satisfaction as the ultimate goal. Where *logos* is dominant, the experience will center on feelings of guilt about one's own inadequacies . . . and perfection will be the ultimate good. (75–78; see also
86–89)

The Bunyan model, it seems to me, is not in any way relevant to the religious content of the *Metamorphoses* or indeed to pagan religious experience in general. This should be evident from the theologically informed
shape of the crisis. Bunyan's account is *too* culture-specific for our purposes; any typicality in it is overwhelmed by fire and brimstone.

Yet I dwell on it at some length precisely because of its irrelevance.
Apuleian critics, whether they were thinking specifically of Bunyan or
not, have consistently made the mistake of attempting to see the religious patterns of the novel in terms of a Protestant scheme of personal
sin and redemption. They view Lucius' transformation as a punishment for his alleged moral sins (carnal lust and striving after forbidden
knowledge) and suggest that Isis serves as an agent of moral purifica-
tion rather than as a metaphysical anchor of meaning.[3] But I argued in
my reading of the text itself in chapters 1 and 2 that Lucius' problems,
like Tolstoy's, are to be understood as epistemological rather than
moral, and I believe that the plausibility of this claim will be borne out
as we examine more parallels in this and the next chapter. Certainly a
"quest" paradigm of some sort would be more in keeping with the traditions of pagan philosophical and religious transformation of which
Augustine is a later Christian representative. In the next chapter I will
discuss how applying a paradigm of quest to the novel requires that we
reformulate the definition of "sin" and morality as it is inscribed in the
Metamorphoses. But now that we have identified the Jamesian model

---

3. So, e.g., Festugière (1954, 68–84), in his chapter "Lucius and Isis,"
assumes from the concatenation of the novel's events that Lucius is being punished for his carnal desire. He then seems puzzled that Apuleius would suggest
this connection when such a stern view of desire is more Christian than pagan.
Yet Festugière is unable to take the next step of reexamining his assumption
that "lust" is Lucius' fundamental problem. Likewise, Sandy 1978 searches in
vain for signs that the *Metamorphoses* is the "History of a Wicked Life" (after
Defoe) that he thinks is required to make it a plausible conversion account. For
more examples of anachronistic religious readings of the novel, see the introduction. For Isis as a metaphysical and epistemological anchor, see chapter 6,
section 3.

that *is* relevant to our purpose—the "Tolstoy" model—let us examine it in more detail.

I have already suggested that, according to James, the basic impulse behind this type of conversion experience is the conviction, suddenly or gradually formulated, that all mortal endeavor is futile and insignificant when measured against the infinite span of cosmic space and time. Once this suspicion creeps in, conventional pursuits lose their old ability to provide a sense of meaning and satisfaction. This is how James reconstructs the motivating obsession of the "melancholy" preconvert:

> All natural goods perish. Riches take wings; fame is a breath; love is a cheat; youth and health and pleasure vanish. Can things whose end is always dust and disappointment be the real goods which our souls require? Back of everything is the great spectre of universal death, the all-encompassing blackness. (1958, 120)

To those whose world view has taken this turn, "all natural happiness . . . seems infected with a contradiction. The breath of the sepulchre surrounds it" (121). Taking his cue from earlier psychology, James adopts the term *anhedonia* to designate the most extreme forms of this sort of existential paralysis. The anhedonic subject becomes unable to derive any pleasure whatever from the whole range of activities that had formerly kept him or her going.[4] As traumatic as this development may be, it provides, according to James, the spark of the religious impulse. It moves those experiencing it to begin asking whether we do not "need a life not correlated with death, a health not liable to illness, a kind of good that will not perish, a good in fact that flies beyond the Goods of nature" and helps us make sense of death, the "worm at the core of all

---

4. James' pathologizing tendency is once again clear here. *Anhedonia* is the "pathological depression" or "melancholy" of the "neurotic constitution" (124–25). "Moreover," he continues, "it is only a relatively small proportion of cases that connect themselves with the religious sphere of experience at all" (127). Conversion is not by any means the only possible result of the failure to engage with conventional structures of meaning that constitutes *anhedonia*, and in fact James' next piece of documentary evidence in this section is a "letter from a patient in a French asylum" (127). In suggesting a potential correlation between religious experience and mental illness, James anticipates the orientation of many modern studies of conversion.

our usual springs of delight" (121). Once again we are reminded of a more recent formulation of the religious impulse: "Religious experience is rooted in dissatisfaction at an existential level." For Lucius, the "good that will not perish" is Isis, who serves as an antidote to the "absence of all permanent meaning" (122) in the "natural" world.

What causes those who had been more or less content with their lives to develop a view that from the "healthy-minded" perspective is so morbid and perverse? This is a complicated question to which James offers the rather simple answer of temperament. Circumstance would also seem to play a part. A recurring motif in accounts of conversion is the unexpected advent of the crisis in the prime of the subject's life and at the height of his or her success in the conventional world. This was true of Augustine, as we will see in the next chapter; and it was true of James' chief exemplar, Tolstoy. James quotes the passage in Tolstoy's *Confession* where the Russian describes with some sense of paradox the enviable state of life he had achieved when things started falling apart for him:

"All this [i.e., his existential crisis] took place at a time when so far as all my outer circumstances went, I ought to have been completely happy. I had a good wife who loved me and whom I loved; good children and a large property which was increasing with no pains taken on my part. I was more respected by my kinsfolk and acquaintances than I had ever been; I was loaded with praise by strangers; and without exaggeration I could believe my name already famous. Moreover I was neither insane nor ill. On the contrary, I possessed a physical and mental strength which I have rarely met in persons of my age [he was 51]. I could mow as well as the peasants, I could work with my brain eight hours uninterruptedly and feel no bad effects." (James 1958, 131)[5]

Yet it was precisely the conventionality of his successes that made them seem so tenuous and transparent. Tolstoy lost faith in this false religion, in the values embodied by the "life of the upper, intellectual, artistic

---

5. James uses his own translation of a French edition of *Confession*. This passage appears on p. 29 of Patterson's translation (hereafter, Tolstoy 1983). The classic biographies of Tolstoy are Maude 1987 (first published 1929); and Troyat 1965. See also more recently Wilson 1988.

classes, . . . the cerebral life, the life of conventionality, artificiality, and personal ambition" (James 1958, 153). As he underwent his "profound transformation," Tolstoy's formerly unexamined way of life seemed to him more and more to have "lost all meaning." It was not real life but a "semblance of life," a parodic system of delusions (Tolstoy 1983, 68, 76).[6]

In choosing as his main spokesman of conversion someone who suffered from what we might now call midlife crisis, James was at variance with a distinct tendency in other early works on the psychology of religion to link conversion with *adolescent* groping at world construction (see especially Hall 1904). Whether or not we are to imagine Lucius as having reached midlife according to the standards of ancient life expectancy, his noble birth and exclusive education, and the general prosperity and privileged status he seems to enjoy at the time of his crisis, all correlate with the preconversion conditions of Tolstoy and Augustine. Mason (1983) has shown that Apuleius has gone to some length to give his hero a distinguished pedigree through references to the fame and antiquity of Lucius' family, the attainment of its members to high office, and their connections to several Greek cities. But, as Mason notes, "Lucius' distinction is of an entirely conventional kind: birth, position, homeland. . . . The lesson that Lucius appears to learn [is] to distinguish conventional social distinction from the true glory he obtains through Isis and Osiris" (141, 143). As the priest of Isis says to Lucius in Book 11 (15), "neither your noble birth nor your social status nor your learning in which you pride yourself did you any good in your hour of need" [*nec tibi natales ac ne dignitas quidem, vel ipsa, qua flores, usquam doctrina profuit*]. This reference to the ultimate impotence of *doctrina* finds a parallel in Tolstoy: disillusioned in his intellectual search for a way out of the morass, he comes to the conclusion that "'all

---

6. Tolstoy's own crisis is anticipated in remarkable ways in his earlier fiction. In *War and Peace* (1869), the frigid artifice of high society in St. Petersburg is a central theme, and the exposure of it finds Tolstoy in fine satirical form. Social artifice and its hollow pretensions are consistently portrayed as a kind of theatrical performance: see, for example, Book 8, chapter 9 in toto, the "natural" woman Natasha's loss of innocence at the opera; and the descriptions of the deluded Napoleon as an actor trying to pull off a *coup de théâtre* (973–76, passim, both in Tolstoy 1966). The reader is reminded of the frequent appearance of theatrical images in the *Metamorphoses* (see chap. 1, sec. 1).

those who before me had sought for an answer in the sciences have also found nothing'" (James 1958, 132).

James is very clear about why he chooses Tolstoy's as an exemplary conversion: it illustrates in an almost textbook way the sequence that James has identified as characterizing the type of crisis and conversion structured around metaphysical quest. As he explains, "it is a well-marked case of *anhedonia*, of passive loss of appetite for life's values; and second, it shows how the altered and estranged aspect which the world assumed in consequence of this stimulated Tolstoy's intellect to a gnawing, carking questioning and effort for philosophic relief" (128). We need to look at each phase of this process in some detail, since each phase has an expression, mutatis mutandis, in Apuleius' representation of Lucius' experience in the *Metamorphoses*. James describes the first intimations of Tolstoy's crisis in this way:

> At about the age of fifty, Tolstoy relates that he began to have moments of perplexity, of what he calls arrest, as if he knew not how to live, or what to do. It is obvious that these were moments in which the excitement and interest which our functions naturally bring had ceased. Life had been enchanting, it was now flat sober, more than sober, dead. Things were meaningless whose meaning had always been self-evident. The questions "why?" and "what next?" began to beset him more and more frequently. (1958, 130)

Quoting extensively from his translation, James then allows Tolstoy to speak for himself: "'I felt that something had broken within me on which my life had always rested, that I had nothing left to hold on to. . . . I could give no reasonable meaning to any actions of my life. . . . Why should I live? Why should I do anything? Is there in life any purpose which the inevitable death which awaits me does not undo and destroy?'" (130–31). In summary, James asks the reader to note the fundamental feature of the early stages of Tolstoy's crisis: his "absolute disenchantment with ordinary life, and the fact that the whole range of habitual values may, to a man as powerful and full of faculty as he was, come to appear so ghastly a mockery" (133). Tolstoy's stark new view of the value of conventional pursuits grew out of his situating them for the first time in a cosmic context. "Is there anything real and imperishable that will come of my illusory and perishable life?" he asks himself.

"What kind of meaning can my finite existence have in this infinite universe? . . . What is the meaning of my life beyond space, time, and causation?" (Tolstoy 1983, 58).[7]

When we scrutinize Tolstoy's newfound aporetic world view more closely, we can see that a paradox lies at its very heart. It is built on the "inversion of natural appearances" that James proposed as the defining feature of the way reality is processed by the twice-born. Fame, money, family, and indeed all the things worth striving for, according to conventional systems of value, are now seen for what they "really" are, mere diversions which keep those who allow themselves to be deluded by them from the real business of life. Tolstoy writes ruefully and at some length about how he came to see the fame and money accruing from his literary endeavors as surrogate gods at the center of the false religion of the intelligentsia and the literati, a religion that Tolstoy himself had served as high priest (Tolstoy 1983, 17–22). Society was a perverse and self-perpetuating system that doled out praise, social status, and monetary rewards for what were really immoral or, at best, amoral activities. The spectacle of what he took to be the inversion of true value struck Tolstoy as a kind of "madness." We will recall this designation when we come to Augustine's (and Lucius') assessment of the conventional world in chapter 4. Tolstoy recalls how even after he began to be disillusioned with the literary life, his disaffection was mitigated by his knowledge that there was still an untapped source of potential satisfaction that "held the promise of salvation: family life." And indeed when he settled into a happy family life it did have the effect of successfully "diverting" him for a while from any "search for the overall meaning of life" (25). But in time the "true" nature of family life as exactly that—a diversion—began to assert itself as well.

---

7. Compare the reflections of Tolstoy's tortured fictional counterpart Pierre Bezukhov in *War and Peace*, who undergoes several crises and conversions in the course of the novel: "It was as if the thread of the chief screw which held his life together were stripped, so that the screw could not get in or out, but went on turning uselessly in the same place. . . . 'What is bad? What is good? What should one love and what hate? What does one live for? And what am I? And what is life, and what is death? What power governs all? . . . Can anything in the world make . . . me less a prey to evil and death?—death which ends all and must come today or tomorrow—at any rate, in an instant as compared with eternity.' And again he twisted the screw with the stripped thread, and again it turned uselessly in the same place" (Tolstoy 1966, 377–78).

At the height of his anhedonia, Tolstoy lost the ability even to think about taking care of any business relating to his work, his family, or his property without being brought up short by the nagging question "So what? What difference does it make?" He knew that even if he fulfilled the desires that came to him out of habit, it would bring him no real sense of satisfaction (Tolstoy 1983, 27–28). He adopts a harrowing image to convey his sense of the precariousness of the human condition or, more precisely, of the condition of humans without God. We are stuck in a well, afraid to emerge for fear of a wild beast above ground, unable to jump to the bottom because of a hungry dragon waiting there. We cling to a branch growing out of the well's crevices, watching that meager support also vanish as it is gnawed away by mice, and knowing that it is inevitable that the branch will break and we will fall into the jaws of the dragon. Yet when some drops of honey on the branch's leaves catch our attention, we stretch out our tongues and try to lick what succor—fame, money, family—we can. "I try to suck the honey that once consoled me," writes Tolstoy, "but the honey is no longer sweet. . . . The two drops of honey which more than anything else had diverted my eyes from the cruel truth were my love for my family and my writing, which I referred to as art; yet this honey had lost its sweetness for me" (30–32). We will see in the next chapter how this growing conviction that "true" values have been inverted in the conventional world—that true value has been falsely assigned to the phenomena of the sensible world when it actually lies in something transcendent—is a central feature in the conversion processes of Augustine and his fictional counterpart Lucius.[8]

According to James' model, it is this urgent sense of aporia about the ultimate meaning of one's life that motivates the sort of quest typical of experiences of conversion such as Tolstoy's. Being of an intellectual bent, Tolstoy's instinct is to do some research:

> I searched for an answer to my questions in every area of knowl-
> edge acquired by man. For a long time I carried on my painstak-

---

8. Tolstoy generalizes by quoting from a very eclectic range of sages who have understood the problem, from Solomon to Schopenhauer (see Tolstoy 1983, 43–46). His breadth of reference corresponds to my own resistance to the idea that existential angst, or some variation of it, is restricted to the modern period and to be associated only with modern intellectual currents. See Barrett 1962.

ing search; I did not search casually, out of mere curiosity, but painfully, persistently, day and night, like a dying man seeking salvation. I found nothing. (Tolstoy 1983, 33)

One of the striking things about this passage in connection with Lucius is Tolstoy's insistence that "mere curiosity" played no part in driving his own search; it was instead earnest, deliberate, and systematic. In contrast it often seems as if idle *curiositas* is the impulse behind virtually everything that Lucius does. But unlike Tolstoy's, Lucius' dissatisfaction can be understood as registering at an unconscious level; in the next chapter I will argue that his curiosity and, indeed, most aspects of his behavior can be read as manifestations of a sublimated discontent and an unconsciously formulated, undirected search for satisfaction.

Tolstoy concludes his critique of conventional values by providing a kind of taxonomy of the different ways in which people grapple with the problem of meaning. Among these ways are two that offer some useful comparative material. The first Tolstoy calls the way of ignorance. Those who follow this path are completely oblivious to their peril. They "see neither the dragon that awaits them nor the mice gnawing away at the branch they cling to; they simply lick the drops of honey." The second is the way of epicureanism. Epicureans are "fully aware of the hopelessness of life," but they choose to divert their attention from it as well as they can by pursuing all the sources of fleeting pleasure available to them (Tolstoy 1983, 49–51). In either case the result is a kind of "intoxication" or anesthetized state; both groups pass their lives in idleness and empty amusement, with their despair lurking just under the surface, albeit at different levels of consciousness.[9] As

---

9. Cf. Pierre: "It was too dreadful to be under the burden of these insoluble problems, so he abandoned himself to any kind of distraction in order to forget them. . . . Sometimes he remembered how he had heard that soldiers in war when entrenched under the enemy's fire . . . try hard to find some occupation the more easily to bear the danger. To Pierre all men seemed like those soldiers, seeking refuge from life: some in ambition, some in cards, some in framing laws, some in women, some in toys, some in horses, some in politics, some in sport, some in wine, and some in governmental affairs. 'Nothing is trivial, and nothing is important, it's all the same—only to save oneself from it as best one can,' thought Pierre. 'Only not to see *it*, that dreadful *it*'" (Tolstoy 1966, 594–95).

James comments, the second tactic "is only a more deliberate sort of stupefaction than the first" (132). Lucius, as we will see, is an expert at diverting and anesthetizing himself. He approaches life relying on a combination of the two strategies identified by Tolstoy, and the frequency with which he finds himself "stupefied" or "dumbstruck" by the diversions he stumbles upon finds a felicitous, if accidental, reflection in James' choice of words here.[10]

In retrospect, Tolstoy realizes, or the retrospective interpretation that he imposes on his experience is, that his restless dissatisfaction was rooted in a longing for God (the proverbial *desiderium dei*), which was misdirected and allowed to light instead on the false gods of conventional systems of value. James quotes Tolstoy's description of this vague but powerful desire:

"During the whole course of [my crisis] . . . alongside of all those movements of my ideas and observations, my heart kept languishing with another pining emotion. I can call this by no other name than that of a thirst for God. This craving for God had nothing to do with the movement of my ideas—in fact, it was the direct contrary of that movement—but it came from my heart. It was like a feeling of dread that made me seem like an orphan and isolated in the midst of all these things that were so foreign." (James 1958, 132)

Of interest here is the notion that the *desiderium dei* had a life of its own and a movement toward fulfillment quite apart from Tolstoy's conscious intellectual ruminations. At the time he experienced this craving he failed even to realize its proper object or what his true desire was— hence his continued search in other spheres for other answers. This phenomenon helps shed some light on Lucius' apparently oblivious state of mind prior to his conversion. While Tolstoy consciously regis-

---

10. On Lucius' strategies of diversion and in particular on the use of verbs of stupefaction (*obstupesco*, etc.) to describe Lucius' responses to his environment, see chapter 4, section 2. Like Tolstoy, Augustine prefers the image of intoxication (*ebrietas*) to convey how deep his complacency was before his dissatisfaction worked its way to the surface and motivated his search for truth; on this, see also chapter 4, section 1.

tered his free-floating longing and felt acutely the dissatisfaction that resulted from his failure to identify its source, he was unable for some time to recognize the "true" nature of his desire. Lucius is represented as being just one grade more obtuse: he fails to register even his dissatisfaction at a conscious level.

Here I have only suggested some parallels between Tolstoy's crisis in values and that of Lucius because this entire phase of the conversion process will be developed more fully in chapters 4 and 5. There I will argue that the scheme of the exposure of "false" values and the discovery of "true" ones is, with certain adjustments for differences in representational modes, a generic feature of conversion narratives, including the *Metamorphoses*. For now, I would like to examine another aspect of Tolstoy's crisis that is of more immediate concern as we think back to the disintegrating face of Lucius' world, which chapters 1 and 2 explored. Basing his description on Tolstoy's case and on other accounts of similar experiences, James notes that once someone is in the grip of anhedonia, the world in that subject's perception can assume an "altered and estranged aspect," which can be very unsettling. This change in how reality is perceived is the result of the preconvert's disengagement from the familiar structures of meaning that had functioned, so to speak, as the glue holding his or her world together and giving it cohesion. James explains the reasons behind this altered perception of one's environment in the following way:

Conceive yourself, if possible, suddenly stripped of all the emotion with which your world now inspires you, and try to imagine it *as it exists*, purely by itself, without your favorable or unfavorable, hopeful or apprehensive comment. It will be almost impossible for you to realize such a condition of negativity and deadness. No one portion of the universe would then have importance beyond another; and the whole collection of its things and series of its events would be without significance, character, expression, or perspective. Whatever of value, interest, or meaning our respective worlds may appear endued with are thus pure gifts of the spectator's mind. . . . [T]he world's materials lend their surface passively to all the gifts alike, as the stage-setting receives indifferently whatever alternating colored lights may be shed upon it from the optical apparatus in the gallery. . . . [T]he practically real world for each one of us . . . is the compound world, the physical

facts and emotional values in indistinguishable combination.
(1958, 128–29)[11]

When the world's customary values have been sucked out of it, only a
vacuum remains. What can occur in the perception of one experiencing
such a crisis is nothing less than the "transformation in the whole
expression of reality." To that subject, James continues, "the world now
looks remote, strange, sinister, uncanny" (129).

It is just this sort of amorphous and unhinged world, bereft of its
usual boundaries and signposts, that Lucius is represented as moving in before his conversion. In particular James touches on the lev-
eling effect that follows the disappearance of conventionally assigned
values, relationships, and hierarchies; this effect is ubiquitous in the
world of the *Metamorphoses:* "No one portion of the universe would
then have importance beyond another; and the whole collection of its
things and series of its events would be without significance, character, expression, or perspective." Later, in discussing the effects of
conversion on the world view of the convert, James observes a kind
of reverse movement in the "objective change which the world often
appears to undergo" when one has achieved the "assurance state."
"An appearance of newness beautifies every object," he writes, "the
precise opposite of that other sort of newness, that dreadful unreality
and strangeness in the appearance of the world" that clouds the view
of melancholy preconverts (199). Book 11 of the *Metamorphoses* presents us with an Isis who has this ability to make the world seem
bright, clear, and new once Lucius begins to reconstruct his world
around her.

The negative transformation of Tolstoy's reality included a persistent sense that he was being mocked, that a "cruel and stupid" joke was

---

11. The idea of the exposure of a raw reality teeming under the surface of
polite convention ("try to imagine it *as it exists,* purely by itself") fairly invites
comparison with later existential writers, in particular Sartre, a twentieth-
century counterpart of Apuleius qua philosophical novelist. See chapter 5, section 2. Of course, the whole premise that there is such a thing as reality "as it
exists, purely by itself" has been problematized in poststructuralist thought,
and James anticipates this by, in his own way, collapsing the opposition
between subject and object.

being played on him, as one by one his cherished values were exposed as delusions. "'[It] was as if some wicked and stupid jest was being played upon me by some one,'" he recalls. "'One can live only so long as one is intoxicated . . . ; but when one grows sober one cannot fail to see that it is all a stupid cheat. . . . [T]here is nothing even funny or silly in it; it is cruel and stupid, purely and simply'" (in James 1958, 131). The radical alienation of Tolstoy's perspective, and in particular his sense of being the butt of a "cruel and stupid" joke, reminds us of Lucius' alienation as the scapegoat at the Risus festival. As, to his horror, "life's phenomena, which [he had] thought to be clear and full of meaning" grew instead more nebulous and value-neutral, Tolstoy became convinced that "the only absolute knowledge attainable by man is that life is meaningless" (Tolstoy 1983, 90, 34). Living according to the values and aspirations of the conventional world was no real life, he came to believe, but a "'parody on life, which its superfluities simply keep us from comprehending'" (James 1958, 154). In Tolstoy's new vision, as in that of Lucius, I think, the comfortable world of convention and conventionally assigned values is exposed as a house of cards, and the situation of any human being dwelling within such a fragile structure is precarious indeed. We have already seen one of Tolstoy's images for conveying this newly appreciated precariousness: the dragon in the well. Later in his *Confession*, he likens the human condition to that of a man resting uncomfortably in bed on a mattress consisting only of a few straining cords. He looks down and sees the "bottomless depths of the abyss," the "infinity below [which] repels and horrifies" him. Thus, before his conversion, Tolstoy found himself "hanging over the abyss suspended by the last of the cords that [had] not yet slipped out from under" him (Tolstoy 1983, 92–93). Once this "altered and estranged" perception of the world and his situation in it had fixed itself in his mind, there was no going back to the happy ignorance of his earlier life.[12]

Descriptions of this sense of the estrangement of one's environment

---

12. The stark new vision of Pierre as he loses his illusions is even more instructive, mutatis mutandis, in connection with the world of the *Metamorphoses*. As he sinks into his first crisis early in the novel, "everything within and around him [begins to seem] confused, senseless, and repellent" (Tolstoy 1966, 379). At his nadir, just before his meeting with Platon Karataev, who puts

are not confined to accounts of religious conversion, as James makes clear. He compares Tolstoy's alienation with that of a group of "asylum patients" whose perceptions of a nebulous and unreal world echo Tolstoy's. In both cases the horrific new vision results from the collapse of, or the failure ever to assimilate, a socially shared nomic structure that orders and valorizes the world's phenomena. In James' view there is no qualitative difference between the experience of Tolstoy and that of the mentally ill. It is only a difference of degree and of the retention (in Tolstoy's case) of the ability to function in the world in spite of unsettling new insights. The dysfunctionally melancholy have simply moved a little further along the continuum of detachment from the conventionally defined world. For them, the world's "color is gone, its breath is cold, there is no speculation in the eyes it glares with":

> "I see everything through a cloud . . . things are not as they were, and I am changed."—"I see . . . I touch, but the things do not come

---

him on the road to rebirth, Pierre sees little hope that any sense can be restored to his life: "[I]t was as if the mainspring of his life, on which everything depended and which made everything appear alive, had suddenly been wrenched out and everything had collapsed into a heap of meaningless rubbish. Though he did not acknowledge it to himself, his faith in the right ordering of the universe . . . had been destroyed. . . . [H]e felt that the universe had crumbled before his eyes and only meaningless ruins remained, and this not by any fault of his own. He felt that it was not in his power to regain faith in the meaning of life" (1072). Likewise, the chronically disillusioned Andrew Bolkonsky reaches his own low point on the evening before the battle of Borodino. This is how Tolstoy describes *his* stripped-down vision of reality: "From the height of this perception [of his coming death] all that had previously tormented and preoccupied him suddenly became illumined by a cold white light without shadows, without perspective, and without distinction of outline. All life appeared to him like magic-lantern pictures at which he had long been gazing by artificial light through a glass. Now he suddenly saw those badly daubed pictures in clear daylight and without a glass. 'Yes, yes! There they are, those false images that agitated, enraptured, and tormented me. . . . There they are, those rudely painted figures that once seemed splendid and mysterious. Glory, the good of society, love of a woman, the Fatherland itself— how important these pictures appeared to me, with what profound meaning they seemed to be filled! And it is all so simple, pale, and crude in the cold white light of this morning which I feel is dawning for me'" (858).

near me, a thick veil alters the hue and look of everything."—
"Persons move like shadows, and sounds seem to come from a
distant world."—". . . people appear so strange; it is as if I could
not see any reality, as if I were in a theatre; as if people were actors
and everything were scenery. . . . Everything floats before my
eyes, but leaves no impression."—"I weep false tears, I have
unreal hands: the things I see are not real things." (James 1958,
129)

The impressionistic, unstable, and capriciously metamorphosing quality of the material world that emerges in these documents reminds us
that the same quality pervades the world of the *Metamorphoses*. I would
note in this connection that the unfortunates quoted above were not
schooled in Platonic doctrine. Insofar as cultural models can be separated from experience, these people's conviction of the sensible world's
unreality comes to them spontaneously and does not represent an
endorsement of doctrinal dualism. There exists a tradition of efforts to
read the *Metamorphoses* as a coded Platonic treatise, but I think that it is
equally legitimate to approach the work as a representation of Lucius'
spontaneous (and, from Apuleius' perspective, composite) religious
experience, although this experience would have been informed by the
dualism that had begun with Plato but which had in the meanwhile
been very much generalized. To return to the correlation between religious experience and mental illness: James has no answer to the question of why some melancholiacs are "saved" by religion and some find
less socially acceptable ways out, or none at all.[13]

By now it should be clear that I think that the *Metamorphoses* can be
read as a running account of the fragmentation of a conversion-ripe
subject's view of the world once habituated values come into question.
The collapsing universe of the *Metamorphoses* in all the aspects and

---

13. James borrows his testimony here from G. Dumas, *La Tristesse et la Joie*
(Paris, 1900). He goes on to suggest the shapes that melancholy can take even
further along the continuum. "The worst kind of melancholy is that which
takes the form of panic fear," he writes, and then invokes the account of one
who suffered from it: " 'Suddenly there fell upon me without any warning, just

expressions of it discussed in chapters 1 and 2 can be taken to represent two stages of the conversion process as it is analyzed by James. At one level the disintegration of Lucius' world represents the comprehensive failure of habituated structures of meaning and, more specifically, the disillusionment with conventional values that marks the initial phase in the type of conversion crisis in question. I will have more to say in the next chapter about how this precipitating disillusionment expresses itself in the novel. At a secondary level the novel's unhinged reality represents the "altered and estranged aspect which the world assume[s] in consequence" of the breakdown of primary structures. In both Tolstoy's and Lucius' cases we see a kind of sequential structural collapse: once the bedrock values go, nothing can make sense any more, and aporia extends itself in concentric circles until all reliable order and self-evident value disappear. An especially intriguing parallel is the linkage in both accounts between the disintegration of the

---

as if it came out of the darkness, a horrible fear of my own existence. . . . After this the universe was changed for me altogether. I awoke morning after morning with a horrible dread at the pit of my stomach, and with a sense of the insecurity of life that I never knew before. . . . I remember wondering how other people could live, how I myself had ever lived, so unconscious of that pit of insecurity beneath the surface of life.'" Such an assertion of a "horrible fear of [one's] own existence" easily could have been taken from later existential writings. It is also instructive for our purposes that this subject sought an antidote in religion: "'I have always thought that this experience of melancholia of mine had a religious bearing. . . . If I had not clung to scripture texts like "The eternal God is my refuge," etc., "Come unto me, all ye that labor and are heavy-laden," etc., "I am the resurrection and the life," etc., I think I should have grown really insane.'" The most extreme stages of melancholy are horrific indeed: "Were we disposed to open the chapter of really insane melancholia . . . it would be a worse story still—desperation absolute and complete, the whole universe coagulating about the sufferer into a material of overwhelming horror, surrounding him without opening or end" (James 1958, 135–36). Here we run into heavy weather indeed, with limited applicability to the novel; but James' comments serve to reinforce his general point about the subjectivity of vision, which *is* relevant to our purposes: "The lunatic's visions of horror are all drawn from the material of daily fact" (138).

social or moral worlds on the one hand and the physical world on the other. Tolstoy's loss of faith in *social* values caused him to perceive his *physical* environment also as hostile and precarious: he came to feel "like an orphan and isolated in the midst of all these things that were so foreign." Likewise the estrangement of the material world and that of the social world proceed alongside each other in some kind of symbiotic relationship in the novel.

There are various ways out of this uncomfortable state of epistemic limbo, according to James. The "process of unification," as he calls it, "may come gradually, or it may occur abruptly; it may come through altered feelings, or through altered powers of action; or it may come through new intellectual insights, or through experiences which we shall later have to designate as 'mystical.'" The path to relief that opens itself to Lucius involves a mystically inspired sudden conversion, about whose mechanics I will have more to say later. However resolution comes, "firmness, stability, and equilibrium" replace the "storm and stress and inconsistency" of the period of crisis (James 1958, 146–47). James insists that the process of finding unity and "reducing inner discord"—of resolving cognitive dissonance, in modern psychological terms—is a generic one. Religious regenerations "are only one species of a genus that contains other types as well." One's new birth might equally be "away from religion into incredulity, or . . . from moral scrupulosity into freedom and license," for example. As an illustration, James offers the "counter-conversion" of Jouffroy, during which the French philosopher moved from religious belief to skepticism:

> "Anxiously I followed my thoughts . . . scattering one by one all [my] illusions. . . . Vainly I clung to these last beliefs as a shipwrecked sailor clings to the fragments of his vessel; vainly, frightened at the unknown void in which I was about to float, I turned . . . towards my childhood, my family, my country, all that was dear and sacred to me: the inflexible current of my thought was too strong—parents, family, memory, beliefs, it forced me to let go of everything. . . . I knew then that in the depth of my mind nothing was left that stood erect. . . . I seemed to feel my earlier life, so smiling and so full, go out like a fire, and before me another life opened, sombre and unpeopled, where in future I

must live alone, alone with my fatal thought which had exiled me thither."[14]

In addition to making James' point that conversion can move in either direction, this passage offers a perfect parallel to the crisis in values experienced by Tolstoy. In both cases disillusionment deepens inexorably as the tenets of a "religion" crumble before the eyes of the believer. And in both cases the subject's disengagement from a habituated structure of meaning leads to a sense of estrangement from the environment in which each had felt at home. We will see that James' assertion that a generic process unifies conversions underneath the incidental details of their "theologies" is expanded in modern studies of conversion, where relevant ideas about the general mechanics of cognitive paradigm shifting are often brought to bear.

William James may be the best remembered of the pioneers in the psychology of religious experience, but he was not the only one, nor was he even the first. In formulating his Gifford lectures, which would become *The Varieties of Religious Experience,* James drew heavily on what little work had already been done at that time in the field. In particular he repeatedly cites the earlier studies of Leuba (1896) and especially Starbuck (1899, revised 1901). Starbuck anticipated James in his division of conversion experiences into two types corresponding to James' "conviction of sin" (Bunyan) and "metaphysical quest" (Tolstoy) models, and in his enumeration of some of the symptoms that tend to precede conversion. He included among these a sense of estrangement and detachment from one's familiar environment—as one of his informants put it, " 'everything seemed dead.' " Like James (and Tolstoy), Starbuck believed that vague yearnings toward the infinite could be misdirected into momentary diversions (1901, 58–70; 85–86). He shared James' view that extreme cases of religious or prereligious fervor were the stuff of abnormal psychology (163–79) and explored at some length the notion of the "subconscious incubation" of forces tending toward conversion (101–17). James and later writers adopted this explanation, and it will be invoked in the next chapter to suggest some ways of understanding

---

14. James (1958, 147–48) quotes from Theodore Jouffroy, *Nouveaux mélanges philosophiques* (Paris, 1842).

sudden conversions such as that of Lucius. Unlike James, Starbuck eschewed autobiographical narratives as documentary evidence for his study, fearing that in many cases they were "written to produce a religious effect, so that the facts are doubtless out of perspective" (22). His suspicions on this score were of course legitimate, but the "facts" extracted from the questionnaires and interviews that he preferred instead were not necessarily any more immune to contamination. It is now a commonplace that *no* verbal account can faithfully represent experience, which in any case is always mediated by cultural models. Starbuck furthermore limited the utility of his study by selecting his informants exclusively from American Protestant communities. He thus unwittingly set the stage for the tendentiousness that characterized much of the work on religious psychology after James and contributed to its being discredited within a larger field increasingly concerned to claim a status as "objective" science.

Even as James relied on earlier work, most of the studies appearing after him in the classic period were to a greater or lesser degree dependent on his own work. The contributions of Coe (1916), Pratt (1920), Strickland (1924), and Clark (1929), who brought the period to a close, are fairly representative of this early spate of scholarly activity. A limitation common to these studies is that the groups selected as informants are so narrow and homogeneous (usually contemporary American Protestants) that the utility of their results for formulating a general, cross-cultural model of the workings of conversion is seriously limited. James, in selecting his documents from a range of religious and nonreligious accounts, seems to me to be less liable to this charge. Some of these later writers of the classic period suggest that a generic psychological process underlies religious and secular conversions, but they do not document or elaborate on their suggestion (for example, Clark 1929, 37). Pratt is unusual in that he makes an effort to expand his sources beyond the usual Christian circle by incorporating two narratives of conversion from the Hindu tradition. One is the autobiographical account of Maharishi Devendranath Tagore, which parallels Tolstoy's *Confession* in striking ways.[15] Pratt's point in casting his net so wide is to expose the tendency of other writers to generalize the con-

---

15. Tagore recalls his life before conversion: "'Darkness was all around me. ... Life was dreary, the world was like a graveyard. I found happiness in noth-

viction of guilt and sin found in the Protestant evangelical tradition and exemplified by Bunyan to the psychology of religious experience as a whole. Feelings of guilt are completely absent in Tagore. His problems, like Tolstoy's, were "objective and metaphysical," in James' terms; his search was for "true" value. Pratt recognized that both the experience of conversion and the narrative describing it can be shaped by theological patterns and that this is especially true in emotional evangelical settings; people can and, in fact, are bound to cultivate the type of conversion experience prescribed by their community (1920, 150). He thus anticipates the later attempts of Beckford (1978) and others to disentangle the complex web of culture, experience, and narrative as it is relevant to conversion. Furthermore, Pratt's insistence that the Bunyan model has limited application might well have been heeded by Apuleian critics, who have attempted to impose it in some form or another on the conversion of Lucius.

Religious experience fell out of favor as a subject of psychological inquiry around 1930, and it did not come to be regarded as a legitimate area of investigation again until some forty years had passed. The decline of the early phase of scholarship in this area was a function of external social forces as well as intrinsic methodological weaknesses in the studies themselves, at least from the point of view of those dedicated to making the youthful social sciences more respectable by modeling their methods at least ostensibly after those of the hard sciences. William James himself has been charged with a number of methodological failings. He neglected, for example, evidence from the experience of ordinary believers in favor of autobiographical accounts by extraordinary religious figures, along the way appearing to take autobiography, a notoriously problematic genre, at face value. Furthermore, according to his detractors, he tended to treat religious experience as an ex nihilo phenomenon without sufficiently considering the

---

ing, peace in nothing. The rays of the midday sun seemed to me black.'" As Pratt paraphrases, "[t]he universe seemed barren to him and life empty and worthless. . . . Life was stale, flat, unprofitable." When a religious resolution—a "new and intense value . . . around which he might unify his life"—began to suggest itself, Tagore felt as if the true nature of his longing had finally been revealed and that this longing was finally being satisfied (1920, 133–37).

cultural factors that might play a role in shaping it. In the same vein he is faulted for making emotion and internal psychodynamics central to understanding religious experience in general and conversion in particular, while ignoring social factors such as the simple desire to belong to a group. James' immediate predecessors and successors avoided the first of these charges with their quasi-scientific collection of data from real religious communities, but left themselves open to other criticisms by their narrow selection of respondents. Meanwhile, social changes such as the shift away from religious world views toward a behavioristic one conspired to further undermine the status of the psychology of religion, so that when it reemerged in the 1970s it was inevitably a very different creature from the one it had been in its infancy.[16]

2

Much has changed in the approaches of social scientists and theorists to the study of religious experience since the time of William James and his immediate heirs. Attempts have been made to standardize and quantify the measurement of religious experience, and a social interactionist perspective has superseded the common earlier view of conversion as the solitary and internally driven psychological struggle of an individual. Yet in spite of radical differences in methodology and the shift to a social psychological or sociological orientation, much of the modern writing on conversion echoes James in its assertion that the initial stage of the process often involves a disintegration of habituated structures of meaning and familiar ways of organizing reality. The basic model established by James, in which conversion is a process of cognitive breakdown and restructuring triggered by a challenge to an established world view, keeps emerging either explicitly or by implication in a wide range of modern studies of conversion itself or of related phenomena. What I propose to do in this section is to survey a selection of the studies that display this strain, drawing attention along the way to their points of contact with James and his exemplary convert Tolstoy

---

16. For a fuller account of the rise and decline of the early movement in the psychology of religion, see the surveys enumerated in n. 2 above, especially Spilka, Hood, and Gorsuch 1985 (chap. 9 on trends in the study of conversion); Wulff 1991 (chap. 10 on William James); and Beit-Hallahmi 1974.

and ultimately with the Apuleian representation of conversion. I will begin with treatments of religious experience and conversion proper, move on from there to consider studies of various kinds of coerced attitude change (for example, "brainwashing" and "deprogramming"), and finally come to analogies between conversion and the psychotherapeutic process. What these have in common is that they are all types of attitude change; they simply take place under different circumstances. Our ultimate concern will be with the underlying process discernible in all three and its relevance to the progression represented in the *Metamorphoses*.

Peter Berger has been a major contributor to the literature in the sociology of religion that has appeared over the last thirty years. In *The Sacred Canopy* (1967), he brings the theoretical perspectives developed earlier with Luckmann in connection with formulating a sociology of knowledge to bear on an analysis of the social function of religion.[17] In the opening chapter, suggestively entitled "Religion and World-Construction," Berger begins with what he as a sociologist regards as the basic fact of the condition of the human organism, namely a "built-in instability" arising from the absence of any given or intrinsic relationship between human beings and the world. We are forced to "ongoingly establish a relationship" with the world, to engage continually in "world-building" in order to compensate for this natural void and to establish some kind of stability (1967, 5). The product of human world-building is, of course, culture, and "its fundamental purpose is to provide the firm structures for human life that are lacking biologically" (6). These structures include categories and values imposed on natural phenomena as well as on purely social ones (although to what extent these can be distinguished is arguable, and culture itself tends to conflate or separate the two categories according to what is needed to validate particular cultural discourses). Berger stresses that humanly produced structures, because they are arbitrary and must be "continuously

---

17. See Berger and Luckmann 1966. For a review of *The Sacred Canopy*, see, e.g., Knudten 1968. As that reviewer notes, Berger's is a synthesizing approach that draws extensively on previous work in the sociology of religion and related fields, most notably that of Weber and Durkheim, among many others: see Berger's copious notes and the bibliography contained there. Knudten, whose review is favorable, also remarks that Berger's scheme is a theoretical one and thus open to limited empirical validation. This will not be true of all the studies cited here.

produced and reproduced," are inherently unstable, "precarious and predestined to change." As he puts it, "while it is necessary that worlds be built, it is quite difficult to keep them going" (6).

One reason why humanly produced worlds keep going as long as they do is the circular process through which they attain the status of objective reality. Once generated, human cultural products are transformed and confront us as a "facticity outside of" ourselves. According to Berger, "the humanly produced world becomes something 'out there'. . . . Although all culture originates and is rooted in the subjective consciousness of human beings, once formed it cannot be reabsorbed into consciousness at will. It stands outside the subjectivity of the individual as, indeed, a world" (8–9). Culture's status as objective reality— as nature—is then maintained by the community's adherence to a kind of social contract requiring collective recognition of it as such. This power of culture to "constitute and impose itself as reality," says Berger, results in society's being "commonly apprehended by man as virtually equivalent to the physical universe in its objective presence" (10–12). The circle is completed when the constructed world is then reabsorbed into consciousness "in such a way that the structures of this world come to determine the subjective structures of consciousness itself" (15). In spite of the insidiousness of this process and the ill uses to which it can be put, the prospect of human life ruled by gross biological imperatives without the mediating presence of culture is a grim one indeed. For "the socially constructed world is, above all, an ordering of experience. A meaningful order, or nomos, is imposed upon the discrete experiences and meanings of individuals" (19). Language is, of course, one of the primary mechanisms for "imposing differentiation and structure upon the ongoing flux of experience" (20); in this connection it is significant, I think, that Lucius' loss of the ability to speak coincides with the breakdown of differentiation and structure in his world. Berger concludes that "to live in the social world is to live an ordered and meaningful life" (21).

The subjective but objectified reality of the social world is continuously reinforced by individuals in conversation with others in their community and can be maintained only so long as this conversation continues. If it is disrupted—if, for example, one finds oneself cut off from one's customary interlocutors, or if something happens to undermine trust in society's system of valorizations—then the world, says Berger, "begins to totter, to lose its subjective plausibility." In other words, he continues, "the subjective reality of the world hangs on the thin thread of conversation" (16–17). This, at last, is where Lucius comes in, and as we continue I will try to show how. Berger writes that any radical separation of an individual from the social world—that is, any slide into a state of anomy—is threatening to that person least of all because of the emotional ties that are lost. Far worse, the anomic individual "loses his orientation in experience. In extreme cases, he loses his sense of reality and identity. He becomes anomic in the sense of becoming worldless." With his epistemological taproot in society cut off,

> the fundamental order in terms of which the individual can "make sense" of his life and recognize his own identity will be in process of disintegration. Not only will the individual then begin to lose his moral bearings . . . but he will become uncertain about his cognitive bearings as well. . . . The ultimate danger of . . . separation [from the social world and its values] . . . is the danger of meaninglessness. This danger is the nightmare *par excellence,* in which the individual is submerged in a world of disorder, senselessness and madness. Reality and identity are malignantly transformed into meaningless figures of horror. To be in society is to be "sane" precisely in the sense of being shielded from the ultimate "insanity" of such anomic terror. (22–23)

This may seem to be heavy-handed stuff to be applying to a comic novel from pagan antiquity, but let us suspend our assumptions about genre and period and see where it leads us. In what sense does Lucius suffer a "radical separation from the social world"? The separation consists, I think, in the crisis in values that is betrayed by his compulsive and aimless casting about for novel and (he hopes in vain) lasting forms of gratification. The values with which he had been inculcated and to which he had become habituated now seem to be leading him nowhere. Tolstoy, of course, was more clearly anomic, or to employ the corresponding Jamesian term, anhedonic, that is, cut off from sharing in the values and norms of his society. In the novel, Lucius' standing outside of his usual social system is symbolized in his status as an exile, which persists in some sense throughout the work, until he finds a home—his true home—with Isis. Even before his transformation, he is traveling in a foreign country, far from familiar people and surroundings; as an ass he finds himself marginalized in ways he had never imagined, beneath the notice and the contempt of even the most marginalized human beings. As for Berger's "nightmare world of disorder and senselessness," in which the anomic individual can lose any orientation in experience, become uncertain about his or her cognitive bearings, and search in vain for the familiar signposts that had always marked out the way, this is, it seems to me, quintessentially the world of *Metamorphoses* 1 through 10. Once it begins, the nightmare that Berger suggests is comprehensive, ultimately encompassing all aspects of existence. Thus, in the novel the signposts in both the physical and the social worlds have been pulled up, revealing the "chaos [that] must be kept at bay" (Berger 1967, 24).

There are, according to Berger, marginal situations beyond the reach and force of nomos that demonstrate the sheltering function of the social order at the same time that they "reveal the innate precariousness of all social worlds" (24). Both of these seem to me to have some relevance to the novel. The first marginal situation is that represented by dreams and fantasy. As Berger describes them:

> They appear on the horizon of consciousness as haunting suspicions that the world may have another aspect than its "normal" one, that is, that the previously accepted definitions of reality may be fragile or even fraudulent. Such suspicions extend to the identity of both self and others, positing the possibility of shattering metamorphoses. (23)

As far as we can tell, Lucius is not dreaming, but his newly anomic world resembles a dream, as Berger describes it. It is volatile down to its very physical matter, and its unstable character raises the suspicion that anything could happen, that "shattering metamorphoses" could occur at any moment. But the "marginal situation *par excellence*," Berger asserts, "is death." Because it makes a mockery of all human endeavor and achievement, death undermines all the ordinarily unexamined "cognitive and normative operating procedures" that order life on an everyday basis (23–24). We saw how it was a clearly perceived and articulated confrontation with his own mortality that caused conventional values to pale for Tolstoy and sent him on his search for cosmic meaning. Death lurks as a problem, indeed the ultimate problem, in the *Metamorphoses* as well, although, as usual, the problem is expressed there in a more indirect way. Flight from the void of mortality, or efforts to compensate for or make sense of it, can be read into Lucius' endless search for satisfaction, misdirected as it is; it can also be imputed behind Augustine's more directed search for meaning in diverse religious and philosophical systems (see chap. 4).

I take the liberty here of quoting Berger at some length because he provides a fine description of precisely the sort of protective and valorizing structure that Lucius has slipped out of and of the "dark, ominous jungle" into which he has wandered:

> Every socially defined reality remains threatened by lurking "irrealities." Every socially constructed nomos must face the constant possibility of its collapse into anomy. Seen in the perspective of society, every nomos is an area of meaning carved out of a vast mass of meaninglessness, a small clearing of lucidity in a formless, dark, always ominous jungle. Seen in the perspective of the individual, every nomos represents the bright "dayside" of life, tenuously held onto against the sinister shadows of the "night." In both perspectives, every nomos is an edifice erected in the face of the potent and alien forces of chaos. This chaos must be kept at bay at all cost. To ensure this, every society develops procedures that assist its members to remain "reality-oriented" (that is, to remain within the reality as "officially" defined) and to "return to reality" (that is, to return from the marginal spheres of "irreality" to the socially established nomos). (24)

But for Lucius these procedures seem to have lost their effectiveness.

Berger extends his discussion—and this is really the substance of his book—to a formulation of the relationship between society and religion; this formulation has implications for the dynamics of conversion that are relevant to our purposes. He argues that once the socially constructed order is taken for objective reality, the process of its objectivation is taken one step further: "there occurs a merging of its meanings with what are considered to be the fundamental meanings inherent in the universe. Nomos and cosmos appear to be co-extensive" (25). They become locked in a circle of mutual reinforcement: the humanly constructed order is projected into the universe and thence reflected in such a way as to "stabilize the tenuous nomic constructions" that were its source in the first place. So Berger: but the question of whether cosmic order is a self-serving human projection or objectively real—the latter would have been the ancient view, predating sociological analysis—is well beyond our scope. Our focus is rather on the function of human communion with the cosmic order, whatever the reality status of that order—that is, the function of religion—in the face of the fragility of the social order. The cosmos posited by religion, argues Berger, transcends human beings and their wobbly social world and locates them in an ultimately and intrinsically meaningful, fixed, and eternal order. In dualistic systems it is opposed to chaos and, as such, functions as the "ultimate shield against the terror of anomy"—a sort of giant safety net stretched over the "abyss of meaninglessness." All nomic constructions, Berger notes, are "designed to keep this terror at bay." But "in the sacred cosmos . . . these constructions achieve their ultimate culmination—literally, their apotheosis" (26–27).

The shielding power of the cosmos expresses itself partly in its ability to integrate into a comprehensive nomos precisely those marginal situations that call the reality of everyday life into question (42). Chief among these, as we have seen, is death:

> Death radically challenges *all* socially objectivated definitions of reality. . . . Death radically puts in question the taken-for-granted, "business as usual" attitude in which one exists in everyday life. Here, everything in the daytime world of existence in society is massively threatened with "irreality"—that is, everything in that world becomes dubious, eventually unreal, other than one had used to think. Insofar as the knowledge of death cannot be avoided in any society, legitimations of the reality of the social world *in the face of death* are decisive requirements in any society. (44)

By placing marginal situations like death in the context of a larger sacred reality, religion mitigates their threat to the social world and enables that world to continue. When people think that even the most apparently unintelligible events and experiences have a place in a cosmic system that makes sense, they are less likely to question the social values that unrationalized experience with marginal situations could well undermine, if not destroy (44). In chapter 6, I will discuss how Isis and the cosmic order that she represents function as a "shield against the terror of anomy" for the Fortuna-battered Lucius. The specter of death lurks in the background of the *Metamorphoses* even as it is identified explicitly by Tolstoy as the cause of his malaise. But once both converts tap into an overarching, deathless order that promises them a share in its deathlessness, the fact of individual physical death takes its proper place, and a rather minor one, in this grand new scheme. A cosmic perspective assigns all phenomena, whether "bad" or "good," a place in an ultimately intelligible order and allows people to carry on.

Berger does not explicitly discuss the voluntary conversion of individuals, but the implications of his scheme for understanding this experience are clear enough. An understanding of conversion, that is, the acquisition of a religious world view, as a (re)construction on the cosmic level of a nomizing structure that has failed on the social level would be consistent with Berger's theories about the sociology of knowledge and the function of religion. He as much as implies that conversion involves just such a general pattern of disintegration and reconstruction in his comments about the forced conversion of whole cultures (45–46). The most effective way of bringing about such conversion is through the destruction of a culture's "plausibility structure," that is, the "processes that ongoingly reconstruct and maintain" a particular world and thus constitute the social "base" for the continuing existence of that world as "real to actual human beings." Taking as an example the Spaniards' destruction of the plausibility structure of pre-Columbian Inca society, Berger notes the "terrifying rapidity" with which the reality of the world based on that plausibility structure disintegrated once the destruction began. The world of the indigenous Peruvians was shattered and redefined in terms of the plausibility structure of European Christianity. As brief as Berger's discussion is, it posits a process at work in the coerced attitude change of a whole society similar in its outlines to the process that emerges in studies of such cult-related phenomena as the "brainwashing" and "deprogramming" of individuals. More important to our immediate purpose, the pattern of disintegration and reconstruction that Berger discerns in the forced conversion of an entire culture constitutes a sort of collective parallel to the progression that I have identified as potentially characterizing the spontaneous conversion of individuals, including Lucius. Insofar as Berger touches upon the conversion of individuals, which he defines as "individual transference into another world" (50), his claim that the possibility of conversion increases with "the degree of instability or discontinuity" in the old plausibility structure is relevant here, since I have argued in chapters 1 and 2 that Lucius' old plausibility structure appears to have become unstable and discontinuous in the extreme.[18]

Batson and Ventis, writing some fifteen years later, recall Berger in their premises about the constructedness of reality and the implications of this for the genesis and function of religious world views. They, however, use these premises as a basis on which to build a model of the conversion experience of individuals, that is, their movement from one world view to another (religious) one. We will see that the pattern of disintegration under stress of a precariously constructed order and the subsequent reconstruction of world view on new organizing principles is central to Batson and Ventis' analysis of religious experience, even as it is implicit in Berger's.[19] They begin with a cross-cultural catalogue of ten very different accounts of conversion, taking from William James the idea that the best way to get at the general psychological processes underlying conversion is to study the most dramatic and intense instances of religious experience because it is here that these processes are most clearly displayed.[20] What Batson and Ventis see as the common thread in these accounts is that they all describe an experience involving "dramatic change, both in the way the person sees the world and in the person's behavior; each [experience] is reality-transforming" (1982, 63). Before proceeding to their conclusions about these narra-

---

18. It should be noted that many question the commonly held view, accepted by Berger and especially identified with Durkheim, that there is an inverse relationship between anomy and religiosity (i.e., that feelings of anomy inspire religiosity and that religion causes those feelings to disappear). See, e.g., Carr and Hauser 1976; and Dean 1968.

19. Batson and Ventis use the terms "conversion" and "religious experience" interchangeably; see their index under both. The revised and expanded edition of Batson and Ventis' 1982 study *The Religious Experience* (Batson, Schoenrade, and Ventis 1993) makes no changes or additions that would alter the applicability of their earlier discussion to my argument.

20. The ten exempla are: Siddhartha, later the Buddha; Moses; St. Paul; St. Augustine; Thoreau; two revival-inspired converts cited earlier by Starbuck (and James); a student acquaintance of Batson and Ventis; Malcolm X; and a psychologist under the influence of LSD (57–63). The wide diversity ("Even within our small sample," they write, "we find four major religions represented—Buddhism, Judaism, Christianity, and Islam; there are also several experiences that involve personal, idiosyncratic beliefs not easily related to any institutional religion") is designed to support one of Batson and Ventis' main contentions: that a generic process underlies a large proportion of all religious experience.

tives, they ask that their readers accept two related assumptions: that behind diverse manifestations of religious experience there lies a common or similar psychological process; and that this process in turn has analogies in other kinds of "reality-transforming" experiences (64–65). The analogous secular and intellectual reality-transforming experience upon which Batson and Ventis choose to concentrate in order to illuminate reality-transforming religious experiences is the process of creativity.

It would take us very far afield indeed to attempt to delve into all that is known about the process of creativity. What I propose to do instead is provide a brief account of Batson and Ventis' synthesized model of creativity, concentrating in particular on the features that will be prominent in their analogous model of religious experience and thus relevant to our reading of the *Metamorphoses*. They identify six propositions or components that seem to be integral to the creative process.[21] The proposition that reality is constructed is fundamental; we impose meaning on what would otherwise be, in the words of William James, a "'booming, buzzing confusion.'" The "structure and stability of 'reality'" that we project onto the world and the "meaning that we attach to our experience" according to the rules of that structure are pure creations of the human mind. Because we arbitrarily "form our experience into meaningful objects and relations," it is possible for two people (or even the same person at different times) to construct "two different realities out of exactly the same sensory input" (1982, 65–67). Batson and Ventis' second proposition is that the character of the reality that we construct is determined by the shape of our cognitive structures. Defining cognitive structures as the "conceptual dimensions on which we scale our experience" and the mechanisms that "allow us to compare one experience with another," they assert that it is this "ability to classify and differentiate experiences [that] enables us to construct a reality" (68). A crucial and obvious question not treated by them is that of how our cognitive structures acquire the shape that they have in the first place; Berger's loop of naturalization is an explanation that would be consistent with their other premises. A third component of Batson and Ventis' scheme that is critical to understanding the creative process

---

21. Batson and Ventis are drawing on a range of currently accepted theory about creativity and on related work in, for example, developmental psychology (Piaget) and phenomenological philosophy: see their citations ad loc.

is the apparently hierarchical arrangement of cognitive structures, with specific dimensions and higher levels of conceptual complexity on top, so to speak, and the most general and abstract organizing principles on the bottom. Thus "when we are presented with a problem that requires organizing principles at a higher level of conceptual complexity than we have developed, it will appear to be insoluble," as indeed it is within the existing cognitive structures (69–71).

Batson and Ventis regard creativity as essentially a problem-solving activity, during which the solution to the problem and an improvement in one's cognitive organization (that is, an increase in its complexity) emerge simultaneously. "When," they write, "some problem is insoluble within the existing cognitive structures, a new organization is needed." One cognitive organization must be abandoned and replaced by another one; when this happens, "a new world or reality is created." Following others, they insist that true creativity involves not just a change but an improvement in cognitive organization (this is their fourth proposition). They define a better organization as "one that, through greater differentiation and integration, makes it possible to think what was previously unthinkable." True creative thought, therefore, is "the process whereby one's cognitive structures are changed toward greater flexibility and adaptability" (1982, 71–73). This is contrasted with various kinds of noncreative cognitive change, such as the acquisition of new knowledge; the movement toward a simpler and more restrictive, rather than an expansive and more complex, organization; and alternation, that is, a lateral "shift from one cognitive organization to another, but at the same level of complexity" (73–74). Creative change, on the other hand, is characterized by "an increase in the number of organizing principles, the level of organization, or the interaction and interpenetration of existing principles." When this happens, "the old reality . . . is transcended; it is seen for what it is, one way of looking at the world that has only a limited range of application" (74). This idea of creative, as opposed to noncreative, cognitive changes will have a parallel in Batson and Ventis' model of religious experience.

Batson and Ventis are very clear that creativity is an adaptive process. It occurs when a problem arises that cannot be solved within the confines of one's existing cognitive organization:

[Creative] changes in cognitive structure appear to result when one's current reality ceases to function effectively. . . . Under such circumstances . . . pressure arises to accommodate our cognitive structures to our experience. It is not, of course, a question of finding the "right" or "true" structures, for rightness and truth can be defined only *within* a set of cognitive structures. It is instead a question of finding a functionally better reality, one that enables the individual to expect and to respond more effectively to experiences of the sort that actually occur. (73)

Batson and Ventis proceed to identify (after Wallas 1926) four stages in the creative process, all of which have parallels in religious experience (the positing of these stages is their fifth proposition). The first stage consists of a period of preparation or "baffled struggle in which the individual attempts to solve the problem in terms of his or her existing cognitive structures." When this approach leads nowhere, that person may begin to "feel trapped within the current organization with no way out" (1982, 77–78). The incubation stage occurs when active pursuit of a solution to the problem ceases and all the possible ways of looking at it are allowed to incubate at an unconscious level. Such a relaxation of the active exercise of existing cognitive structures "appears necessary if one is to be able to think about the problem in a new way, if a more adaptive organization is to evolve" (78). This stage would seem to represent the Jamesian idea of the "subconscious incubation" of forces tending toward conversion and to parallel the surrender of will that James asserts is necessary before conversion can take place. The stage of illumination is the point at which "new, more appropriate cognitive structures may emerge," structures that allow the individual to see all the elements of the problem in a new way. Finally, during the verification stage, the new insight is elaborated and tested for validity against experience (78). To illustrate these four stages of creative problem solving, Batson and Ventis cite four cases of scientific or mathematical discovery ("eureka-experiences," one might say) that hinged on creative cognitive restructuring or, in the terminology of Thomas Kuhn, paradigm shifts (75–77). This movement into the realm of scientific problem solving does not involve so radical a detour from our path as may first appear, for an analogy between the dynamics of Kuhnian paradigm shift and those of religious conversion is one that is frequently implied, if not explicitly posited, in studies of conversion, as we will see.[22]

After briefly discussing how the process of finding solutions to personal problems also can be analyzed in terms of the restructuring of constructed reality, Batson and Ventis turn to their analogous model of religious experience, which concerns us most directly.[23] They maintain that in many cases the process of conversion can be broken down into four stages, each with a corresponding phase in their model of creativity.[24] In connection with James' discussion of Tolstoy's conversion, I invoked a fundamental premise in Batson and Ventis' understanding of religion and religiosity: that "religious experience is rooted in a dissatisfaction at an existential level" (1982, 82). And indeed existential crisis—a sense that "there is a discrepancy between what is and what one feels ought to be with regard to one or more questions of existence"—marks the first stage in the religious experience, according to their sequence (82–83). Existential crisis often takes the form of grappling with mortality and with what it means about our values and the proper conduct of our lives. This first stage corresponds to the preparation stage in the creative process, with the existential conundrum presenting itself as the problem that cannot be solved within present cognitive structures. One can of course try, but most likely will find oneself spin-

---

22. The sixth proposition in Batson and Ventis' model of the creative process is that "the creative sequence outlined may have a physiological base" (79–80) and need not concern us. On "subconscious incubation" as it is developed in James and others, and as it appears in the *Metamorphoses,* see chapter 4, section 2.

23. Personal problem solving also works in stages, according to Batson and Ventis. These stages are: (1) personal conflict or crisis; and (2) confusion and exhaustion if the problem cannot be resolved within current cognitive structures; but "this disintegration can have a positive function, for the most dramatic personality growth often takes place during such periods of personal crisis and ego disintegration" (the relevance to the conversion experience of this idea that disintegration can ultimately have a positive effect will become clear in my discussion of parallels between conversion and the psychotherapeutic process); (3) new self-image or new way of seeing ourselves in relation to the world, "a way that provides a foundation for building a new reality that is more in tune with our experience"; and (4) improved social functioning (1982, 81–82).

24. In their discussion of the stages involved in religious experience, Batson and Ventis draw especially on Bertocci (1958), Clark (1958), Loder (1966), May (1975), and Rugg (1963).

ning one's wheels in any number of dead ends, such as, for example, Tolstoy's ultimately unsatisfying conventional pursuits. Batson and Ventis, in fact, cite as exemplary statements of existential crisis some of the same passages of Tolstoy's *Confession* quoted above.

In spite of the comic components of the *Metamorphoses*, I think that this sort of crisis can be read in Lucius' behavior as well. His thoughtless, unproductive behavioral patterns indicate that he has hit a wall, that (as Batson and Ventis say of the preparation phase in the creative process) his "current reality has ceased to function effectively," and he is "trapped within the current organization with no way out" (1982, 73, 77–78). We will look more closely in the next chapter at Lucius' (and Augustine's) habituated patterns of thinking and action and at how these strategies have outlived their usefulness. Batson and Ventis make another point that will be especially important when we return to scrutinizing Lucius in more detail. They suggest that existential crisis can be experienced at an unconscious level, that there might be only a vague and inarticulate perception of it on the part of the sufferer. This could provide us with a clue as to why the narrative represents Lucius as failing to dwell on the problem before his conversion, which then appears to be completely unmotivated at the beginning of Book 11. Just as the paradigm shifts necessary for the solution of problems in science often are brought to completion by unconscious processes and result in sudden understanding, so the early stages of religious experience can be hidden from view and have a resolution that appears similarly abrupt to the observer. Batson and Ventis conclude their description of the first stage of religious experience by noting, as James did before them, that crisis and conversion often take place in the prime of life, when, in the terms of Maslow (1954), "all deficiencies are met." They cite Tolstoy, Augustine, and the Buddha; we have already noted that Lucius, although a young man, seems, because of his privilege, to exemplify this pattern as well.

Batson and Ventis identify self-surrender as the second stage in religious experience, analogous to the incubation stage in the creative process (1982, 83–84). After repeatedly battering against the wall of one's existing reality in an effort to regain existential meaning and after getting nowhere with that approach, one comes to despair and hopelessness. There is a "loss of direct contact with one's day-to-day reality" as "the grip of one's old way of thinking about the crisis loosens." This, in short, is what the narrative represents as happening to Lucius in

Books 1 through 10 of the novel, as I have argued in chapters 1 and 2. A resolution of the crisis finally comes when a "light of a new vision" blazes into this dark night of the soul. This event corresponds to the flash of illumination in creativity and, like it, occurs when "old ways of thinking based on the old cognitive structures (e.g., one's desire to live versus the inevitability of one's own death)" are superseded. Such a disentanglement from former modes of thought "permits a new way of looking at the elements of the crisis (e.g., one has already died to the old life and is living an eternal life)" (84). The experience of new vision often includes a sense that physical reality itself has been transformed. I would qualify Batson and Ventis' analogy between creative and religious insight by noting that whereas creative insight really does seem to involve thinking things that have not been thought before, insofar as this is possible, religious insight is not so much creative as adhesive, that is, the answer is found in an established religious discourse. This distinction is meaningless to the convert, however, in whose perspective that discourse is entirely new.

The breakthrough for Lucius comes with his vision of Isis on the beach near Corinth. In connection with her appearance it is worth noting Batson and Ventis' observation about creative illumination: "Often . . . the insight first appears in the form of a visual image" (1982, 78). Isis embodies a system of alternatives to Lucius' old approach to life and the values that it represented, as we will see in more detail in the following chapters. It is important to remember, however, as Batson and Ventis do, that the sort of crisis that they describe need not always have such an apparently happy outcome. On the contrary, the process may involve disillusionment without any kind of compensation or reconstruction; the insight may be that "the only meaning is to be found in being able to live without meaning" (85). This is the progression William James illustrated when he cited the "counter-conversion" of Jouffroy. Batson and Ventis move into existentialism proper for their exemplum; it is Camus' Stranger, who expresses his new vision this way: " 'For the first time, the first, I laid my heart open to the benign indifference of the universe' " (85). I will argue in chapter 5 that in spite of the worlds separating the *Metamorphoses* and the sort of twentieth-century philosophical novel of crisis without the conversion, so to speak, that *L'étranger* represents, there are still enough common threads that they can be instructively compared.

To complete their model of religious experience, Batson and Ventis, noting that "a dramatic shift in reality should work to produce a dramatic shift in behavior as well," designate the final stage as one in which a "new life" is built (1982, 85–86). They conclude by reiterating their thesis that in many cases the religious experience of individuals is a process of cognitive restructuring that occurs in response to one or more existential questions. In emphasizing this strain of religious experience, with its primarily cognitive operations, they seek to counterbalance another common line of investigation, one which stresses the emotional aspects of the experience as the key to understanding it (they cite Otto 1923 and Pruyser 1968; we will encounter others as we proceed). Batson and Ventis, on the contrary, are convinced that it is the cognitive process and not attendant emotions that "reveals the basic nature of the experience" (86–87). The final observations in their discussion of personal religious experience involve the proposition that religious experience (as a solution to existential problems), like intellectual problem solving, can be creative or noncreative (87–89). Noncreative religious experience might take the form of escapism; alternatively, it might involve a closed, nondynamic solution "in the form of dogmatic beliefs and rules of conduct" that impose "rigid and arbitrary conceptualizations on one's experience" (87). Creative religious experience, on the other hand, is dynamic and open to further transformation. As Batson and Ventis summarize the distinction:

> One may have a reality-transforming religious experience that invites further transformation or one that forecloses it. In the former case, the new reality is recognized as a tentative and transient construction, one that will probably undergo future change. . . . In the latter case, the new reality is perceived as *true* reality. It is assumed that one has been given an insight into the mysteries of life that cannot be improved upon, an insight that has definitively answered one or more existential questions. Although such insight may have dramatically positive effects in infusing life with meaning and direction, it would seem to discourage further religious development. . . . Both of these types of religious experience involve new vision, but the former is more creative than the latter. (88)

The distinction between these two modes of religiosity has something of an Apuleian analogue in the two attitudes toward the conversion of

Lucius that are inscribed in the Isisbook. As much as it may seem to the *actor* that everything has finally fallen into place, the detached and skeptical author suggests, through the ironic undertow in his representation of the experience, that Lucius the *actor* is naïve in thinking that he has found true reality. Instead of mounting to a "higher" order of reality, he has simply made a lateral move; all the convert has done is trade one arbitrary system of constructs for another and then delude himself by elevating the latest system to the status of "truth." Apuleius implies that for the sake of security, Lucius the *actor* buys into the sort of "rigid and arbitrary conceptualization [of] experience" that, according to Batson and Ventis, characterizes noncreative and nondynamic religious experience. In contrast, the recognition that the new religious reality— or any reality—is a "tentative and transient construction" is to be identified in the *Metamorphoses* with the *auctor* Apuleius, although of course it is not open *religion* in Batson and Ventis' sense that this attitude represents.[25]

Many other studies either anticipate or echo Batson and Ventis in their focus on the cognitive aspects of conversion, and in particular on

---

25. Batson and Ventis conclude their discussion of the stages of religious experience with an addendum in which they consider the empirical status of their model (1982, 89–95). Their examination of the hypothesis that there is a correlation between existential crisis and religious experience is most relevant to our purposes. Citing a number of studies from the 1970s, they find that the empirical evidence is "generally consistent" with their correlation, "although the evidence is far from conclusive." Batson and Ventis acknowledge certain methodological failings in some of the studies, such as the absence of control groups and the old problem of the reliability of narratives composed after the fact. The fact would appear to be that one could cite studies to support virtually any view of the genesis of religious experience; the dispute between Heirich and Ullman, noted below, is only one case of contradictory findings. This might be a good place to remind the reader that we are not so much concerned here with recovering actual religious experience (if indeed that is possible) as we are with situating the *Metamorphoses* in a system of representations and analyses of it.

It is also worth noting, although incidental to our main purpose, that Batson and Ventis in the same addendum cite two studies that suggest a correlation between a temperamental "openness to experience" and life-transforming religious experiences. We recall Lucius the wide-eyed *credulus* of *Metamorphoses* 1 and his stated credo, *nihil impossibile arbitror*.

the disintegrative aspects of the period before conversion. These studies stress the primacy of cognitive elements, as opposed to emotional, moral, or social factors, in paving the way for conversion (although of course these elements can coexist, especially the cognitive and the social if we accept the proposition that cognitive systems are socially determined and maintained). I will limit my discussion to a few representative studies, beginning with the important and frequently cited article of Heirich (1977). Heirich starts by observing that social scientists have tended to explain conversion as a way of coping with emotional stress or as the result of certain kinds of social interactions. He isolates three general lines of assumption and inquiry in the previous literature (656–57). Conversion is viewed, first of all, as being a "fantasy solution to stress"; this is the implicitly disapproving perspective of much of the later psychological and psychoanalytical literature (beginning with Freud 1927), as well as of a prominent strain of political analysis going back to Marx. The second common explanation of conversion is framed in terms of previous conditioning; it looks, writes Heirich, for circumstances of socialization "that . . . leave one ripe for the plucking." A third explanatory theme concentrates on immediate social interactions, "patterns of interpersonal influence," and changes in reference group that draw the impressionable preconvert into the sphere of another world view.

In his discussion of previous efforts to support or refute these claims, Heirich notes that the results are variable, but that the tests to which the hypotheses are put consistently lack rigor, the absence of control groups being one of the most glaring deficiencies (657–60). The substance of Heirich's article is a description of his own test of emotional stress, previous socialization, and immediate social influence as factors leading to conversion, based on the responses of a group of converts to Catholic Pentecostalism (660–72). In brief, he found that his indicators for all three factors occurred with enough frequency among the control group to undermine the claim that those factors are necessarily to be associated with conversion. Heirich argues that the methods of previous studies are misguided. As he puts it:

[T]he organization of evidence in this form is specious. To show that something influences the likelihood of conversion, one should group respondents in terms of the presence or absence of that influence on them. Then one should note the proportion of converts present within each group. One need not argue that the influence will lead everyone to convert. (There could be a variety of ways to respond to that influence.) Nor need one argue that no one lacking that influence will convert. (There could be several routes to conversion.) But if the influence works as claimed, the proportion of converts should be noticeably higher when the influence is present than when it is absent. (664–65)

When he reorganizes his own study along the lines that he suggests here, he discovers that "support drops away for theories that explain religious conversion entirely in terms of psychological stress or previous socialization" (673).

Rather than continuing to design studies that simply replicate invalidated presuppositions and methods, Heirich suggests that those investigating conversion should fundamentally shift their analytical focus. They should begin to conceptualize conversion not as a form of emotional dysfunction or a type of adaptation to social environment, but rather as one manifestation of a cognitive "process that seems fundamental to human existence": the "assertion of a sense of ultimate grounding—one that provides a clear basis for understanding reality, that provides meaning and orientation for understanding one's situation and acting in relation to it" (673). Once we begin to think of conversion as the "process of changing a sense of root reality" (674), two basic questions present themselves for further investigation. First, under what circumstances does clarity about one's old root reality disintegrate? Second, how does an alternative sense of grounding emerge, and what must it be able to do that the old one failed to do? Heirich notes that beginning the study of conversion with these questions would tie it more closely to "the growing body of literature that treats religion . . . as efforts to discover a ground of being that orients and orders experience" (674).

Heirich formulates his two questions primarily as a starting point for future investigation. He does, however, offer preliminary suggestions as to the lines along which he thinks such investigation might proceed. The religious tradition suggests, he writes, that "a person's sense of ultimate reality" might shift when one of three circumstances arises. The first set of circumstances concerns us most. It involves "experiences or encounters" that "cannot be encompassed within current explanatory schemes yet cannot be ignored"; such experiences can destroy the hold of "present understandings of root reality" (674). This is the condition in which Lucius finds himself (as did Tolstoy) as he struggles in his own inept way with questions of human values and the meaning of life in the face of death.[26] Heirich continues by predicting that the new reality adopted by converts will "offer a solution to the particular experiences that have broken the hold of past explanations" (675). The question of whether Isis offers such a particular solution for Lucius will be central to my discussion of the Isisbook in chapter 6. In conclusion, Heirich suggests that the literature in the history and philosophy of science concerning the shift to "new paradigms" that often occurs in the course of scientific inquiry could be used to illuminate the dynamics of how an alternative sense of grounding emerges in the conversion process (675–76); he cites Kuhn (1962) in particular. He ends with a statement of the value of the approach that he proposes for understanding attitude change in general:

> Rather than treat [converts] as deviants, we might learn more about both their experiences and social processes generally if we approach them as offering a unique vantage point for examining the establishment and disestablishment of root senses of reality. (677)

We should not treat conversion as an "odd experience" but as "one form of a fundamental human encounter," as a particular expression of a generic phenomenon.[27]

---

26. Heirich's other two sets of circumstances are: (1) "when . . . unacceptable outcomes appear imminent . . . if current understandings of root reality are correct"; and (92) (he is more tentative about this condition) when "respected leaders publicly abandon some part of past grounding assumptions" (675).

27. Ullman (1982) (see also 1989) takes issue with Heirich by offering a critique of cognitive approaches, including his, her main complaint being the lack of empirical testing. She then designs and conducts her own test of cognitive vs. emotional antecedents to conversion, which yields results indicating that psychodynamic factors (such as turmoil in childhood and adolescence) are much more important than cognitive ones. But Ullman's indicators for cognitive stress—low tolerance of ambiguity and *conscious* cognitive quest—seem very limited. It bears remembering that the psychiatric tradition in which Ullman is working harbors a set of unfavorable assumptions about religion.

Heirich's reference to Kuhnian paradigm shifts comes as a kind of postscript in his study. Jones (1978), on the other hand, moves the analogy to a central place in his analysis of conversion (which he calls "alternation").[28] He tests the Kuhnian model not on religious converts in the usual sense but on secular converts, such as new members of Alcoholics Anonymous and the British Socialist Party, and finds that it can be applied to these groups. Jones thus provides further support for the claim that a generic psychological process can underlie superficially disparate conversions. Jones' interest in Kuhn's work lies in the latter's argument that socially constructed paradigms—that is (in Kuhn's words), "'set[s] of conceptual, methodological, and metaphysical assumptions'"—control problem solving in a scientific setting and in effect limit the ways in which problems can be approached (Jones 1978: 66). When a paradigm can no longer account for empirical reality, it crumbles under the strain and is replaced by another one that can. Jones notes that Kuhn himself speaks in religious terms about paradigm shifts in science. In writing of the "'neural reprogramming that . . . must underlie conversion,'" Kuhn observes that:

> "Scientists . . . often speak of the 'scales falling from the eyes' or of the 'lightning flash' that 'inundates' a previously obscure puzzle, enabling its components to be seen in a new way that for the first time permits its solution." (Jones 67, quoting Kuhn 1962, 204; 122–23)

As Jones observes, this is exactly the sort of language found in accounts of conversion, "whether it is gradual or sudden, secular or supernatural" (67). The parallels discernible from one type of paradigm shift to another bring to the fore a general truism of which we often lose sight: that ways of seeing are relative. It is possible for both social and natural phenomena to come to be viewed in a way radically different from the usual one if the foundations of the old perspective are shaken (68).[29]

---

28. Jones' chapter from 1978 is substantially the same as his article of 1977. A work as original as Kuhn's is not, of course, without detractors: see Jones (1978, 67) and the citations there.

29. Jones' stress on the idea that both social and natural phenomena can take on a new and different aspect reminds us that the altered world of Lucius has two components: the physical or natural and the social. Jones points out that Wittgenstein, among others, was very interested in the phenomenon of transformed perception: "'But what is different: my impression? my point of

Jones incorporates this truism and the magnitude of its implications into his definition of conversion: it is not just some "internal," emotional experience but a matter of interaction between inner consciousness and the external universe. It is "a reorganization of the 'world' in a transformative manner with a concomitant plausibility structure to maintain the new reality" (69).

Throughout his work Jones stresses, as do others, that a generic process of alternation can take place within any number of cultural systems. He also maintains that this process is essentially the same whether it takes place spontaneously as the result of natural ripening, so to speak, or is the object of some form of externally imposed psychological engineering. In connection with this latter set of circumstances, Jones describes how one's world view "can be changed or managed by covert and overt manipulation" through a process of directed "stripping down" and "remodelling." He cites as examples of engineered attitude change the sort of "rehabilitation" or resocialization that goes on in drug treatment programs and in prisons (60–62; see also McHugh below). The guided dismantling and reconstruction of world view takes less obviously coercive forms as well; one such form is the shift aimed for in the psychotherapeutic process, as we will see. The important thing for us is that, growing out of a range of impulses and meshing with a variety of discourses, there is a common "process of transformation from one world view to another [which embraces] both secular and transcendental areas of activity" (60).[30]

To illustrate this further, Jones cites the language used by converts to socialism, homosexuality, and a newly adopted abstinence from drugs and alcohol to describe both their period of drifting and the moment of truth when the "scales fell from their eyes" (70–71). He also invokes

---

view?—Can I say? I describe the alternation like a perception; quite as if the object had altered before my eyes.' Something has become reorganized; a new organization has emerged; 'My visual impression has changed.' Situations and objects are *interpreted*, but there is no 'inner picture' but 'a chimera; a queerly shifting construction'" (Jones 1978, 68, quoting from Wittgenstein 1953).

30. Mitchell (1973, 137) puts it this way: "'Conversion from liberal democracy to Marxism or from humanism to naturalism . . . involves as radical a transformation as conversion to or from Christianity. . . . [I]t involves, intellectually, a massive shift in the overall appreciation and assessment of an immense range of facts and experiences and, with this, a new pattern of feeling and acting'" (cited in Jones 1978, 77 n. 10).

Arthur Koestler's account of his conversion to communism, in which the latter remembers how at the moment of "enlightenment," after a long intellectual struggle, he felt as if "'the whole universe [fell] into a pattern like the stray pieces of a jigsaw assembled by magic at one stroke'" (Koestler 1951, quoted in Jones 71).[31] My point in stressing the generic nature of the conversion process is this: if the comparison of disparate religious and secular accounts in modern studies suggests a common process at work from conversion to conversion, then it stands to reason that the same process could underlie conversion in an ancient pagan religious and philosophical setting, in spite of the tradition of assuming that pagan religious conversion was a rather bloodless affair, long on ritual and short on cognitive or emotional content. If this inference is valid, then the pattern of cognitive disintegration and reconstruction that keeps asserting itself as the defining feature of the process in modern accounts and studies would be at home in an ancient narrative of conversion such as the *Metamorphoses*.

It would be needlessly repetitive to belabor my point by continuing to summarize studies of religious conversion that seek to explain it by comparing other kinds of attitude change exhibiting the same underlying pattern.[32] But now that this pattern has been established as being integral to much of the discussion of conversion in general, it will be useful to consider descriptions of coerced or directed paradigm shifting, such as "brainwashing" and "deprogramming," because their language is equally evocative of Lucius' preconversion experience as rep-

---

31. In a note Jones mentions briefly several other cases of secular conversion, of which perhaps the most evocative is that of Patty Hearst to the world view of the Symbionese Liberation Army. Quoting from an affidavit published in a newspaper, Jones describes Hearst's sojourn in paradigm limbo before the world view of her captors established itself: "'All sorts of fantastic shapes and images kept coming and going before her eyes, so that the faces of the kidnappers and jailors appeared to her as weird and horrible masks. . . . [H]er mind became more distorted and confused. . . . She finally came to the realization that she was becoming insane'" (1978, 77 n. 11). This surreal vision suggests parallels with Lucius' preconversion perspective.

32. For argument in the same vein as that paraphrased above, see, e.g., Greil 1977 and Jules-Rosette 1975. Greil builds his analysis around the idea that one's cognitive reality has several components, including perspective and stock of knowledge, both of which can be discredited when they fail to mesh with empirical reality. When that happens, one must search for a new perspective that will restore meaning and a viable world view. Although Jules-Rosette does

resented in the *Metamorphoses*. One such description, or, more pre-cisely, prescription, is that of McHugh (1966). He accepts the hypothe-sis that a disintegration of one's established world view is a prerequi-site for any radical change in outlook and applies it to the rehabilitation (that is, resocialization) of members of prison populations. In order to alter the antisocial attitudes and behaviors of these subjects, McHugh proposes that the efficacy of their old values must first be erased through a deliberately engineered process of (in his terms) "desocial-ization" or "programmed alienation" from their current social order. For rehabilitation to be successful, McHugh asserts, it must be pre-ceded by unlearning, which necessarily will be attended by a sense of disorientation and disintegration. Such a period of alienation and normlessness—of anomy—must be engineered because this state encourages the disintegration of previous systems of value, which is in turn a condition of change in the form of resocialization according to the values of the dominant culture. As McHugh puts it, "disintegration [is] the social condition which precedes rehabilitation" (356).

McHugh offers a program detailing how the powers that be might create programmed alienation in the target population (360–62). The two basic components of this program are the dislocation of the sub-jects' sequence of activity and the subversion of their interpersonal rela-tionships. To achieve the first goal, measures must be taken to "decon-stitute" the subjects' social organization, so that events begin to seem unpredictable and "normatively meaningless." Imposing a random sequence of events will destroy the assumption that events can be

---

not offer any such systematic scheme, her account of her own almost inadver-tent conversion to membership in an indigenous African Christian church, the Apostles of John Maranke, is of great cross-cultural interest. It contains much relevant, if unelaborated, talk about a "new order of reality," changes in her "perceived body of knowledge," the "reconstruction of assumptions," a "new vocabulary and set of cognitive operations," "conceptual and emotional restructuring," and the "suspension of ordinary expectations" (passim). Under the shock of the "shift from one realm of thought and action to another," she writes, "the very physical terms of existence seem to alter. . . . The candidate on the threshold of conversion begins to orient toward objects and events in a new way" (135). The physicality in this description reminds us of the shifting nature of Lucius' physical world in *Metamorphoses* 1–10. It is worth noting that Jules-Rosette invokes William James at several points in her article and consistently frames her account of her experience in his terms.

ordered, influenced, or categorized on the basis of past observation for the purpose of predicting cause and effect. The resulting fragmentation or absence of connection among discrete occurrences causes the meaning of those events to cease to be self-evident. To achieve the second goal of the program, those in charge must arrange for a continuous turnover in the subjects' group composition, so that their social interactions will appear to consist of a series of contacts with individuals so random and fleeting that systems of reciprocity cannot develop. Given the crucial role that social interactions play in maintaining structures of knowledge, the resulting isolation of the subject further undermines his or her habituated ways of processing reality.

Reducing the subject's physical and social environment to a chain of "suspicious encounters between strangers and meaningless links between events" produces over time the desired state of "desocialization," that is, the breakdown of the authority of old systems of valorization. The subject, as McHugh writes, " 'becomes *tabula rasa* as to the previous conceptions of the meaningful life.' "[33] Now, "*tabula rasa* as to the previous conceptions of the meaningful life" is precisely what I have argued Lucius is by the end of *Metamorphoses* 10. Certainly, a "dislocated sequence of activity" and the episodic character of his social contacts are central features of his experience before he is "resocialized" by Isis. The only difference between McHugh's prisoners, on the one hand, and Lucius and Tolstoy, on the other, is that the former have their disorientation induced for them from without, whereas for the latter the "previous conceptions" are erased through a spontaneous process. In both types of change we see the correlation between the collapse of values or "desocialization" (Berger's "separation from the social world") and a fragmentation of one's perception of the world in both its material and social aspects. The equation can work in two directions: the undermining of coherence and connection can lead to the breakdown of rationalizing values, or such a breakdown can lead to a perception of incoherence and lack of connection. In any case, new values emerge as a kind of glue reuniting the world's fractured parts.

In an article on the forced "deprogramming" of cult members, Kim (1979) delineates essentially the same steps in the process of resocialization. Religious deprogramming, he argues, is an instance of the "social construction of subjective reality," like conversion itself or vir-

---

33. McHugh (1966, 363), quoting Leites 1953.

tually any kind of socialization. It is a reverse conversion or "deconversion" and, like the former, a process during which one is "led to dismantle and disintegrate the nomic structure of his/her subjective reality and, then, [to switch] to another world—a new or the previously held reality" (197). The process is managed in three distinct phases. In the "unfreezing" phase, the existing epistemological equilibrium of the cultist is destabilized, so as to create a need or motive to change systems of belief. The cultist's "locked mind is opened," so that his or her current subjective reality is seen in a critical light and the beliefs inscribed in it begin to seem misguided and false (202–3). This is McHugh's tabula rasa phase. The next step is "changing" or reorienting the cultist's cognitive structure toward a new equilibrium, presumably one that is more in conformity with that of respectable society (204–5). Finally, during "refreezing," the new equilibrium is integrated into the personality and reinforced by a system of social rewards, a tactic that had figured in the subject's seduction by the cult in the first place (205–6).

Kim lays a great deal of stress on the importance of an "agent of change" (a deprogrammer) and external influence and reinforcement, which is not surprising since the subject of his analysis is coerced attitude change. We will return to this idea in chapter 6, when we consider Lucius' encounter with a cult in the Isisbook. But I think that the experience of Lucius as represented in *Metamorphoses* 1 through 10 is to be understood as essentially one of spontaneous "unfreezing"; this acts as a kind of inadvertent preparation for his opportune encounter with the cult at a point when he is ripe, even desperate, to be "refrozen." The analogy that I am suggesting here between the "unfreezing" of a cult perspective and the "unfreezing" of Lucius' (or Tolstoy's or Augustine's) conventional values is perhaps more clearly appropriate if we view both the cult perspective and conventional values as products, the one "deviant" and the other normative, of processes of indoctrination that are heavy-handed or more subtle and protracted, as the case may be. Tolstoy understood this when he compared the St. Petersburg literary and social establishment to a religious cult.[34]

---

34. The subjects of Kim's study were former members of the Unification Church (the "Moonies"), Hare Krishna, the Children of God, and the Way of God. The literature on brainwashing and deprogramming from the 1950s (with its obsession with the communist threat) through the 1970s (and its concern

A less violent but equally goal-oriented form of guided attitude change is psychotherapy in all its forms. One of the major differences between the psychotherapeutic process and the kind of coercive persuasion discussed above is that in the former, disengagement from habituated perspectives is not deliberately induced in the initial stages by an outside agent, but rather begins to unfold on its own in response to circumstances or experiences in one's life. Thus the therapist steps in at some point after the process of disintegration has already begun, to direct the change toward a desired type of reconstruction. In this sense the psychotherapist acts as the priest or guide figure of cult—the Mithras, if you will—intervening with his appealing alternative world view just when the resources of the preconvert's old cognitive structures have been exhausted. The analogy between priest and psychiatrist is a commonplace, in fact, and is one that the literature is unabashed about making. Several studies make explicit comparisons between conversion experience (religious or otherwise, induced or spontaneous) and psychotherapy and stress the crucial role of disintegration of world view in both. Adler and Hammett (1973), for example, use their analysis of the psychosocial dynamics involved in the sequence of "crisis, conversion, and cult formation" to illuminate what happens during psychoanalysis.

They begin—and this will be familiar by now as a common starting point for discussion of conversion in any guise—with the idea of a shared cognitive system. This they define as "a comprehensive, integrated, coherent organization of cognitive structures concerning the total environment . . . [that provides] an understanding of how things 'hang together,' [and enables] man to locate himself spatially and historically [so that he] can face the present without the insecurity of chaos and the future with some assurance of predictability" (1973, 861–62). These structures of meaning are maintained primarily through membership in and interaction with a social group. Adler and Hammett's model of what happens when these structures are strained as a result of their failure to accommodate the subject's empirical reality, or as the result of the subject's separation from his or her reference group, will

---

that religious cults were seducing alienated youth) is enormous. See, for example, Sargant 1961; Schein 1971 (on whom Kim draws extensively); Shupe, Spielman, and Stigall 1977.

also be familiar.[35] An unstable condition of crisis ensues; restabilization comes through the encounter with a new reference group (this phase constitutes conversion proper) and finally through resocialization and the new sense of security that grows out of it (863). Adler and Hammett's perspective on crisis and conversion is essentially a social interactionist one, with its stress on social reference groups and particularly on an agent of change who manipulates the resourceless preconvert. But they also admit the possibility of spontaneously generated crisis when they write that "the motive for change is crisis (*natural* or iatrogenic)" (862, emphasis mine).

Adler and Hammett's point is to suggest that although the discourses involved may vary, the process that they outline is a "common psychosocial sequence" identifiable in many kinds of radical attitude change, including the kind in which they are especially interested, change during psychoanalysis (863–64). Like crisis and conversion in the more standard sense, psychotherapeutic change involves the discrediting and discarding of a crumbling structure of meaning, followed by a period of "cognitive chaos" or crisis as the old system dissolves. It is the responsibility of the analyst qua priest to oversee this process of change and to direct the client's "security-seeking behavior" toward a "stable, cohesive, integrating superstructure" modeled after that of the therapist. When Adler and Hammett style this new structure of meaning a "haven of safety" for the beleaguered analysand, they inadvertently—or perhaps not, given their system of analogies—evoke the conventional language of religious conversion and relief. This language is exemplified in the Isisbook when the priest Mithras informs Lucius that he has anchored himself at last in a "harbor of rest" [*ad portum Quietis*] (11.15). Likewise, the period of "cognitive chaos" that they prescribe as necessarily preceding the safe landing in new conceptual territory has its correspondent in the representation of Lucius' reality in *Metamorphoses* 1–10.

Although his tone and orientation are different in many respects from those of Adler and Hammett, Rogers (1968) also voices the

---

35. The "cults" that provide the material for Adler and Hammett's model of conversion are strictly regimented programs for substance abusers, such as Alcoholics Anonymous and Synanon, as well as regimens designed to "deprogram" "brainwashed" prisoners of war. The range of groups and ideologies finding themselves placed under the "cult" (as the "conversion") umbrella simply underscores the generic character of the processes involved.

repeatedly expressed belief that cognitive collapse and disorder ultimately can be constructive and in fact are necessary ingredients of
growth. He opposes this proposition to the conventional wisdom cor-
relating order with mental health and "reality," and chaos with mental
illness and alienation (249). On the contrary, Rogers asserts, the construction of order on both the personal and the objective or cosmic levels is often deceptive and defensive; he echoes Berger in his assertion of
the defensive character of world construction. The minds of the mentally ill, according to Rogers, are not chaotic and disintegrated, but
rather locked into systems of defensive hyperordering. Mental illness is
a private quest for order, begun when the appearance of threats to the
established cognitive structure—for example, an event or problem that
cannot be incorporated into that system—creates anxiety (249–50,
252–54). In this analysis it is the perception of a rigid order and not of
fluidity that is "distorted" (258). The details of Rogers' philosophical
and theological musings need not concern us, but his main point
should: that chaos must be embraced and integrated both at the level of
personal psychic maintenance and at the "cosmic" level, that is, the
level of religious experience. Like Adler and Hammett, Rogers advises
that the client be allowed to experience a period of deep ambiguity and
"disturbed, disordered" feelings and encouraged to assimilate these
somehow into the reconstructed order. Here, as in so many treatments
of conversion of one stripe or another, disintegration is the first step
toward reconstruction, often but not always on a firmer foundation
(250, 259–60).

Rogers recommends the same approach to religious experience: one
must open oneself to "the chaos of alienation and meaninglessness" in
order for a "new integrative order" to be able to materialize (260).
Rogers' conviction of the "chaotic undercurrents of religious experience" (261) is one for which we could find an abundance of documen-
tation in pagan antiquity. Similarly, his view, asserted by others as
well, that disorder and indeterminacy, as traumatic as they may be
when actually experienced, can ultimately lead to apparently positive
results is discernible in our ancient narrative of religious experience,
the *Metamorphoses*.[36] I argued in chapter 2 that Lucius' affair with the

---

36. Besides Rogers, the others holding this view include Dabrowski (1964),
Boisen (1936), and Frankl (1963). Boisen and Frankl are interested in explicitly
associating what is commonly viewed as mental breakdown with spiritual

Corinthian matron is represented in such a way as to suggest that an event that makes a mockery of conventional boundaries has the potential to begin to exhibit a sense and integrity of its own when viewed from a new perspective. We are afforded a similar glimpse at the liberating potential of the old order's disintegration in the picture of the carnivalesque *anteludia* leading the procession at the festival of Isis in *Metamorphoses* 11.8. There, indeterminacy is symbolically embraced in ritual and celebrated rather than resisted. Thus the novel incorporates both the horrific and the liberating aspects of disorder. Which of these aspects is seen by any given subject is largely a function of whether an obsolete structure is clung to out of fear or let go with equanimity.

I have attempted to show that there is a persistent strain in the literature on conversion and related phenomena, going back to James, that regards a sequence of cognitive disintegration, disorientation, and reconstruction as central to the process. This literature, along with autobiographical, poetic, and fictional representations of crisis and conversion that are built around the same sequence, comprises the generic tradition, if you will, in which I seek to resituate the *Metamorphoses*. Regardless of the impetus behind the conversions in the studies cited above, the descriptions in them of the disintegrative phase—the crisis—are all strongly evocative of the representation of Lucius' reality in the first ten books of the novel. To be sure, there are differences between the preconversion experience of Lucius and the experience as it is described in some of the above discussions. The most obvious is that Lucius' conversion is unambiguously religious; he is not being psychoanalyzed or brainwashed in political ideology, nor is he a scientist working through a paradigm shift. But the apparently generic features of fundamental attitude change that assert themselves in a variety of settings make all these descriptions of the process useful for understanding what Lucius is depicted as going through. The fact that Lucius'

---

growth and religious experience; Dabrowski confines himself to developmental psychology. For classically psychoanalytical (Freudian) analyses of conversion, see, e.g., Allison 1969 and Salzman 1953. In general, these have too much of a focus on parent-centered complexes and too pathologizing a view of religious belief to be useful for our purposes, but our pattern of disintegration and reconstruction emerges in them as well. See especially Allison: conversion brought structure, wholeness, integration, and meaning to the subjects' previously fragmented, undifferentiated, and structureless reality.

crisis and conversion occur spontaneously without external coercion or guidance further distinguishes his experience from the conversions in some of the studies above; but again, the underlying process is the same. Finally, it would appear that the nature of his crisis in values is not clearly formulated in his mind; accordingly, his search for a "new paradigm" is presented as misguided and inept. We will see in chapter 4 that a crisis thus experienced and acted out is not without parallel in both narratives of conversion and analyses of it. All these differences are compatible with my general model of crisis and conversion.

3

In conclusion, it will be useful to look briefly at four important schematizing studies of conversion that are not centrally concerned with paradigm shift but that are nevertheless relevant to assessing the "authenticity" of the picture of crisis and conversion presented in the *Metamorphoses*. Lofland and Stark (1965) worked with a contemporary American millenarian movement flourishing on the West Coast in the 1960s to develop a "value-added model of the conditions under which conversion occurs" (862).[37] This model entails seven steps or conditions, all of which are necessary and sequential. The first three are factors of the subject's predisposition: a feeling of tension between reality and life as it "should" be; a tendency to solve problems within a religious perspective; and self-definition as a religious seeker. The last four are situational factors: arrival at a "turning point" shortly before the encounter with a cult, a point at which all the old lines of action have been exhausted and the necessity of trying a different approach is inescapable; then, encounter with a cult and the development of strong affective bonds with one or more of its members; next, the neglect of ties with those outside the cult; and finally, intensive interaction with cult members.

Does the conversion of Lucius as represented by Apuleius conform to this pattern? Lofland and Stark formulate the character of the precipitating tension in a way that is general enough to allow us to equate it with the frustration implicit in Lucius' dogged but ultimately unsatisfying pursuit of gratification in the sources to which he has always

---

37. For critiques of Lofland and Stark see, for example, Seggar and Kunz 1972; Austin 1977; Snow and Phillips 1980; and Lofland's own reassessment (1977).

turned for it in the past. His arid voluptuary patterns are, as I will show, symptomatic of his "existential crisis." The question of whether Lucius' regular problem-solving perspective can be understood as a religious one is more complicated. It is true that when Fotis implores him not to divulge her mistress' magical feats, she says that she trusts him because he has been "initiated into many mysteries" and therefore knows how to keep a secret. But it is unclear how she would know this about him, or that her remark is anything more than a proverbial way of expressing her confidence that he knows how to keep his mouth shut.[38] Further, even if Lucius is to be taken as a multiple initiate—and this would not have been unusual for a young man with his status and connections in a syncretistic age—there is no reason to believe that by participating in these rituals he was slaking anything more than his chronic thirst for novel experiences. These previous religious initiations could have consisted entirely of formal actions devoid of the metaphysical, cognitive, and emotional content evident in his relationship with Isis and implied as the goal of a "religious problem-solving perspective" in Lofland and Stark's conception of it.

I think that Richardson (1979) comes closer to describing Lucius' problem-solving perspective when he includes among the possibilities the "physiological" and the "conventional" perspectives (238–39).[39] Richardson defines the former as "the use of elements or activities to affect the body and mind in a way that furnishes some 'meaning' for the person," and gives as examples indulgence in sex and drugs, the first of which at least is consistently an impulse of Lucius before his conversion. But I think that the "conventional" perspective—which Richardson also calls the "muddle through" perspective—is an even more fitting formulation to describe Lucius' approach to life. When confronted with the profound questions of life, people committed to this perspective respond by even more aggressively pursuing the activities that they have been socialized to think will make them happy—in Richardson's list of illustrations, "getting a divorce, getting married, moving, changing jobs, taking a holiday, dropping out of school, affili-

---

38. This is Winkler's view of Fotis' comment (1985, 319 n. 77 on *Metamorphoses* 3.15).

39. Richardson's other perspectives are the psychiatric, the political, and the religious. He and his associates based their conclusions on observation of a Christian commune that typified the "Jesus Movement" popular among youth in the United States in the late 1960s to the mid-1970s.

ating with a conventional religious (or another type of) group," throwing themselves into child rearing, or resorting to "mass media addiction, . . . immersion in work, and, more spectacularly, alcoholism, suicide, and promiscuity." Lofland and Stark recognize these activities as indirect responses to unarticulated existential questions, too, when they comment on the human capacity to grasp at "compensations for or distractions from problems of living" by executing "a number of maneuvers to put the problem out of mind" (1965, 868). According to Richardson, it is often the case that these "quite 'normal' activities are deliberate or even unconscious attempts to solve felt problems" (1979, 239). I will argue in the next chapter that Lucius' stubborn persistence in looking for satisfaction where he has always found it can be read as part of an elaborate and unconsciously driven diversionary strategy.

Richardson takes issue with the claim of Lofland and Stark that in order for a religious conversion to take place the preconvert's perspective must be a religious one. It is possible for problem-solving perspectives to shift in the course of crisis and conversion, he argues, if the former perspective is discredited by its clear inability to move one out of one's current rut and toward some kind of solution (257, 259). The way to a shift in Lucius' perspective toward one that allows for a religious resolution is paved, I think, by the manifest bankruptcy of his habituated approach, which keeps him on a treadmill of wearily repetitive desires and pleasures. If we accept Richardson's view that perspectives can be crossed in the course of the conversion process, then the status of Lofland and Stark's third condition (that the preconvert must define himself as a religious seeker) as a necessary one is undermined. This is especially true in view of the unconscious character of much seeking and the fact that, as Richardson puts it, "felt needs" can be "amorphous and little understood" (259). Lofland and Stark's fourth step and the first of the situational factors—the arrival at a turning point when old lines of action have been exhausted and the issue of a new approach is forced—would seem, however, to characterize Lucius perfectly as he makes his escape from the arena at Corinth and collapses in an exhausted heap on the beach at the end of Book 10.[40]

Lofland collaborated with Skonovd to produce another schematizing study, organized this time not around steps or conditions but rather around "conversion motifs" or types of conversion experience.

---

40. See chapter 6, section 3 for discussion of Lofland and Stark's final three conditions as they relate to Lucius.

Of their six motifs, the conversion of Lucius, while fictional, would seem to represent a combination of three: the intellectual, the mystical, and the affectional. Intellectually centered conversions involve conscious investigation and an active quest for answers to clearly perceived cosmic questions; they have a heavy cognitive element (1981, 376–77). Lucius too is on such a quest, I think, and his cognitive organs are being restructured; the difference is that none of this is happening in a clearly formulated, conscious way. In mystical conversions, on the other hand, the subject is passive and prior to the conversion experiences a long period of stress and a "sense of estrangement and unreality" (377–78). No adjustment is needed to make this an apt description of Lucius. Finally, conversions in which the affectional element is primary hinge on the role of the preconvert's emotional attachments to believers in pulling him into the new reference group (379–80). In chapter 6 we will look more closely at Lucius' relationship with his mentor/father figure, Mithras, and how it influences the direction that his solution takes.[41]

A final study warranting mention is that of Sarbin and Adler. Like many others, they consider religious conversion to be one manifestation of a generic process of "self-reconstitution," which can also occur in political, military, and social contexts and be set in motion by coercive and psychotherapeutic persuasion, as well as by religious longings. Their schematizing framework identifies themes that they found to be common across a range of manifestations of this process. The first theme, that of "death and rebirth," takes in the entire sequence of cognitive strain and restructuring that occurs in response to the failure of customary beliefs and values (1970, 606–10). There is no need to reiterate the importance of this theme to the representation of Lucius' experience, but it will also be noted that the entire protracted process of cognitive death and rebirth experienced by the *actor* in Books 1 through 11 is symbolically reenacted during his initiation in the Isisbook (especially 11.23). For now, I am still concerned primarily with the sort of crisis that can precede conversion. In order to demonstrate the persistence across social scientific and literary genres of the type of narrative of crisis that I have identified, I now turn to autobiographical, fictional, and poetic representations of it.

---

41. Lofland and Skonovd's other three motifs or types are the experimental, the revivalist, and the coercive.

4

Autobiographical Representation

1

In chapter 3, I drew on a range of modern studies of conversion and related phenomena to establish an operative model of preconversion experience that involves a comprehensive alienation of the subject from what Ebel calls the "structures of understanding that enable us to locate ourselves in the universe" (1970, 161). My focus there was on the way conversion is theorized in William James and his heirs as a shift in cognitive paradigms, and on how preconversion experience is widely understood as the disintegration of old paradigms of knowledge and value. As a result of this epistemic rupture, the world constructed according to those old paradigms—a world that had been familiar and comfortable—becomes palpably defamiliarized in the subject's perception. In many cases the old paradigms are the site for the inscription of a conventional system of goals and rewards whose value has always been unquestioned but which now seems inadequate to the task of making sense of other, newly obtruding aspects of reality. Thus the literature of religious conversion is full of enlightened narrators' recollections of how the values and pursuits of the conventional world were gradually exposed to them as "false" and diversionary, and the pleasures deriving from them as fleeting and therefore (to this way of thinking) meaningless. It is this new way of perceiving familiar activities, the narrator typically recalls, that drove him or her to embark on a quest for some source of enduring satisfaction to compensate for the failure of the achievements of conventional life to truly satisfy, overshadowed as they are by the specter of death. That the impetus for the search lies in anxiety about death may or may not be explicitly stated. In Tolstoy it emphatically is, as we have seen; it will become clear that the *Metamorphoses* has its own ways of expressing this anxiety.

Narratives of conversion thus often represent a longing and search for a transcendent center to anchor the slippery and unstable and therefore (again, in this view) ultimately meaningless semiotic field of every-day experience. The idea of the exposure of "false" values and the dis-covery of "true" ones in the divine, especially as it expresses itself in the notion that there are proper and improper objects of desire and sources of pleasure, is therefore one construction or interpretation that can be imposed on a breakdown of habituated structures of meaning, and it is the one that will especially concern us in the present chapter. This is because it is this particular form that paradigm shift tends to assume when it is played out in a religious (or philosophical) context, when the subject, for whatever reasons, experiences and expresses the shift in religious terms. The reader should, therefore, bear in mind that in spite of the moralistic coloring of accounts in this tradition and the appar-ently circumscribed character of the model, a scheme of conversion as a crisis in values is one particular manifestation of the generic shift in cognitive paradigms discussed in chapter 3. Values are, after all, a kind of knowledge. Socially constructed valorizations determine the kind of world that we build and call objective. Thus when one experiences the obsolescence of an old structure of values, this constitutes a crisis of meaning as well as of morals; it represents an epistemological break as well as an ethical one. It is this interpenetration of values and knowl-edge that connects the following discussion with the previous chapters and their focus on epistemological instability.

The pattern of the gradual exposure of conventional values as "false" and the subsequent floundering of the subject until "true" val-ues reveal themselves can be richly illustrated by examining how it appears in what is commonly regarded as the paradigmatic narrative of conversion in Western literature, the *Confessions* of St. Augustine. I will argue that the pattern can be discerned mutatis mutandis in the *Meta-morphoses* as well, and that it is an integral element in the representation of Lucius' preconversion crisis. As has consistently been the case, the point of my comparison of the novel with later narratives of conversion is to establish a new context for reading the *Metamorphoses* in the absence of comparable first-person accounts of pagan conversion either contemporary with or earlier than the novel itself. The common North African origins of Apuleius and Augustine and the rhetorical profes-sion that they shared have suggested comparison of the *Metamorphoses* and the *Confessions* on certain limited points, such as the theme of curiosity. What has not been understood is that in spite of the one being an ultimately unresolved polysemic fiction and the other a solemn religious autobiography, the two accounts are bound together by a much more fundamental and persistent thematic link. The crisis in values from which each *actor* is represented as suffering constitutes the first stage in the comprehensive paradigm shift that characterizes a large proportion of conversions generically. Each work has its own ways of expressing the Tolstoyan anhedonia—the listless loss of appetite for life's ordinary values—that accompanies the growing suspicion that there must be more to life than the conventional pursuits on which most people unthinkingly expend their energies.

In Lucius' case, once the pleasures that had produced meaning in his life seem no longer capable of performing that function—in other words, to put a slightly different cast on it, once the underpinnings of his epistemic system fail—he finds himself in a sort of free fall involving the slippage of foundations at all levels and in all aspects of his reality. I have discussed in chapters 1 and 2 how the novel represents this disoriented state of epistemological limbo—of anomy, in Berger's terms. I went on to argue in chapter 3 that Tolstoy's account of his pre-conversion state of mind involves a similar sense of being suspended in a formless void. Augustine does not go quite this far, at least not in any overt way. Still, the core of the movement from crisis to conversion in all these cases involves a gradual and complete inversion in the order of what is to be valued, which is often expressed in terms of whether it is a proper or an improper object of desire. This makes the *Confessions* a very instructive parallel to the *Metamorphoses*, since the way in which the initial slippage is formulated in the two works is strikingly similar across the apparent gulf of genre. Furthermore, both the crisis in values and the resulting anhedonia in themselves constitute a state of anomy, a kind of epistemological break, and represent the first stages of movement toward a shift in basic paradigms, that is, toward conversion to participation in the realm of "true" value. Among all the narratives that I have treated or will discuss, what we have are differences in the degree of extremity and in the ways of representing the crisis, rather than any fundamental difference in what the components of that crisis are.

The basic pattern uniting the *Confessions* and the *Metamorphoses* goes deeper than any conventional act-oriented notion of sin and redemption. Rather, it hinges on the idea that the sensible world in all its aspects is characterized by *fallacia*—deception—or, in the words of a modern student of Augustine, on the growing conviction that we mortals inhabit a "bodily world of mendacious imitations of Truth" (O'Connell 1969, 15). Both narrators describe a past when they found themselves entangled in a widely accepted web of false values. Both formulate this system of false values as an equation involving desire and pleasure: their problems began, each narrator suggests, because virtually all their activities were driven by misguided desires. The narratives follow the same logic on this point: because desire had as its objects things that were ephemeral, any pleasure produced by the fulfillment of these desires was bound to be likewise fleeting, and any happiness deriving from the accumulation of such pleasures a mere illusion. Each narrative in its own way indicts a whole range of secular pursuits, from the plainly trivial to the supposedly serious, as mendacious and ultimately empty and exposes an assortment of common values, from the unabashedly hedonistic to the allegedly respectable, as inadequate to satisfy definitively the deepest needs of human beings.

The motif of the "falseness" of human wishes and of any enjoyment growing out of their fulfillment thoroughly pervades the *Confessions*. Augustine deploys a system of *cup*-rooted words to designate these misplaced desires (*cupiditas, concupiscentia, cupire*); less frequently he uses the words *desiderium* (a longing) and *studium* (a passionate interest in or zeal for something) in connection with "false" desires. It comes as no surprise that he condemns the classic Christian nemesis, sexual desire, on the grounds that it wastes the energies of its victims on a futile and spiritually destructive obsession that by its cyclical nature can never be truly dispelled. "The habit of trying to satisfy that insatiable desire tortured me and held me captive," he recalls in Book 6 [*consuetudo satiandae insatiabilis concupiscentiae me captum excruciabat*] (6.12.22). He later remembers that he worried that God would cure him of the "disease of sexual desire" [*morbus concupiscentiae*] too quickly, for he preferred to have to keep satisfying it than to have it extinguished altogether (8.7.17).[1] What is remarkable, as we will see, is that Augus-

---

1. The text of the *Confessions* is that of M. Skutella (1981); translations are mine. The standard biography of Augustine in English is Brown's (1967); for commentary on *The Confessions*, see O'Donnell 1992. The scholarship on Augustine is of course vast; here I will only mention the useful recent discussion of the *Confessions* by Morrison (1992), who pays special attention to the gap between conversion experience and narrative.

tine employs this language of misguided or displaced desire not only in connection with sexual libido but also to designate the whole range of other urges, both sustained and momentary, that diverted his attention and prevented him from recognizing that his longing was really for God.

It should already be clear that this particular expression of the generic cognitive paradigm shift discussed in chapter 3 very centrally involves ideas of the false as opposed to the true; of delusion as opposed to true knowledge; of psychic perversity as opposed to psychic health; and of the ephemeral and the temporal as opposed to the eternal and the ideal. In other words, we recognize very clearly the workings of a system of ontological dualism. We ourselves can question the premises of such a system, but all that matters for our purposes now is that this was the larger discursive framework within which both Augustine and Lucius, constructing reality or being represented as constructing reality within the Platonic tradition as they were bound to do, experienced and narrated their crises and conversions. One could even say that their experiences and subsequent narratives could not have taken the particular forms that they did outside the preexisting discourse of dualism within which they moved and thought. In this respect the construction that they put on their experience had a script, at least in the general structure of the narrative. Ultimately, however, on this point the *Metamorphoses* is more complex, which is not surprising given the different stances of the two authors toward the experience represented. Instead of swallowing the discourse of truth and falsehood hook, line, and sinker, so to speak, the *Metamorphoses* incorporates a detached, critical voice to balance the *actor's* uncritical immersion in that discourse.

Augustine traces the roots of his epistemological and, secondarily, ethical derailment to his early childhood. Recalling his notorious theft of the pears, a formative experience to which he attaches extreme importance, he laments the familiar impetus behind it: the "itch of desire" [*pruritus cupiditatis*] (2.8.16). Earlier on he had likewise identified the motive for his boyish hooky playing as an itch to gratify his "love of playing and desire to watch frivolous performances and to imitate what transpired on the stage" [*amor ludendi, studium spectandi nugatoria et imitandi ludicria*] (1.19.30). The lure of public games and shows is a trap that later snares Augustine's virtuous friend Alypius upon his arrival in the big city:

The cesspool of Carthaginian morals had absorbed him with its passion for frivolous shows and had drawn him into a mad obsession with the games in the circus . . . but I myself neglected to try to persuade him not to destroy his good character by his blind and headlong desire for empty spectacles.

[gurges tamen morum Carthaginiensium, quibus nugatoria fervent spectacula, absorbuerat eum in insaniam circensium. . . . Sed enim de memoria mihi lapsum erat agere cum illo, ne vanorum ludorum caeco et praecipiti studio tam bonum interimeret ingenium.] (6.7.11–12)

In the last two passages we see but two instances of a theme sounded repeatedly by Augustine in the *Confessions*: that one of the most common, and the most destructive, objects of misguided desire was popular entertainment—*spectacula*—in the various forms that it took in provincial cities of the empire. We will soon see that it is the desire to be diverted by a show that frequently leads characters astray in the *Metamorphoses*. In both works, the quest for the amusement provided by *spectacula* becomes a sort of symbol for the generally wrongheaded cognitive orientation of those living with their backs turned to the realm of "true" value.

Two additional false desires that Augustine condemns as pernicious have as their objects things as disparate as food and drink, on the one hand, and natural beauty on the other. It is notable that in discussing the dangers presented by the desire for gustatory enjoyment, Augustine points explicitly to the allegedly deceptive nature of that desire as the crux of the problem. He warns that in order to avoid being tricked into the sin of gluttony, one must determine whether one is continuing to eat out of necessity or because of the pleasure that one derives from it: "Often it is unclear whether the body honestly requires nourishment or whether the pleasure-seeking deception of desire is being served instead" [utrum adhuc necessaria corporis cura subsidium petat an voluptaria cupiditatis fallacia ministerium suppetat] (10.31.44). If one fails to stop at necessity, one falls victim to *fallacia* on two counts: the self-deception of allowing oneself to believe first that it is survival and not sensuality that motivates self-indulgent behavior, and second that the indulgence of this sensuality will make a real contribution to one's happiness. Similarly the love of natural beauty rends the soul with "diseased desires" [*desideria pestilentiosa*] and lulls the lover, stuck in the "glue of desire" [*gluten amoris*], into a precarious comfort derived from things that will only wither and die (*non stant: fugiunt*, 4.10.15). From this passage it is clear that it is precisely the transitory nature of their objects that lies at the core of Augustine's conviction that the desires that drive most of humanity are somehow "mendacious."

The same principle emerges in the scorn he heaps upon the values of his former profession as a teacher of rhetoric. He makes it clear that it is fundamentally desire that lies behind this activity as well, the objects in this case being fame and fortune. Augustine's inculcation with the values of the profession began at a tender age: "In my tenderest youth I was studying books of rhetoric, in which I desired to excel" [*imbecilla tunc aetate discebam libros eloquentiae, in qua eminere cupiebam*] (3.4.7). The choice of the final verb here is, I think, not a careless one. Later he describes himself as having been a "most worthless slave of evil desires" [*aequissimus malarum cupiditatum servus*], again using *cupiditas* in the context of his widely ranging scholarly activities and professional ambitions. He continues in the same passage to express regret that the time he spent pursuing the fulfillment of these "meretricious desires" [*meretriciae cupiditates*] was a waste of his innate quickness at learning (4.16.30). The scathing adjective that he uses here gives a new vividness to the thematic idea of deceptive blandishments and specious attractions, which Augustine now locates in the intellectual sphere.

But at least his voracious reading in philosophy, as misguided as he came to believe it had been, was inspired by a desire to get at Truth. In contrast, he presents himself as gradually coming to the conclusion that his advancement in the field of rhetoric had no redeeming value whatsoever. The most effective way for the narrator Augustine to convey his enlightened view of the utter worthlessness of rhetorical education is to characterize the forces behind it in language reminiscent of that which he uses to condemn sexual desire:

They did not consider to what ends I might put the things that they compelled me to learn. They assumed that I would try to satisfy the insatiable desires for the poverty that they call wealth and the infamy that they call glory.

[illi enim non intuebantur, quo referrem, quod me discere coge-
bant, praeterquam ad satiandas insatiabiles cupiditates copiosae
inopiae et ignominiosae gloriae.] (1.12.19; cf. esp. 6.12.22)

In this passage we find Augustine enjoying the fact that ultimately the
joke, so to speak, was on the teachers of rhetoric. It shows very clearly
that he conceived of rhetorical ambition as a manifestation of spurious
and insatiable desire, its particular objects being wealth and fame. (We
might note that the formulation is framed in a polished rhetorical
jingle.) It was this *cupiditas* for professional success that Augustine
claims drove him to leave Carthage with its rowdy students and come
to Rome. He describes this move as happening at a time when God
"snatched him away using his [i.e., Augustine's] own desires as a goad,
on the road to finally putting an end to those desires" [*cum et me cupi-
ditatibus meis raperes ad finiendas ipsas cupiditates*] (5.8.15)—an indication
that God himself is not above using a little *fallacia* on occasion if it
enables him to accomplish his purposes.

What is objectionable to Augustine about professional achievement,
therefore, is that it represents the displacement of desire onto an inappropriate object. It results from deluded activity grounded in a false
understanding of how the world really works and of what is truly valuable. But rhetoric, he came to believe, was additionally abhorrent for its
sophistic amorality, its cavalier willingness to argue either side of a
question. At 9.2.4, he disparages his former academic position as a
teacher of rhetoric by calling it the "chair of lies" [*cathedra mendacii*].[2] It
was a position in which the praise won was in proportion to the deception perpetrated ("the bigger the liar, the greater the reputation" [*hoc
laudabilior, quo fraudulentior*] (3.3.6); it deliberately disseminated fraud
in a world where there was a natural abundance of it already. So, as
was the case with excessive eating and drinking, success in rhetoric was
built on two kinds of *fallacia:* the kind that the art of persuasion is by
definition, and the process of self-deception that allows its practitioners to believe that its rewards are what they really desire.

Augustine's narrative presents his past self as only growing more

----

2. Cf. 6.6.9, ". . . when I was preparing to recite a speech in praise of the
emperor, in which I would lie lavishly and thus earn the approval of the
experts" [*cum pararem recitare imperatori laudes, quibus plura mentirer, et mentienti
faveretur ab scientibus*].

aware that for all the success he had met in realizing his desires, not only his declamations but his entire life had the quality of a lie about them. In Book 6 he describes the disillusionment that he remembers as overwhelming him after years of following conventional roads to a stubbornly elusive happiness. Having dutifully pursued for some thirty years the desires of his class for social and professional status, material wealth, and good marriage, the Augustine who is the *actor* of the narrative is here made to despair of these achievements ever leading him "to solid happiness" *[ad securam laetitiam]*. On the contrary, these *cupiditates* bring him no end of trouble *(amarissimae difficultates)* in the conflict they cause in his soul; and, more crucially, the attainment of their objects, contrary to expectation and conventional wisdom, only seems to engender ever more unhappiness and psychological pain. Paradoxically, the more fully Augustine participates in the received system of values, the heavier the burden of his unhappiness becomes: "Driven by the goads of my desires I dragged the baggage of my unhappiness, and the longer I dragged it, the heavier it became" *[sub stimulis cupiditatum trahens infelicitatis meae sarcinam et trahendo exaggerans]* (6.6.9).[3] Augustine remembers feeling as if he were caught in a system that fed on itself, in which desires fulfilled yielded not an end to desire, but ever more and newer desires, all demanding to be gratified. He recalls that his frustration with this roller-coaster approach to life finally produced in him a resolve to "leave behind all the empty hopes and the mendacious madness of vain desires" *[relinquere omnes vanarum cupiditatum spes inanes et insanias mendaces]* (6.11.18).

If the initial desire was wrongheaded, then the pleasure afforded by its satisfaction inevitably falls short of the expected result and is therefore, to Augustine's mind, as "mendacious" as the initial impulse. As with desire, it is the pleasure *(voluptas)* associated with sexual activity that provokes some of the shrillest condemnation. But also as with desire, Augustine speaks with equal disappointment about a whole

---

3. The prevalence in the *Confessions* of the image of delusion-induced unhappiness as oppressive "baggage" *(sarcina)* invites comparison with the motif of the repeated oppression of Lucius, the recalcitrant beast of burden, with all manner of literal *sarcina* whose weight only grows heavier with the journey. Cf. *Conf.* 4.7.12; 8.5.12; 8.7.18; 9.1.1 (in contrast, God's *sarcina* is light, cf. *Matt.* 11: 30); 10.40.65 (the "baggage of habit": see below on the force of habit as an obstruction to reconceptualizing reality) with *Met.* 4.4; 3.28; 6.25, 26; 7.15, 17, 18, 19; 8.15, 28, 30; 9.29; 10.1.

range of "false" pleasures (he calls them *voluptates, suavitates, iucundi-tates, delectationes,* and *deliciae*), from the childish excitement of the pear caper to the fruits of his study of literature, philosophy, and rhetoric. The theft of the pears, which inspires all the more guilt in retrospect because it was enjoyed for its own sake without even a pretense of any practical object, is linked to an act so apparently dissimilar as that of sexual intercourse by the use of *voluptas* to designate the desired goal in the former case as well: "For me the pleasure was not in the pears them-selves, but simply in the act of being bad" [*in illis pomis voluptas mihi non erat, ea erat in ipso facinore*] (2.8.16).

A childish prank and the primal act: these could be viewed as the opposite extremes on a scale of activities whose resulting pleasures Augustine indicts as dangerously seductive because of their place in a system of mistaken values. In between them fall countless other activi-ties, some of them seemingly innocent and even potentially connected with the higher life. Of particular interest is his suspicion of the plea-sures associated with eating and with listening to music—even sacred music, after his conversion—since he says here specifically that they are characterized by the *fallacia* that he implies also of virtually all the other pleasures upon which ordinary mortals rely to infuse some meaning into their lives. Augustine worries about the ever present threat that he will allow his senses to be seduced by the music of hymns and con-fesses that the fear of this deceptive pleasure sometimes leads him to err in the direction of excessive severity (10.33.50). We have seen how the desire for food and drink beyond what is strictly necessary to sus-tain life is regarded as deceptive; so is the pleasure deriving therefrom (10.31.44). What gluttony offers is "delight full of danger" [*periculosa iucunditas*] because of its insidious diversionary power, and this indeed is Augustine's view of all temporal pleasures. In retrospect he realizes that the pleasure he took in his education was empty also—he calls its staples *vana*—and so insidious that it made him a miserable sinner without his even knowing it: "I happily learned these things and took a wretched pleasure in them, and for this I was called a boy with a great future ahead of him" [*libenter haec didici et eis delectabar miser et ob hoc bonae spei puer appellabar*] (1.16.26).

Augustine the *actor*'s problem as Augustine the narrator recon-structs it, then, was that his desires could not really be satisfied, his pleasures did not seem to last. It was this vague but deep sense of dis-satisfaction that caused him to begin suspecting his pursuits and values of "falseness." Until he found "true" happiness in God, all his happiness *(felicitas, laetitia, gaudium)*, resting as it did on tenuous foundations, had a hollow ring. Augustine remembers, for example, becoming gradually more aware of the "falseness" of the happiness that attended his youthful studies and subsequently his successful academic career, to name but one source of *falsa felicitas*.[4] The problem with happiness deriving from temporal sources, in Augustine's view, is that the ephemeral character of its underpinnings makes the happiness itself precarious, unstable, and unreliable: "Woe to those who define prosperity by the world's standards, because they are vulnerable both to fear of adversity and to disappointment when their happiness does not last" *[vae prosperitatibus saeculi semel et iterum a timore adversitatis et a corruptione laetitiae]* (10.28.39).[5] Temporal happiness is built on transitory material phenomena, mere phantoms *(imagines)*, which hungry but misdirected souls vainly "nibble at with starving minds" *[famelica cogitatione lambiunt]* (9.4.10). By contrast, "true" happiness, his reasoning goes, would be by definition indestructible and in no way tied to the sensible world and its mortal inhabitants.

Augustine recalls that he observed the "false happiness" syndrome being acted out all around him by others. For example, he cites the pride of his own father, overcome by narcissistic joy at the prospect of having grandchildren to perpetuate his line.[6] What distinguishes

---

4. He uses this phrase to describe the lure exerted by Rome, with its greater opportunities and better working conditions for teachers ("To be sure I deplored my genuine misery at Carthage, but what I sought in Rome was false happiness," *[ego autem qui detestabar hic veram miseriam, illic falsam felicitatem appetebam]* 5.8.14).

5. Augustine comes very close here to sounding the Fortuna theme that is so central to the *Metamorphoses*. Cf., e.g., 5.12.22, the root of the viciousness of Augustine's Roman students was that they "were in love with the fleeting diversions of the temporal world and they tried to embrace a world that would always slip through their fingers" *[amando volatica ludibria temporum . . . et amplectando mundum fugientem]*.

6. 2.3.6: "When my father saw my maturing body in the public baths, he began on the basis of this to eagerly anticipate grandchildren, rejoicing as he told my mother, rejoicing and drunk on the invisible wine of his own perverse and earthbound will" *[ubi me ille pater in balneis vidit pubescentem . . . quasi iam ex hoc in nepotes gestiret, gaudens matri indicavit, gaudens . . . de vino invisibili perversae atque inclinatae in ima voluntatis suae]*.

Augustine from these others in his presentation of matters is that he has the introspective power to recognize that something is wrong, while they are altogether oblivious to the emptiness of their lives, or perhaps, as he implies, the thoroughness of their delusion simply prevents them from registering and formulating that emptiness consciously, as he himself was doing. This matter of "quiet desperation"—of a disillusionment with learned values that fails to formulate itself as such in the mind, but which is nevertheless clearly acted out in a desperate casting about for that always elusive definitive pleasure—is something to which we will return when we continue our scrutiny of the representation of Lucius' crisis. Furthermore, the device of reinforcing what is suggested about the protagonist's experience by surrounding him with other characters who are struggling with the same problems (whether they realize it or not) is one used to great effect by Apuleius as well as by Augustine, as we will soon see.

Augustine writes that at the height of his success and the depth of his malaise, he saw a drunken beggar in the streets of Milan and was moved to reflect on this man's lot as compared with his own (6.6). The beggar appeared to be happy because it had been a good day for him: he had managed to beg enough money to buy a drink. But of course he, like everyone else, was deluded; what he was enjoying was not *true* happiness (*verum gaudium*). Still, because of the spontaneity and the simplicity of his pleasures, the beggar's happiness seemed to Augustine less blameworthy than his own, founded as it was on a much more convoluted system of sophisms and lies. Augustine's bankrupt *ambitiones* and the ill-used learning (*doctrina*) that he put in their service made the *gaudium* that he sought by circuitous routes (but was never quite able to find: *non inde gaudebam*) much "falser" [*multo falsius*] than that of the mendicant. At least the drunk would wake up sober in the morning; in contrast, Augustine likens the whole of his existence before his enlightenment to an insentient drunken stupor.[7]

---

7. The equation of life devoted to conventional values with a drunken binge is recurrent. Cf., e.g., Alypius at the games: "He drank in the madness without knowing what he was doing and he delighted in the criminal contest and was drunk on the bloody pleasure that they offered" [*hauriebat furias et nesciebat et delectabatur scelere certaminis et cruenta voluptate inebriabatur*] (6.8). The reader

At this point in the narrative Augustine's moment of truth is not to arrive for another two books, with the famous exhortation of the mysterious childlike voice to "take this book and read" it in the garden at Milan (8.12). Still, from the heavy world-weariness that emerges in the chapter on the Milanese beggar, it is apparent that Augustine remembers reaching the end of the line, so to speak, long before his sudden scriptural revelation—the experience that he himself clearly regarded as his conversion proper. He presents himself as being trapped on the treadmill of conventional values and feeling acutely that it was taking him nowhere for a considerable period of time before he suffered what William James might have called the collapse of psychic interstices. Augustine's old system for ordering reality had failed, but he had only just begun to discern the lines along which he would construct a replacement. He therefore found himself floundering in an epistemological and moral void, clearly needing to make a radical change but not quite knowing how or in what direction to make it. His habituated ways of valorizing phenomena no longer seemed to be working, but new ways had yet fully to emerge. In Berger's terms, this is Augustine's anomic phase, and its defining features can be detected in the parallel phases of the crises of Lucius and Tolstoy.

Needless to say, there are crucial issues in the interpretation of Augustine's narrative of crisis and conversion that are beyond the scope of the present discussion. One such fundamental question is whether Augustine is a reliable narrator of his own past. Are we justified in believing that events happened as he describes them as happening, or that his thoughts and responses to these events were as he says they were? The writing of any autobiography is a process of selection, governed by the tricks and imperfections of memory as well as by the

---

is reminded that both Tolstoy and Lucius also ultimately reject *doctrina* as a means of attaining happiness, and that images of inebriation and stupefaction figure prominently in Tolstoy's account of his life before conversion (see chap. 3, sec. 1). I will argue below that *stupor* has the same metaphorical function in the *Metamorphoses*.

narrator's conscious reshaping of his past experiences to conform to his present understanding of their meaning and to his purpose in recounting them. It is inevitable that the final account is to a greater or a lesser degree stamped in the mold of the discourse adopted and assimilated by the narrator at the time of narrating, so that the construction that he puts on events is circumscribed and dictated by what that discourse allows.[8] Whether or not Augustine is "telling the truth," however, is not really a question in which we need to become mired, since it is the patterns recurring in conversion *narratives* that we are concerned to identify in order to situate the *Metamorphoses* among those narratives. As I suggested in the introduction, there is no doubt a complicated interdependence between such narratives and actual experience. But the more the *Confessions* can be seen as a generic or paradigmatic narrative of conversion rather than a wholly objective account of unique individual experience, the more useful it is for our purposes.

And in fact Hawkins (1985) maintains in her recent study of "archetypes of conversion" that Augustine's work is precisely such a paradigmatic narrative. It is a prototype of the "quest" model of conversion narrative and in turn became a paradigm of conversion *experience* for later converts, as narrative and experience came to reinforce each other in a closed discursive loop. The quest type of narrative typically describes a search for metaphysically rooted meaning in the unstable flux of experience. The search is motivated by "feelings of inchoate longing, vague yearning, and unappeasable desire [that] are the affective and libidinal counterparts to the intellectual search for wisdom and truth." According to this model of crisis and conversion, life before conversion "is perceived as a kind of labyrinthine maze with numerous false passages and wrong turnings," in which "the soul errs in choosing the wrong object for its love" (30; 34).[9] My contention is that the *Meta-*

---

8. O'Meara (1954, 5) maintains that Augustine never intended the *Confessions* to be a "purely personal history," but rather, at least to some extent, a paradigmatic or generic account. For a discussion of the place of the *Confessions* in the literary tradition, see Courcelle 1963. For a recent analysis of how Augustine may have consciously allowed ideological motives to shape his narrative, see Fredriksen 1986.

9. On misdirected desire in the *Confessions*, see also Hawkins 1985, 57, 62–63, 66–67, 78, 89, 126.

morphoses also belongs to this tradition of conversion narratives, and that the pagan novel, at least in its "serious" aspects, may therefore be the prototype rather than the *Confessions*. Lucius' separation from his accustomed epistemological anchorage and his anomic drifting before coming upon Isis as his transcendental signified have been explored at length in chapters 1 and 2. I will argue below that his apparently aimless wandering as an ass represents a search for meaning driven off course by misdirected desire and thus stands, mutatis mutandis, very much in what would become the Augustinian tradition.

In this discussion of Augustine I isolated a fundamental and, I would argue, generic pattern in the *Confessions* that involves the endless circular movement of misguided or displaced desires and misbegotten pleasures, which never produce any real satisfaction. I suggested furthermore that although words like "desire" and "pleasure" might strike the reader as primarily moral terms, the character of the crisis embodied in Augustine's awareness of the inadequacy of his old values is epistemological or cognitive as well as moral. This is because the construction of objects of desire is an epistemological process drawing on culturally produced values, which are a form of knowledge. When the old structures of meaning built upon these pieces of social knowledge break down, as they do for Augustine, the subject finds himself the disoriented inhabitant of an unhinged world showing some or all of the qualities that characterize the world of Lucius. In other words, when we clear away the moralistic overlay and adjust for the ontological framework of dualism that is ultimately accepted as the given nature of reality in the *Confessions* (and ultimately in the *Metamorphoses* as well, at least from the *actor*'s point of view), what we can discern in Augustine's description of his experience is a cognitive paradigm shift along the lines of those described in chapter 3 as characterizing conversions of all kinds, and not just religious ones. Augustine never articulates as explicitly as Tolstoy that the impulse behind his search for "true" value is provided by the prospect of death, with its power to annihilate the meaning of temporal achievements. Still, his obsessive concern with the ephemerality of phenomena in the real world of matter and his repeated assertion that this is the reason for their ultimate worthlessness (an equation whose validity is far from self-evident) would seem to suggest that mortality is not unproblematic for him.

2

The Augustinian scheme of "false" values is a central one in the *Meta-morphoses* as well, and, as in the *Confessions*, the problem of "false" val-ues expresses itself in the novel in terms of misguided desires and mis-begotten pleasures. It is not difficult to show that desire motivates a large proportion of the novel's action. As is the case with the *Confes-sions*, the sexual manifestation of desire has been considered the most significant, to the extent that many critics have assumed that it is this "sin," along with the other of dabbling in black magic, that earns Lucius the "punishment" of transformation into an ass. In my reading, on the other hand, Lucius' real and fundamental error, like that of Augustine, is his failure to calculate correctly where "true" value and knowledge lie.[10] To be sure, philandering is a way of life in the *Meta-morphoses*. The tryst of Lucius and Fotis provides the occasion for extended erotic interludes throughout the first three books, described in terms similar to those Augustine assigns to his own dalliances and sexual impulses (for example, *cupido, Met.* 2.10; 2.16). Lucius' suscepti-bility to sexual temptation is not diminished after his transformation into an ass, as he demonstrates as soon as he finds himself in the same pasture with a herd of attractive fillies (7.16). The distracting sexual passions of others mirror the hero's weakness in this area. For example, there is Socrates' affair with the witch Meroe as related by Aristomenes in Book 1 (5–20) and the extramarital escapades of the baker's wife (9.22–31); although these begin as lighthearted diversions, both end in disaster. In the tales of Thrasyllus (8.1–14) and the treacherous step-mother (10.2–12), on the other hand, we see sexual desire at its most obsessive and destructive from the very beginning of each account. Both stories are constructed around terms that Augustine regularly applies to false desires generically—*cupido* and *studium*, for example.[11]

But in the *Metamorphoses*, as in the *Confessions*, sex is only one of a

---

10. MacKay (1965) expresses a similar view when he proposes that Lucius' "sin" is his willful wrongheadedness in general.

11. Thrasyllus: he falls "into the deep ruin caused by desire" [*in profundam ruinam cupidinis*] (8.2); his desire for Charite is a *summum studium* (8.2); he is driven by a "desire to physically possess the woman" [*studium contrectandae mulieris*] (8.7); and he forgets about everything else except for this desire [*uno potiundi studio postponens omnia*] (8.10). The stepmother: she also is driven by *cupido* (probably personified, 10.2).

whole range of inappropriate objects of desire. Furthermore, the application of equally strong language to other types of desire, from the potentially dangerous to the apparently benign, suggests that it is not any particular act engendered by the desire that is being indicted so much as the desire itself, for its "falseness," that is, its focus on nugatory objects. Another important entry on the list of offending objects of desire is knowledge of magic. Lucius describes his interest in magic in language that is, if anything, more passionate than that which he enlists in his recollection of Fotis' charms. He remembers being "desirous of learning things that are rare and wondrous" [*cupidus cognoscendi quae rara miraque sunt*] in the early days of his sojourn in Thessaly's enchanted regions and recalls being in the grip of a suspenseful *studium* to break into the forbidden realm of magic (2.1). Lest the reader still not appreciate the compelling character of his impulse, he goes on to call it not only a *cupido* but an "excruciating desire" [*cruciabile desiderium*] in the next chapter (2.2). In his attempt to gain Fotis' aid in satisfying it, Lucius impresses on her that he is "very ardently desirous of learning about magic" [*magiae noscendae ardentissimus cupitor*] (3.19). Clearly, this is erotic language transferred to a nonsexual context, but, as we will see, the realm of magic is only one of many nonsexual contexts in which desire operates. The prospect of witnessing a magical event stirs a desire in others similar to that of Lucius. So, for example, a crowd is captivated by the feats of the necromancer Zatchlas, who "arouses in those present a desire [*studium*] to see a great miracle" (2.28). Likewise, the unfortunate Thelyphron is glued to this scene "with curious eyes" (2.29); it will become clear that in both the *Metamorphoses* and the *Confessions* curiosity is to be seen as a type of false desire.

Misdirected desire can be the driving force behind a variety of behaviors in the novel outside the more sensational realms of sex and magic. For example, *cupido* is used as a synonym for *avaritia* at 9.19, where the slave Myrmex allows his loyalty to be corrupted by his greed for money: "His desire [*cupido*] for the seductive money did not abate, but rather destructive greed had invaded even his dreams." But it is the desire that lies behind the widespread tendency of characters in the *Metamorphoses* to be instantly transfixed by any novel sight or story that is perhaps the most striking expression of false desire in the novel. The passages in which this happens involve more than an incidental depiction of idle curiosity. From the words that he chooses to describe these scenes, it is clear that Apuleius means for us to regard the indulgence of curiosity as another of several manifestations of wasted desiderative energy. When all the citizens strain for a view of the slain Tlepolemus, they are driven by a *studium* for a good look at the spectacle (8.6), and when the Corinthian crowds later assemble, bent on being amused by the novelty of a trained ass, they are "filled with desire" *[cupientes]* to see Lucius perform (10.19). Furthermore, as we will see below, the satisfaction of curiosity produces a kind of pleasure *(voluptas, iucunditas, delectatio)*, which is the projected result of the satisfaction of any desire.

Lucius himself, as a man and as a beast, is of course the worst offender when it comes to allowing himself to be led astray by curiosity. He boasts at 1.2 that he is the sort of person "who would like to know everything or at least most things" *[qui velim scire vel cuncta vel certe plurima]*. Here Lucius does not say explicitly that he is consumed by a *desire* to accumulate all manner of knowledge and experience indiscriminately, but his compulsive endeavors to do so throughout the novel are in fact fueled by precisely that. This is most apparent in connection with Lucius' magical aspirations. His interest in magic is clearly motivated by curiosity, but he enlists "desire" words to describe his feelings, as we have seen (2.1–2, 3.19). His mention, moreover, in 1.2 of *iucunditas* ("pleasurable delight") as the reward he will reap if the traveler obliges him with a story further strengthens the identification of curiosity as a type of desire, since *iucunditas* (or *voluptas* or *delectatio*) is what one ordinarily experiences once a desire has been satisfied. In this connection we might recall Augustine's warning that eating more than one needs to live can produce a forbidden *iucunditas* (*Conf.* 10.31.44). To a great extent *cupidus* and *curiosus* are interchangeable adjectives in both the *Metamorphoses* and the *Confessions*, or, to put it another way, curiosity is represented in both as a category of false desire and one of the most common manifestations of the displacement of the desire for a transcendental signified, that is, a god. I will have more to say below about this conception of curiosity and how it links the two works.

Now, to the casual reader Lucius' desire to be entertained by an amusing story and the stepmother's desire to enter into an illicit sexual relationship with her stepson in Book 10 may seem to be qualitatively different propositions. But we have seen how Augustine equates the desire that motivated his bankrupt social and academic ambitions and his early sexual activities with that which caused him as a child to skip school and go to a show or engage in various other apparently harmless boyish pranks. Likewise, Apuleius strongly suggests that it is essentially the same drive that is at work, whether it is directed in such a way as to produce grave or ostensibly benign results. In a sense the consequences are incidental. It is really the persistent and usually randomly directed impulse—the desire—of Apuleian characters to grasp at any sort of momentary diversion that is meant as the chief measure of the degree to which they have gone off track in their estimation of the value of their activities in the larger scheme of things.

Like desires themselves, the fleeting pleasures following upon their attainment are central to the *Metamorphoses*, just as they are to the *Confessions*. Again, it is easy for the reader to focus on sexual pleasure, and indeed Lucius does speak of *voluptas* as the fruit of his affair with Fotis. For example, he describes the sensation he felt while watching her provocatively stirring a cauldron of stew as the "torture of intense pleasure" *[cruciatum voluptatis eximiae]* (2.10).[12] Likewise the prospect of sexual *voluptas* is the lure that leads Socrates (1.8), Thrasyllus (8.9), and the Phaedra-like stepmother (10.4) astray. Yet sex is only one of many sources of *voluptas* in the novel. The slave Myrmex, for example, anticipates that his ill-gotten gain will bring him *voluptas* (9.19). But by far the largest class of extrasexual and extramagical pleasures in the novel is constituted from those associated with the waylaying impulse of curiosity. We have seen that it is curiosity that is at the root of Lucius' (and others') obsession with magic. But it is also a synonym for the desire that drives him (as it drives others) to seek momentary pleasure indiscriminately in any novel sight, tale, or experience.[13] When this

---

12. Cf. 2.17, Lucius and Fotis drink more wine in the midst of one of their bedroom bouts in order to "relieve their weariness, excite their desire, and renew their pleasure" *[lassitudinem refoventes et libidinem incitantes et voluptatem integrantes]*. To this cf. *Conf.* 10.34, "God is right there but people do not see him, because if they did they would not move away from him and waste their energies in pleasures that only cause weariness" *[et ibi est et non vident eum, ut non eant longius . . . nec [fortitudinem] spargant in deliciosas lassitudines]*.

13. Sights: e.g., his pleasure at the incidental resemblance of the robbers' old cook reining in the ass to a scene from mythology (6.27); his hope of gratification from being a spectator at the bandits' capture (7.13); and his enjoyment of

happens, a causal connection is implied between *curiositas* qua desire and the diversionary pleasure that is its product.

The ubiquitous casting about of chronically curious minor characters or crowds for the idle pleasure of an unusual sight provides a background for the representation of the same compulsion in Lucius. Socrates' troubles begin when he is on his way to gratify his desire for the "pleasure of a gladiatorial spectacle" *[voluptas gladiatorii spectaculi]* (1.7). Further, the rich man Demochares knows that he can curry public favor by financing entertainment to provide the citizens with the *voluptas* that can be derived from such shows (4.13). This generalized quest for pleasurable *spectacula* reaches a peak of frenzy when news of the trained ass circulates in Corinth. Lucius' current master, Thiasos, happily takes pleasure in the novelty of the sight (*delectatur . . . novitate spectaculi laetus dominus*, 10.16); and Lucius' trainer eagerly teaches the ass new tricks to increase the master's pleasure even further (*studiosissime voluptates [domini] . . . instruebat*, 10.17). The public is quickly infected with Thiasos' enthusiasm for the diversion, and later, when the show expands to include cross-species sex, interest in the "voluptuary spectacle" *[voluptarium spectaculum]* (10.35) is all the more rabid. And so, here, as elsewhere in the novel, Lucius' bad habits, in this case his curiosity, are put in high relief against a background of like behavior in others.

These examples show that desire and pleasure are important motivational forces in the novel's action. Furthermore, we can see even from this selection of episodes that Apuleius consistently applies what might be called the Augustinian vocabulary of spurious desire and pleasure to a similarly wide range of activities. This suggests that both narratives are making the same point about the futility of *all* these activities, regardless of their relative status on conventional morality's scale of taboos. The failure of Apuleian characters to find satisfaction in their

---

the show in Corinth while waiting for his own cue to perform (10.29). Experiences: e.g., his pleasure *(delectatio)*, simply because it involved a new experience for him, of the miserable conditions at the mill (9.12). In most of these passages curiosity is explicitly named as the driving force behind Lucius' behavior. Tales: e.g., the "Tale of the Tub" (9.4), the grisly tale of the bailiff (8.22), the tale of the baker's adulterous wife (9.14–31), and the countless other "pleasant tales" that absorb his attention in the course of his wanderings.

accustomed pleasures is pointedly illustrated in the ways their patterns of behavior are represented. Unlike Augustine, Lucius the narrator never labels the dead-end desires and pleasures of his past self or others "mendacious" or "fallacious," but the overall, carefully wrought impression that the novel gives, particularly in the books immediately preceding the intervention of Isis, of a whirlwind of frenzied activity going nowhere fast carries this message as effectively as Augustine's systematic commentary.[14] The novel's inhabitants, with Lucius in the forefront, are represented as acting out of an imperfectly understood, unarticulated restlessness that drives them to seek relief in any pleasure, from the most consuming to the most inane. But the "true" nature of the restlessness and the misguided means by which they try to quell it make it inevitable that they will always go away unsatisfied.[15] Like Augustine despairing in the streets of Milan, but considerably less self-aware, they have clearly reached the end of the utility of their old way of life; but it does not seem to occur to them that there might be another way. The failure of their usual system of desires and pleasures to continue ordering their lives in a satisfying way represents a highly dramatized form, in fact almost a reduction to absurdity, of the crisis in values that can be the precipitating phase in the conversion process and which appears in other forms in other narratives.

Perhaps the foremost symbols of malaise in the novel are the many idle, diversion-seeking mobs that appear at regular intervals and demonstrate their tendency to drop everything and gape whenever something out of the ordinary happens to engage their attention. In the course of the novel, crowds are riveted by the sight of necromantic feats

---

14. In spite of the absence of direct commentary from the narrator, the motif of mendaciousness and duplicity is in fact incorporated into the novel in other ways. Lies and deception motivate most of the action in the major episodes of Books 7 through 10, and these episodes depend on an elaborate vocabulary of deceit, which appears later in the *Confessions* in connection with "false" values. See chapter 2, section 1.

15. Skulsky (1981, 74–82) suggests a similar reading of the behavior of Apuleian characters. They are driven by "misdirected love" and by "half articulate and distorted religious aspirations," which end in "cruel misdevotion" because of the failure of the characters to understand their impulses as religious longings. Lucius and the people in his world are united by their "panicky groping toward the reunion," which apparently only Lucius will find.

(2.28, 10.12), dead bodies (8.6), captive bears (4.16), a trained ass (10.15–17), and the impending performance of Lucius and the condemned woman in the Corinthian arena (10.35).[16] The reader is given the strong impression of severely limited powers of concentration. Any object upon which the attention of these crowds lights quickly loses its novelty, and we can imagine them moving listlessly on to another source of amusement, which will soon tire them in its turn. Indeed, this is the way Lucius himself conducts his entire life. Ultimately, it is this mindless, distracted casting about, more than any sexual tryst, that is the novel's primary expression of Lucius' moral bankruptcy. It is important to remember, however, that this is first and foremost an epistemological bankruptcy, since he literally does not know what he is doing. And so, in Book 11 (15), when the priest of Isis seems to rebuke Lucius for having allowed himself to slide down the slippery slope of "servile pleasures" [*serviles voluptates*], he refers, I think, not just to the affair with the slave girl but to the whole range of empty pleasures to which not only Lucius but most of the people around him are enslaved. Likewise, in indicting Lucius' "profitless curiosity," Mithras invokes the general tendency and what it betrays about Lucius' larger "soul-sickness," rather than referring only to his reckless interest in magic.[17]

---

16. The pathology of these crowds is represented as being rooted in boredom; in contrast, the vaguely sinister crowd at the Risus festival (3.1–10) seems to be additionally motivated by a streak of sadism.

17. Relieving *serviles voluptates* of an exclusively sexual/moral charge allows us to make sense of the *innocentia* and *fides* that the crowd attributes to Lucius at 11.16. Others have regarded this as contradicting the priest's indictment (e.g., Griffiths 1975, 257). Since Lucius' "sin" is not moral badness but simple ignorance—allowing himself to be epistemologically derailed—then he can have been a slave to servile pleasures (i.e., the false values of his mistakenly constructed old world) without that ruling out his possession of *innocentia* and *fides*. Winkler (1985, 210–13), on the other hand, takes Mithras' and the crowd's apparently contradictory assessments as two different constructions of evidence whose unclear relationship to fact continues Apuleius' ongoing sabotage of the idea of definitive construction. Winkler does, however, recognize the significant fact that sex per se is never condemned in the *Metamorphoses* (146–47; 192–93: to insist that it is condemned is to "supplement the sense of the text to fit an imposed moral pattern"). For a similar suggestion, see Skulsky 1981, 88–89. For more conventional readings of the status of sex in the novel see, e.g., Sandy 1974 and Penwill 1975.

In the *Metamorphoses* the point is dramatized when the narrative concentrates the idea of the inadequacy of gratification arising from any temporal source in the image of the mobs' insipid stupefaction.

The point is further epitomized in the numerous scenes in which Lucius or others are instantly struck dumb and transfixed *(attonitus, defixus)*, or paralyzed by *stupor*, when they stumble onto a magical, erotic, or simply novel situation. Lucius is dumbstruck (*attonitus . . . stupidus*, 2.2) by his passion to witness something magical, and later is transfixed (*stupidus defixus . . . attonitus*, 3.22) at the sight of Pamphile's actual transformation into a bird. Sexual desire can have the same effect on him. Upon encountering the tempting Fotis in the kitchen, he "stood there dumbstruck and transfixed" *[defixus obstupui]* (2.7), entirely forgetting the magic that had preoccupied him just a few short minutes earlier. But the sources of paralysis extend beyond magic and sex directly experienced. The household of Thiasos, for example, is *attonita* as it anticipates the unusual performance to be enacted in the arena (10.35), and Lucius himself is "dumbstruck with curiosity" *[curiositate attonitus]* at the unfamiliar surroundings of the mill (9.12). The vivid image of thoughtless distraction created in these scenes is central to the Apuleian strategy of using recurrent images and types of action to convey the critical view of human endeavor that Augustine expresses explicitly and abstractly in his running commentary on the events of his past life. Yet the latter's metaphor equating his life before conversion with a drunken stupor (*ebrietas*, 6.6) should not be forgotten in this connection.[18] Moreover, at least twice Augustine uses forms of the verb

---

18. Nor should William James' choice of words in paraphrasing the newly anhedonic Tolstoy's estimation of the conventional pursuits of men of his class: these pursuits were diversions, thoughtlessly exploited to avoid the stark reality of the human condition; they offered a kind of anesthesia bringing on senseless "stupefaction" (1958, 132). Apuleius' use of *defixus* to conjure up this image would doubtless have magical connotations for the ancient reader (cf. *defixionum tabellae*, tablets of magical incantations). The double charge with which the word is invested is consistent with the view that Apuleius uses magic to represent epistemological aporia metaphorically. Significantly, a similar invocation of magic comes naturally enough to Augustine, who, quoting Paul *(Galatians* 3:3), asks this question of the unconverted, i.e., those with an incorrect cognitive orientation: "Who has cast a spell on you?" *[quis vos fascinavit?]* (13.13.14).

In connection with the dual allegiances of motifs, I should point out that the

stupere in the Apuleian sense of being gullibly impressed, even mesmerized, by something that is, in a word, not God: at 4.4.16, of an audience's awe at an orator's skill; and at 5.3.28, of people's amazement at the calculations of astronomers.

And so the sort of energetic and conscious pursuit of largely "respectable" diversions that is faulted in the *Confessions* is pointedly reduced in the *Metamorphoses* to a passive and unthinking susceptibility to the lure of *any* diversion. Yet each work in its own way captures a Tolstoyan anhedonia, or failure to take any real pleasure in life's ordinary values. Some expression of disillusionment with conventional values would be consistent with the satire of Lucius' bourgeois smugness and self-righteous moralizing that appears at intervals throughout the *Metamorphoses*. However the narrative expresses it or at whatever level the characters are depicted as understanding it, the growing suspicion that one's learned system of goals and rewards is fundamentally flawed represents a serious challenge to cultural paradigms and socially generated knowledge. If the desires and pleasures—the values—upon which this system is based are "false," then the happiness (*gaudium, laetitia*) resting on them is tenuous in the extreme. Augustine spells this out, but Apuleius demonstrates it indirectly, by structuring his novel around a seemingly endless series of rising and then disappointed expectations. This cycle is the stuff of the ass's life until Isis rescues him from it. In the episodes shortly after Lucius' transformation, when he is tantalized three times in rapid succession by roses that promise to restore his human shape, the plot expresses just how elusive the ingredients for lasting happiness are (3.27, 3.29, 4.2). Whenever the ass spies some roses, an obstacle to eating them appears at the last minute, or they are revealed to be mere facsimiles. The real thing can come, significantly, from divinity alone.

But the elusive roses mark only the beginning of the ass's cycle of rising expectations and dashed hopes. Every time he seems to have

---

pursuit of spectacle that I have identified as a symptom of malaise in the *Metamorphoses* is a recurring motif in ancient prose fiction in general, without necessarily having this connotation. Yet there it is again in the *Confessions*, and it carries there an explicitly expressed epistemological and moral charge. See chapter 2, section 3 on the *Metamorphoses* as a site for the transformation of literary conventions and their significations.

reached a respite from his travails, his happiness is shattered by impending disaster. To name but a few instances: Lucius is "joyous and happy" [gaudens laetusque] at the prospect of a life of leisure as his reward for rescuing Charite, only to discover that "no pleasures nor even freedom" await him, but rather forced labor at the flour mill (7.15); he is "happy and enthusiastic" [laetus et . . . gestiens] when he learns that he is to be put out to pasture with a herd of eligible mares but immediately finds himself fending off a vicious attack by jealous stallions (7.16); he rejoices (gaudebam) at his escape from a cook who was preparing to disguise him as venison for dinner but immediately must face another danger when he is suspected of having rabies (9.1–3); as a pampered circus novelty he allows himself to feel secure in his impression that Fortune is finally smiling on him after allowing him to be mistreated for so long (10.16) but soon discovers that he is expected to participate in an offensive and dangerous performance in the arena.[19] One can almost hear the strains of Augustine's warning, "Woe to those who define prosperity by the world's standards, because they are vulnerable both to fear of adversity and to disappointment when their happiness does not last" (10.28).

The figure in the *Metamorphoses* that represents instability in human affairs is, of course, that of Fortuna. For both Lucius and Augustine, adopting "true" beliefs and values means finding a realm beyond the reach of this principle. Indeed, once Lucius devotes himself to Isis, he is (he believes) at last safe from the whims of Fortuna and secure in his

---

19. At 7.15, Lucius' short-lived *laetitia* stems also from his anticipation of finding roses when he is freed; thus the important leitmotif of the frustrated search for roses reappears in the novel's later books. For *gestire* (as at 7.16) in the sense of complete absorption in the (false) desire or pleasure at hand, cf. 2.6 (of Lucius' desire to be privy to Pamphile's secrets); 10.19 (of the Corinthians' desire to view the novel animal act); and *Conf.* 2.3 (Augustine's father's enthusiasm at the prospect of having grandchildren). As usual, the experiences of others mirror those of Lucius. For other instances of teasing *gaudium/laetitia* with disaster close at its heels, see, e.g., 1.17 (Aristomenes); 2.26–30 (Thelyphron); 4.16–18 (Demochares); 7.13, 8.1–14 (Charite and Tlepolemus). Occasionally, a reversal results in a happy ending, e.g., when the father of the scapegoated stepson has both his children restored to him (10.12), but in view of the novel's dominant patterns we must view any joy as accidental and precarious (with the notable exception of the happy ending of the tale of Psyche [6.23–24], where happiness significantly is bestowed by divinity).

happiness. In both cases, conversion reveals (or in the case of the *Metamorphoses*, reveals on one level of reading) a world of "true" desire, pleasure, and happiness, and exposes the temporal world's versions of these as cheap imitations that kept the converts mired in the shifting quicksands of Fortuna.[20] Thus, in a very real sense what tapping into a transcendent realm offers to both converts is *solid knowledge*, since discourses of dualism posit true and false as the leading epistemological categories. Religion gives both converts a superstructure of meaning and an unchanging source of values and valorizations to replace the ones that they have lost. In other words, religion's primary function is to stabilize and order reality.

In spite of their clear thematic links, there are obvious differences in narrative technique between the *Confessions* and the *Metamorphoses* that are great enough to have obscured the similarities in most critics' minds. To a large extent these differences are of course a function of the difference in genre, but Apuleius compounds the problems beyond what is dictated by generic constraints. Stated succinctly, the problem is this: in the *Confessions*, as in other autobiographical accounts of conversion, the narrator is constantly present in the text as a commentator on and interpreter of the events of his past life. From the vantage point of the present, that is, the time of writing, the narrator imposes a narrative and conceptual framework on past experience that situates it in a larger context and gives it coherence and meaning. The narrator takes this hermeneutic role in all autobiography but perhaps especially so in autobiographies of conversion insofar as the discovery of a structure of meaning is what is explicitly being recounted. Moreover, the *actor* or past self typically is represented as having been keenly aware that something was amiss all along, and the narrative tracks the subject's conscious efforts to find a solution. Augustine's *Confessions* perfectly illustrates these two principles of spiritual autobiography. Augustine the narrator in fact actually addresses much of his work to the God,

---

20. In his speech at 11.15, the priest Mithras makes it clear that Isis offers protection against the vicissitudes of Fortune. The last word of the novel is *gaudebam*, suggesting that Lucius the *actor*-convert has found the lasting happiness that only divinity can bestow—if one reads it, as one might, without irony. Of course, Book 11 and in fact the novel as a whole have features that problematize the apparently neat closure represented by Lucius' conversion. See chapter 6, section 3.

whom he fully knows only at its end, but who informs every aspect of his present interpretation of the past.

But the *Metamorphoses* is different, and more different than it needs to be simply by virtue of its character as a fictional confession as opposed to a "true" autobiography. There is a glaring absence in the novel of any retrospective narrator providing a running commentary on past action and where it is tending. All the reader gets is Lucius the *actor*'s experiences *as they happen*, in all their meaningless randomness, devoid of the overarching sense-making apparatus ordinarily emanating from the narrator-convert. Lucius the narrator (or Lucius-*auctor* in Winkler's terms) strangely withholds all reflective commentary, and we are utterly surprised when the *actor*'s picaresque adventures are brought to a screeching halt by his sudden conversion in Book 11. To complicate matters further, Lucius the *actor* himself is represented as being completely unreflective; he betrays no trace of being engaged in a conscious search for meaning in the chaos of his experience. On the contrary, he just bumbles along from crisis to crisis, apparently oblivious to the possibility that the inane and episodic character of his life suggests that it may be time to try something new. This inescapable absence of any indication of "moral" growth on Lucius the *actor*'s part has long frustrated critics determined to see in the *Metamorphoses* a *Bildungsroman* constructed along more familiar lines. Such critics assume moreover that conversion must be moral in its focus, and so take a stance that only complicates their doomed search for "growth" on the *actor*'s part.

I have argued above that Lucius and Augustine are to be seen as suffering from the same sort of malaise, but that it is expressed very differently in the two works. The "message" conveyed explicitly in Augustine's tortured soul-searching commentary is implicit in the action of the novel and in the way it is presented. The failure of conventional values to provide real satisfaction is symbolized in the repetitive and unproductive behavior of the novel's characters and especially of Lucius himself. In the *Confessions*, the pursuit of false values is represented for the most part by Augustine's systematic fulfillment of societally sanctioned ambitions. In the *Metamorphoses*, on the other hand, it is reduced to the compulsive and undirected absorption of Apuleius' restless characters in the most fleeting, frivolous, and randomly appearing diversions. Yet Lucius the *actor* never seems to recognize or diagnose the syndrome, and Lucius the narrator never imposes an Augustinian explanation. This silence is curious indeed. Critics before Winkler for the most part pretended that the problem did not exist. In Winkler's view, the narrator's destabilizing absence from the narrative (which continues into Book 11) is a function of the novel's multivocality. It is an integral component in the Apuleian strategy of resistance to authorized interpretations, a strategy devised to convey the author's point that all knowledge is subjective and arbitrary. Apuleius threads the *Metamorphoses* with (at least) three major tracks or voices: those of Apuleius-*auctor*, Lucius-*auctor*, and Lucius-*actor*. But these voices never converge, not even at the very end; what we are left with instead are loose ends and a longing for closure that will not come. "The gap," as Winkler (1985, 241) puts it, "is never closed."

It seems to me that at another level—the level of our *actor* Lucius and the representation of *his* perceptions and experiences—a principle other than that of overarching indeterminacy is at work, namely the principle of psychological verisimilitude. It is well documented that sudden conversions do happen, preceded by no conscious or systematic search on the part of the convert and indeed adumbrated by no evident preparation of any kind. By presenting Lucius the *actor* as altogether oblivious to his deeper need, his thoughts never extending beyond the moment or, more often, the crisis at hand, Apuleius vividly recreates for the reader the experience of a hapless chosen one "slouching toward Bethlehem" by indirection, as in fact many others after and perhaps before him have done. The failure of the narrator, Lucius the convert, to provide any commentary from the beginning that would prepare us for the conversion further reproduces its suddenness for the reader. Thus, the evidence for Lucius' "moral progress" and growing self-awareness long sought in the text by critics as being indispensible to a proper account of conversion is not as indispensible as has been supposed. The model of conversion preceded by conscious intellectual or ethical striving is, after all, in origin a Platonic one. But the religious content of the novel is syncretizing; the absence of any indication that this was the pattern of Lucius in the *Metamorphoses* is one argument for liberating the novel from the exclusively Platonic frameworks into which it has often been forced. Other models allow for a sublimated search and for the "quiet desperation" of a far less introspective experience.[21]

---

21. It is worth noting here that although Augustine's own conversion was a protracted and self-conscious affair, he is very much impressed by the story of an imperial official's sudden conversion to Christianity (8.6.15).

Under the heading "The Phenomenology of Grace," Winkler (1985, 242–47) allows for the explanation outlined above in the course of reviewing other approaches to the problem of the persistent separateness of *auctor* and *actor*. Ultimately he dismisses it (along with all the others) because in its previous incarnations it has failed to acknowledge the indeterminate and "purposely problematic" character of the text, instead falling into the trap of looking for a higher authority to make sense of the novel. It is his favorite among the wrongheaded monolithic theories, however, because it "comes to grips with the surprise of the new meaning introduced in Book 11 and with Lucius' reticence to address the issue of its concealment in Books 1–10" (228). In Winkler's words, the "Phenomenology of Grace" school holds that the *Metamorphoses* is designed to "reproduce in the reader an *experience* of grace granted"—granted suddenly and without its being sought. "The reader is made," his summary continues, "to participate not only in the events of Lucius' fictional life but in the original helplessness of not knowing where they might lead."[22] Religious revelation does not involve the "educational transaction" that Platonizing interpreters have sought; rather it is a "brute experience" full of "surprise and wonder," which the narrative technique of Apuleius very effectively reproduces (242–44). The reservations expressed by Winkler about this view begin to fade, it seems to me, if we understand that indeterminacy and religious experience are not mutually exclusive, and that, in fact, a perception of the former can be integral to the latter when religious experience is taken to include not only conversion itself but the crisis leading up to it. In my reading, moreover, the operation of the "phenomenology of grace" in the *actor*'s reality in no way rules out the simultaneous presence of a skeptical authorial voice offering a circumspect (and often ironic) commentary on the subjective nature of Lucius', and all, religious experience.

The phenomenon of what William James would call "subconscious incubation" and his analysis of sudden conversion have never been scrutinized for their possible relevance to the way religious experience is represented in the *Metamorphoses*. James takes full advantage of then embryonic ideas about the unconscious—"whole systems of underground life," as he puts it (1958, 189)—to formulate a preliminary the-

---

22. Winkler cites B. Kenny (1974) as one who had previously developed this view.

ory about sudden conversion, which in its essentials is still accepted today. Speaking about the operation of the unconscious in general, James posits that any "shifting of men's centers of personal energy" (of which conversion is one type) *might* be the result of "conscious processes of thought and will" of the sort that critics have tried to impute to Lucius. But such shifts are just as likely to be the product of the "subconscious incubation and maturing of motives deposited by the experiences of life," whose results "when ripe . . . hatch out or burst into flower" (186). The unconscious, James continues, is a place existing for "the accumulation of vestiges of sensible experience (whether inattentively or attentively registered), and for their elaboration . . . into results that end by attaining such a tension that they may at times enter consciousness with something like a burst" (190). For our purposes James' aside that experiences do not need to be "attentively registered" in order to incubate and surface in some form at a later time is of obvious relevance in connection with the apparent failure of Lucius to register his discontent the way Augustine presents himself as doing.

Of course, these ideas are axiomatic to most of us living in the post-Freudian world, and they have been indelibly inscribed in the literature on religious experience in general and sudden conversion in particular. As is often the case, however, James expresses the connections as well as or better than any of his successors. He makes a well-known distinction between two types of conversion: the volitional conversion, which involves a conscious quest for meaning and a gradual and considered change of views, and the sudden, or crisis, conversion, which is preceded by striving (often in a disguised or misdirected form, that is, not aimed in the direction in which the final solution will lie), frustration, abandonment of the effort, and then a sudden revelation of the "truth" (1958, 168–76). Apparently crucial to this self-surrender type of conversion is the condition that conscious effort must be given up; will starts the process, but the relevant mental activity goes on toward its conclusion involuntarily and unconsciously after the effort has ceased. James compares the common experience of trying hard, but unsuccessfully, to remember something, giving up, then having the information dislodge itself and come to the surface when we least expect it. He explains the psychodynamics behind sudden conversion this way:

> A man's conscious wit and will, so far as they strain towards the
> ideal, are aiming at something only dimly and inaccurately imag-

ined. Yet all the while forces of mere organic ripening within him are going on towards their own prefigured result, and his conscious strainings are letting loose subconscious allies behind the scenes, which in their way work towards rearrangement; and the rearrangement towards which all these deeper forces tend is pretty surely definite, and definitely different from what he consciously conceives and determines. It may consequently be actually interfered with (jammed, as it were like the lost word when we seek too energetically to recall it), by his voluntary efforts slanting from the true direction. (172–73)

This is a very interesting analysis for the light it sheds on Apuleius' representation of the religious experience of Lucius. I have argued that Lucius' conscious efforts seem to be engaged in just the sort of misdirected search suggested here by James. In religious discourse, Lucius' true desire (the *desiderium dei*), which he does not recognize as such, is for connection with the transcendent realm of divinity, but his "voluntary efforts slant from the true direction" and lead him down all sorts of dead-end streets, beckoning with their "false" senses of fulfillment. James' formulation allows for the kind of complete obliviousness to the "true" problem and the "true" solution that Lucius seems to display, as well as for the more consciously registered appreciation of need expressed by Augustine. For a long time Lucius' continuing efforts to satisfy his desire in the only ways he knows "jam" the emergence of a new approach to the problem, one lying altogether outside his old range of vision. It is the force of habit—the unthinking reliance on habituated structures of meaning to provide answers and the inability to step outside of those structures in order to see the problem from a different angle—that obstructs change and keeps him spinning his wheels in the same rut. James discusses the role of habit in blocking cognitive progress. "Formed associations of ideas and habits are usually factors of retardation in such changes of equilibrium," he writes. "A mental system may be undermined or weakened by . . . interstitial alteration just as a building is, and yet for a time keep upright by dead habit" (1958, 163). I know of no better description of Lucius' dogged and episodic preconversion lurching than that provided inadvertently by James in the last phrase.

James also makes a case for the role of simple exhaustion in the process of (apparently) sudden conversion. When the struggle, whatever its character or ostensible character, becomes too much to bear, we get "so exhausted . . . that we have to stop, so we drop down, give up, and don't care any longer. Our emotional brain-centers strike work, and we lapse into temporary apathy" (1958, 173). Just so does Lucius "drop down" from exhaustion on the beach at Corinth after escaping from the arena at the end of Book 10, and that is the moment when his life changes completely. What are we to infer has happened to him? James provides an answer when he argues that a "small . . . stimulus will overthrow the mind into a new state of equilibrium when the process of [unconscious] preparation and incubation has proceeded far enough" (148). "When the fruit is ripe," he explains succinctly, "a touch will make it fall" (150). Precisely what the precipitating "touch" is for Lucius is not entirely clear. It is clear enough, however, that *something* about the prospect of performing in the arena with the condemned woman—be it the danger, the humiliation, or simply that it focuses in his mind his weariness with his old life and its pointless absurdities— sends him, so to speak, over the edge. Whatever impels Lucius to make the break at this point, his reorientation gels with such suddenness that to any reader or onlooker there appears to be, as James notes is often the case, "an element of marvel" in it (163).[23]

There are many subsequent versions of William James' "subconscious incubation" in the literature on religious conversion, and it would be otiose to enumerate them all. One of the more instructive expressions of it is found in the work of Batson and Ventis, whose

----

23. As usual, James provides a collection of case histories to support his theory: for example, Jouffroy and his "counter-conversion" ("'this . . . revolution had not taken place in the broad daylight of my consciousness. . . . It had gone on in silence, by an involuntary elaboration of which I was not the accomplice; and although I had in reality long ceased to be a Christian, yet . . . I should have shuddered to suspect it, and thought it calumny had I been accused of such a falling away'") (1958, 163); a contemporary Oxford graduate and correspondent of Leuba who was converted suddenly one day, at a time when he "'was in no way troubled about [his] soul'" (179–81); an irreligious French Jew who experienced a sudden conversion to Roman Catholicism, about whom James notes that the "predisposing conditions appear to have been slight" (181–84); and G.C. Finney, whose *Memoirs* (1876) record that "'without any expectation of it, without ever having the thought in my mind that there was any such thing for me, without any recollection that I had ever heard the thing mentioned by any person in the world, the Holy Spirit descended upon me in a manner that seemed to go through me, body and soul'" (204).

approach to religious experience relies on an analogy between it and the creative process, as we saw in chapter 3. In describing this process, so similar in their view to the psychodynamics of conversion, Batson and Ventis observe that it is the straitjacket of our dominant and habituated cognitive organizations that keeps us from approaching apparently intractable problems in fresh ways. They cite four cases of scientific creativity, all culminating in a "eureka-experience" that came in a flash when it was least expected and after all concerted effort had been given up (1982, 74–76).[24] What happens in such moments is the final collapse of the impeding cognitive structure against which the solution has been straining and the falling into place of a new structure that acknowledges and accommodates the problem's realities. Batson and Ventis echo James on the matter of will as well as of habit. In their schematization of the stages in the creative process, they posit that the process begins "with a period of baffled struggle in which the individual attempts to solve the problem in terms of his or her existing cognitive structures" and "begins to feel trapped within the current organization with no way out." There follows a phase of incubation brought on by exhaustion, in which active pursuit of an answer ceases and effort is given up. It is only then that illumination and a release of long accumulated tension comes. They note that "psychoanalytic writers suggest that this illumination occurs at the level of the unconscious or nonconscious mind" (77–78). According to Batson and Ventis, religious experience can follow a parallel trajectory. A new vision emerges only after a period of "trying and failing to regain existential meaning within one's existing reality," in an effort that leads to exhaustion and giving up (83–84). Again, we think of Lucius on the beach.[25]

One further citation from a modern study will serve to demonstrate

---

24. The cases are: Archimedes and the principle of specific gravity; the mathematician Poincaré and Fuchsian equations; the chemist Kekulé and the benzene ring; and Darwin and the theory of evolution.

25. Like James, Batson and Ventis provide supporting case histories. An especially interesting one for our purposes is that of a Princeton undergraduate who had a completely unexpected mystical experience in his dormitory room. The student insisted afterwards that "he had no serious problems or concerns at the time and had no idea why or how this 'white light' experience occurred." Batson and Ventis comment that the "experience does not appear to have been precipitated by an existential crisis, *at least not a conscious one* [emphasis mine]" (1982, 83 n. 2).

that an oblivious and distracted preconvert is not so inconsistent with the realistic representation of religious experience, at least as it is understood in the narratives of social science, as many critics have assumed it to be. We encountered the work of Richardson (et al. 1979) in chapter 3 (section 3), in connection with the question of the problem-solving perspective within which Lucius is represented as operating. In the theoretical framework that he and his colleagues establish for their study of a "Jesus Movement" commune of the late 1960s and early 1970s, Richardson includes five "major perspectives for interpreting and dealing with felt problems" (239). They are, as we have seen, the psychiatric, the political, the religious, the physiological, and the conventional. Critics of the *Metamorphoses* have made the mistake of assuming that Lucius ought to be represented as trying to solve his problems within a religious perspective in order for his preconversion experience to make sense as such. But Richardson suggests that it is just as likely that efforts toward resolution will take place within one or more of the other problem-solving perspectives before the subject finally realizes, and not always consciously, that he has exhausted those possibilities and moves to a religious perspective. Of particular interest in connection with Lucius' behavior as it is represented in Books 1 through 10 are the physiological and the conventional perspectives. Again, Richardson defines the first as the "use of elements or activities to affect the body and mind in a way that furnishes some 'meaning' for the person" involved, sex and drugs being the most perennially popular items from the menu of potential "elements and activities" (238). It hardly needs pointing out that the Lucius of Books 1 through 10 has a proclivity in this direction, but this proclivity has never been read by critics as evidence of dissatisfaction and searching, as it clearly can be.

Even more illuminating is the application of the idea of the conventional perspective to the picture of Lucius. Significantly, Richardson gives this approach the alternative name of the "muddle through" perspective, like James inadvertently conjuring up an image of our ass as he lurches from crisis to crisis in the *Metamorphoses*.[26] According to

---

26. Straus (1976, 253–58) calls it "creative bumbling": "The sense that 'I am a seeker (after transcendence)' only arises after the person has repeatedly acted and interacted as a seeker over some period of time. A novice's self-conception rarely involves more than a vague sense of wanting change" (254).

Richardson (quoting Lofland and Stark 1965), those trapped inside this perspective tend either to "'persist in stressful situations with little or no relief'" or to take stabs at executing "'a number of maneuvers to put the problem out of mind.'" The latter tactic results not in true solutions but rather in mere "'compensations for or distractions from problems of living.'" These compensations can involve the entire range of conventional values and common pleasures available in any given era, pursued perhaps with inordinate zeal, as well as more obviously diversionary measures (Richardson et al. 1979, 238). It is my contention that the behavior of Lucius can be read as exemplifying the "muddle through" approach. Of further interest for our purposes is Richardson's observation that "quite 'normal' activities [can be] deliberate or *even unconscious* attempts to solve felt problems" (emphasis mine). "Most people," he continues, "will try to 'muddle through' before dealing with their problem in more dramatic ways" (239). In other words, the lack that precedes conversion need not be specifically and consciously formulated, even by the preconvert; on the contrary, it might be "amorphous and little understood" and, accordingly, any attempts to address it not easily recognizable as such (258–59).

Richardson thus affirms the Jamesian view that the inadequacy of the preconvert's old values and paradigms can be felt at an unconscious level and that the only evidence of this type of crisis accessible to the eye of an observer is the sort of distracted and aimless casting about for diversion practiced compulsively by Lucius. Lucius' behavior therefore is in itself evidence of striving and searching for meaning, and critics have been prevented from seeing this by their attachment to a set of assumptions about what such a search, and any literary representation of it, ought to look like. Self-conscious rumination is not the only evidence of existential crisis, and Lucius' failure to engage in it does not mean that he cannot be read as having one. This failure and the failure of Lucius the narrator to provide a retrospective structuring commentary can be understood as two interlocking components in the representation of a certain kind of crisis and conversion. When the differences in how the narratives represent their crises as being experienced and acted out are accounted for, the *Metamorphoses* and the *Confessions* are very much alike indeed.[27]

---

27. For other discussions of sudden conversion, see, e.g., Hawkins 1985, 45–46, 167 n. 39 (she offers as the classic example the conversion of St. Paul on

3

The previous section was devoted to discussing some of the features of Apuleius' narrative technique that seem to create difficulties for anyone trying to take the *Metamorphoses* seriously, so to speak, as a narrative of conversion. The refusal of the experiencing and the narrating ego to give any indication that they are the same entity, or at least to converge in the end as they "should," according to generic conventions, has been a major factor in preventing critics from seeing important thematic connections between the *Metamorphoses* and other works unquestionably accepted as "serious" (if otherwise problematic) narratives of conversion. It is for this reason that I have suggested that there are ways of reading these Apuleian differences according to which they are consistent with the "authentic" representation of religious experience. But for now I want to return to the main thread of this chapter and to my argument that the crisis in values so much in evidence in both the novel and the *Confessions* is an expression of the sort of epistemological breakdown and subsequent paradigm shift discussed in chapter 3 as integral to one type of conversion. In Augustine's case the discovery that conventional values and valorizations are "false" is about as far as the breakdown goes, although this in itself represents a degree of cognitive crisis sufficient to support a reading of the *Confessions* as exemplifying the pattern that I have isolated. Still, the exposure of his old values as inadequate does not seem to lead in Augustine's case to the kind of comprehensive cognitive disorientation that I have attributed

---

the road to Damascus as it is described in *Acts of the Apostles* 9:3–9); Paloutzian 1983, 97–99; Scobie 1975, 105. As is often the case, ancient understanding prefigures the findings of modern social science: Lucretius' picture of the bored, distracted, and desperately unhappy rich man casting about for diversions and "muddling through" constitutes a pre-Apuleian version of sublimated existential crisis and the misdirected searching that seeks to ease it. It concludes: "Thus each man flees from himself . . . and hates himself because he is a sick man that knows not the cause of his complaint. . . . [B]y living we cannot forge for ourselves any new pleasure; but while we have not what we crave, that seems to surpass all else; afterwards when we have attained that, we crave something else; one unchanging thirst of life fills us and our mouths are forever agape" (*De rerum natura* 1053–84, trans. W.H.D. Rouse [London and New York: Loeb Classical Library, 1924]). Of course, Lucretius is quite clear that the root of such behavior is anxiety about death.

to Lucius in chapters 1 and 2, although there are glimmers of "things falling apart" around Augustine in the *Confessions* as well, as we will soon see. The discussion in chapter 3, however, certainly provides a framework for reading the radical anomy of *Metamorphoses* 1 through 10 as a symptom—a more advanced stage, one might say—of Lucius' preconversion crisis, and we will see that there are parallels in other conversion narratives to this sort of radical disintegration of perspective.

In addition to the fundamental thematic parallel of the exposure of "false" values, the *Metamorphoses* and the *Confessions* share other motifs related to this basic scheme and thus to the portrayal of the breakdown and shifting of paradigms in general. Both narrators suggest that the ongoing devaluation of conventional activity caused the world around their experiencing selves to show itself to them in a new light. As the structuring discourses whose function is to impart meaning to these activities disintegrates, the world of the *actors* acquires a nebulous and threatening quality, even in its physical aspects. They seek solid ground but find only illusions, traps, and snares. We recall that Tolstoy was beset by a horrific sense of the "altered and estranged aspect which the world assumed" (James 1958, 128) once its phenomena had been stripped of their assigned meaning. Tolstoy was experiencing the sort of Bergeresque "terror of anomy" that can occur when structures of meaning collapse. Similarly, Augustine repeatedly describes his benighted preconversion life as a period of tentative groping on a "dark and slippery path" (*[per tenebras et lubricum]*, 6.1.1; cf. 4.2.2, where he worries that his faith is "slipping and sliding on a slippery path" *[lapsans in lubrico]*). He recalls his sensation that he was constantly losing his footing on this treacherous ground, covered as it was at every turn with traps and snares (*insidiae* and *laquei*) in the form of "worldly" values and "false" beliefs.[28] It is only after his conversion that Augustine the narrator fully understands that these temptations were, as he now believes, sheer illusion: "I had loved vanity and I had sought falsehood. . . . For in the illusions which I had taken as truth were only vanity and falsehood" [*dilexeram enim vanitatem et quaesieram mendacium. . . . in phantasmatis enim, quae pro veritate tenueram, vanitas erat et mendacium*]

---

28. For figurative *insidiae* and *laquei* in the *Confessions*, see, e.g., 3.6.10; 4.6.11; 5.3.3; 7.13; 6.12.21; 7.21.27; 10.31.44; 10.34.52; 10.35.56; 10.36.59.

(9.4.9; cf. 3.7.2, passim). But long before he diagnoses the problem, suspicions that this was the case nag at him more and more.

Lucius too finds his footsteps planted on *terra infirma*. The priest Mithras is a problematic figure; nevertheless he appears to speak something like the truth when he chastises Lucius for having allowed himself to be diverted onto the "slippery path of uncritical youth" *[lubricum virentis aetatulae]* (11.15) in his earlier life. This echoes the words of Socrates to Aristomenes in Book 1 (6), when Socrates laments that he has fallen victim to the "slippery meanderings" of Fortuna, the symbol of random, structureless experience. In the course of his adventures, Lucius is beset by actual traps and snares (*insidiae* and *laquei*), even as Augustine is surrounded by metaphorical ones.[29] These physical pitfalls moreover have their social counterpart in the deception routinely practiced by the novel's duplicitous characters, in treacherous acts often characterized as *insidiae* and *laquei*. For example, the deranged Corinthian murderess commences her crime spree by "ambushing the girl [her husband's innocent sister] with the cruelest snares of death" *[crudelissimis laqueis mortis insidiari]*, into which the girl falls unsuspecting (*laqueos insidiarum accessit,* 10.24); and the doctor's wife is duped into tripping in the "snares of deceit" *[laqueis fraudium . . . inducta]* (10.27). These images operate within a larger network of deceptive appearances in the novel and thus are to be connected with the slippage of reliable correspondences and the progressive disintegration of the structures formerly relied upon to fix reality in a more general sense.

Thus both narrators recall that they found themselves tentatively groping their way through a treacherous and highly suspect *terra infirma*. The inhabitants and the features of this landscape often turn out to be the opposite of what they appear to be, or to have an opposite value to that conventionally assigned to them. I have already touched

---

29. Physical traps: e.g., 2.18, Fotis' warning to Lucius that he is likely to be the target of a mugging (*insidiae*) in Hypata; 7.25, on the verge of escaping from the evil boy and the shepherds who had planned to castrate him, Lucius is disappointed in his hopes when "Fortuna lays a fresh ambush" *[insidiae]* for him; 8.15, the escape of the dead Charite's household, including Lucius, through the wolf-infested countryside where "ambushes lie hidden" *[latentes insidiae]*; and 8.16, they fall into a "far worse trap" *[peiores laquei]* when they are attacked by suspicious farmers instead. On duplicity and deception, see chapter 2, section 1.

on the thorny, if not intractable, problem of sorting out what "really" happened from what is retrojected into the past by the narrator of auto-biography or quasi autobiography. Even granting this qualification, however, it does still seem that the sense of alienation from their envi-ronments that both Augustine and Lucius the *actors* experience (as did Tolstoy after them) is represented as developing gradually and sponta-neously, and as constituting a major component in their perception *before* conversion. It does not appear to be a feature of a newfound belief in some doctrinal paradox about the unreality of material reality, which the convert-narrators then project back onto their past experience from the comfort of their assurance states. Of course this does not mean that such a doctrinal paradox was not in the discursive air in which the experience materialized or was imagined, or that other doctrinal con-structions and interpretations are not imposed by the narrator upon each "experience" in retrospect. In fact, the entire scheme of "false" as opposed to "true" values is just such a construction, in the general sense that it represents a typical framework for interpreting past aporia when its resolution is a religious one.

In view of the newly inhospitable quality that their worlds have acquired, it is not surprising that both *actors* would be depicted as responding to it with a sense of dispossession, of being cut off from what is familiar—exiles in search of a home. Augustine remembers his misguided past as a time when he wandered "far from God into a dis-tant region" (*[in longinquam regionem]*, 4.16.30; cf. 12.11.13, passim). As a convert, he is convinced that God's realm alone is his true homeland (his *patria*, e.g., 7.20.26; 7.21.27). Significantly, exile is a common fate in the novel also. Both Aristomenes and Thelyphron are barred from their homelands and consigned to rootless wandering for the rest of their days.[30] The fact that both Aristomenes and Lucius speak of their exiles as voluntary is in itself significant, insofar as perverse willfulness is invoked explicitly in the *Confessions* and implicitly in the *Metamorphoses* as an important force in keeping the misguided pilgrims on the wrong course. Among Lucius' many sweet-talking pledges to Fotis is one in

---

30. 1.19, "I fled through remote and pathless wilderness and embraced a voluntary exile after leaving behind my homeland and ancestral hearth" [*per diversas et avias solitudines aufugi et . . . relicta patria et lare ultroneum exilium amplexus*]; 2.30, "Nor was I able to return to my ancestral hearth" [*nec . . . lari me patrio reddere potui*].

which he swears that he is "neither thinking about his ancestral hearth nor contemplating a homecoming"; all he cares about, he continues, is spending the night with her (*nec larem requiro nec domuitionem paro et nocte ista nihil antepono*, 3.19). He willingly postpones his literal homecoming for the pleasure of the moment, little suspecting that this decision is inviting on himself an exile of far greater dimensions than the geographical. The affair with Fotis is at one level depicted in an exuberant and carefree spirit, one apparently far from the guilt over carnal pleasures that plagues Augustine; I have argued moreover that it is not sex per se that is demonized in either work. Nevertheless, the motif of the scorned homecoming links Lucius' fling with the more lurid and unambiguously ruinous sexual tryst of Socrates. According to Aristomenes, Socrates "preferred carnal pleasures and a wrinkly whore to his hearth and children" [*voluptatem Veneriam et scortum scorteum lari et liberis praetulisti*] (1.8).

In the limbo where both Lucius and Augustine find themselves floating, ordinary human activities begin to impress them differently. Conventional life, with its ever more transparent mistaken premises and spurious goals, presents itself to them as a mad delusion, a frenzied search for meaning that lights instead on inane diversions. This view is dramatized in both works by the use of images of reckless rashness and even madness in connection with all the activities once thought worthwhile but now increasingly suspected of "falseness." Augustine claims that he vowed in the midst of his inquiry that after he found truth (*sapientia*), he would renounce the "mad delusions" [*insaniae mendaces*] upon which his current life was based (6.11.18; cf. 8.2.4, passim). These delusions range from conventional ambitions and his belief in the value of rhetoric to his wrongheaded theological formulations and, at the other end of the spectrum, the impulses of teenage lust. Rhetoricians, he says, are driven by their own "madness" and "hallucinations" [*furor*] and [*deliramenta*] to persuade their "crazy" [*insani*] admirers of the value of the "mad delusions" [*insaniae mendaces*] passed off as truth by the craft (1.17.27; 8.2.5; 9.2.2). Likewise, his early mistaken understanding of the exact nature of the trinity was "madness" (*insania*, 7.14.20), as was something of such an apparently different order as the first stirrings of sexual desire (*vesania libininis*, 2.2.4). Augustine presents his past self as rushing blindly and headlong into the abyss of false beliefs (e.g., *praeceps ibam tanta caecitate*, 2.3.7). The image of a headlong and blind dash to perdition is repeated in the description of the effect that the games had on Alypius: the "madness of the games" [*insania circensium*] awoke in him a "blind and headlong desire" [*caecum et praeceps studium*] (6.7.11–12) to immerse himself in the perverse pleasures that they offered. The stark image of the abyss (*abyssus*) as a symbol of cognitive, and thus moral, free fall occurs very frequently in the *Confessions* (e.g., 2.4.9; 9.1.1; 13.13.14; 13.14.15).

We recall that as his preconversion crisis progressed Tolstoy too had a growing sense of human activity as a lot of sound and fury, signifying nothing. It was a joke, it was madness, it was driven by delusion. The quickening pace of frenetic and counterproductive activity in the *Metamorphoses*, and especially in Books 7 through 10 as the turning point draws closer, in itself creates an impression of *insania*. But in several passages in the novel, as in the confessional narratives of both Augustine and Tolstoy, the language of madness and of reckless and willful persistence in a misguided course is enlisted to support the point. For example, Lucius is described as being out of his mind with excitement at the spectacle of Pamphile's transformation (*exterminatus animi attonitus in amentiam*, 3.22). Earlier, in spite of (or perhaps because of) Byrrhena's admonition that he avoid the magical doings at Milo's house, Lucius is in a blind frenzy of desire to be admitted to them:

> Far from heeding her warning, I yearned to hurl myself willingly headlong into the bottom of the abyss with one quick leap. I flew like a madman in a great rush back to Milo's house.
>
> [*tantum a cautela Pamphiles afui ut etiam ultro gestirem . . . me volens . . . prorsus in ipsum barathrum saltu concito praecipitare. . . . vecors animi . . . ad Milonis hospitium perniciter evolo.*] (2.6)

The images here—of a mad, willful, headlong leap into a metaphorical abyss (here, *barathrum*)—are strikingly similar to those regularly used by Augustine. The pagan narrative as a whole, in fact, teems with frenzied but ultimately futile sound and fury. Often it is provoked by erotic desire. The wicked stepmother is driven "headlong by madness" [*vaesania praeceps*] (10.4) to plot her destructive acts. Likewise, Thrasyllus had "hurled himself headlong [*sese . . . praecipitaverat*] and, without knowing it, little by little into the deep ruin that desire [*cupido*] brings" (8.2). But madness can have other sources—greed and pride, for example, as in the case of the arrogant young landlord, a "mad, raving bandit" [*vaesanus . . . furiosus latro*] (9.36, 9.38).

What motivates all this frantic casting about? I think that both narratives offer fundamentally the same answer, although as usual it is much more explicitly stated in Augustine because of his systematic imposition of an interpretive framework on the events and perceptions of his past life. In the mind of Augustine the convert, the impulse behind all human striving, however secular it might appear, is an innate and unconscious "desire for God" [*desiderium dei*], which is deceived and diverted toward a wide range of temporal god-surrogates. As he muses to God at 10.27.38, "you were inside all along but I was seeking you in things of the world" [*ecce intus eras et ego foris et ibi te quaerebam*]. When the *desiderium dei* is directed toward objects other than God, the deceived lover inadvertently serves a demon who "imitates God in a perverse and distorted way [*te perversa et distorta via imitanti*] (10.36.59; cf., e.g., 2.6.14). Augustine repeatedly characterizes the *desiderium dei* as a kind of hunger (*esurio*) or thirst (*sitis*), thereby making it clear that he considers it a basic human drive.[31] Yet in spite of its power, it generally goes without being correctly named, and he makes it clear that it was not so named by him until after his conversion. He speaks of his distracted and desperate preconversion activities as representing a wrongheaded response to this desire when it was only vaguely apprehended and not yet recognized for what it truly was. The activities in question could be as apparently different as his early studies in science and philosophy (for example, at 3.6.10), on the one hand, and on the other his effort to find "someone or something to love" upon arriving in Carthage (3.1.1). In both these passages, Augustine speaks of himself as sampling diverse "dishes" in a misguided attempt to satisfy an *esurio* and a *sitis* that were actually (realizes Augustine the narrator) for God.

In keeping with Apuleius' avoidance of the type of retrospective commentary that unifies the *Confessions*, Lucius the narrator never diagnoses his (or others') illness as a longing for divinity that goes unsatisfied because its "true" character is not understood. Yet the parallels with Augustine in the representation of Lucius the preconvert as

---

31. Hunger and thirst: see, e.g., 3.1.1; 3.6.10; 7.17.23; 9.4.10; 10.27.38; 11.1.1; 11.2.3; 11.30.40; 12.11.13; 13.13.14; 13.17.21. See Hawkins 1985, 56–57 on hunger as a metaphor for spiritual need in the *Confessions*.

a deluded pursuer of "false" values, along with the religious resolution
of the plot, allow us to read Lucius too as bumbling along, driven by
some kind of *desiderium dei*. He has no awareness of what his true need
is until it unexpectedly catches up with him at the beginning of Book
11. Moreover, Apuleius seems to have Lucius unwittingly diagnose his
own disease when, in the course of persuading Aristomenes to tell his
tale at the beginning of Book 1, Lucius remarks that he is someone who
"thirsts after novelty" (he is, he says, a *sititor novitatis*, 1.2). Like Augustine, Lucius knows that he thirsts after something; the problem before
his conversion is that he persists in attempting to satisfy this thirst with
"novelty"—that is, with new and untasted, but ephemeral, pleasures—
when it can be truly quenched only by Isis. In both narratives, the
explanatory trope of a desire for God, whether suggested or explicitly
articulated, is necessarily a feature of the narrator's perspective, as
opposed to that of the *actor* or the experiencing self. As a concept, it is
not part of the *actor's* cognitive apparatus. Frustrated *desiderium dei* is
part of a larger interpretive code used by converts to explain the causes
of cognitive and moral aporia *after* it has been resolved by adopting a
religious master narrative. The idea of an innate human desire for
union with the divine is central to how religious world views explain
any vague and wistful longing for any transcendental signified that
will make sense of the *disiecta membra* of experience.

Critics have long pointed to curiosity as an important thematic link
between the *Confessions* and the *Metamorphoses*.[32] What has not been
noticed is that both works either explicitly or implicitly represent
curiosity as one of the primary forms that the displaced desire for God

---

32. For discussion of what curiosity seems to have meant in a range of
ancient authors, including Apuleius and Augustine, see Mette 1956; Labhardt
1960; Joly 1961; 1966; and Walsh 1988. On curiosity in the *Metamorphoses*, see
Lancel 1961; Schlam 1968b; Sandy 1971; deFilippo 1990; also Schlam 1992, 48–57
(= chap. 5, "Curiosity, Spectacle, and Wonder"). These discussions on the
whole tend to focus on the idea of curiosity as the impulse behind the search for
forbidden knowledge. But in both the *Metamorphoses* and the *Confessions*, the
curiosi are just as likely (and in the novel more likely) to be distracted spontaneously by trivial pursuits as they are to be engaged consciously in a directed
quest. Again, by equating apparently harmless and clearly dangerous objects of
curiosity, both authors suggest that it is the impulse itself that is to be faulted,
insofar as it represents being derailed from the right path and being oriented
toward the wrong paradigms of value.

can take. Curiosity is a "false" desire, and when it is gratified by being directed toward novelty the result is distraction and the accumulation of random experiences and information, but not wisdom. *Confessions* 10.35 contains a lengthy discussion of curiosity and the reasons why Augustine regards it as a symptom of spiritual derailment. Curiosity, he asserts, is a "lust for experience and knowledge" [*experiendi noscendique libido*] for its own sake, with no consideration of its actual value in the moral life of the subject. Curiosity is to the mind what lust is to the body: it is a mental desire *(cupiditas)*, a thirst to gratify the eye (or the other senses or the intellect) with knowledge or experience of meaningless things *(vana)*. It can impel people to direct their attention even toward ghastly sights in order to create in themselves, just for the sake of the experience, sensations of horror or sorrow.[33]

The list of common objects of curiosity that Augustine assembles at 10.35 includes freaks and prodigies displayed in public shows, natural phenomena, and theatrical productions, as well as astrological and other sacrilegious rites. Of special interest in relation to Lucius' weaknesses is the inclusion on Augustine's list of magical arts, but also foolish tales and unexpected sights, which can be as unspectacular as that of a spider catching flies. The crucial thing is that Augustine equates these apparently disparate objects of curiosity, insofar as all of them represent a focus of the desiderative impulse on "trivial and insignificant matters," which divert the mind from serious thought and reduce people to "idle gaping" [*vanus hebescere*].[34] The concern about curiosity expressed by Augustine at 10.35 is amply illustrated throughout the *Confessions*. The objects of curiosity proscribed by Augustine at some point or another include *spectacula* of various sorts, from shows in the theater (1.10.16) and gladiatorial games (where Alypius is "conquered by curiosity" [*curiositate victus*], 6.8.13) to the *curiosae visiones* conjured up by sacrilegious rites (10.42.67); the "false tales" of drama (1.10.16) and other literature (1.13.22); unfamiliar experiences (for example, when Alypius contemplates getting married out of sheer curiosity about the married state, 6.12.22); and new pieces of scientific or miscel-

---

33. Here Augustine gives the example of a mutilated body as the object of curiosity. We recall the desire *(studium)* of the citizens to view the body of the dead Tlepolemus at *Metamorphoses* 8.6.

34. For other general condemnations of curiosity in the *Confessions* apart from 10.35, see, e.g., 1.14.23; 3.3.5; 10.3.3; 13.20.28; 13.21.30.

laneous knowledge (5.3.4; 10.37.60). It is significant that in the above passages, as in the *Metamorphoses*, curiosity is equated with desire *(desiderium, cupido)* in two of them (6.12, 10.42) and associated with pleasure *(voluptas)* in two others (6.8, 10.37).

No one would deny that curiosity is one of the primary engines of action in the *Metamorphoses*. We have already seen some of the major instances of curiosity's indulgence in the novel and noted that Apuleius, like Augustine, formulates curiosity as a kind of misguided desire. Indeed, at the story's very outset Lucius identifies himself as one who is "curious about everything" *[curiosus alioquin]* (2.6) and who would like to know "if not everything then at least most things" (1.2). The objects to which Lucius applies this urge in the course of the action include many of the diversions condemned by Augustine: magic; *spectacula*, from the institutionalized (that is, shows and games) to the most randomly appearing; and the numerous allegedly "pleasant" *[lepidae]* tales that bind the novel together. In the scenes in which Lucius comes to a dead stop in the midst of a pressing crisis to take note of an unusual sight (for example, as he is being attacked by mad dogs at 8.17; immediately before his dreaded performance in the arena at 10.29), the warning of Augustine that curiosity has the power to distract us from serious business is graphically, and absurdly, illustrated. All these diversions are united by the common property of *novitas*, the thirst for which, it will be remembered, Lucius admits is one of his own chief motivating impulses (1.2). The thirst for novelty drives others in the *Metamorphoses* as well. For example, the crowd gathering to get a glimpse of Demochares' new bear (actually the bandit Thrasyleon in disguise) casts "curious looks" *[curiosi aspectus]* toward the pseudo-animal, which is said to offer the sort of *novitas* that often suddenly grabs people's attention (4.16). Likewise, at 10.16, Thiasos is thrilled at the "novelty of the spectacle" *[novitas spectaculi]* of the ass eating human food; and at 10.23, Lucius' keeper sees the possibility of pleasing his master with a "novel spectacle" *[novum spectaculum]*.[35] Augustine never explicitly connects curiosity with novelty, but the implica-

---

35. Related are the "contrived novelty" *[commenta novitas]* (3.11) of the Risus festival, which the citizens of Hypata so heartily enjoy; and the "excessive newness" *[nimia novitas]* (9.18) of the gold coins that tempt Myrmex. Here *novitas* carries a double meaning in that the coins are newly minted but also offer the slave a novel experience, that of possessing wealth.

tion at 10.35 and elsewhere is certainly that the thrill of novelty is the desired object of activities driven by curiosity. Moreover, he identifies the appeal of the new as the force that is at least partially responsible for luring him into worldly vices, which he calls the *novissimae res* of his youth (2.2.3), and later into his attraction to the Manichaean heresy, which is described as a "novelty" [*novitas haeresis illius*] (3.12.21).

Thus, curiosity is not only a dominant theme shared by the two works; it also has the same negative connotations in both works, apparently for the same reasons. As usual, Augustine is explicit in his condemnation and his rationale for it, but we can glean the same attitude from the earlier picture of curiosity and its destructive effects. At best, curiosity in the *Metamorphoses* represents a palliative, and Lucius the narrator seems to realize this when he recalls that in the sordid surroundings of the mill it was only the continuing indulgence of his "inborn curiosity" that provided him with any solace at all in a life that had become "torturous" (*nec ullum uspiam cruciabilis vitae solacium aderat, nisi quod ingenita mihi curiositate recreabar,* 9.13).[36] But this solace

---

36. *Metamorphoses* 9.13 on the whole is an important passage for pinning down the meaning of curiosity in the novel. After observing that his curiosity provided him with some relief at the mill, Lucius continues: "Not without reason did the divine inventor of the earliest poetry among the Greeks, when he desired to portray a hero of the greatest good judgment [*prudentia*], sing of one who had acquired the highest virtues [*virtutes*] by visiting many cities and by getting to know many peoples. In fact, I now remember with gratitude being an ass, because while I was concealed in his skin and tossed around by various misfortunes, that ass rendered me much-knowing if less prudent [*etsi minus prudentem, multiscium reddidit*]"—presumably less prudent than Odysseus. These musings of Lucius have presented critics with a number of problems. First, there is the apparent implication that Lucius the convert is still only *multiscius*, which is a state that results from the indiscriminate application of curiosity, when we might expect him to be more advanced at that point. This problem arises when *reddidit* is read as a present perfect rather than an aorist or historical perfect, which is equally possible. What Lucius is meant to say is, "*at that time* the ass rendered [not *has* rendered] me *multiscius*, which was better than nothing—it was somewhat comforting." (Hanson in his Loeb translation [1989] seems to understand this: he renders, "[the ass] made me better-informed.") It is clear that Lucius the convert has moved, or thinks that he has moved, into a world of something more than *multiscientia*, or the uncritical accumulation of bits of knowledge, as we will see in chapter 6. Against this interpretation, see Winkler 1985, 166–68. Second: what are we to make of the exemplum of Odysseus? It seems to imply that curiosity is not always a bad

consists of momentary relief rather than genuine or lasting satisfaction. An explicit statement of disapproval comes at 11.15, when the priest of Isis, for what his words are worth, includes Lucius' "fruitless curiosity" [curiositas inprospera] among the habits of the convert's old life that are to be renounced. Moreover, at 11.23 Lucius the converted narrator himself warns the reader against letting "rash curiosity" [temeraria curiositas] cause him or her to ask about the details of Lucius' initiation into the mysteries of Isis. The rationale for the condemnation of curiosity in both works lies not so much in the particulars of the acts that it inspires as it does in the view that chronic curiosity in itself, like any "false" desire, whatever its objects, is a primary symptom of incorrect spiritual orientation or, to put it in nonreligious terms, of orientation toward the wrong cognitive paradigm. In a very real sense, it is incidental whether curiosity motivates a foray into the forbidden realm of black magic or a moment of idle diversion by an unusual sight or sound. One is calculated and overtly dangerous, the other impulsive and apparently inconsequential; but both betray the same profound need and the same reliance on "inauthentic" sources for satisfying it. Both authors make

---

thing, that it can bring prudentia and virtutes, that it can have proper objects, or at least better and worse objects. Outside the scope of the novel, in the various strains of traditional thought about curiosity, there may have been a view that curiosity, while almost always somewhat suspect, could be exercised in intellectually respectable ways: see, e.g., Skulsky 1981, 88–97 and Walsh 1988 on "good" vs. "bad" curiosity. But prudentia (acquaintance with or knowledge of something, skill, good judgment, discretion, etc.) is really just a mature form of multiscientia. It is not religious knowledge or anything like grace; it is not even secular wisdom. We must remember the setting of 9.13: it is a "bad scene," the sort in which curiosity offers some (paltry) relief; curiosity can serve a purpose, but the implication is that it also has serious limitations. Odysseus, like Lucius, was good at making the best of bad situations, and curiosity helped both of them to do this. The praise of Odysseus here presents him as exemplifying the highest level a mortal can attain relying on reason and intelligence alone (which Lucius used less prudently; it was only a difference of degree). In this sense the Apuleian Odysseus could be compared to Dante's Virgil, who has many virtues and whom Dante loves like a mother and a father; yet Virgil's reason has limits, he cannot be saved, and ultimately he must be left behind. Interestingly enough, Dante's Odysseus has evolved into an exemplum with no redeeming virtues whatsoever. His "lust" [ardore] for new experiences—i.e., his curiosity—epitomizes the sort of willful derailment from the true way that inevitably leads to damnation in Dante's universe (Inferno 26.90–142).

this clear by the range of objects that each ascribes to curiosity, with the implication that the differences among them are only of degree.

A final similarity between the two works with relevance for my argument is the stress in both on habit as a force that prevents the two *actors* from seeing their situations from new angles and formulating new approaches to their problems. Both Lucius and Augustine exemplify the sort of slavery to old cognitive paradigms that blocks the ability of the subject to remap reality in ways that more closely correspond to actual needs and more accurately reflect his or her empirical experience. We saw in chapter 3 that running up against solidly established structures of meaning and spinning one's wheels there is not uncommon in the crisis phase of cognitively oriented experiences of conversion and narratives about them. The force of habit or, more precisely, of habituated modes of conceptualizing reality accounts for both Lucius' and Augustine's uncritical adherence to old approaches to the problem of meaning—for example, seeking it in the satisfaction of curiosity and of "false" desires in general—in spite of mounting evidence that the possibilities of these approaches have been exhausted.

Of course, Augustine presents himself as having been less uncritical even in the throes of the crisis than Lucius seems to have been, and his narrative is informed by conscious reflection on the problem of habit (*consuetudo*). We fall into sin, he says, because of the "force of habit" [*violentia consuetudinis*], by which the mind is dragged down and held unwillingly, yet deservedly, since it slipped into the habit of its own accord" (8.5.12). Many times elsewhere he laments the nearly insurmountable difficulties involved in breaking out of familiar modes of thought and the behaviors resulting from them, which one must do if one is to adopt a religious world view (which is not, of course, the way Augustine himself would formulate his aspirations).[37] Truth and habit engage in a kind of tug-of-war for the soul, which finds itself "lifted up by truth, but weighed down by habit" [*veritate sublevatus, consuetudine praegravatus*] (9.2.1). At 7.1.2, Augustine berates himself for having been hindered by a mind "stopped up" [*incrassatus corde*] with conventional images that circumscribed his efforts to formulate a true Christology. This reminds us of the spirited injunction to the skeptical traveler in *Metamorphoses* 1.3; Lucius advises him to loosen his "clogged ears and

---

37. See, for example, 3.7.13; 7.17.23; 8.7.18; 9.11.26; 10.30.41; 10.40.65.

stubborn heart" [*crassae aures et obstinatum cor*] in order to comprehend the part of reality that is "beyond the grasp of ordinary thought" [*supra captum cogitationis*]. This is Lucius' advice, but the irony is that at this point in the narrative it is only with respect to his belief in wonder-tales that he himself displays an unfettered mind. In other cognitive spheres he is as clogged up as the traveler whose intellectual complacency he condemns with characteristic self-righteousness. His thoughtless and compulsive behavior vividly illustrates the tendency of those slouching toward conversion in spite of themselves to "keep upright by dead habit," to invoke again the eminently applicable image of William James.

5

Poetic and Fictional Representation

1

In the previous chapter, I refined the idea of religious crisis as a breakdown of received cognitive structures and a shift in paradigms of knowledge by beginning to examine how this experience often formulates itself after the fact in religious discourse. Both the *Confessions* and its seriocomic precursor, the *Metamorphoses*, exemplify how this shift can be constructed as a movement from "false" and deceptive values to solid and "true" ones. As in the confessional writing of Tolstoy, the collapse of once reliable values (especially as they express themselves as objects of desire and sources of pleasure or satisfaction) is, for both Augustine and Lucius, the first step in the collapse of the subject's whole world. With the basic values that had structured reality and prescribed what was worth and not worth doing now gone or tottering, all aspects of that reality begin to be processed differently. In different ways and to different degrees in each narrative, reality appears newly defamiliarized, estranged; the preconvert moves in a void, and this development represents a transitional stage in the conversion process. Because values are themselves a kind of knowledge and because they inform our comprehensive structure of knowledge at every level, the exposure of habituated values as "false" constitutes an epistemological as well as a moral crisis. The apparently intractable problem that Lucius, Augustine, and Tolstoy all run up against and which they are unable to solve within the constraints of their old world view is the problem of meaning: what brings true and lasting satisfaction or pleasure and therefore makes life meaningful? In spite of the moral cast that the expression of the problem can take on in their narratives (especially Augustine's), our three preconverts are primarily experiencing knowledge trouble, since it is being oriented toward the "wrong" epistemological paradigm that has led to their frustration.

We have now come to the appropriate point for discussion of the tale of Cupid and Psyche (*Metamorphoses* 4.28–6.24), for this tale represents not so much the generalized anomy of Books 1 through 4 and 7 through 10 as it does the underlying crisis in values that is at the root of such anomy. Because I was concerned in chapters 1 and 2 with examining the ways in which Apuleius represents Lucius' transformed perception of his environment, I concentrated there on the books of the novel that are set in or depict the "real" physical and social world of the ass-man. Clearly the tale of Cupid and Psyche falls into another category. Unlike the other tales, it does not narrate an "actual" event occurring in Lucius' own milieu, but rather is a fairy tale or myth set in a remote and unreal place and populated by divinities. As such, it provides a sort of magical interlude in Lucius' travails rather than an occasion for the continuation or duplication of them; the tale temporarily lifts the ass out of his own increasingly problematic reality. It does, however, represent a parallel expression-in-miniature of Lucius' own movement from "false" to "true" values, of his shift in cognitive paradigms. In particular, the tale describes Psyche's habit of allowing her desire to be displaced onto "false" objects, and her tendency to derive pleasure from spurious and transient sources. This incorrect orientation is the substance and the cause of her separation from pristine union with divinity, and results, as it does for Lucius, in a period of trials and exile. Only with the realization that the divine is the "true" object of her desire does Psyche at last experience (or, in the symbolic language of the tale, give birth to) enduring pleasure.[1]

The tale opens with a very vivid picture of the displacement of desire onto a false god—in a word, of idolatry. Their religious longings veering off course, the citizens of Psyche's city worship the mortal girl as if she were a goddess. Not only her fellow citizens, but also foreign-

---

1. Critics have written more about the tale of Cupid and Psyche than about any other single episode of the *Metamorphoses* (with the possible exception of the Isisbook). Their sometimes myopic focus on this tale, central though it surely is, at the expense of the rest of the work has in my judgment led to the neglect of other important aspects of the novel and how it works as a whole. There have been four basic approaches to the tale of Cupid and Psyche: those concentrating on its literary antecedents; its folkloric features; its psychological symbolism; and its mythic significance or allegorical function. Parts of what I have to say about the tale will overlap with the latter in particular. For the tale as Platonic allegory, see the end of this section and note 7. For annotated bibliography through 1970, see Schlam 1971. For a selection of more recent work, see Kenney 1990a and his references.

ers swarm into the city in "zealous crowds," driven by the rumor of a "remarkable spectacle." Once they feast their eyes on Psyche, they are "dumbstruck with wonder" at her ineffable beauty and worship her with religious rituals as if she were the goddess Venus herself (*multi denique civium et advenae copiosi, quos eximii spectaculi rumor studiosa celebritate congregabat, inaccessae formonsitatis admiratione stupidi . . . eam ut ipsam prorsus deam Venerem religiosis venerabantur adorationibus*, 4.28). We recognize immediately the language and imagery of false values and misdirected desire that are applied to the proclivities of Lucius and others in the main action of the novel and in the other parallel tales. The devotion of Psyche's admirers is driven by zeal or eagerness—in other words, by desire—and their absorption in her mesmerizing power is total, as is that of Lucius when he encounters a diverting sight and is "transfixed" or "struck dumb," as he often is. Psyche moreover becomes a *spectaculum*, and this is very much stressed; at 4.29, tourists arrive from all over the world to view this "glorious sight of the age" [*saeculi specimen gloriosum*]. We have seen how in Augustine as well as in the rest of the *Metamorphoses*, objects of false desire and especially of curiosity regularly appear as objects of vision. Finally, the ineffability of Psyche's beauty (*nec exprimi ac ne sufficienter quidem laudari sermonis humani penuria poterat*, 4.28) signals the inversion of religious desire, as the ineffability of religious experience is a standard feature of narratives about it.

The problem is, of course, that Psyche is *not* a true god, that she is not the Venus that her worshipers come to take her for. She is a mere mortal inhabitant of the illusory sublunar realm. It is Psyche's mortality that seems especially to infuriate the real Venus as she raves about the injustice of this "outrageous transference of divine honors to the cult of a mortal girl" [*haec honorum caelestium ad puellae mortalis cultum inmodica translatio*] (for *translatio* read: displacement, 4.29). Venus alludes to Psyche's mortality three times in the course of this short first speech (4.29–30) and complains that she herself must settle for "indirect worship" [*vicaria veneratio*] through the mediation of her *imago*, Psyche. Meanwhile, all this veneration ruins Psyche's chances of marriage: although all gaze at her (*spectatur ab omnibus*), their wonder at her "divine appearance" [*divina species*] is of the sort they would feel at a statue (*simulacrum*) polished to a high sheen by a craftsman (4.32). It is true that Venus, the "real" goddess in this sequence, ultimately comes to represent *false* desire or bad love in the tale, and indeed in the novel as a whole. Her nasty behavior toward the innocent, if slow-witted, Psyche associates her with the world of deception and furor that Psyche in the end transcends. This identification is borne out by Venus' appearance in the lascivious masque celebrating fleeting pleasures in Book 10 (29–34), participation in which Lucius precipitously flees.[2] It is worth noting that in the tale of Cupid and Psyche, Venus has a handmaiden named Habit (*Consuetudo*, 6.8), which, as we have seen, plays a major role in perpetuating "false" or accustomed structures of value, according to Augustine as well as to modern analyses of the conversion process. In her capricious and gratuitous cruelty, Venus is to Psyche what the goddess Fortuna is to Lucius. Yet in spite of her apparently negative symbolism in the total scheme of the novel, the indignation of Venus as the slighted deity in the early chapters of the tale of Cupid and Psyche, along with the striking picture of the misguided idolatry practiced by the members of Psyche's cult, creates a sustained programmatic representation of the central issues of the tale: misdirected desire, spurious pleasure, and the bad habits that cause people to indulge them.

About halfway through the tale we learn where Psyche ought to be directing *her* desire. After accidentally pricking her finger with one of Cupid's arrows, she "fell in love with Love without knowing it [and] burned more and more with desire for the god of love" [*ignara Psyche . . . in Amoris incidit amorem . . . magis magisque cupidine fraglans Cupidinis*] (5.23). In the novel's scheme what this scene represents is "true" love, the desire for god. The "spectacle" of this vision of the divine and the pleasure (*voluptas*, 5.26) that she derives from it are the objects that Psyche should have kept her sights trained on—metaphorically, at any rate, since in her original state of grace and blissful union with Cupid, she has never seen the god and in fact is forbidden from doing so. But Psyche, like Lucius, keeps veering off course. And as with Lucius, one

---

2. On the role of Venus in the pantomime of the judgment of Paris in Book 10, see, e. g., Tatum 1979, 79–80 (a section entitled "Venus Where She Belongs: The Arena at Corinth"). He concludes, "Nothing that has gone before exposes the illusory nature of the beguiling, 'earthly', Venus quite so starkly as the arena at Corinth" (80). This is true, but as I suggested earlier, I think that Tatum is mistaken in thinking of "bad" desire in the novel more or less exclusively in terms of sex. On the significance of the mime, see also more recently Finkelpearl 1991. On Venus in the *Metamorphoses* in general, see, e.g., Singleton 1977; and Schlam 1978.

of the primary indications of her derailed desire is the frequency with which she is led astray by the impulse of curiosity. Curiosity is explicitly and repeatedly named as the force that drives her to sneak the forbidden peek at Cupid in the first place and to handle his potent arrows, in acts of faithless disobedience that cause him to abandon her (5.6, *sacrilega curiositas*, 5.19, 5.23). At 5.23 this curiosity is associated with her "insatiable mind" [*insatiabilis animus*]; this is significant insofar as curiosity in the novel as a whole is identified with desires that by their nature cannot truly be satisfied and with pleasures that cannot ever satisfy. In her quest to be reunited with Cupid, Psyche allows herself to be very easily pulled off course a second time. Disregarding the warnings of the talking tower, she indulges her "rash curiosity" (*temeraria curiositas*, 6.20) and opens the box containing Proserpina's beauty, which she is bringing back to Venus to fulfill the condition of one of the trials imposed upon her. This results in her falling into a deathlike sleep that apparently would have been permanent had not Cupid intervened.[3] Is Psyche's curiosity merely idle, as that of Lucius appears to be, or is it something more substantive, the quest for forbidden knowledge that critics have often read into both cases? Essentially, it is the former, I think, and when it appears to be the latter it is an accident. More than anything else, curiosity represents in both cases a habit of mind, an easy and thoughtless divertibility from the serious business of life. The curiosity of both Lucius and Psyche lights on anything, great or small, that catches its interest.

This dangerous habit of mind is illustrated very clearly in Psyche's responses to the luxury of the palace in the enchanted valley where Zephyr deposits her. She "eagerly" examines the treasures of the palace (*prolectante studio pulcherrimae visionis; studium* being one of the novel's synonyms for desire) and derives much pleasure *(voluptas)* from the sight (5.2). Her *voluptas* is intensified when invisible servants treat her to a sumptuous meal and a bath. One of these disembodied voices asks

---

3. Sleep and stupor are generic metaphors in religious and philosophical writing for life without God or some other transcendental signified. We have seen the metaphor in Tolstoy and Augustine; we will see it in Dante and Sartre. The other passages where curiosity appears as a diversionary force during Psyche's quest for Cupid are 6.19 and 6.21 (where Cupid himself scolds her for giving in to it). *Temeraria curiositas* at 6.20 anticipates Lucius the convert's warning to the reader against letting rash curiosity violate the secrecy of the mysteries (11.23).

her why she is "dumbstruck" [*obstupescis*] by the opulence; apparently, Psyche has assumed the attitude of mindless diversion that we have come to associate with Lucius. Eventually, though, Psyche grows accustomed to her new situation, and the details of Apuleius' description of this development are significant: "Soon the novelty, once she became accustomed to it, brought her pleasure, and the sound of the mysterious voice was the solace of her solitude" [*novitas per assiduam consuetudinem delectationem ei commendarat et sonus vocis incertae solitudinis erat solacium*] (5.4). Novel experience, then, is what provides Psyche, as it does Lucius, with solace or relief in an otherwise unsure or difficult situation, and habit plays a role in this process of anesthetization.

The entire setting recalls the shimmering and opulent unreality of Byrrhena's house (2.19), and the parallel is anchored by the echoing epigrammatic summations of the wonder of each scene: "There was nothing that was not there" [*nec est quicquam quod ibi non est*] (5.2), of Cupid's mansion, and "Whatever could not be, was there" [*quicquid fieri non potest ibi est*], of Byrrhena's. In the earlier scene, the focus was on the apparent instability of the material artifacts of the banquet as one manifestation of the instability of Lucius' whole world, but in both we find ourselves in a miragelike realm that seems to epitomize the idea of seduction by randomly appearing and fleeting pleasures. Of course, the irony here is that Psyche is inadvertently enjoying "true" pleasure inasmuch as this is the palace of the god Cupid. But this is an accident, the result of her habit of taking idle pleasure wherever it happens to present itself, and ultimately (the tale suggests) one's focus on God needs to be conscious and committed.[4] I think that the point of the scene is to

---

4. Psyche's initial union with Cupid is at another level the result of divine grace. There is an uncannily Calvinistic strain in the tale in that, on the one hand, it seems to be trying to convey the "message" that Psyche's easy divertibility almost leads to her ruin, but on the other, suggests persistently that she would have been rescued by divine intervention—grace, providence—no matter what she did. Note, e.g., the repeated supernatural interventions that save the fainthearted Psyche's skin and get her back on track: 5.25, 6.10, 6.12, 6.15, 6.18–19. It is completely unclear that either Psyche or Lucius is to be understood as learning any lesson that *earns* them salvation, although it may be implied that *after* their salvations-by-grace they finally understand what they have been doing wrong. This absence of any indication of conscious progress (spiritual, intellectual, moral) in the preconversion stages seems to me to be one of the single most un-Platonic features of the tale and indeed of the entire work.

establish Psyche's Lucius-like lack of discrimination, her inability to concentrate on the problem at hand, her tendency to allow herself to be diverted and lulled into complacency, all as a way of life. The lesson with which Psyche is finally presented, after all, is that she ought to have *concentrated* on her goal of reuniting herself with Cupid rather than allowing herself to be diverted so easily by the pull of her curiosity.

It is the dynamics of Psyche's relationship with her wicked sisters that most clearly illustrates the dangers of false desires and false pleasures. These sisters embody the inimical world of deception and error—the world of false values—that dualistic religious discourses exhort us to strive to transcend. Cupid is bending to Psyche's insistent desires (*cupita*, 5.6) when he agrees to let the sisters visit, and she experiences a kind of (false) "happiness" and "joy" [*laetitia, gaudium*] (5.7, 5.13) when all three are finally reunited. But it is of course her sisters who lead Psyche seriously astray by stirring up her fears about the identity of her husband. Her separation from Cupid is the direct result of her continuing participation in the world of false desires and pleasures that the sisters so vividly represent. Like the preconversion world of Lucius (and of Augustine), it is a world of treachery, dangers, fraud, and furor. The sisters are experts at dissimulation; they lie, they mask their *fraus*, they cover their treachery with smiling faces (5.14, 5.15). They will deceive anyone who stands in the way of their plan (one of them "deceives her husband with a lie" [*mendacio fallens maritum*] [5.27] about where she is off to), as they methodically go about surrounding their little sister with the "daggers of treachery" [*gladii fraudium*] (5.19). As in the world of Lucius, this duplicity has a contagious quality: in her only demonstration of assertive ingenuity, Psyche gives her sisters a taste of their own medicine when she tells lies to cause them to hurl themselves off Zephyr's rock after she discovers how they have misled her (5.26–27). By continuing to operate by the rules of the world exemplified by the sisters, Psyche sentences herself to a period of being beset by the dangers, traps, and snares (*pericula, insidiae, laquei*, 5.11, 6.4, 6.5, 6.17) that characterize their world (as they characterize the preconversion realities of Lucius and Augustine).[5] The picture of this negative, disorderly world is completed by the *furor* with which it is thoroughly

---

5. The parallel between the trials of Psyche and those of Lucius, in which they thread their way through "dangers, toils, and snares," to quote the hymn

saturated. The evil sisters are "inflamed" and "swollen with madness" (5.17; 5.11, *vesania turgidae;* also 5.27) and at one point are likened to Furies (5.12). They pass their affliction on to Psyche as she becomes mad with fear at their insinuations about her mysterious husband (5.18, 5.21). In spite of the sisters' maliciousness, it is the shrewish Venus, the queen of bad love, who is the most extreme incarnation of *furor* and cruelty *(saevitia)* in the tale.[6] This is exactly the sort of dangerous world through which Lucius picks his way, especially in Books 7 through 10.

Thus Psyche, like Lucius, is in a sense a slave to "false" desires and pleasures, and in fact she is called the "handmaiden of Venus" [*Veneris ancilla]* (6.8), even as Lucius is upbraided for having been a slave to pleasure by the priest in Book 11 (15). But in neither case is their weakness to be taken as being connected exclusively to sex, and in fact this is obviously not the case with the naïve and virginal Psyche. Rather, the problem lies in their tendency to allow themselves to be oriented toward the "wrong" paradigm of desire and pleasure, a paradigm that can encompass not only certain kinds of sexual encounters but also a whole range of inconsequential and ephemeral pleasures, which because of their very ephemerality are "bad" in religious discourses turning on notions of idealism and transcendence. It is important to observe that neither Psyche nor Lucius engages in "wrong" behavior because she or he is "bad" or "sinful"; they are instead merely misguided and plagued with a childlike inability to focus their attention. To different degrees, they simply do not *know* any better. This would seem to be even more the case with Lucius, who apparently does not have a clue where his "true" desire tends until it literally stares him in the face, whereas Psyche is at least fitfully aware during her trials that her "true" course is toward Cupid. Psyche is explicitly described as "simple-minded" (*simplex, animi tenella,* etc.) many times as the tale unfolds (5.11, 5.15, 5.18, 5.19–20, 5.24, 6.15), and she appears to remain,

---

"Amazing Grace," is signaled by the echo between 6.4, where Psyche prays that Juno will aid her as she is "worn out by the many labors [that she has] endured" *[meque in tantis exanclatis laboribus defessam],* and 11.15, where Mithras welcomes Lucius, who is "driven by many diverse labors that he has had to endure" *[multis et variis exanclatis laboribus . . . actus].*

6. It is widely recognized that this Venus is modeled on Virgil's illtempered Juno. The Virgilian allusions continue in the narrative of Charite (8.1–14), with its clear invocation of Dido. See chapter 2, n. 10.

like Lucius, as *simplex* at the end as she was at the beginning. It is true that this *simplicitas* is partially responsible for getting them both into trouble, but it also represents a kind of essential moral innocence. It is perhaps this attribute that explains why they are chosen for salvation in spite of their false starts and apparently incorrigible bumbling. Psyche's salvation and, in fact, her apotheosis (6.23) come through the intervention of Cupid, when she ("Soul") is redirected toward the "true" object of her desire, namely the god Cupid ("Desire") himself, and united with him (6.24). The product of this union is the immortal child *Voluptas,* a reference to the sort of deep and enduring pleasure that can only come from connection with the transcendent realm.

For obvious reasons, the tale of Cupid and Psyche traditionally has been read as a Platonic allegory. There is in evidence, after all, an overarching scheme of the soul's ascent to an abstract transcendent realm and a suggestion that this is accomplished when erotic or desiderative energies that have been dissipated on transient objects are now harnessed and directed toward that realm. This is, of course, the subject in particular of the *Phaedrus* and the *Symposium.* In addition, certain details of the Apuleian text seem deliberately to echo Platonic passages. For example, Venus orders Cupid to see to it that Psyche falls in love with the lowest of men, lacking rank and wealth (4.31). In view of the fact that Psyche's lover ultimately turns out to be Cupid himself, the allusion to *Symposium* 203c–d, where Socrates insists against the claims of the other speakers that Eros is rough, poor, and homeless, is unmistakable. Likewise, the tale's suggestion of a struggle between a low sort of love, embodied in Venus, and a higher kind, represented by Cupid and ultimately revealed in Isis, recalls the distinction between Common and Heavenly Love in the speech of Pausanias (*Symposium* 180d–185c). One could, in fact, take the view that the pattern that I have argued structures the novel as a whole qua conversion narrative—a pattern whose basic features are a turning from "false" to "true" values, a reorientation of displaced desire toward its "true" object, and the dualistic world view that all this implies—is in general simply an expression of Apuleius' Platonism. The *Metamorphoses* would then be a fictional representation of Platonic concepts of conversion, and the parallels in modern studies and in other conversion narratives that I invoke would suggest that the basic movement of Platonic conversion in antiquity followed a generic model of conversion. This in itself would add something to our understanding of the possible shape of philosophical conversion in the Greco-Roman world.

But my goal is to expand and shift the field of vision against which the *Metamorphoses* has traditionally been seen. Others have identified the novel's Platonic features and keyed its content to systems of Platonic thought; there is no reason to duplicate their efforts.[7] A major part of my purpose is to suggest that the constraints of genre that have been accepted as determining the range of valid readings of the novel have been too narrow. Broadly speaking, the approved generic frameworks have included those of Platonic allegory as well as of comic romance and paradoxography. This is not to deny that the *Metamorphoses* embodies elements of all of these and more. But it seems to me also to display other credentials that have not been adequately appreciated, with a currency outside the realm defined by certain second-century literary conventions and philosophical concerns. The generic context of the *Metamorphoses* should be expanded to include narratives of conversion as a genre, one spanning many periods and cultural settings. Once this community is established, then, assuming some correspondence between narrative and experience, we can draw at least a preliminary inference that the generic patterns identified here also structured experiences of personal conversion in pagan antiquity. This would give us new footing in connection with a phenomenon about whose internal workings we know next to nothing.

Reading the *Metamorphoses* as a narrative of conversion in more general terms obviously does not rule out its representing a particular expression of the generic pattern, that is, a second-century Platonic one. Its author was, after all, a self-styled Platonist. Later accounts—Augustine's, for example—that seem to replicate the pagan work's basic patterns would then serve as witness to the generalization of Platonic tropes in religious narratives operating outside of and later than Platonism strictly speaking. At the risk of appearing reductive or of seem-

---

7. On the Platonic aspects of the tale of Cupid and Psyche, see Hooker 1955; Penwill 1975 (who ultimately argues that Psyche is a negative exemplum of proper Platonic experience); and Kenney 1990b. On the Platonic features of the *Metamorphoses* as a whole, often with heavy reference to the tale of Cupid and Psyche, see Portogalli 1963; Moreschini 1965; Thibau 1965; Schlam 1970; Pottle 1978; Heller 1983; DeFilippo 1990. For more general studies of the Middle Platonism of Apuleius, see Mortley 1972; Dillon 1977, 306–38; Moreschini 1978; and Donini 1979.

ing to oversimplify, however, it seems to me worth saying that there is a real sense in which all conversions and narratives about them are Platonic, at least in the West. Both the concept and the language are in origin Platonic (see, for example, *Republic* 518c–d), but have since lost that specificity. The question for us is when this generalization began. My own view is that in the second century it was well under way, and that it was inevitable that certain Platonic patterns would appear in a work such as the *Metamorphoses,* whose purpose was to explore issues of religious experience and belief in a *general* way. Winkler shares my view of the ultimately composite character of the novel's religious content and Apuleius' reasons for making it that way. The point is to provide the reader with "an *instance* of that leap to a higher, integrating hypothesis that transforms the meaning of earlier episodes in one's life," in order to ask hard questions about how any such claim of metaphysical closure should be interpreted. In view of this design, "any cosmic power would have done as well" as Isis (1985, 277), and a broadly based and nonspecific central structure would allow the reader to concentrate on these more general questions.

The *Metamorphoses,* like the culture that produced it, is syncretistic; it is a composite picture of religious experience. Some of its specific features—for example, the idea of misguided eros—may seem to be Platonic, but they too may have been generalized at this point. One might say, after all, that a struggle to find the "proper" object of erotic energy is at the center of the *Aeneid* as well. On the other hand, there are conversion motifs in the novel that are in no way Platonic, even in a general way. Two of the most important ones are the subliminal incubation of preconversion stress and its resolution in revealed religion and by grace in the absence of any suggestion of directed and systematic intellectual striving on the part of the convert. To paraphrase C.S. Lewis, by the time we get to Book 11 of the *Metamorphoses,* there is as much *agape* darting down as there is *eros* steaming up. Psyche does not come to redirect her desiderative energies as a result of conscious reflection and choice; they are redirected for her. Moreover, the entire picture of epistemological or cognitive breakdown that I have argued is central to the novel's representation of crisis and conversion, especially insofar as it is conveyed as Lucius the *actor*'s spontaneous experience rather than as encoded philosophical dogma, is not ordinarily identified with Platonism. One might think of the Platonism of the *Metamorphoses* this way: Augustine and Dante (to whom we will come shortly) were clearly working within a Platonic tradition when they produced their narratives of conversion, but the telos of their search is Christ. Something like this applies as well to the *Metamorphoses,* which represents a search whose telos is Isis qua representative transcendent deity. Of course, the novel and its author are much closer to Platonism, but the parallel has its uses. The *Metamorphoses* should, I think, be thought of as a bridge or a transitional text in which we can see the scheme of "false" values and displaced eros becoming a feature of conversion narratives generically; it represents a step, and a fairly advanced one, in the generalization of basic Platonic tropes.

2

We have seen how the tale of Cupid and Psyche epitomizes a basic pattern typical of narratives of conversion and prominent in our exemplar of autobiographical conversion narrative, the *Confessions* of Augustine, as well as in the *Metamorphoses* itself as a whole. I now continue with the task of establishing features that characterize the narrative of conversion as a genre by studying more representatives of that genre, with the ultimate purpose of showing how the pagan novel emerges as one of those representatives. Again, the community between the *Metamorphoses* and these other texts, be they autobiographical, poetic, or fictional, has significant implications for our understanding of personal religious experience in antiquity and for our view of the capacities of ancient prose fiction as both a medium for the representation of and a model for that experience. This is because that community allows us to read back into ancient conversion experience not only the subject's changing understanding of the nature of reality, which is found across our range of narratives, but also the recurring tropes through which that new understanding is assimilated and expressed. The features of these narratives that will especially concern us are the movement from "false" to "true" values (even if the truth is that all truth is a delusion), the related motif of displaced desire, and the ways in which this movement represents a radical shift in the subject's paradigms of knowledge. I will examine first Dante's great poetic allegory of conversion, *The Divine Comedy,* as kindred in spirit to the *Metamorphoses* in these respects, and then a modernist variation on these themes, Sartre's philosophical novel *Nausea.* I expect this last choice to raise some eyebrows, but its apparent implausibility as a parallel to the *Metamorphoses* is part of my point: mutatis mutandis, the patterns in question here are remarkably persistent. I think that it will become clear why *Nausea* can, in fact, be considered a narrative of conversion and, moreover, why it is in some respects closer to the *Metamorphoses* than more obvious *comparanda*.

The central thematic threads of Dante's narrative of conversion are the same as the ones that we have detected in the *Confessions* and the *Metamorphoses*. Indeed, the proposition that desire drives all human action, good and bad, is explicated at great length in the very heart of the poem, in Virgil's discourse on love at *Purgatorio* 17.85–139. As a prelude to this, in the previous canto Dante the poet has Dante the pilgrim come upon Marco Lombardo, who explains why the soul needs the guidance of the Church, which in Dante's view has been seriously derelict in its duty. The "simple little soul" [*l'anima semplicetta*] comes forth ignorant, like a child, and instinctively lets its attention fall on whatever gives it delight (*volentier torna a ciò che la trastulla*), explains Marco.[8] It is the task of the Church to guide the soul's desiderative impulses, in other words, its love (*l'amore*), to their proper object (*Purg.* 16.85–102). Two points in particular jump out here as relevant in connection with the *Metamorphoses*. First, Marco's epithet for the soul, *semplicetta*, can only remind us of the *simplicitas* that is explicitly attributed to Psyche and implicitly to Lucius. Second, and related to this point, is the fact that "sin" is clearly conceived of in this passage, as it is throughout the poem, as being the result of ignorance; it is an epistemological problem.

In the next canto Virgil elaborates on the topics introduced by Marco Lombardo. Love is innate in both creature and creator, he explains to Dante, and goes on to distinguish between "natural" and "intellectual" love. The latter (*l'amore d'animo*) can stray from its true object, which is the "primal good," by targeting the wrong object (*per malo obietto*) or by

---

8. I will be citing Dante from Sinclair's bilingual edition of *The Divine Comedy* (1961), providing the Italian only when particulars of diction seem relevant to my purpose. Citation is according to the line numbers of the Italian text. Any sustained translation, i.e., of anything more than a word or short phrase, is that of Sinclair, with some modernization of his archaic second-person verbs and pronouns. It is difficult to know where to instruct the reader to dip into the sea of Dante criticism. A good place to start is Freccero 1986, insofar as his central concern with the "poetics of conversion" links his study with mine. He provides copious bibliography in his notes.

being excessive or defective in degree when directed toward objects that are in themselves neither bad nor good (*Purg.* 17.91–102). Here we see a typically scholastic refinement of the inherited notion of "bad" or inferior love: not only can love err in finding the wrong object, but one can also be faulted for applying too much or too little love to otherwise acceptable objects. These complications notwithstanding, we can see the same principle operating in this conversion scheme as can be identified in the *Confessions* and the *Metamorphoses:* desire, or love (here, *l'amore*) drives all action, be it "sinful" or virtuous. Virgil states this principle explicitly at 103–5. The bulk of Virgil's discourse is devoted to an explanation, also quintessentially scholastic, of how Purgatory is structured on this principle: the mountain is divided into terraces representing different manifestations of perverted, deficient, and excessive love as one ascends (106–39). He touches again toward the end of the canto on the idea that it is a misunderstood *desiderium dei* that is the impulse behind all the distracted expenditure of desiderative energy for which the souls in Purgatory are now paying. "Everyone confusedly apprehends a good in which the mind may be at rest, and desires it *[e disira],*" he says (127–28). The trouble comes when that desire goes astray, but again, it is cognitive confusion and not moral corruption that initially causes people to take the wrong course.[9]

Indeed, *desiderium dei,* experienced as the burning, erotic longing familiar from mystical writings, pervades *The Divine Comedy,* and the picture of it intensifies naturally enough as Dante moves through Paradise, where this desire finds its true object. What Dante the pilgrim experiences there is not only the satisfaction of his desire but the revelation of true knowledge, in a linkage that is important as we contemplate the connections between values and knowledge, between morality and epistemology. These manifold fruits of conversion make the condition of the virtuous pagans in Limbo especially poignant: they are doomed to live on eternally in desire without any hope of ever satisfying it (*Inf.* 4.42). The proposition that the natural, proper, and ultimate object of human desire is a transcendent and metaphysical one sets up the binary opposition that forms the foundation of the *Confessions* and the *Metamorphoses* qua narratives of conversion as well. In all these nar-

---

9. Virgil's discourse on love continues in the next canto (*Purg.* 18.16–75), where he expands on the topic of good and bad desire and in the process seems to take the Epicureans in particular to task.

ratives, this opposition involves the conflict between "false" and "true" values as it plays itself out in distinctions between "false" and "true" desires and pleasures. *The Divine Comedy* describes the process by which Dante the pilgrim gradually comes to realize, often under the stern tutelage of the relentless Beatrice, that his desire has been displaced onto "false images of good," as she puts it: "He bent his steps in a way not true [*per via non vera*], following after false images of good [*imagini di ben . . . false*] which fulfill no promise" (*Purg.* 30.130–32). "Present things with their false pleasures [*col falso lor piacer*] turned my steps," confesses Dante himself in the next canto (*Purg.* 31.34–35). Beatrice continues to hammer away at him: he had sought his pleasures in, he had wasted his desire on "deceptive things" [*cose fallaci*], on "vain and fleeting things" [*vanità con sì breve uso*] (*Purg.* 31.54–56, 60). One is reminded of the frequency with which *fallax* and *fallacia* appear in the *Metamorphoses* and the *Confessions*. By the time Beatrice finishes with Dante's reeducation, it seems to him that "that which had most bent [him] to the love of it became for [him] the most hateful" (*Purg.* 31.86–87). His paradigm of value has been completely inverted.

There is no reason to discuss every instance of the topos of false values that structures *The Divine Comedy* as it does the *Confessions* and the *Metamorphoses*, for they are countless. "As fire may be seen to fall from a cloud, so the primal impulse, diverted by false pleasure [*torto da falso piacere*], is turned to the earth," Beatrice explains again at *Paradiso* 1.133–35; and, on the problem of displacement specifically: "If aught else beguile your love it is nothing but some trace of this [the eternal light of God], ill-understood, that shines through there" (*Par.* 5.10–12). The idea is perhaps most poignantly expressed by the unjustly damned Guido da Montefeltro, whose conversion narrative in *Inferno* 27 parallels Dante's own. "That which had formerly given me pleasure [*pria mi piacea*], now grieved me," he says simply (27.82). This movement from "false" to "true" values, and the accompanying "corrective" reorientation of derailed desire, is what marks at a fundamental level both the experience and the narrative of religious conversion in their complex, mutually reinforcing relationship. Both experience and narrative involve the disintegration of an old framework of values, and the cognitive restructuring and reorientation necessitated by this loss. What happens is nothing less than the systematic revalorization of all the world's phenomena.

No image in *The Divine Comedy* represents the seduction by false pleasures and the displacement of desire more vividly than the Siren who appears in Dante's dream at *Purgatorio* 19.7–33. At first she seems grotesque, "stammering, cross-eyed, and crooked on her feet, with maimed hands and of sallow hue." But as the dreaming Dante gazes at her, she is transformed into a suitable object of his desire; he becomes blind to her meretriciousness and is mesmerized by her song, which brings him great pleasure (*tanto son di piacere a sentir piena*, she sings, 21). But Virgil and a holy lady, presumably Beatrice, intervene in the dream and break the Siren open, exposing the real rottenness beneath the alluring facade. The Siren's claim to offer true satisfaction (*sì tutto l'appago*, 24) is striking because we know that in Dante's universe this is precisely what she cannot give. The reference to satisfaction links the Siren to other figures in the poem that represent the temptations and obstacles that conspire to pull well-meaning but weak-willed sinners from the true way. From the very beginning Dante has had his ascent obstructed by creatures whose menacing gestures cause him to lose heart in a way that can only remind us of Psyche's faintheartedness; unfortunately she lacked a Virgil to provide encouragement at these critical junctures. This obstruction begins in *Inferno* 1, with the three beasts (the lion, the leopard, and the she-wolf) that block Dante's path and prevent him from taking an easy detour out of the Dark Wood of Error. The viciousness of the she-wolf seems to surpass that of the other beasts, and Virgil explains it this way: "Her greedy appetite is never satisfied and after food she is hungrier than before" (97–99). Thus the beast is associated with insatiability, which everywhere characterizes "false" desire. Those who seek satisfaction in the realm of the three beasts are destined to live on in desire, without hope of true satisfaction, as do the lost pagans in Limbo. With certain comic adjustments, it is possible to imagine the life of the fictive Lucius continuing as an episodic and perennially frustrated search for satisfaction had Isis not intervened.

Another Homeric figure adapted to his own purposes by Dante is Ulysses, whom the poets encounter among the evil counselors in *Inferno* 26. When considered in an Apuleian context, this figure resonates even more deeply than the Siren because of his identification, both traditionally and in Dante's version, with curiosity. In a series of twists that are pure Dante, Ulysses tells the tale of his final voyage and shipwreck; unlike his Homeric predecessor, he never makes it home to Ithaca and Penelope. Instead, he is driven to the ends of the earth and to disaster by his "passion [*l'ardore*] . . . to gain experience of the world" (97–99)—in other words, by his curiosity, formulated as desire. Dante stresses Ulysses' willful perversity in going off course: "Not fondness for a son, nor duty to an aged father, nor the love . . . owed Penelope" were stronger than his more wayward desires, and he pays for this neglect of duty by being denied his homecoming. We have seen the motif of self-imposed exile and self-sabotaged homecoming before: recall the words of Lucius to Fotis in Book 3 (19), likewise motivated by derailed desire ("In fact I don't miss my home and I'm not planning any homecoming; all I care about is spending the night with you"), as well as the straying Socrates of Book 1 and the words used by Aristomenes to reproach him ("You deserved to suffer the worst, since you preferred sensual pleasures and a wrinkled whore to your home and children," 1.8). Dante's Ulysses casts his lot in the world of sense and experience (115–16), thinking that this way lies the acquisition of virtue and knowledge (*virtute e canoscenza*, 120). And of course in the monistic Homeric world, that would have indeed been the case, but in Dante's it is only evidence of the depth of Ulysses' delusion. In view of the persistent characterization of the sinners in Hell as brutish because of their rejection of reason, there is irony in Ulysses' exhortation to his men when he tells them that they were made to follow his brand of virtue and knowledge rather than live as brutes (*come bruti*, 119). Ulysses' search is, in fact, a "mad flight" [*folle volo*] (125), propelled by unrestrained and misdirected desire (his companions too are *aguti* for the journey, 121).[10]

Lucius is not portrayed as elevating the goal of his own "mad flight" to the level of "virtue and knowledge," in spite of efforts to see a search for forbidden knowledge behind his fascination with magic. His flight is nevertheless driven, as is that of Ulysses, by curiosity and a voracious and indiscriminate thirst for variegated experience, and in both cases this is presented as the wrong course. At other points in *The Divine Comedy*, curiosity distracts the pilgrim Dante himself, and its quality in these passages reminds us more of the clearly idle curiosity of Lucius. For example, in *Inferno* 21 Dante's attention is caught by the sight of the bubbling tar in the fifth bolgia, and his preoccupation causes him not to notice a devil sneaking up behind him (22–30). The description of Dante's response to the diverting sight reminds us of how the fre-

---

10. For additional remarks on Ulysses in *Inferno* 26, see chapter 4, n. 36.

quently *fixus* Lucius and *his* instantaneous absorption in novel sights
are characterized: Dante "gazed in wonder, transfixed" [*fisamente
mirava*] (22). Later, in *Inferno* 30, Dante allows himself to be diverted
again, this time by the sordid spectacle of a squabble between the falsi-
fiers Sinon and Master Adam. Again, Dante is *fisso* by the sight, and
Virgil scolds him for this second lapse (130–32). Slow (but not as slow
as Lucius and Psyche) to take the lesson to heart, Dante slips back into
gawking in Purgatory, this time curious about the whispers and pointing of a group of souls who are themselves curious about his corpore-
ality. At this point Virgil gives him an extended rebuke and hortatory
lecture: "Stand like a firm tower that never shakes its top for blast of
wind; for always the man in whom thought springs up over thought
sets his mark farther off, for the one thought saps the force of the other"
(5.14–18). In other words, *pay attention*.

Dante, in fact, characterizes himself and his chronic curiosity in
terms very similar to those used by Lucius at 1.2, when the latter calls
himself a "thirster after novelty under any circumstances" [*sititor alio-
quin novitatis*]. When Virgil points out the souls of the proud for
scrutiny in *Purgatorio* 10, Dante complies without hesitation, since (he
says) he is the sort of person who is always eager for novelty (*novitadi*,
104). It happens that the "novelty" in this case has a didactic function
and is approved for viewing by Virgil the sage and guide. As in the
Metamorphoses, it is all a matter of directing one's attention—one's
desire—to the right objects. The many images in *The Divine Comedy*,
especially in the *Inferno* and the *Purgatorio*, of Dante stopping to stare,
transfixed and amazed, distracted by some trifle, his destination forgotten, are strikingly similar to the equally numerous images of the
dumbstruck Lucius in the *Metamorphoses*, and they have, I think, the
same metaphorical value in both texts, that of representing easy seduction from the "true" way. But when the attention of our pilgrims is
finally fixed on its true object, their engagement is often described in
the same terms: as transfixion, as amazement, as the gratification of
desire. The impulse remains the same; the difference is that it has now
found its proper object.

Perhaps the most poignant episode of symbolic distraction
(although in this case it is not driven by curiosity) followed by a harsh
but necessary staying of the course occurs at the beginning of the *Purgatorio*, when Dante meets the soul of his old friend, the musician
Casella. The allegorical charge of the scene is given a preview even

before Dante identifies his friend. Amazed to see a living man in Purgatory, the group of souls with which Casella arrives stands amazed, their eyes fixed on Dante's face *(al viso mio s'affisar)*, "as if forgetting the way to make themselves fair" (2.67–75). At the first diverting sight that they happen upon, these childlike souls forget where they are supposed to be going. Delighted to see someone he knows, Dante asks Casella to sing one of his old songs to make the way lighter, to give solace *(consolare)* on such an arduous journey (106–11). Casella complies, and immediately Dante and all the souls, including the ordinarily sober Virgil, are transported: "My Master and I and these people who were with him seemed as content as if nothing else touched the mind of any. We were all rapt and attentive *[fissi e attenti]* to his notes" (115–19). But their relief from care is short-lived: immediately the stern Cato the Younger, for complex reasons Dante's choice as the guardian of the foot of the Mount of Purgatory, breaks up the party, chastising the souls for their sloth and negligence (120–23). By the beginning of the next canto, the souls are back on track, their faces turned to the mountain's summit (3.1–3). Again, there are several remarkably Apuleian features in this episode. There is the stereotyped transfixed response of the audience/spectators, with its suggestion of easy divertibility and deficient powers of concentration. Furthermore, when he asks for a song, Dante just wants a little consolation, a brief respite from care; this is the motive that is implied behind much of Lucius' diversion seeking and is explicitly stated as such at 9.13. The bulk of Lucius' diversions (as well as many of the diversions enumerated by Augustine) is *apparently* harmless. One might likewise ask what harm there is in easing the climb up the Mount of Purgatory with a little campfire song. But these apparently harmless activities *are* pernicious, in that they are manifestations of a habit of mind that must be purged if the aimless wandering is to end and the way home is to be found.

Many of the metaphors used by Dante (as earlier by Augustine) to describe his pilgrim-self's benighted state before conversion are also used by Apuleius in representing the condition of Lucius. The equation of sin with blindness is ubiquitous in *The Divine Comedy*. Blindness appears in the *Metamorphoses* chiefly in the epithet of the goddess Fortuna, who as the symbol of a world without order or meaningful connection is not as far from Dante's godless world as she might seem. In spite of its circumscription in the novel, the metaphor of blindness as it appears in Dante is relevant for our comparison because it signifies the absence of "true" knowledge and the sort of epistemological confusion that is central to the *Metamorphoses*. The *Divine Comedy* is only secondarily an account of moral purgation; its primary concern is to represent the process by which the convert's perception is fundamentally changed as he comes to a radically new way of seeing, knowing, and constructing reality. This is especially evident in the *Paradiso*, as Dante comes closer to the brightness of true vision and "real" knowledge. Before that climax, there are points of allusion to the ways in which an attachment to old habits of thought and to limited paradigms of how things must work blocks the attainment of this new vision. When Dante and Beatrice zip spontaneously toward heaven from the earthly paradise at the top of Purgatory, he is understandably puzzled about what is happening to him. Beatrice begins her explanation of the workings of gravity and matter in Paradise by noting that Dante's perceptions are dulled by "false imaginings" [*col falso imaginar*] and that his rigid preconceptions prevent him from understanding this new experience (*Paradiso* 1.88–93). In other words, he is a prisoner of his old paradigms of knowledge. In *Purgatorio* 13, Dante himself attributes the same sort of blocked (but gradually loosening) consciousness to the souls of the envious. His address to them is: "O people assured of seeing the light on high which alone is the object of your desire . . . may grace soon clear the scum of your conscience" [*resolva la schiume di vostra coscienza*] (85–90). We recall that the idea of clogged or stopped-up consciousness appears in both the *Metamorphoses* and the *Confessions* (1.3 and 7.1.2, respectively). In all three works it is a minor component in the representation of conversion as a process of refiguring reality and of breaking out of epistemological constraints, which are symbolized by Dante regularly in the metaphor of blindness.

The works share other metaphors denoting the cognitive dullness and the misconstruction of reality that mark life before conversion, and the innate desire that strives, often in vain, against these limitations to find its true object. For example, the chronically displaced *desiderium dei* is a hunger and a thirst, and the godless life was a period of temporary insanity or heavy sleep.[11] Finally, Dante uses the very highly developed

---

11. Thirst and hunger: e.g., *Purg.* 18.4; 21.1–4, 39, 74; 27.115–17; 32.12; *Par.* 2.19–20; 7.12; 8.35. Madness: *Purg.* 1.59, passim. Sleep: e.g., *Inf.* 1.11; *Purg.* 33.33; *Par.* 30.82–84. See chapter 4, section 3 for the use of these metaphors in Apuleius and Augustine.

metaphor of gravity and weightlessness throughout the *Purgatorio* and the *Paradiso* to indicate the transition from the conscious application of will and effort by the preconvert to the breakthrough of grace, which makes this effort no longer necessary. This transition is religious discourse's version of the "eureka-experience" in creativity and other kinds of paradigm shifts. As I suggested in my discussion of Lucius and sudden conversion in chapter 4, the *Metamorphoses* has its own ways of expressing this moment of truth when change becomes effortless and spontaneous, after a long period of often misguided effort.

At this point we might pause to return momentarily to the question of Platonism and specifically to ask whether there are ways in which *The Divine Comedy* also could be said to be a Platonic artifact. After all, the displacement and reorientation of eros and an ascent to God from the world of cheap imitations are in origin important Platonic motifs, and these we see in Dante in abundance. Furthermore, Dante's poem, like the tale of Cupid and Psyche, contains references that seem calculated to invoke Plato: Dante the pilgrim's desire to know God is so strong that he feels as if he is growing feathers for flight (*Purg.* 27.121–23), and Beatrice chides him for allowing his wings to be weighed down by false desires (*Purg.* 31.58–60). All this aviary imagery has to remind us of the association between wings and the soul's immortality in the *Phaedrus,* not to mention Lucius' original plan of being transformed into a bird. But ultimately the answer to the question of whether *The Divine Comedy* is Platonic is yes and no, as is often the case when we put this question to literary texts. Dante's is a Christian poem produced when the Platonic tradition in its essentials and, more important, Platonic ways of thinking and their reproduction in literary forms were so deeply established as to be virtually unmarked or naturalized. Insofar as it is Platonic, it is a Platonism highly mediated by Aquinas, among others. I stress this only because I think that with certain adjustments this is a productive way to think about the religious content of the *Metamorphoses,* or at least those elements of its religious content that I have isolated. The features of *The Divine Comedy* discussed here are motifs of conversion narratives generically, motifs that appeared much earlier in the pagan novel, where they were, I think, also generic and synthesizing. The difference is that Dante's poem ultimately has an uncompromising Christian agenda, whereas Apuleius' purpose was to explore religious experience in a more general, and critical, way.

It is a very great leap from the world of Dante to that of Sartre, but the choice of a text that seems as far removed from the others as it could possibly be to serve as my prose fiction exemplar of conversion narrative is deliberate. I think that it will become evident that there are good reasons for regarding Sartre's philosophical novel *Nausea* as a narrative of conversion. Such narratives involve basic patterns common to otherwise apparently disparate texts, and the assertion of these patterns in an existentialist novel of the 1930s will provide an especially clear demonstration of their persistence. These are patterns reaching back, I think, to the seriocomic novel of Apuleius. Like that work, *Nausea* displays the conventional structure of conversion narratives. This structure is built around a central crisis in meaning or values, which inspires a quest that in turn leads to some sort of resolution of the crisis. As we will see, the solution of Sartre's *actor* Roquentin raises the same possibility of irony, even parody, and suggests the same strains of multivocality that assert themselves in the *Metamorphoses* as a whole, and especially in Book 11. Roquentin's search, like those we have already considered, exposes the "falseness" of his established system of values and leaves him a disillusioned and broken man.

Beyond this fundamental similarity, there are particular features of *Nausea* that make it especially evocative of the *Metamorphoses*. Foremost among these is the clear cause-and-effect relationship between the crisis in values and an altered perception of reality down to its physical matter on the part of the subject experiencing the crisis.[12] Roquentin's crisis and search are explicitly represented as an experience of epistemological breakdown and disorientation of the sort discussed in chapter 3 as characterizing an early stage in the process of conversion. Ultimately, Roquentin's problem is, of course, that he has the bad luck to suffer his crisis in a world where God is dead, where there is nothing to convert to. Because of this, he is to a very great extent stuck in the void that is exposed when the layers of conventional values papering it over are peeled away. He has to learn to live with anomy, although he does come to find some solace in a source that performs the service of divinity without being divinity, namely, music. Also Apuleian, apart from the ambiguities and ironic twists at the end, is the fact that *Nausea* is written as a diary and therefore lacks the retrospective narrator's voice that is likewise conspicuously absent in the *Metamorphoses*. The reader

---

12. On this relationship, see also chapter 3, section 1: James and Tolstoy, and James on Tolstoy.

is exposed to the perceptions and experiences of Roquentin and Lucius as they unfold, without benefit of the kind of integrating commentary offered by Augustine the narrator to explain what it all means. Fundamentally both novels are about the structures we project onto the world, and what can happen when those structures fall apart.

Roquentin's problems begin when one day, apparently quite unexpectedly, he begins to have the sensation that he is seeing through essences or the characteristic qualities of things, and through the conventional systems of valorization that assign things their qualities, to bare existence itself. It is the intrinsic meaninglessness of unmediated reality that mocks Roquentin and makes him sick. He is struck by the hard truth that all order and meaning are arbitrarily imposed—a fiction—and that what lurks behind appearance is not some stable and transcendent source of meaning, but nothingness. This experience results in Roquentin's world being drained of its former coherence. In his perception, all the world's phenomena begin to look strange, distorted, and lacking in any rational or predictable connection among themselves. This is precisely what Tolstoy describes as happening to him in his *Confession*, and I have argued that Books 1 through 10 of the *Metamorphoses* can also be read as a representation of just such a changed perception. It seems to Roquentin that he has become "subject to these sudden transformations" [*sujet à ces transformations soudaines*] of the objects in the world around him or of the situations in which he finds himself; his life has taken on a "jerky, incoherent aspect" [*cet aspect heurté, incohérent*] as the result of the piling up of "a crowd of small metamorphoses" [*une foule de petites métamorphoses*] (5).[13] Everything looks different to him now, unfamiliar, volatile, and grotesque. He can scarcely recognize ordinary objects, such as his pipe, a fork, a doorknob in his hand; the hand of an acquaintance becomes "like a fat white worm in [his] own hand" (4). He becomes alienated from his own body, and his own materiality becomes strange to him as he stares in the mirror and tries to make sense of the collection of features that are his face (16–18). He is disoriented, he seems to float, others float also and are merely "flabby masses" (18–19; 24).

Attempting to work in the library, Roquentin has an overwhelming

---

13. Quotations are from Alexander's translation of *Nausea* (1964), with the French provided from the Gallimard edition (1938) when the details seem relevant. Page numbers are those of the translation.

sensation of the instability of his physical surroundings and of their potential to transform themselves suddenly into entirely different shapes and substances:

> The inconsistency of inanimate objects! . . . [Ordinarily] these objects serve at least to fix the limits of probability. Today they fixed nothing at all: it seemed that their very existence was subject to doubt, that they had the greatest difficulty in passing from one instant to the next. . . . Nothing seemed true; I felt surrounded by cardboard scenery which could quickly be removed. The world was waiting, holding its breath. . . . I looked at these unstable beings which, in an hour, in a minute, were perhaps going to crumble. . . . [W]hat feeble barriers! I suppose it is out of laziness that the world is the same day after day. Today it seemed to want to change. And then, *anything, anything* could happen. (76–77)

Here, Roquentin's impressions of the material world are remarkably similar in their essentials to those of Lucius on his first morning walk in Hypata (2.1), and his conviction that "anything could happen" reminds us of Lucius' declaration at 1.20: "I consider nothing impossible." There is a crucial difference in that Lucius' response to these sensations is one of wonder and eager anticipation; Roquentin's, one of terror and a desperate desire to "stop [objects] in the midst of their metamorphosis" (78). But we have seen how the objects of Lucius' perception become less wonderful and more disturbing as his life as an ass grinds on, and certainly at the Risus festival his attitude toward the inscrutability of what is going on around him is similar to that of Roquentin. As a mark of modern insight on the part of the *actor* that is absent in the *Metamorphoses*, Roquentin does seem to understand that it is not objective reality that has changed but he himself, or, more precisely, his ways of processing that reality (4).

The spontaneous disintegration of Roquentin's world drives him to consider systematically his own past sources of meaning, structure, and comfort, or those of others, in an effort to rediscover a glue that will hold together the newly undifferentiated and empty phenomena of his experience. All this search reveals, however, is the thinness of the patina of significance and rational order that is spread over existence by conventional values and pursuits. The list of activities and their associated values that Roquentin interrogates is Augustinian indeed and is represented in the *Metamorphoses* by the futile cycle of desire and pleasure in which Lucius and his fellow travelers are trapped. The first idol to fall in *Nausea* as its inadequacies are exposed is time as an orienting and structuring device. Roquentin has spent his adult life as a scholar of history, but he now sees that the past is a chimera that cannot be grasped. The orderly march of events in the history books is merely a narrative constructed by historians and has no connection to the actual past, which is amorphous, dead, and unrecoverable (see especially 13; 94–103). Likewise, the reality of his own past slips away from him. One's past experiences, it seems to him now, have meaning only in retrospect, after they have been fitted with a narrative that transforms them from meaningless experiences to meaningful stories with coherent linear sequences of cause and effect (see, e.g., 32–33; 36–40). These insights result in Roquentin's very Augustinian rejection of the professional ambitions that had driven him up to that point. After the dishonesty of his project (a historical biography) impresses itself upon him, Roquentin loses his ability to concentrate on it. The exposure of the "falseness" of its value leaves a vacuum: What am I going to do with my life? he asks himself (94). He becomes listless: "I want to get up and go out, do anything . . . to stupefy myself" [*de faire n'importe quoi pour m'étourdir*] (97). We recall the ubiquity of images of stupefaction in both Apuleius and Tolstoy, conveying in both texts the idea of mindless diversion from hard realities.

The other stops in Roquentin's search for meaning are humanism, the values of the bourgeoisie, and finally, love. His rejection of humanism and of the belief that the accumulation of knowledge is a marker of individual and social progress is related to his new attitude toward his academic endeavors. Humanism is embodied in the novel in the figure of the Autodidact, whose pathetic naïveté reveals both the *actor*'s and the *auctor*'s estimation of the philosophy that the Autodidact embraces with such childlike faith. His mechanical mouthing of the values of humanism is a kind of incantation whose barely disguised purpose is to orient and valorize his own life. He is working his way alphabetically through all the books in the library, a project that creates for him the illusion that "there is a universe behind and before him," as Roquentin remarks with (as often) a certain wistful envy (30). The Autodidact's exposition of his religion during a lunch with Roquentin only fills the latter with rage at his *simplicitas*. By the end of this meeting Roquentin is having visions of stabbing the Autodidact in the eye, ruminating on how the only constraints preventing him from doing so are utterly arbitrary social rules that he has complete freedom to take or to leave (103–23). The exposure of the extreme tenuousness of social constraints is a major concern in Books 7 through 10 of the *Metamorphoses*, as the reader will recall. The Autodidact is, however, not quite so obtuse as Roquentin imagines: "Life has a meaning if we choose to give it one," he observes with an insight all the more striking because of the inadvertently evasive quality in his other pronouncements (112).

Roquentin's scathing assessment of bourgeois values makes it clear that in his view any attempt to cover ontological nothingness with them is a deluded enterprise as well. He sees the bourgeois world as one of inane posing and artifice, where gestures and speech are at variance with real meaning.[14] Several sequences convey this view. The Sunday promenade of the Bouville elite on the Rue Tournebride (41–54) gives Roquentin the opportunity to observe and disparage their complacency and absurd self-importance. The brittleness of the social performances in which they engage each Sunday afternoon makes the fragility of the entire social hierarchy, which is their fundamental source of meaning, order, and their own sense of value, glaringly evident. These pillars of the community have been quite successful at stupefying themselves as Roquentin on occasion longs to do, as it seems to Tolstoy he has done all his life, and as Lucius and those around him do habitually in their own way. A woman starts and comes momentarily out of her dream *(sortant d'un rêve)* to answer a question, then falls back into the dream *(est retombée dans son rêve)* after this social duty is discharged (48). On the boardwalk, people's "wide-open, staring eyes" *([leurs yeux grands ouverts et fixes]*, like those of Dante and of Lucius) "passively reflected" their surroundings; "only their breathing, deep and regular as that of sleepers, still testified that they were alive" (52). This is the day that they live for, and the evening with its visit to the cinema for another of the much anticipated but ultimately unsatisfying diversions of which their lives are made: "They were greedily awaiting the hour of soft shadows, of relaxation, abandon, the hour when the

---

14. The distinction here and throughout the novel between appearance and reality, surface and depth, form and substance, signals that Sartre too (perhaps in spite of himself) is working within Platonic paradigms involving the very dualities and binary oppositions that poststructuralism seeks to undo.

screen, glowing like a white stone under water, would speak and dream for them. Vain desire *(vain désir):* something would stay, taut in them. . . . Soon, as every Sunday, they would be disappointed" *(elles allaient être déçues)* (50–51).

Two other sequences further expose the hollowness of bourgeois values. The exemplary bourgeois Dr. Rogé seems to have the power to reestablish order and almost magically to delineate safe and firm categories, simply by pronouncing that the marginal figure of Achille is crazy (67–69). The boundaries conjured up by this vessel of authority create a semblance of stability, but Roquentin knows that both the boundaries and their source are a sham. "Experienced professionals" like Rogé are as blind as everyone else: they drag out their lives "in stupor and semi-sleep" [*dans l'engourdissement et le demi-sommeil*]; they pursue conventional goals unthinkingly and have no real grasp of what is happening to them (68). This last symptom is a fitting description of Lucius' level of self-awareness as he stumbles through life in his unwitting movement toward Isis. In spite of Rogé's prestige and his elaborate diversionary tactics, death looms for him as it does for all and undermines the value of all his achievements (69–70). The culmination of Roquentin's contemptuous reflections on conventional values comes when he studies the portraits of Bouville's founding fathers in a gallery consecrated to preserving their memory (82–94). In a tone only partly ironic, Roquentin admires their confident world-building, aided in its progress as it was by their lack of doubt, their disinclination to introspection, and their unquestioned expectation of order in the world and privilege for themselves. This sureness about their own rights gave them pleasures free of the "aggressive futility" that Roquentin himself so acutely feels in his *(le plaisir . . . perdait son agressive futilité)* (85). So palpable a sense of entitlement emanates from the portraits that under their stern scrutiny Roquentin begins to feel the weight of their judgment. Compared to these grand figures, he has no right to exist. His life is utterly devoid of their solidity and purpose; instead, it randomly "puts out feelers toward small pleasures in every direction" [*poussait au petit bonheur et dans tous les sens*] (84). This is, of course, exactly what Lucius is represented as doing habitually, and in spite of Roquentin's potential susceptibility to seduction by bourgeois mythology, he realizes that this is precisely what its promulgators are doing too. The confidence with which they assert the objective reality of their values cannot ultimately hide from him the diversionary character of those values. The fact that their discourse has been naturalized cannot conceal its status as mere discourse.

The conclusion that Roquentin cannot avoid after reflecting on these common strategies of world construction is that nothing is intrinsically meaningful or ordered; all value and structure are purely arbitrary, and all existents depend on others for their significance rather than containing it within themselves. This conclusion fills him with despair and makes all human activity seem pointless to him.[15] This is Roquentin's state of mind when he arrives at *his* moment of truth, analogous to that of Augustine in the garden at Milan or Lucius on the beach at Corinth. The details of its portrayal make it clear that Sartre is consciously reworking the traditions of conversion narrative or spiritual autobiography for a postreligious age and, in the process, adding a distinct element of black humor and parody. Roquentin's description of his revelation in the park relies on the inherited terminology of religious, and even mystical, experience: he feels a "horrible ecstasy" [*une exstase horrible*] and an "atrocious joy" [*cette atroce jouissance*] at his "deliverance" [*délivrance*] (131–32). Furthermore, the words he enters in his diary immediately after the experience convey in a formulaic way the mystic's absolute sureness that true knowledge has been revealed: "Suddenly, the veil is torn away, I have understood, I have seen" [*le voile se déchire, j'ai compris, j'ai vu*] (126). The existentialist twist is that the truth revealed is not God or any transporting cosmic mystery but simply gaping nothingness, the void. On the streetcar from which he jumps in a panic before wandering into the park, Roquentin is assaulted again by the instability of objects and their spontaneous metamorphoses. Names no longer stick to things and delineate their characteristic functions and qualities: "I murmur: 'It's a seat,' a little like an exorcism. But the word stays on my lips: it refuses to go and put itself on the thing" (124). Language (Roquentin realizes) is a kind of magical incantation to make things behave themselves. It is the central structure around which all the interpenetrating systems constructed to order reality are built. But when signifiers are cut off from their referents, when the arbitrariness of the connection between them is exposed, the result (in

---

15. With Roquentin's response Sartre again clearly marks his *actor*, if not himself, as a modernist and not a postmodernist, who would greet precisely these propositions as liberating rather than oppressive.

Roquentin's perception) is that the world becomes unintelligible, it falls apart: "The words had vanished and with them the significance of things, their methods of use, and the feeble points of reference which men have traced on their surface" (127). The functions, qualities, and essences carried in language disappear, and the brute, raw stuff of existence asserts itself, pulsating and metamorphosing before his eyes, with all its puny constraints broken.

The culmination of Roquentin's new vision comes in the park itself and centers on the root of a tree, suddenly and radically defamiliarized. He "sees" that humanly constructed categories and abstractions cover over the root's bare existence and that these categories do not exist in nature. This is what happens when the categories fall away:

> [T]he root, the park gates, the bench, the sparse grass, all that had vanished: the diversity of things, their individuality, were only an appearance, a veneer. This veneer had melted, leaving soft, monstrous masses, all in disorder—naked, in a frightful, obscene nakedness. (127)

Roquentin desperately tries to stabilize things by locking them into some familiar relationship with each other: "[E]ach of them escaped the relationship in which I tried to enclose it. . . . Of these relations (which I insisted on maintaining in order to delay the crumbling of the human world, measures, quantities, directions)—I felt myself to be the arbitrator" (128). In other words, Roquentin now understands that meaning is not intrinsic but contextual and relational; the problem is that the relationships too are coming unglued, and without them meaning is impossible. It seems to him that everything in the world has always been practicing a "passive resistance" (130) to arbitrary human categorization and that finally this resistance has grown to all-out war. All distinctions give way to continuity, fusion; the world is a "gelatinous slither," a "flowing larva" (134), even as it is in the *Metamorphoses*. Given their community of vision, it would seem that a quintessentially modernist novel and a piece of seriocomic prose fiction from Greco-Roman antiquity can share substantial conceptual territory, in spite of the common belief that alienation was invented in the twentieth century and requires a more highly developed sense of an autonomous subject than the ancients had mustered. Roquentin and Lucius the *actor* inhabit essentially the same anomic world.

Roquentin has one last card to play, one last value to cling to: love. From early on in the novel, there has loomed his impending reunion with an old flame, Anny, whom he comes to regard as his last hope and refuge from disillusionment. Her function as such becomes all the more crucial to him after he has his vision in the park, but when they finally meet he discovers that her disillusionment is as deep as his, though different in its details (135–54). Thwarted communication is a major issue in the *Metamorphoses;* similarly, Roquentin's and Anny's attempts to communicate are strained and awkward. They find that they no longer understand or know each other, if indeed they ever did. This is nowhere more painfully evident than when she says to him: "'I'm glad you've stayed the same. My milestone. If you'd moved . . . I would have nothing fixed to orient myself'" (143). There is a poignant irony in Anny's regarding Roquentin as her fixed point for anchoring her own fluidity just when all his fixed points have slipped irretrievably away. He learns that she is a kept woman, listless and in the habit of traveling to distract herself, but that nothing gives her any real satisfaction (153). In the end the encounter with Anny marks just another episode in the cycle of anticipation and disappointment, of desire titillated but unsatisfied, that constitutes his life, as it does the lives of all our preconverts. After leaving her, Roquentin struggles no more: he is resigned to his fate, his paradigm shift is completed. "[T]here is absolutely no more reason for living," he writes in his diary; "all the ones I have tried have given way." "The Nausea," he knows, "is here for good; "it is [his] normal state." In a reprise of the Augustinian and Apuleian conception of habit as a force inhibiting cognitive change, Roquentin sees that in the past, habit was what propelled his going through the motions of living, while blocking his comprehension of the ugly "truth" (156–57). He mocks the naïve faith of others in the solid structure of their worlds:

> They aren't afraid, they feel at home. . . . They have proof, a hundred times a day, that everything happens mechanically, that the world obeys fixed, unchangeable laws. . . . Idiots. . . . I know that it has no laws: what they take for constancy is only habit and it can change tomorrow. . . . It can happen at any time . . . [a]nd a crowd of things will appear for which people will have to find new names—stone-eye, great three-cornered arm, toe-crutch, spider-jaw. (158–59)

Again, with some adjustment for the differences in tone and manner of representation, this is the wildly volatile world of Lucius.

At several points in this discussion, I have alluded to Sartre's allegiance to Platonism, or, more precisely, to his taking certain Platonic ways of thinking for granted. These particular ways of thinking are currently vilified by poststructuralists under the broader rubric of humanism, but Plato is their source. Recognizing these tropes in *Nausea* is important here for two reasons: it allows us to continue our consideration of the generalization of Platonic discourse, which I think was well under way in the second century; and it provides us with the key to understanding why the prognosis for Roquentin is not so bleak as it appears to be. By generalization I mean the insinuation of Platonic modes of thinking into the cognitive structure of a culture, to the point that they are no longer marked as Platonic. We (humanists) routinely speak in terms of appearance and reality or of the real and the ideal, for example, as if the validity and even the objective reality of these opposing categories were self-evident, and certainly without thinking of ourselves as practicing Platonism when we do so. This shows how thoroughly Platonic discourse has been naturalized, and I think that the *Metamorphoses* reflects the early stages of that naturalization. Virtually all the patterns and motifs that I have discussed as identifying the *Metamorphoses* as a typical narrative of conversion were, I think, no longer marked as exclusively Platonic in Apuleius' time. They were generic even then; they might have appeared in any narrative, or experience, of conversion, regardless of its particular ideological refinements, as indeed they appear nearly two millennia later in *Nausea*.

This novel is shot through with assumptions rooted in Platonism. Roquentin's is a world of dualities, of binary oppositions. He naturally thinks in terms of appearance versus reality, surface or veneer versus depth, text versus truth. He is attached to the belief that in order to really mean anything, meaning must be intrinsic and not contingent. Far from reflecting a self-evidently true description of objective reality, these received Platonic ways of thinking are only ways of thinking, and pernicious ones at that, in the critique put forward by other discourses, most recently and notably poststructuralism. Roquentin is devoted to the idea of a transcendent realm where meaning can be anchored; he longs for it, although such a realm is apparently nowhere to be found. His metaphysical longing, a clear vestige of Platonism, marks him as a phallogocentric humanist patriarch in spite of his own expressions of contempt for humanism and for conventionality, but it also provides the opening for his "salvation." One of Roquentin's insights during his fateful visit to the park is that people have "tried to overcome . . . contingency by inventing a necessary, causal being," in a word, by inventing God (131). He scoffs at this notion as pathetically naïve, but in the final pages of the novel Sartre caps his reworking of the conventions of conversion narrative by introducing a variation on this theme that allows Roquentin, while still suspended over the void, to find some respite in another realm. We have seen in what straits our preconverts find themselves; in the next chapter we will consider the paths that they take out of those straits.

Part 3
The New World

6

Book 11: Conversion as Integration

1

Conversion, in spite of how it might appear to observers or even to the one who experiences it, is not an overnight affair. On the contrary, when it is measured from the first symptoms of slippage in old paradigms to the point when the new ones are locked firmly in place (if indeed that is the outcome), conversion under any guise is a protracted process. Until now we have been concerned with the changes that take place in the interactions between the preconvert's consciousness and his or her environment in the period before the new world view actually takes root. Several different patterns and types of preconversion crisis are discernible both in analytical descriptions and in literary narratives, but the one upon which this discussion has focused has as its precipitating event some fundamental challenge to the comprehensive structure of meaning within which the subject has always operated. Initially, this challenge often takes the form of an erosion in the ability of conventionally sanctioned or habituated pursuits to be self-evidently valuable or to continue to provide the satisfaction that they once had. There ensues a consciously or unconsciously formulated search for a definitive source of satisfaction and for new paradigms of value to accommodate the newly felt needs and the changed empirical reality of the subject. Frequently, this changed reality is a consequence of a heightened awareness of the threat that mortality poses to humanly constructed systems of meaning.

But as I have stressed in the previous chapters, paradigms of value are paradigms of knowledge. Once the basic and unquestioned values that have formed the foundation of an individual's world are shaken, other components in the subject's old organization of reality crumble in a kind of domino effect. This sequence of events constitutes primarily an epistemological or cognitive crisis and only secondarily a moral one, insofar as epistemology precedes or at least informs ethics in the process of world construction. The crisis consists ultimately in the failure of an entire system of world construction, beginning with that system's undergirdings in basic values, which are a form of socially constructed knowledge. These values function as a kind of glue holding the world together, and when this glue evaporates the subject's whole world comes apart. It can even *look* different, amorphous and flat, with a glaring and disorienting absence of the hierarchy, differentiation, and predictable interconnectedness that are the benefits of a fabricated and imposed nomic structure. The preconvert grows more and more alienated from that entire structure, which from the new vantage point seems unstable and hollow.

Conversion is not the only course out of cognitive straits such as these, and indeed the vision of a slipping and sliding reality is not always regarded as problematic or as needing to be brought under control. But before poststructuralism made living with, and even exulting in, the fleeting and the unstable a viable alternative, the impulse to find a metaphysical anchor has been a remarkably constant feature of intellectual and cultural history. Consequently, it has also been a consistent feature in the experiences and narratives of individuals who have found themselves suddenly worldless while operating within an idealistic intellectual and cultural tradition. For them the satisfaction of this impulse has often taken the shape of religious conversion. What I propose to do now is posit in general terms the features that religious world views would need to possess and the benefits that they would have to offer if they are to solve the problems that characterize the type of crisis with which we have been concerned. As this discussion proceeds it is important to keep in mind the axiom that in order to take precedence a new cognitive paradigm must correct the deficiencies of the old by addressing the specific issues that have come to seem intractable within the confines of the exhausted system. Then I will examine the extent to which my formulation of the function of religious world views is supported in some of the modern analyses of religious experience in general and conversion in particular that I invoked in chapter 3, as well as in literary representations of it, culminating in the *Metamorphoses* itself.

First and foremost, a religious world view must provide epistemological stability. This is accomplished through the operation of religious systems as superstructures of meaning with much grander claims than most purely social structures, although we will see that religious systems have often been used to legitimate the secular status quo. At the center of such a superstructure is the longed-for transcendental signified—that is, God or a god or gods—which acts as the ultimate standard of truth, knowledge, and reality-definition. Given an origin in a metaphysical center and source and from there informing all empirical phenomena, meaning is no longer contingent and relational but fixed and absolute. The basic problem for all our preconverts is that in some sense the center of their worlds no longer holds; with the adoption of a religious world view, a center is again located, and the result is that the entire world is reanchored and restabilized. This new and definitive point of reference is a sort of fulcrum around which everything else falls into place in an orderly way. Structure, hierarchy, unity, and coherence replace the dispersal and fragmentation of a centerless world; categories and divisions are reestablished. Above all, this center is the locus of solid knowledge and serves as a standard against which the contingent knowledges of the empirical world can be checked. We can see that the convert is once again simply going about the business of world construction, but this time the world is built, as it seems to the convert, on solid, higher ground.

Second, since the impetus behind the collapse of conventional systems of value is often a newly pressing awareness of the power of death to annihilate human achievement and its ordinarily adequate meanings, religious world views must integrate death in such a way as to blunt its capacity to constitute the quintessential anomic event. As a rule, they accomplish this by offering the convert the opportunity to participate in some way in an infinite and permanent metaphysical realm that transcends the spatial and temporal limitations of mere mortals. Additionally, rituals of death and rebirth signify the erasure of the convert's old structure of meaning and his or her resocialization in another one, the "true" one. Third, this transcendent realm with its unchanging center is perceived as the realm of "true" value, as the home of the real and genuine version of the countless "false" and imitative values of the secular world. This benefit is related to, and is essentially another way of stating, the principle that religion provides the convert with a structure for determining what is "true" knowledge and what is not. The realm of the divine, and specifically the divine center itself, is now identified as the "true" object of the convert's deepest desire. Retrospective accounts, as we have seen, tend to represent this desire as having been applied in the past to unworthy objects and therefore as having gone chronically unfulfilled. Since eros is now directed toward its proper object, "true" pleasure and "true" happiness replace their paltry secular imitations, and this nexus of metaphysically anchored values replaces the conventional values that had previously grounded the convert's structure of meaning (although again, from an analytical rather than the convert's point of view, there is often a suspicious interpenetration between the metaphysical realm and the conventional world).

Fourth, once everything is in order again, once the world's "glue" is reapplied and organizing principles are reinstated, we would expect the convert's vision to be freed from the flatness and lifelessness, the defamiliarization and estrangement that marked his or her perception of the environment during the crisis phase. Conversion will involve quite literally a new vision of reality and a concomitant sense of renewal and even rebirth. Fifth and finally, a point that involves not so much the function of religious world views as the ways in which they establish themselves: the new orientation of the cognitively reconstituted subject often gels, so to speak, in what might be called a gateway experience to the state of assurance. This is the transforming moment when, after being under strain for some time, the cognitive templates finally and dramatically shift once and for all, and the convert's perspective is changed for good. Such events include what are commonly called mystical experiences, and they are analogous to the "eureka-experience" in the creative process. Mysticism is a vast and complex subject in its own right, and I will only be touching on it in a circumscribed way. But an obvious point of interest for us is what William James called the noetic quality of mystical experience. This refers to the typical and unshakable conviction of the mystic that a *knowledge* and a *reality* transcending all others have been revealed, a conviction that has obvious relevance in an inquiry whose focus has been the epistemological features of conversion.

Obviously, religious traditions differ from one another in their details if not in their basic features and patterns. My list of the benefits accruing from the decision to live within a religious world view is meant to be very general, and as general as it is, it still would be inappropriate to apply to religious experience in nondualistic traditions. Within these parameters, however, I think that many would intuitively agree that my first four propositions encompass some of the more important attractions of religious systems generically. And indeed these are the terms found in much theoretical writing on religious experience and conversion. Although he does not use Kuhnian language, William James nevertheless seems to conceptualize conversion as a variety of paradigm shift, one occurring within a tradition or an attributional system that causes it to be seen not as a mere lateral move but as the discovery of the "right" paradigm. Conversion is the moment when "religious ideas, previously peripheral in [the convert's] consciousness, now take a central place, and . . . religious aims form the habitual centre of his energy." James imagines the sentiments of the convert as the latter reflects on, and wonders at, the completeness of his or her turnaround: "My soul stands now planted in what once was for it a practically unreal object, and speaks from it as from its proper habitat and centre." A rudimentary form of the Kuhnian idea of paradigm shift is evident, especially when James writes that conversion happens when "one aim grows so stable as to expel definitively its previous rivals from the individual's life." Conversion is a change in one's center of energy, a shift in or rearrangement of one's mental system (1958, 160–63). In other words, it is a process involving the dismantling of one cognitive structure and its replacement by another.

Related to James' stress here on the cognitive aspects of conversion is the fact that he speaks repeatedly of conversion as a process of locating or relocating a center, toward which the individual now directs his or her emotional energy, to be sure, but first and foremost a metaphysical center around which the rest of the subject's reality can be constructed. The need for such a center and its subsequent discovery are a response to the "soul-sickness" that James sees as lying at the heart of preconversion crisis. The chief symptom of this "sickness," it will be recalled, is a kind of anomic shock brought on by a thorough disillusionment with conventional values, which have for the first time been measured on a larger scale and found wanting. James imagines the preconvert's dismay and the grinding of the subject's mental gears toward a model of reality that will bring comfort: "The strangeness is wrong. The unreality cannot be. . . . [A] metaphysical solution must exist. If the natural world is so double-faced . . . what world, what thing is real?" (130). A little earlier, James had summarized the problem and suggested the form that its solution might take, this way:

> The lustre of the present hour is always borrowed from the background of possibilities it goes with. Let our common experiences

be enveloped in an eternal moral order; let our suffering have an immortal significance, . . . and [our] days pass by with zest; they stir with prospects, they thrill with remoter values. Place round them on the contrary the curdling cold and gloom and absence of all permanent meanings . . . and the thrill stops short. (1958, 122)

What we need, says James, and what the soul-sick need acutely, is "a life not correlated with death, a health not liable to illness, and a kind of good that will not perish" (121). By making contact with and partici- pating in a world that is infinite, eternal, and unchanging, the convert erases the boundaries of the individual's finitude and mortality; the finite and the eternally realized become one (344). Several points are striking in James' comments, apart from the idea that communion with an immutable deity residing in a remote transcendent realm acts as an antidote to the flux and contingency of "this" world. We see further- more the identification of this new center with "true," fixed values, with permanent meaning, with "real" reality as opposed to its many seductive imitations ("eternal moral order . . . remoter values . . . per- manent meanings").

Clearly the crux of James' view of the function of religion is that it involves the location of a point, a seemingly invulnerable one, from which to begin world construction. His prime witness confirms impor- tant aspects of this view. The source of Tolstoy's preconversion anguish is in these nagging questions: "Is there anything real and imperishable that will come of my illusory and perishable life? What meaning can my finite existence have in the infinite universe?" (1983, 58). After his conversion he comes to believe that "the essence of any faith" (that is, the acceptance of religious discourse as a true description of reality) "lies in giving life a meaning that cannot be destroyed by death." This is accomplished when the finite and the infinite are brought into a rela- tionship of continuum, a relationship that had always existed but which the convert only now understands (78; 62). We recall the image of the broken-down bed that Tolstoy uses to illustrate his precarious preconversion state. Now, with the protective superstructure of divin- ity installed above, Tolstoy no longer fears dropping into the abyss: "I can see that I am no longer dangling or falling but am firmly sup- ported. . . . [I] see that there is a single cord underneath the center of my body, that when I look up I am lying on it firmly balanced" (93). The typical preconversion need to locate solid reality and real meaning, both of which are identified with permanence and infinity, emerges here. Furthermore, the related role of the transcendental signified as a stabilizing force is vividly illustrated when Tolstoy describes himself as physically regaining his balance with its aid.

Later scholars tend to be more forthright and systematic than James was in their critical deconstruction of religious discourse. Berger is a case in point, but his rationalizing orientation still rests on the premise that religious systems work to stabilize the world and to provide a structure within which order and meaning can be located. One of Berger's aims is to show how religion has been used by the powers that be to legitimate and perpetuate the humanly constructed (and often unjust) social order. It is in this sense that he ultimately means for his description "world-maintaining" to be applied to religion. Much of his discussion involves an analysis of ways in which religious systems have been invoked to undergird and stabilize precarious social structures by anchoring them in a transcendental realm beyond contingency. As Berger puts it:

> Religion legitimates so effectively because it relates the precarious reality constructions of empirical societies with ultimate reality. The tenuous realities of the social world are grounded in the sacred *realissimum*, which by definition is beyond the contingencies of human meanings and human activity. (1967, 32)

In other words, this legitimating and stabilizing operation works by making nomos and cosmos coextensive, by projecting the meanings of the humanly constructed order into the universe (25).[1] Paradoxically, however, religious discourse can also pose a threat to the social order; it can be a world-shattering as well as a world-maintaining force. This has generally been the official position taken by religious rhetoric itself, regardless of the world-maintaining that it might be accomplishing simultaneously (it hardly being the case that those "using" religion to legitimate the status quo present the matter thus to the credulous

1. See also Berger 1967, 28; 89 ("[R]eligious legitimation . . . provides a semblance of stability and continuity to the intrinsically tenuous formations of the social order"); passim. In spite of this overtly critical stance, Berger is hardly dismissive or contemptuous of religion as (say) a Marxist might be. On the contrary, his ultimately nonjudgmental empathy with the human need for stability seems to me to stand very much in the Jamesian tradition.

masses). In its world-shaking incarnation, religion can reveal the artifice of the social order rather than informing it with a borrowed legitimacy. When the empirical world is seen *sub specie aeternitatis*, it can suffer a radical relativization and depreciation; institutions can be exposed as humanly constructed, with no inherent sanctity or authority (98–100).

The notion that the adoption of a religious world view can be a world-shaking act is, as a rule, central to the self-representation of religious discourses themselves, as I have suggested. This belief, and not the more skeptical and rationalizing one, is obviously also basic to the perspective of any wavering preconverts in or converted narrators of accounts describing how they came to reject the world of conventional values and subsequently to embrace values as they are measured on a cosmic scale. As far as the convert is concerned, the transcendent realm qua source and seat of absolute truth is not an idea cynically fabricated and manipulated by the powerful to exercise social control and prop up an unjust social order. Rather it represents a, or *the*, real and authentic order glimmering eternally behind an unstable social order that has failed. In chapter 3, we encountered Berger's claim that when individuals participate in the social order, that is, when they agree to "co-inhabit its nomos" and to accept "the cognitive and normative edifice that passes for 'knowledge'" in that particular society (21), they receive in return a shield against the frightening loss of cognitive and moral bearings—the anomy—that can result when one is not integrated into a system of social knowledge. By the same token, religion offers a sort of deluxe reinforced shield against anomy, insofar as its foundations, or at any rate its claims about its foundations, are so much firmer. In Berger's words:

> The sacred cosmos, which transcends and includes man in its ordering of reality, thus provides man's ultimate shield against the terror of anomy. To be in a 'right' relationship with the sacred cosmos is to be protected against the nightmare threat of chaos. To fall out of such a 'right' relationship is to be abandoned on the edge of the abyss of meaninglessness. (27)

How do religious systems accomplish what "mere" social systems, lacking sufficient or sufficiently persuasive cosmic grounding, often fail to accomplish?

Their success lies in their "unique capacity to 'locate' human phenomena within a cosmic frame of reference" and an "ultimately meaningful order." With this centering and anchoring of the world, "the inherently precarious and transitory constructions of human activity are . . . given the semblance of ultimate security and permanence" by being "grounded in a sacred time within which merely human history is but an episode." "God," Berger notes, "becomes the most reliable and ultimately significant other. . . . Ambivalences are removed. Contingencies become certainties" (26; 35–38; 94). The fact that religious systems, in the process of conferring order and meaning in general, incorporate and explain—in Berger's terms, nomize—the otherwise anomic phenomenon of death accounts in no small part for their appeal. Placing them in the context of some cosmic system gives anomic events an intelligible place in the larger scheme of things. Religious discourse, according to Berger, "legitimates marginal situations in terms of an all-encompassing sacred reality," so that people are able to go about their ordinary business "in the 'knowledge' that even these events or experiences have a place within a universe that makes sense" (44). What conversion does is transfer the individual into another cognitive world, one that integrates what has been marginal and fixes what has been precarious.

Many other scholars of the psychology and sociology of religion echo Berger's claims about the utility of religious belief and the nature of its function in people's lives. Spilka (et al. 1985), for example, devotes an entire chapter to the relationship between religious belief and various forms of anxiety about death, from the immediate and concrete to the abstract and philosophical. Virtually any religious tradition represents an attributional system with "a ready set of explanations about the meaning of death" (127; and see their chap. 6 in toto). On a more general level, in a discussion headed "Why are people religious?" Spilka paraphrases the answers to this question formulated by various schools of thought in religion and related fields. Of particular interest is the tradition that sees religious belief as a matter of cognitive growth, or at least of the desire for cognitive growth and for the discovery of ultimate meaning. This tradition includes certain strains of developmental psychology, whose practitioners explain religious impulses as one manifestation of a basic human need to locate "permanence amidst a world of change," and to satisfy an "associational urge" to understand how the self is linked to others and to the world as a whole in a meaningful and comprehensive system.[2] Turning to the dynamics of conversion itself, Spilka confirms the view of Batson and Ventis and others that conversion is a matter of moving from one set of cognitive constructs to another. According to Spilka and his coauthors, "humans need to have an organized framework within which their life takes on meaning and purpose." We need to orient ourselves toward *some* system of meaning, and a religious system fills the bill as well as, and in many ways better than, others. Conversion is a process of finding an "alternative meaning system" possessing features that correct the "now-perceived deficiencies of previous systems" (204, 208).

In chapter 3, we encountered the work of Heirich and its insistence that conversion needs to be understood in terms of world construction rather than emotional maladjustment (the premise of another major approach). He describes conversion as a shift in "a person's sense of ultimate reality" and as a process of acquiring a "sense of ultimate grounding . . . that provides a clear basis for understanding reality [and establishes] meaning and orientation for understanding one's situation and acting in relation to it" (1977, 273–75). Thus, like James and Berger, Heirich formulates adherence to a religious system as a way of forging an indestructible epistemological anchor. Likewise, the work of Schweiker (1969) on religious belief as a "superordinate meaning system" (borrowing the phrase and the idea from Bellah 1964) operates in the same vein. But I doubt the need to document this analysis any further, for as the anthropologist Clifford Geertz notes, "[t]he notion that religion tunes human actions to an envisaged cosmic order and projects images of cosmic order onto the plane of human experience is hardly novel."[3] Let us consider this and related points established as a recurrent claim in writing about religion and in belief about belief, and move

2. See Spilka, Hood, and Gorsuch 1985, 12–16 and their references, especially Elkind 1970; Polanyi and Prosch 1975; and Dewey 1929. I wonder about the implication that these "basic human needs" are intuitive and innate; but their status as the product of culture more than nature would not make them any less urgent.

3. 1973, 90. After noting that the proposition is self-evident, Geertz goes on to elaborate on it at some length and quite eloquently in his chapter "Religion as a Cultural System." See especially 99–125. For other, more sociological or psychological expressions of the same view, see, among others, Batson and Ventis 1982, 3–16; Gorlow and Schroeder 1968 (many of the "motives for participating in the religious experience" revealed in their research confirm this general analysis); Jules-Rosette 1975, passim; Rambo 1993, 10, 50, 56, 64, 82, 162.

on to the next of my proposed features of religious experience that would specifically counterbalance deficiencies perceived in the crisis phase.

If during the crisis phase the world around the preconvert appears unfamiliar, incoherent, and flat, with a "dreadful unreality and strangeness" (James 1958, 199), then the metaphysical recentering of the world and its subsequent reinfusion with meaning ought to result in a literal renewal of the convert's vision and an optimistic sense that all is again right in the world. Such a sense of "clean and beautiful newness" is indeed recounted in the testimony marshaled by James to document what he calls the "hour of the conversion experience" (199, 195)—those transformative moments when everything falls into place, so to speak, and after much confusion and struggle the "state of assurance" is finally achieved.[4] James takes note of the recurrent claim that at such times "an appearance of newness beautifies every object" (199). As one convert puts it, " 'I felt myself in a new world, and everything about me appeared in a different aspect from what it was wont to do'" (175). This sensation is common to a range of converts or veterans of religious revelation, from luminaries such as Jonathan Edwards to alcoholics recovering in urban missions. All are, to be sure, reporting experiences generated within the context of American and British Protestantism, which is James' primary point of cultural reference. Edwards describes his attainment of the state of assurance this way:

"The appearance of everything was altered; there seemed to be . . . a calm, sweet cast, or appearance of divine glory, in almost everything. God's excellency, his wisdom, his purity and love, seemed to appear in everything; in the sun, moon, and stars; in

---

4. We recall the writer Arthur Koestler's account of how the process of his conversion to communism culminated in literally a moment when "the whole universe [fell] into a pattern like the stray pieces of a jigsaw assembled by magic at one stroke" (quoted in Jones 1978, 71). Obviously, not all conversions happen this way, with a clearly identifiable moment of truth or "eureka-experience"; James stresses this type, in part because he is interested in dramatic and radical religious experience. But whether "truth" comes in a cataclysmic moment or more gradually, the reimposition of a meaningful structure on the world would result in its coming back to life in ways similar to those described by James' informants.

the clouds and blue sky; in the grass, flowers, and trees; in the water and all nature."[5]

Humbler souls too testify that they witnessed a transformation in the objective world, which in fact would seem to be the result of a change in their dialectical relationship with that world: "'[E]verything seemed new to me, the people, the fields, the cattle, the trees. I was like a new man in a new world,'" says one; and another, a woman: "'I exclaimed, "Old things have passed away, all things have become new." It was like entering another world, a new state of existence. Natural objects were glorified. . . . I saw beauty in every material object in the universe, the woods were vocal with heavenly music'"; and another, the most poignant, I think, in its *simplicitas:* "'[O]h, how I was changed, and everything became new. My horses and hogs and . . . everybody seemed changed'" (James 1958, 199–200). Or, as the abolitionist Henry Ward Beecher encapsulates the transformation of perception that marked his moment of truth: "'[A]ll the world was crystalline, the heavens were lucid.'"[6]

---

5. James (1958, 199), quoting from Dwight's *Life of Edwards* (1830).

6. James 1958, 204–5 n. 21. It is true that James draws primarily on accounts from American and British Protestantism in the revivalist tradition of the eighteenth and nineteenth centuries, but the transformation of vision described in his case histories is not limited to conversion, or, more broadly, to religious experience, occurring in that milieu. To take just one instance of a similar account from a very different environment: Jules-Rosette, the American anthropologist who went to Africa to study an indigenous black church (Christian, it is true) and ended up being seduced into it, reports having visions that left her in an "elated, almost dazed state" and suggest a transformation in her perception of the physical world: (e.g.) "The sky, which was already bright, seemed almost florescent" (1975, 154). Furthermore, her claim of a special, superior reality status for the content of her visions (157) is consistent with the noetic claims of mystical experience in general, as we will see. A final relevant parallel emerges in connection with the potential definitiveness of shifts in paradigms, that is, the extent to which a set of cultural constructs that had seemed absolutely natural can, under certain circumstances, become utterly alien. After her conversion, Jules-Rosette ventures from her adopted home in the hinterlands on a short trip to an urban center and confronts the values of her old life as represented in European and American magazines: "I was so shocked to see the style of life portrayed in [them] that I was certain that I would never return to the West. None of these images would have seemed the least bit remarkable to me before" (160). On the newness of transformed reality, see also, e.g., Batson and Ventis 1982, 60 (especially the "warm, luminous glow" and the "iridescent light" in which the subject's reality is bathed); 84.

Something else emerges in these accounts that takes us back to the reconstructive properties of religious belief. Specifically, it leads back to the ability of religious discourse to provide a center around which to orient the rest of reality and from which emanates an absolute form of truth against which the "truths" of the empirical world can be measured. For in James' reports of new or transformed vision, of times, often fleeting, when the weight of habituated or conventional ways of seeing is shed (albeit perhaps only to be replaced by another set of conventions, conversion conventions), the claim that with the state of assurance come joy and pleasure of a quality never before experienced occurs with remarkable reliability. In the convert's conviction, this is happiness of an entirely different order from the "relief" or the momentary escape that "commonplace happinesses" represent (James 1958, 55). Often the description (and presumably the experience) of this joy is eroticized, so that it is represented as the satisfaction of sexual desire, now properly harnessed, purified, and directed toward the divine center; the result is a "pleasure" of "indescribable" intensity (204 n. 21).[7] What emerges in these diverse accounts is a common narrative about the location of the realm of "true" value as it expresses itself in the discovery of "true" objects of desire and sources of pleasure. Furthermore, this narrative regularly describes an unshakable conviction that its subjects have found not only true pleasure and happiness but *true knowledge* as well (for example, 182–83). In fact, the individual's "sense of perceiving truths not known before" is prominent on James' list of characteristics that mark the state of assurance. "The mysteries of life become lucid," he adds (199). Because of the overwhelming power of these unchanging verities, moreover, those who grasp them typically report that mere human language is inadequate to the task of conveying what the experience was really like.

Although James' subject here is, strictly speaking, still conversion and the attainment of the state of assurance, it is obvious that his discussion is beginning to move into the area of mysticism and mystical experience. James' points about such experiences will nevertheless also be relevant when we turn again to the *Metamorphoses*, since that is exactly what seems to happen to Lucius in his initial encounter with Isis on the beach at Corinth. Mystical experiences can

---

7. See also James 1958, 174–75 ("joy unspeakable"); 177–79; 180–85 ("ardent joy"; "delight" in God); 203–5.

be a kind of gateway to the state of assurance, an official marker and, in some religious cultures, even the necessary and anxiously awaited proof of conversion. Even though their concentrated intensity passes, the impressions received during such experiences can leave a lasting imprint. The mystic narrator's insistence that the experience is utterly ineffable and that it opened up the realm of absolute knowledge and truth are two of the most consistent features of mystical narratives. James takes note of these conventions or identifying markers of both mystical experience and narrative when he does come to his explicit discussion of mysticism in chapters 16 and 17. Significantly, he takes the formulaic narrative claim that the experience "defies expression, that no adequate report of its contents can be given in words" as evidence that "its quality must be directly experienced; it cannot be imparted or transferred to others" (293). He thus reveals his faith in the possibility of original unmediated experience and betrays his blind spot with regard to the circular relationship of experience and narrative.

Of more immediate interest for our purposes is James' isolation of the "noetic" quality in mystical experience as it is represented in narrative. This is not primarily an emotional event but an epistemological one; what the mystic achieves above all is a state of sure and "higher" knowledge, to be distinguished from mundane knowledge arrived at through rational operations. In contrast, this superior knowledge consists of "insights into depths of truth unplumbed by the discursive intellect," which "carry with them a curious sense of authority in the after-time" (293). As far as the mystic is concerned, these moments involve the "direct perception of fact" (324). James offers a wide range of selections from accounts of such experiences, all expressing the conviction that ultimate truth and reality have been unveiled and that they possess an authority to be found nowhere in the increasingly "unreal" and meretricious empirical world.[8] It seems to me that, for our purposes, later writers do not add much to James' discussion of mystical experience, which is, it is true, more descriptive than analytical. Spilka

---

8. 1958, 294–307. At 307, James begins a discussion of how mystical experience is cultivated in various religious traditions, thus offering one of several hints of some understanding on his part that constructions of experience are culturally inherited. His other two characteristics of mystical experience, besides ineffability and noesis, are transience and passivity (293).

(et al. 1985), for example, largely reproduces James' list of criteria for identifying mystical experience, stressing as did James its noetic quality and its elevated ontological claims. As Spilka puts it, it "is not perceived as a mere 'subjective' experience nor an 'emotional' experience. Rather it is a valid source of knowledge" in an objective sense (176).

Spilka does add to the list a commonly reported sense that there is a "unity to the diversity of things" that causes everything to be "seen as distinct, yet somehow . . . simultaneously as part of a whole, as one thing" (177). This organic coherence of vision will ultimately interest us as a remedy to the fragmentation of the world that typifies narratives of preconversion experience, including that of Lucius. James does not discuss this aspect of mystical vision explicitly, but he implies that one of its benefits is a glimpse at the big picture, so to speak—at the spectacle of all the world's parts working together to create a harmonious whole—when he describes those who fail ever to achieve such vision this way:

> In common people there is never this magnificent inclusive view of the topic. They stumble along, feeling their way . . . from point to point, and often stop entirely. In certain [subjects] consciousness is a mere spark, without memory of the past or thought of the future, and with the present narrowed down to some one simple emotion or sensation of the body. (1958, 187)

Thus once again, it seems to me, James inadvertently provides a remarkably fitting description of our ass before his transformative moment.[9]

2

There is no evidence in his writings that Augustine was a mystic in any ordinary sense of the word.[10] Still, the state of assurance that he won

---

9. For their list of attributes of mystical experience, Spilka, Hood, and Gorsuch draw explicitly on Stace 1960, but it seems to me that Stace must have drawn on James. See also Spilka, Hood, and Gorsuch 1985, chapter 8 in toto; Laski 1961; Louth 1983; Melchert 1977; Wainwright 1981; but, as I have suggested, the literature on mysticism is enormous.

10. Although it could be argued that the "take this and read" experience in the garden (8.12) had mystical features. At any rate, it certainly qualifies as a

after many years of consciously and systematically considering alternative epistemologies is represented in the *Confessions* as resting on his belief that he had found a coherent "superstructure of meaning" of the very sort postulated by modern scholars when they discuss the functioning of religious systems in the lives of individuals and communities. Furthermore, the component parts of this structure address and correct specific failings in Augustine's old system of values. They accomplish this in a degree to which the other possibilities that he investigated presumably did not, and while satisfying other requirements of his that the alternatives presumably did not satisfy. We recall that one of the primary symptoms of his crisis was that he no longer seemed to be able to derive any real pleasure from those things dictated by social convention as proper objects of desire. The failure of this established nexus of desire, pleasure, and happiness represents the failure of Augustine's entire learned epistemic and moral system. But, with the fixing of his once distracted sights on what he now believes is the metaphysical center of everything and the genuine source of all value, he finally discovers what the "true" object of his desire has been all along, and by concentrating on it reaps the reward of "true" and lasting pleasure and of immeasurable joy.

Accompanying this shift is the transference of the vocabulary of secular desires and pleasures to the desire felt for and the pleasure now bestowed by a deity located in the transcendent realm. But when these words are used in connection with the latter, they refer not to cheap imitations but to the "real" thing; as Augustine puts it, God is the source of a "sweet pleasure that is not false but rather the unfailing foundation of happiness" [*dulcedo non fallax, dulcedo felix et secura*] (2.1.1).[11] At 9.1 he explicitly formulates the opposition between two

---

transformative moment or, in James' terms, "the hour of the conversion experience." Augustine seems furthermore to have shared with his mother at Ostia something like a mystical experience or a fleeting moment of what they took to be mystical union with the divine, which he describes at 9.10.

11. Likewise, Augustine's *amor* and his *desiderium* are now directed toward the transcendental signified rather than toward objects in the empirical world, and his pleasure, satisfaction, and happiness (*voluptas, deliciae, suavitas, iucunditas, satietas, gaudium, laetitia*) are now derived from that source rather than from temporal ones (*Confessions*, passim). Although Augustine is not as explicit about this as some religious writers are, it is clear from the double duty performed by these systems of vocabulary that he is describing a transformation and redirection of erotic energy.

systems of value perceived as ontologically distinct, one "false" and one "true," the latter being concentrated in God:

> How pleasant it suddenly became for me to do without the frivolous pleasures of the secular world, and it was pure joy to let go of what I had always feared losing. You cast them away from me, you true and highest pleasure, you cast them away and took their place, you who are sweeter than all pleasure.

> [quam suave mihi subito factum est carere suavitatibus nugarum, et quae amittere metus fuerat, iam dimittere gaudium erat. eiciebas enim eas a me, vera tu et summa suavitas, eiciebas et intrabas pro eis omni voluptate dulcior.] (9.1.1)

Those whose feet remain planted in anything other than metaphysical soil are doomed to pursue a mere "phantom of joy" [imago gaudii] and will never experience "true joy" [verum gaudium] (10.22.32) until they radically shift the center of their world view and the focus of their desiderative energy. At 10.6 Augustine rhapsodizes about why loving God is more satisfying than loving another human being, for example, ever could be. When he loves God, he says, it is like listening to a sound that does not die away, like smelling a fragrance that the winds cannot scatter, like tasting food that eating does not diminish, and finally, like clinging to an embrace from which satiety does not tear him away (ubi sonat, quod non rapit tempus, et ubi olet, quod non spargit flatus, et ubi sapit, quod non minuit edacitas, et ubi haeret, quod non divellit satietas). Clearly the crux of this desiderative and voluptuary system's appeal is its organization around ideas and claims of permanence.[12]

Another therapeutic feature of Augustine's new superstructure is its ability to make him feel as if he is a unified and coherent self in a unified and coherent universe. Where distraction and fragmentation once had characterized both his self and the world with which that self inter-

---

12. For "false" versus "true" values and the language of desire and pleasure upon which both depend, see also, e.g., Conf. 8.1.2; 8.5.10 (God represents the sola certa iucunditas); 10.2.2 (tu . . . amaris et desideraris ["you are loved and you are desired"]); 10.23.34 (false versus true gaudia); 10.31.43 (God provides satietas mirifica, as opposed to the hollow satisfaction accompanying conventional pleasures); 12.16.23 (God brings castae et fortes deliciae et solicum gaudium); 13.21.29–30 (deliciae mortiferae versus deliciae vitales); passim.

acted, the world now impresses him as a harmonious whole, and Augustine has his proper and ordained place in it. God is a kind of cosmic housekeeper picking up the pieces of broken lives and gluing them back together to approximate their original wholeness. "You drew me back together when I was in a state of dispersion. For I had been shattered in pieces when I abandoned the oneness that is you and vanished in many different directions," Augustine says gratefully [*colligens me a dispersione, in qua frustatim discissus sum, dum ab uno te aversus in multa evanui*] (2.1.1; cf., for example, 12.16.23). If another metaphor can be forgiven, God is a supremely powerful magnet at the center of the universe, toward which all else is naturally drawn and around which all else is thus ordered—that is, if human perversity does not interfere. This idea of the universe as an organic whole with God (or some other transcendental signified) as its heart is central to all metaphysical discourses. Operating as he does within such a discourse and having internalized its values, Augustine needs some sort of unifying agent in his life. He comes to believe that his salvation lies, as he puts it, "not in distention [*distentio*] but in intention [*intentio*]," that is, not in allowing himself to be pulled away from the center, but in concentrating on it with all his might in order to maintain the integrity and the good order of both his self and his world (11.29.39).

All of this has very marked epistemological implications, which is to be expected since, as I argued in chapter 4, Augustine's precipitating crisis is essentially epistemological; it is a crisis in world maintenance, in Berger's terms. At 4.15.24, Augustine as much as identifies states of *divisio* (as opposed to *unitas*) with the promulgation of *errores et falsae opiniones*. And indeed there is a consistent correlation, in Augustine and in dualistic religious discourses in general, between the conceptualization of divinity as unified, transcendent, and immutable, and the identification of that same divine center as the source and seat of solid, absolute, and noncontingent knowledge, of Truth. God becomes the unchanging standard against which other realities and competing truths are judged. This is a welcome antidote to the slippery knowledge of the empirical world, knowledge that refuses to be pinned down. If Augustine's (and our other preconverts') problems are essentially knowledge problems, then religious conversion is just the thing to solve them. Now whenever a vexing epistemological question presents itself, Augustine has a place to go for a definitive answer. "You are the constant light," he writes, "which I was consulting in connection with all things, to determine whether they were, what they were, and how much they were to be valued [*an essent, quid essent, quanti pendendi essent*] . . . and in all these investigations it is only in you that I find a safe place [*tutum locum*] for my mind" (10.40.65).

Confessions 2.6 as a whole is noteworthy as an elaborated statement of how the convert Augustine divides the universe into the transcendent realm of full presence and reality, on the one hand, and on the other the temporal world of absence or lack and parodic imitation. Of particular interest is his contrast between false knowledge, which he connects with curiosity, and true knowledge, whose locus is God (*tu omnia summe noveris*, 2.6.13).[13] Poststructuralist critics could not ask for a better concise description of how a transcendental signified works than the one that Augustine provides at 1.6:

> In you stand fixed the causes of all unstable affairs, and in you abide the immutable origins of all mutable things, and in you live the eternal rationales of everything irrational and temporary.

> [et apud te rerum omnium instabilium stant causae et rerum omnium mutabilium immutabiles manent origines et omnium irrationabilium et temporalium sempiternae vivunt rationes.]
> (1.6.)

This is a very clear statement of how religious discourse posits an invisible system behind the world of visible and empirical phenomena, structuring them from afar in such a way that they make sense, so that they are, in Berger's terms, nomized. In Augustine's system, God is the ultimate origin and cause of everything and the ultimate measure of truth; these attributes are inextricably tied up with the status of the deity as an immutable point fixed in an otherwise fluid and unstable universe.

Unlike the *Confessions*, *The Divine Comedy* frames the *actor*'s shift in cognitive orientation—his conversion—as a protracted mystical experience. Dante's representation of this shift is like Augustine's, however, in two of its crucial features, namely the twin claims that, when it is over, "true" value and "true" knowledge have been unveiled. As often,

---

13. God is *Veritas*, man is *mendax*: e.g., 6.4.6; 12.1.1; 13.18.23; 13.25.38; passim.

value is expressed in terms of objects of desire and sources of pleasure; after conversion innate desire is no longer displaced onto "false" objects, and pleasure is no longer spurious, because now it is derived from its proper source. As in Augustine, the disintegration of one network of desires and pleasures and the reconstruction of another to replace it represent a radical change in the organization and content of Dante the pilgrim's entire structure of meaning and values. Furthermore, owing largely to the assimilation of much of Dante's account to the conventions of mystical narrative, the descriptions of the convert's newfound love are eroticized to an extent not found in Augustine, although, as we have seen, Augustine does transfer his vocabulary of secular desire and pleasure to their new focus in the metaphysical realm. The difference is that Dante's representation of this transference is unabashedly erotic. There are hints all along in *The Divine Comedy* that this will be the mode in which the divine is ultimately experienced, but not surprisingly it is in the *Paradiso* that the fireworks intensify as desire finds its true object at last.[14]

Even on the outskirts of Paradise, in canto 1, Dante fixes his sight on the sun (as a symbol of God) with powers of concentration of a sort that he seems to have been incapable of mustering in the transitory world of momentarily diverting phenomena (54). As the mysteries of Paradise begin to unfold, he feels being kindled within him a burning desire such as he has never felt before to know their cause (82–84: *La novità del suono e 'l grande lume / di lor cagion m'accesero un disio / mai non sentito di cotanto acume*). After all his aimless wandering in the Dark Wood of Error, Dante the pilgrim is finally nearing his true home, and the closer he gets, the keener his yearning grows. This internally generated system of propulsion drives Dante through all the successive spheres of heaven until he achieves mystical union in the final three cantos of the *Paradiso*. There the center of the universe is represented as a veritable

---

14. For previews of the highly eroticized mystical union with which the *Paradiso* closes, see, e.g., *Purg.* 15.52–53, Virgil tells Dante that "love [*l'amor*] of the highest sphere" will ultimately bend his desire (*disiderio*) upward; *Purg.* 31.118–32, "desires hotter than flame" keep Dante focused on his mystical vision, which is mediated by the Griffin's eyes, and he gains from the experience a deep satisfaction marked primarily by a desire that this moment be protracted indefinitely. In this chapter I again rely on Sinclair's translation of *The Divine Comedy*.

orgy of ardent desire, enduring pleasure, and supreme joy; it is not only
Dante who experiences these things but all the blessed who have been
rewarded by being seated eternally near God in the mystical rose. In
this "secure and joyful kingdom" [sicuro e gaudioso regno] the sight and
desire [amore] of every soul are fixed "on one sign" [ad un segno]
(31.25–27). Dante's penultimate rapture, which is inspired by contemplation of Mary and which he shares with Saint Bernard and the angel
Gabriel, among others, is especially striking for the degree to which it is
described in erotic terms: Bernard is "all on fire with love" for her [io
ardo tutto d'amor] (31.100–101); Gabriel is "so enamored that he seems
on fire" (32.105); and Dante's own eyes are "fixed and intent" [fissi e
attenti] on the Queen of Heaven, becoming more ardent [ardenti] by
contagion when he notices the visible effects of Bernard's passion
(31.139–42).

But for all the ardor generated by Mary, it is union with God that
spells the "end of all desires," and which Dante knows will "[end] per-
force the ardor of [his] craving" [E io ch'al fine di tutt' i disii / appropin-
quava, sì com' io dovea, / l'ardor del desiderio in me finii] (33.46–48). Thus
we have in Dante a very dramatic and highly eroticized representation
of the shift in cognitive orientation from (in the language of religious
discourse) the "love of what does not endure" to love everlasting (Par.
15.11); from the world of false and fleeting pleasures to the world of
purified and concentrated desire, deep and lasting satisfaction, true
value. Even in the bare selection offered here of expressions of this idea
in The Divine Comedy (for the motifs and the language that I invoke are
absolutely pervasive in the work), it is clear that a central image for
marking the change is that of transfixion, of entrancement, of the fixed
gaze. We recall that Dante the pilgrim was often transfixed (as was
Lucius before him) by intriguing sights or diverting sounds in the earlier, and less lofty, stages of his journey. But that was idle amusement;
this is an attitude of wonder inspired by wonder's true and proper
source. It is worth noting that the image and the language remain the
same in spite of the radical shift (at least in the convert's view) in the
attitude's center and inspiration, because we will see in the Metamorphoses the same investment of one image with both negative and positive valuations, depending on the imputed orientation of the represented viewer.

As is the case with the Confessions, it would be easy for the reader to
allow all this talk about desire and pleasure in The Divine Comedy to

cloak the essentially cognitive character of the experience being represented. Even when the long-awaited vision of God brings on the culminating explosion of mystical pleasure in *Paradiso* 33, it is clear from the
description that epistemological issues are still central and that desire
and pleasure are simply the terms in which these issues are being
worked out. Underlying and bound up with Dante the pilgrim's affective responses to God is the operation of the deity as an anchoring and
stabilizing agent and a fixed reference point in a world of flux (for
example, 33.111, *che tal è sempre qual s'era davante*). At the heart of
Dante's mystical insight is an image of unity behind the world's diversity, a unity whose center is God:

> In its depth I saw that it [the Eternal Light] contained, bound by
> love in one volume, that which is scattered in leaves through the
> universe, substances and accidents and their relations as it were
> fused together in such a way that what I tell of is a simple light.
> (33.85–90)

Dante does not say that he "felt" or "inferred" this "truth"; rather he
saw it. It is objective, material fact, clearly apprehended and not
arguable.[15] The murky obscurity of the world of blind error and ignorance represented so vividly in the *Inferno* gives way to an absolutely
crystalline vision of the truth.

This moment is the climax of Dante's mystical knowledge, but he
has had foretastes of it at several points during his ascent. Frequently,
these intimations of ultimate knowledge are represented in terms of
changes in Dante's physical organs of perception as he adjusts to the
blinding brightness of the essential reality that he is gradually
approaching. His old modes of perception are literally burned away to
enable him to see things in a new way without the interference of old
perceptual and cognitive detritus. For example, in canto 30 (46–81),
Dante is momentarily blinded, as he often is, by the searing brightness
of the phenomena of Paradise, but almost immediately he has a sensation of "rising beyond [his] own powers" and realizes that his vision
has improved: "[S]uch new vision [*novella vista*] was kindled in me that
there is no light so bright my eyes would not have borne it." This expe-

---

15. Cf. Roquentin in *La nausée:* "le voile se déchire, j'ai compris, j'ai vu."

rience engenders the desire for further knowledge *(notizia)*, although Beatrice warns Dante that his ability to grasp new insights is still limited because his vision has not yet been perfected.[16] Clearly Dante the pilgrim's conversion involves centrally the development of new ways of seeing and knowing, ways which moreover do not depend on reason (for example, *Par.* 2.43–45). These new modes of cognition and perception give him a glimpse of the ordered and unified reality that is the realm of "higher" knowledge.[17]

Finally, we turn to the preconvert (of sorts) whom we left in what might appear to be the direst straights of all, Roquentin in Sartre's *La nausée*. Roquentin's crisis of values and meaning is enacted in a modernist landscape where no religious system looms large on the horizon of cultural discourse to lift him out of the "gelatinous slither" of existence. It is, moreover, a landscape where resort to such a system would be indicted by men such as Roquentin himself as a delusionary tactic rivaling adherence to bourgeois values in its transparency. For these reasons the prognosis for him appears to be bleak indeed. Yet in spite of these odds, and in spite of himself, Roquentin ingeniously manages to forge a transcendental signified that performs much the same function

---

16. Dante's improving vision: cf., e.g., *Par.* 26.70–79.

17. The conventional claim of mystical narratives that the experience is ineffable is also recurrent in *The Divine Comedy* and especially in the *Paradiso* (e.g., 1.4–6, 70–71, passim), where Dante the poet makes much of his futile struggle to express the inexpressible in words. On a related note, it seems to me that when Dante's ancestor Cacciaguida spins up to him in *Paradiso* 15, nattering an unintelligible language (37–46), this could be read as a comment on the ordering function of language and the status of particular languages as a component of particular cognitive worlds. I have suggested a correlation between Lucius the ass's new muteness and the collapse of his constructed world. By the same token, because Cacciaguida is operating in a different world and playing by different rules, so to speak, that are entirely outside Dante's familiar cognitive paradigms, he is naturally unintelligible to his progeny. The poet so much as says this when he writes that Cacciaguida's speech was "deep" because his "conceiving was set above the mark of mortals," but that when he made an effort he could make his speech come "down towards the mark of our intellect." This is only to suggest that there is something more complex here than the obvious point that Cacciaguida speaks not Italian but a heavenly language. The episode invites speculation about the extent to which Dante understood the connection between language and world view.

as God, in a demonstration of the resilience of metaphysical thought. There have been hints all along in the novel that some sort of solution, some means of transcending the existence that is so problematic for Roquentin, might be available through art, especially music. From the beginning, Roquentin's only moments of anything like peace come when he listens to an old jazz record in a café that he frequents. Something remarkable happens when he hears this music: then and only then, the Nausea stops. He takes in the music as a series of notes and expresses their appeal this way:

> [The notes] know no rest, an inflexible order gives birth to them and destroys them without even giving them time to recuperate and exist for themselves. . . . It seems inevitable, so strong is the necessity of this music: nothing can interrupt it, nothing which comes from this time in which the world has fallen. . . . It filled the room with its metallic transparency. (1964, 21–22)

Later, in the manic diary entry devoted to his horrific revelation in the park, Roquentin writes, "[S]trains of music alone can proudly carry their own death within themselves like an internal necessity: only they don't exist" (133).

Clearly, Roquentin is investing music with some of the same attributes projected onto God in more religious ages. It draws him to itself and comforts him because it seems to be located above, beyond, and outside the material world; it transcends material existence. Moreover, it is made up of fixed relationships and has a fixed and unalterable purpose; in the words of a recent critic, "[t]he song has a beginning, middle, and end, and true necessity, each part belonging to the whole in a set of unchanging relationships."[18] Roquentin perceives the music as somehow organic and self-contained, as having its own internal laws and as not being subject to interference from the world of contingency. Toward the end of the novel, when Roquentin is at his lowest ebb, having sought meaning in various systems of value and having failed to find it, it is hearing this song again that gives him something like a new lease on life. We are a long way from the ecstasy of Dante's mystical vision, but there is comfort here and it allows Roquentin to continue.

---

18. Brosman (1983, 47), whose discussion of *Nausea* as a quest narrative parallels my own reading of the novel.

He is especially struck by what seems to him to be the music's independent existence; it is untainted by materiality:

> It does not exist. . . . [I]f I were to get up and rip this record from
> the table which holds it, if I were to break it in two, I wouldn't
> reach *it*. It is beyond—always beyond . . . it veils itself, thin and
> firm, and when you want to seize it, you find only existants, you
> butt against existants devoid of sense. It is behind them. . . . It does
> not exist because it has nothing superfluous: it is all the rest which
> in relation to it is superfluous. It *is*. (175)

"[C]'est tout le reste qui est de trop par rapport à elle." Roquentin's song, like Augustine's God, represents full presence and full reality; everything else comes up short—is superfluous, deficient, derivative—when measured against either.

Like God, moreover, and unlike the gross world of existence behind which it floats, the melody is unchanging: it "stays the same, young and firm, like a pitiless witness" (176). The extent to which Roquentin thinks of it as having a life, even a mind, of its own, immune to the contingency and relationality that determine everything in the material world, is illustrated when he imagines the process of its creation through the agency of an American songwriter: "It is the worn-out body of this Jew with black eyebrows which it chose to create it" (176). Roquentin imagines the music preexisting even its author, who is, along with the phonograph record, only a conduit through which the music makes itself manifest, much like an eternally existing deity. Roquentin's response to his glimpse of an ultimate and ordered reality to counterbalance the vision of bare and chaotic existence in the park is described in language that marks the culmination of *La nausée* as a secular and at some levels ironic recasting of conventional narratives of religious conversion. He muses that both the composer and the singer of the song are "saved" (*En voilà deux qui sont sauvés*) because by participating in the music's transcendence they have "washed themselves of the sin of existing" (177). So habituated is Roquentin to cynicism that he surprises himself when this idea fills him with "something [he] didn't know any more: a sort of joy" *[une espèce de joie]* (177). We recall the ubiquity of "joy" as a response to moments of religious revelation in James' case histories as well as in Augustine and Dante; we will come to it again in the Isisbook.

As the result of his using music to fix points in a transcendent realm, the formerly despairing Roquentin leaves Bouville with a glimmer of hope or at least with a project for the future. He is encouraged by the possibility that he too could be "saved" by participating in this transcendence, not by being a conduit of music but perhaps by producing some kind of writing, since that is his area of expertise. But the redemptive text cannot be a history, because historical writing has a referent in existence: "[H]istory talks about what has existed—an existant can never justify the existence of another existant." Roquentin's projected book must have no referents, it must be completely outside material existence: "you would have to guess, behind the printed words, behind the pages, at something which would not exist, which would be above existence" (178). It sounds as if Roquentin is going to become a novelist. He imagines that his creation will be pure, unified, and self-contained like the song, working according to its own internal laws.

The question that arises at this point is whether we are not to read Roquentin as deluding himself as surely as if he had embraced the values of the Bouville bourgeoisie. Certainly, his absurdity is evident in the self-importance with which Sartre has him imagine his new life as a famous novelist, which ordinary people would think of as "something precious and almost legendary" (178). Related to this question is a more vexing one, the ultimate question posed by both *La nausée* and the *Metamorphoses:* Even if the structures of meaning that we project onto reality are arbitrary and open to being put to "bad" uses, are they not in some sense necessary if all human activity is not to grind to a halt? Can idealism be categorically suspect if it enables some people to carry on? It is true that the same possibility of irony asserts itself at the end of each work, with the same possibility of our not taking the *actor*'s solution seriously. But it seems to me that this irony is balanced by the fact that both *auctors* take a complex stance toward the conversions of their *actors:* bemusement and skepticism to be sure, but also a kind of sympathetic understanding. The two voices, the *actor*'s and the *auctor*'s, coexist in both works, and in both the voice of the *auctor*, while critical, is ultimately indulgent.

3

I turn now to Lucius the *actor*-convert's experience of conversion as it is represented in Book 11 of the *Metamorphoses*. Does he reap the same benefits from turning toward the divine that are said to accrue from conversion in other sources, and do the realities that Isis represents to him address in specific ways the problems that arose in his interactions with reality before the conversion? Lucius' first encounter with his saving goddess comes in the form of a dream vision, which appears to him as he rests on the beach at Cenchreae, where he has fled from participating in the Corinthian spectacle. From its very beginning the episode is indeed marked by the characterization of Isis and her realm, and Lucius' response to them, in terms similar to the ones that emerged above as typical of descriptions of religious experience. Isis is perceived by Lucius as embodying precisely the qualities necessary to fill the deficiencies that have opened up in his old world.

Lucius' initial communion with Isis is represented as having very pronounced mystical elements. All the blinding brilliance of Dante's God emanates also from the pagan goddess. The first intimations of her impending epiphany course through him as he awakens from his nap and immediately is struck by the sight of the "full moon shining with extraordinary brilliance" [video praemicantis lunae candore nimio completum orbem] (11.1). When she herself follows at 11.3, light blazes from her every feature: the "radiant image" [perlucidum simulacrum] of Isis emerges from the sea, and her identifying lunar headdress "sparkles with white light," her tunic "shines with bright whiteness," and her cloak "glistens with a dark sheen" [super frontem . . . argumentum lunae candidum lumen emicabat . . . tunica . . . albo candore lucida . . . palla . . . splendescens atro nitore]. Along with the brilliance commonly reported in mystical visions, we have the claim that mere human language is inadequate to the task of satisfactorily conveying the impact made by the vision on the one who experienced it: "I will try to describe to you this wondrous sight," says Lucius the narrator, "if only the poverty of human speech gives me the ability to express myself" [mirandum speciem ad vos etiam referre conitar, si tamen mihi disserendi tribuerit facultatem paupertas oris humani] (11.3). Both of these conventional mystical motifs will persist throughout Book 11.[19]

---

19. Brightness: e.g., 11.7, 10 (the initiates' garb); 16 (the ship of Isis); 20. Ineffability: e.g., 11.11; 24; 25.

Rambo (1993, 25) quotes the former Black Panther Eldridge Cleaver's description of his moment of conversion, which is in some of its features remarkably similar to that of Lucius as it was represented by Apuleius almost two millennia earlier. Cleaver's revelation also occurs on a Mediterranean

From the qualities of Isis that are stressed in these initial chapters, it is also clear how she will function in Lucius' new world as the metaphysical anchor and center that his old world had so sorely lacked. The goddess is the reference point around which structure is restored to his universe. In the instant when he awakens and sees the moon, Lucius experiences a cognitive state entirely unfamiliar to him during the events that led to this lonely stretch of beach: he is *sure* that a supreme deity is taking everything in hand (*certus etiam summatem deam praecipua maiestate pollere*, 11.1). In this *certus* we see a suggestion of the noetic quality of mystical experience identified by James and borne out in his and other testimony.[20] Furthermore, the description of Lucius'

---

seashore, at Cannes on the Riviera: "'I . . . began thinking of putting an end to it all by committing suicide. . . . I was sitting up on my balcony, one night, on the thirteenth floor. . . . It was a beautiful Mediterranean night—sky, stars, moon hanging there in a sable void. I was brooding, downcast, at the end of my rope. I looked up at the moon and saw certain shadows . . . and the shadows became a man in the moon, and I saw a profile of myself. . . . When I saw that image, I started trembling. . . . As I stared at this image, it changed, and I saw my former heroes paraded before my eyes . . . passing in review . . . and then dropping out of sight, like fallen heroes. Finally, at the end of the procession, in dazzling, shimmering light, the image of Jesus Christ appeared. That was the last straw. . . . I just crumbled and started crying. I fell to my knees'" (*Soul on Fire* [1978], 211–12, quoted in Rambo).

The reader is encouraged to consult Griffiths' commentary on the Isisbook (1975) for the historicity of particular features of Apuleius' representation of Isis: her appearance, the practices of her cult, prayer formulas, the range of powers attributed to her in prayer, etc. As a rule, these aspects of the Apuleian Isis are well attested in other sources, which Griffiths exhaustively compiles. (There are, however, significant exceptions, for example, Isis' apparent demand, unusual in paganism, that Lucius devote himself exclusively to her: 11.6; see Griffiths 164.) Griffiths' focus is on the specific practices and trappings of Isiac cult, and in its treatment of these issues his commentary is magisterial. It is, however, typical of Isis-oriented approaches to the religious content of the novel in that it has little to say on the less tangible issue of how Isis satisfies the fundamental cognitive (and emotional) needs of Lucius as they are expressed in Books 1 through 10 of the *Metamorphoses*. Griffiths provides a fine bibliography for further reading on the historical Isis (360–87).

20. To the testimony already examined, add that of Simone Weil: "In such matters, she liked to say, one does not believe or disbelieve, one *knows* or does not know" (Fiedler in Weil 1973, 9).

mental processes at this critical moment encapsulates the idea of the subjectivity that permeates any closed system of knowledge: since fate seems finally to be offering some hope of deliverance *(spes salutis)*, Lucius *decides (statui)* to try praying to the goddess (11.1). It is a personal decision, and an arbitrary one. Lucius *chooses* a particular closure for his crisis, just as the reader must decide if and how the novel is to be closed.[21] The first thought that enters his mind about Isis, and the first comfort that he derives from her, are alike connected with her power to regulate all human affairs by her providence, and this too he grasps with "certainty" (*certus . . . resque prorsus humanas ipsius regi providentia,* followed by a catalogue of her areas of influence, which encompass all levels of the cosmos, 11.1).

Isis' primary appeal as a locus from which cosmic order emanates is further illustrated in Lucius' prayer to her at 11.2. Following an established ancient imprecatory formula, he names the *regina caeli* by all the other divine names and functions that might be subsumed under her; all the goddesses whom he invokes (and especially Ceres and Venus) are eminently concerned with the ordering and regulation of nature and human behavior. When Isis herself speaks she confirms the role projected onto her by Lucius as the point of origin and the enforcer of a grand design:

> Behold, Lucius, I am present, stirred by your prayers, the mother of the universe, the mistress of all the elements, the first progeny of the ages, the greatest of gods, queen of the dead, foremost of dwellers in heaven, the one face behind all other divinities. With my nod I regulate the bright heights of heaven, the therapeutic sea winds, and the dread silences of the underworld. My divinity is one although it takes diverse forms and is worshipped in many rites under various names.

---

21. "In the absence of clear and final authorization from the *auctor* (whether narrator or author) we might imitate the action of Lucius: 'I decided' to invoke the goddess (*statui,* 11.1). . . . Apuleius inveigles the reader into a peculiar state of knowledge *about his novel* as an illustration of the structure of religious knowledge in general. The book is made to become, like life, a thing that can only be unified by the reader's decision to see it in a certain way" (Winkler 1985, 131–32).

[En adsum tuis commota, Luci, precibus, rerum naturae parens, elementorum omnium domina, saeculorum progenies initialis, summa numinum, regina manium, prima caelitum, deorum dearumque facies uniformis, quae caeli luminosa culmina, maris salubria flamina, inferum deplorata silentia nutibus meis dispenso: cuius numen unicum multiformi specie, ritu vario, nomine multiiugo totus veneratur orbis.] (11.5)

In her self-representation Isis is made to touch on several of the important features and capacities of transcendent divinities that enable them to counterbalance the tendency of centerless worlds to "fall apart." Apart from the sheer range of areas where her powers are felt—she is present simultaneously virtually everywhere in the universe, making sure that all its parts work together in a harmonious whole—there is the stress on her identification with origins ("first progeny of the ages," cf. 11.9, she is the source [*stirps*] of the heavenly stars) and her repeated claim that she represents a cohesive unity behind the diversity of appearance.

A little later in the same speech she comforts Lucius by assuring him, "now by my providence your day of salvation is dawning." The attribute of *providentia* appears consistently in connection with Isis throughout Book 11. This attribute is linked to her status as the focal point of a world operating according to a reliable system of organizing principles and thus opposed to the chaotic and capricious realm of Fortuna. The function of Isis as metaphysical anchor is symbolized on her robe in the representation of stars ordering themselves obediently around a moon, which of course is to be identified with the goddess herself ("around the embroidered hem and on the surface of the cloak twinkling stars were scattered, and in their center [*earumque media*] a full moon was breathing fiery flames," 11.4). Finally, at the end of her long speech at 11.5–6, Isis suggests that if he makes the decision to ally himself with the transcendent realm that she oversees, Lucius will find the problem of death mitigated by his postmortem assignment to the Elysian fields, where he will enjoy a happy afterlife and she will continue to favor him. She further hints that if he is really exceptional in his devotion, she could reward him by prolonging his life beyond the limits mandated by fate (11.6).[22]

---

22. The clearly transcendent properties of the Apuleian Isis place her largely outside the realm of immanent, numinous deities ordinarily identified

Thus begins Lucius' new life. The reader will recall that a recurrent claim in narratives about the "hour of the conversion experience" is that this moment is accompanied or immediately followed by a strong and palpable sense of renewal and rebirth and by a transformation in the convert's vision of the very face of reality. The world, which had appeared dissonant, flat, and dead, suddenly becomes animated, harmonious, and bright, as the subject makes the transition into the state of assurance. Directly after his initial encounter with Isis, the perspective of Lucius too undergoes just such a transformation as the world around him begins to bloom with new life (11.7). A golden sun arises and drives away the black cloud of night. Lucius himself is filled with joy, and it seems to him that not only all living creatures but even inanimate things such as the houses and the day itself are joining him by "rejoicing with happy faces" [serena facie gaudere]. The conversion of Dante the pilgrim is set symbolically in the spring, in the Easter season; similarly in the *Metamorphoses*, the warmth of spring banishes winter's frost, and the songbirds warble "lovely melodies" [concentus suaves] in honor of

---

with classic Greco-Roman paganism. In his schematization of the evolution of religious systems, Bellah (1964) distinguishes between "archaic" or "primitive" and "historical" religions. The former are characterized by monistic conceptions of the universe and involve little tension between religious demands and social conformity because of the intertwinement of religious and social or civic life. Historical religions, on the other hand, involve a world-rejecting, dualistic cosmos and a transcendent, "demythologized" god. Bellah further posits that this type of religion depends upon a more highly developed construction of individual selfhood and a sharper distinction between subject and object than is evident in archaic religion. Bellah's distinctions correspond to Nock's between "primitive" or "traditional" and "prophetic" religion, and Berger's between religion as a "world-maintaining" and a "world-shattering" force. The Apuleian Isis could be viewed as a transitional deity showing properties of both systems. But ultimately her transcendence, and the dualistic cosmic structure suggested in the novel as a whole and encapsulated in the opposition between Isis and Fortuna, outweighs any residual archaic pagan features. Apuleius did not invent this conception and use of Isis: Egyptian religion was inherently more dualistic than was Greco-Roman, to the extent that it suggested the possibility of a synthesis between it and Platonic philosophy of the sort formulated by Plutarch in *de Iside et Osiride*. While it is obvious that some sort of synthesis of the Platonic and the Isiac is at work in the *Metamorphoses* as well, I think that Apuleius puts it in the service of his larger purpose of exploring *general* issues of religious experience as they arose in the incipiently transcendent religious systems of the second century A.D.

Isis, "soothing with their charming greetings the mother of the stars, the parent of the seasons, and the mistress of the universe." Even the trees come to life, as the breezes cause them to "whisper sweetly with the benign motion of their arms." All traces of threat are gone; everything and everyone in the world is friendly and well disposed. Tempestuous waves subside and the sea grows calm; the sky "shines with the bare and clear brilliance of its own light" [*caelum . . . nudo sudoque luminis proprii splendore candebat*]. "All the world was crystalline, the heavens were lucid": James' examples of the effects of conversion on the subject's perception of physical reality echo the description of Lucius' new world in striking ways. To remind the reader of another: a "calm, sweet cast" lay over all, and God's goodness "seemed to appear in everything: in the sun, moon, and stars; in the clouds and blue sky; in the grass, flowers, and trees; in the water and all nature." That is Jonathan Edwards, moving in a system of cultural discourses as different from those of Lucius as they can be. Yet in both cases an organic coherence and friendly harmony are infused into the world when contact is made with a transcendent reality that informs and structures the everyday one from behind. With a new structure of meaning undergirding them, things make sense again.

After his dramatic transformative moment, Lucius carefully follows Isis' instructions for procuring the regenerative roses, which she provides through the agency of one of her priests. Upon eating them, Lucius is said to shed his "deformed and bestial skin" [*mihi delabitur deformis et ferina facies*] (11.13); (cf. 11.6, where Isis refers to his *deformis facies*). Later Augustine will speak of his old unredeemed self in the same terms: "In your sight it was pleasing to correct my deformities," he writes thankfully to God [*placuit in conspectu tuo reformare deformia mea*] (7.8.12); (cf. 10.27.38; 12.16.23). One of the primary markers of Lucius' new (or the recovery of his original) state is that he regains the faculty of speech. This is stressed in 11.14 (*nova vox, renata lingua*). The reassertion of language, the quintessential structuring mechanism, is thus connected with the general restructuring of Lucius' world as it is accomplished when he locates the starting point for world (re)construction in a transcendent reality.

In his speech at 11.15, the priest Mithras reprises the conception of Isis as the linchpin in a method behind the madness. His explication relies in particular on the dualistic opposition between the world of Isis and that of Fortuna, the goddess who has hounded Lucius through the

first ten books of the *Metamorphoses*. Those consigned to Fortuna's disordered realm are not guided by organizing principles of any kind.
Only "hostile chance" [*casus infestus*] and "random wickedness"
[*improvida malitia*] determine what will happen, and they do so quite
unpredictably; there are no patterns in events or fixed relationships of
cause and effect from which those in the midst of them can extrapolate
for future reference. Instead, being able to see neither behind them nor
in front of them, they are doomed to wander aimlessly in blindness
(*caecitas*) and *error*, Mithras suggests (we think of Dante's Dark Wood of
Error and of the "blind" souls suffering in the *Inferno*). In contrast, Isis
and those who devote themselves to her are endowed with the clearest
sight. She is a "Fortuna who sees" [*Fortuna videns*], who illuminates
everything with the splendor of her light and oversees all the activities
unfolding in the universe, guiding them into euphony through her
providentia.[23] This picture of Isis as the eternally existing (*perpetua*,
11.25) origin of cosmic order and the implement of its maintenance persists to the end of Book 11.

It is an image put forward with particular fullness in Lucius' emotional farewell speech to the goddess before his departure for Rome
(11.25). In his new world view she reigns supreme as the one who conducts the cosmic symphony down to the tiniest, most fleeting note. The
motions of the stars and the planets, all the elements and the cycle of
the seasons, the threads of Fate and the vicissitudes of Fortune, spirits
in the underworld and those in heaven, including all the other gods,
and all creatures on earth—all these are regulated at the nod of Isis. The
stress in Lucius' conception as he reveals it in this speech is on system
and structure, on regularity and predictability, on the idea of an organically cohering whole in which there is a clear division of labor, so to
speak, and clear categories and roles, where everything has its proper

---

23. In his speech Mithras also hints at Lucius' imprisonment on the treadmill of spurious pleasures, a condition related to the difficulty of locating
"true" reality and which devotion to Isis is about to terminate. Lucius' life, he
says, has been (as Hanson translates) a series of "twists and turns of the harsh-
est journeys that end where they begin" [*asperrimorum itinerum ambages reciprocae*]. In other words, Lucius was getting nowhere traveling under the auspices
of his old values, which the priest connects with *serviles voluptates* and *curiositas
inprospera*. But, as I argued in chapter 4, he refers here not so much to Lucius'
weaknesses for sex and magic as to his generally incorrect cognitive orientation.

place and function. In other words, Lucius finds in Isis' world a grand system of replacements for the organizing principles that had slipped out of his old world; he finds in her what he needs. Furthermore, one of the crucial functions and attractions of totalizing systems such as this, that of integrating anomic phenomena and, in particular, death, is evident in Lucius' description of his actual initiation into the mysteries of Isis (11.21, 23; see Griffiths 1975, ad loc.). This series of rituals is experienced as a symbolic death *(voluntaria mors)* and rebirth; they symbolize death to his old life and rebirth into the new. Although the details provided by Lucius are cryptic because of the prohibition against divulging the cult's secrets, it is clear that some sort of elaborate enactment of a journey to death's door, or the realm of Proserpina, and back again is involved (23). On the whole these rituals work to concretize the spiritual rebirth undergone by the initiate, but Isis is also credited with the power to extend the physical lives of her favorites (21), and we have already seen how the greatest reward for service to her is a happy eternal afterlife in the Elysian fields. Like Tolstoy dangling over the abyss and then lifted out of danger by God's lifeline, Lucius now has a safety net with a comprehensive range of features.

Another one of these features, and perhaps the fundamental one, is epistemological stability, which is intimately connected with the cosmic anchoring function of the goddess. Lucius' proem to his account of the initiation proper rings with the zeal of the convert in the passion with which the truth claims of the cult and what it stands for are asserted: *crede, quae vera sunt,* he announces—"believe, these things are true" (23). This is an assertion that he could not have made anywhere in the unstable world of Books 1 through 10. We saw in chapters 4 and 5 that epistemic structures often express themselves in terms of values—that is, in terms of what should be desired, what should give pleasure—and that this aspect of structures of knowledge is one that especially informs narratives of conversion, including the *Metamorphoses*. Typically, the enlightened narrator of such accounts presents the converting self as arriving at the conviction that the goals pursued in the benighted earlier part of life were the "wrong" ones, and that this explains the chronic sense of frustration which fed the search for something "more." Insofar as epistemic structures and systems of value are linked, the relocation of the center of one's epistemic structure in the divine results in the redirection of one's desiderative energy toward the divine as the one true and proper object of that energy. Narratives of religious conversion abound with claims about the "falseness" of the desires and pleasures blindly pursued in the fragmented secular world and the "trueness" of those enjoyed through contact with the transcendent one. This is true of the narratives of Augustine and Dante, and it is true of the *Metamorphoses*. After Isis rescues Lucius, all the desire that he had directed indiscriminately at a range of moving targets without being rewarded with real satisfaction now becomes focused exclusively on her, and the pleasure that he derives from communing with her is of an entirely different order from the fleeting pleasures of his old life.

The first hints that we will witness a wholesale transfer of Lucius' erotic energy appear in the very beginning of Book 11. One of the names by which he addresses Isis in his initial prayer at 11.2 is "heavenly Venus" [*caelestis Venus*]. With this appellation Lucius suggests that Isis will come to represent for him the realm of "higher" or "true" love, as opposed to the "bad" or "false" loves pursued in the sensible world and emblemized in the figure of the shrewish Venus who terrorizes Psyche in the old woman's tale.[24] Even before this there is evidence that the Apuleian vocabulary of desire and pleasure is moving to new applications in the nonmaterial realm. After the lunar intimations of the impending appearance of Isis, Lucius is said to rise up happily *(laetus)* from his sleepy state, moved by a "zealous desire" *(studium)* to purify himself (11.1). Later, during the procession, the unmistakably flagged desire with which he gobbles up the therapeutic roses ("I took them in my greedy mouth and, desirous of their promised effect, I devoured them with great desire" [*avido ore suspectam cupidus promissi cupidissime devoravi*] (11.13) prefigures the intense desire that he will fix on the goddess herself, and her alone, after his transformation. The gratitude of Lucius is so great that he makes no effort to return home but instead remains at Cenchreae and spends the better part of his time communing with Isis by contemplating her image.

This activity is the only aim of his desire and apparently the only source of pleasure for him now. For the first time in the novel the

---

24. Interestingly enough, Griffiths has nothing to say about the potentially Platonic implications of *caelestis Venus*, although he does, as usual, offer a wealth of parallels from other sources for pagan religion. My own view of the Platonic features of the *Metamorphoses* as a whole, as I argued in chapter 5, is that they work in conjunction with a range of other religious motifs to produce a composite narrative designed to represent and explore religious experience in general.

desiderative energy of the previously mercurial Lucius is focused on one object. He becomes an "inseparable devotee of the great deity" [*numinis magni cultor inseparabilis*], and after any interruption he immediately returns to contemplating the goddess, which gives him his greatest pleasure (*me rursum ad deae gratissimum mihi refero conspectum*, 11.19). That we are meant to understand Lucius' devotion as a redirection of erotic impulses is especially clear at 11.24, where he represents himself as a veritable slave of love, "caught in the nets of the most ardent desire" [*ardentissimi desiderii retinaculis*], which when gratified through contemplation gives him "ineffable pleasure" [*inexplicabilis voluptas*]. So great is Lucius' desire (*cupido*) to be initiated that the priest is compelled to gently rebuke his *aviditas*, "as parents often restrain the rash desires of their children" (11.21). This desire persists at the same high pitch after he goes to Rome and increasingly puzzling demands for further initiation are made of him (11.26, 27, 30: as *studium*, especially *studium pietatis*). When we consider as well that curiosity was formulated in Books 1 through 10 as an especially prevalent and dangerous form of "bad" desire, and one to which Lucius himself was particularly susceptible, that he disparages curiosity twice in Book 11 (22, 23) makes it clear that he is on a new desiderative path. The satisfaction and, indeed, the happiness that Lucius receives from being connected to Isis and her world give every indication of being as lasting as those felt by the converted Augustine.

We recall the pervasiveness of claims of joy in narratives of transformative experiences. Joy (*gaudium*) is everywhere in the Isisbook as well (for example, 11.12, 14, 19), and in fact that is the note on which the entire *Metamorphoses* resoundingly ends:

> Then again I shaved my head completely, and neither concealing nor covering up my baldness, but displaying it wherever I went, I carried out the duties of that very ancient priesthood founded in the time of Sulla, joyfully.

> [rursus denique quam raso capillo collegii vetustissimi et sub illis Syllae temporibus conditi munia, non obumbrato vel obtecto calvitio, sed quoquoversus obvio, gaudens obibam.] (11.30)[25]

---

25. Resoundingly perhaps, but not unambiguously. As Winkler points out, Lucius the narrator's use of the imperfect here (*obibam*) is one of several obstacles in Book 11 preventing the *actor* and the narrator from converging as they

Thus the representation of Lucius qua convert involves the unification of his once fragmented desires and their transference to one object that becomes the recipient of his complete and exclusive devotion (be the object Isis or Osiris or the two of them together: they both function as central points in the transcendent realm on which he can now fix his sights and in relation to which he can orient himself). In contrast to his earlier distracted casting about for satisfaction, Lucius' desire now has a constant object and his pleasure a constant source. A "true" system of values has been restored to his world, and with it the "glue" of basic values that holds any world together. His energy now has an unchanging focus in the imagined center of the transcendent, eternal order that Isis represents. Because of its grounding in metaphysics rather than matter, this order is reliable and fixed in the relationship of its parts in a way that Lucius' old order proved incapable of remaining. By communing with Isis he forges his own link in the chain of that eternal order, which allows him to pull himself above the ordinary spatial and temporal limitations of mortals and the vicissitudes of their worlds. In

---

"should" in the end or, as Winkler puts it, preventing the past from catching up with the present (1985, 224). See end of this section.

Back on the *actor*-track, however, the joy, happiness, and wonder inspired in Lucius by Isis are mirrored in the responses of other characters, even as his preconversion experience had parallels in the ancillary narratives: e.g., the joyful *(laetantes)* women in the procession, the people's and the priest's wonder at Lucius' transformation, and the crowd's *gaudium* (11.9; 13; 17). Moreover, we see the same sort of inversion of images of transfixion and stupefaction that comes into play in *The Divine Comedy*. For example, Lucius is *stupore defixus* when he finds himself a man again, and Mithras is *attonitus* at the same sight (11.14). As in *The Divine Comedy*, these attitudes are to be related, I think, to the shift in the focus of Lucius' erotic energy and the transference of the language used to describe it. We are meant to understand that in the convert's world at least, this dumbfounded amazement is of the "approved" variety, as opposed to the kind inspired by fleeting and frivolous novelties, because it is in response to divinity, which is *truly* awesome. Related inversions occur at 11.16, where the publicly rehumanized Lucius is the cause of the townspeople's pointing fingers and their whispering exchange of information (a replay on a positive note of 3.12, his humiliation after the mock trial); and 11.24, where he becomes a *spectaculum* in his elaborate Isiac garb. Again, within the discourse of the *actor*-track, it is acceptable, and in fact a positively good thing, to be fixated on *this* *spectaculum*, because of its connection with the goddess. These scenes could, of course, also be read ironically, i.e., convert and devotees are deluding themselves into thinking that they have found a definitive "wonder." It is this view that Winkler identifies with the *auctor* Apuleius.

Lucius' new world Isis is positioned as the transcendental signified from which meaning and value, defined in relation to her, are interwoven down through all the less lofty phenomena of existence.

There is one final related point of "authenticity" in the Apuleian representation of the cognitive dynamics of Lucius' conversion or, to put it another way, one final point of consistency between the Apuleian representation and other narratives of conversion. This point relates to the character of structures of meaning as cultural products of particular communities, which retain their status as objective reality through the largely unconscious and unarticulated collective agreement of the community to treat them as such. A corollary to this proposition is that social interaction is crucial both in creating and maintaining and in destroying such systems. There is an integral relationship between one's social contacts and one's attitudes. As Lofland and Stark stated the relationship in connection with conversion, "final conversion [is] coming to accept the opinions of one's friends" (1965, 871). This principle has been documented extensively in recent work on the social dynamics of cults. Two thousand years and significant changes in the way the self is constructed and related social processes may separate the cult of Isis and (for example) the Unification Church. If, however, we can trust the account in Book 11 of the *Metamorphoses*, there are also striking parallels between the two cultic worlds, especially in connection with what we might call the impressionability of the preconvert. Adler and Hammett (1973, 863) encapsulate the process of the assimilation of an individual into a cult as one involving essentially three steps: the disruption of the preconvert's original group system and his or her subsequent unstable and vulnerable condition; the introduction of the subject at just this point into a new group system by a leader or disciples of that system; and the confirmation of the convert's newfound security through membership in the new group and progression through its ranks.

Richardson (et al. 1979, 259–61) echoes this scheme when he describes the process as being set in motion after the preconvert loses meaningful ties with mainstream society or, at any rate, with his former reference group and the structure of meaning attached to it. At that point a cult can exert a "pulling effect," which grows stronger as the interactions between potential converts and those who are already members of the group intensify. Affective bonds thus play a major role in attitude change; as Richardson puts it, "[s]trong positive interactional ties between sect members which are more rewarding than out-group ties provide the basis for maintenance of faith" (270). It is true that Lucius does not prefigure the proverbial alienated youth of the 1960s and 1970s in the specifics of his "loss of meaningful ties with society." He retains a network of friends and family, who are overjoyed to discover that he is safe and bring him gifts and money at 11.18. Still, the exile that he endures as an ass, not only from his old social world but from his former ontological condition; the persistence with which the futility of pursuing his old values asserts itself during that period; and the fact that in the end he chooses to reject those values in favor of a new life with new organizing principles all indicate slippage in the degree to which he is integrated into his old world and its values.

Scholarship on the dynamics of cult recruitment also stresses the formation of strong affective bonds between the potential convert and an established leader or guide figure who acts as the preconvert's mentor in the transitional period. The figure of Mithras certainly fulfills this function; at 11.25, Lucius describes him as not only a *sacerdos* but a *parens*, whom Lucius will never adequately be able to thank for his services. It is this mentor who bridges the gap between the preconvert's first exposure to the cult's world view and the final acceptance of it as objective truth. A strong affective attachment to someone who is already a member often exists alongside the new recruit's intellectual reservations, but not uncommonly the affective bonds win out and the preconvert assimilates the member's construction of reality and becomes a convert himself (Lofland and Stark 1965, 871–72). Lucius' reservations actually come later, when demands for further initiation are made of him at Rome, but the solidity with which his new perspective is established in Greece through the agency of Mithras apparently enables his belief to weather these doubts. At the crucial early stages of assimilation, intensive interaction between the new convert and the group reinforces the former's initial assent; this prolonged association allows the new perspective to "come alive." Steps often encouraged at this point by established members of the sect include a move by the new convert into the cult's quarters, which is crucial in order for the reinforcing exposure to the cult's perspective to occur on a daily basis, and the surrender of all the convert's "personal and material resources" to the cult (Lofland and Stark 1965, 873–74). Lucius, of course, is drawn into making both of these gestures.

Sarbin and Adler also insist on the importance of an "Other" as a role model who facilitates the new convert's process of resocialization (and who, depending on the context, might be called a "sponsor, priest, therapist, shaman, doctor, guard, guru, or captor"). The function of this figure is to act as an "evaluative audience for the adaptive measures the actor takes in handling the strains involved in the change process" (1970, 610–11). The same theorists also note the role of "elementary ritualistic and imitative activity" in acclimating the convert to the new perspective and in enabling the convert to master his or her behavior so that it will conform to the requirements of the new life. These activities can be manipulated by recruiters to intensify the desire of the new member to belong fully; the imposition of a waiting period and the postponement of ceremonies marking full acceptance into the cult are typical forms that such manipulation can take (612–13). We recall Lucius' extreme eagerness to be initiated; this eagerness only intensifies each time he is told by Mithras that he must be patient and await the nod of approval from Isis herself. In the terminology of Straus, Lucius' zeal seems to indicate that he is in the "redhot phase" of conversion to a sect. In this phase the convert acts the ideal cult member "to the point of exaggeration," in order to place his "subjective psychological transformation within the world of other people" and thereby to have it validated. During this "proving" phase, according to Straus, in addition to displaying the proverbial "zeal of the convert," the new member identifies himself "as transformed by symbolic behaviors or props that promote instant recognizability" as a cult adherent (1976, 266–67).

What is really behind this aggressive identification with the new group, although converts would rarely formulate it thus, is a need on their part to *use* "institutional provisions of a [cult] toward . . . their own life-changing ends" (Straus 1976, 267). In other words, they see in interactions with cult members the opportunity to create a new objective world for themselves, a world with features that they need personally. The social interactionist perspective on cult formation and adherence is in its origins clearly a phenomenon of the 1960s, which marked the birth in the social sciences of the premise (typified in the writing of Berger) that "all systems of social knowledge and beliefs are sustained by an underlying 'sentimental order'," and that "truth is a function of what is defined as such in the individual's social and emotional milieu" (Lofland and Skonovd 1981, 380–81). But the fact that this modern theoretical framework can be applied on so many points to a representation of conversion and adherence to a cult that comes to us out of the cultural milieu of pagan antiquity suggests that the phenomenon preceded adequate modes of understanding and describing it by many hundreds of years.[26]

Up to this point in my discussion of the Isisbook, I have given the impression that it is a monolithic paean to the realm of "true" value and represents a moment of grand Augustinian closure. But Book 11, and indeed the entire *Metamorphoses,* is much more complicated than that. All is not well when the narrative ends. The *actor's* resolution is not the only perspective built into the final book, many features of which pull against that resolution and sabotage the closure that the narrative seems at another level to be trying to achieve. There is, for example, the inescapable suggestion that Lucius is a dupe, a gullible sucker who is so enamored of his new love that it blinds him to the possibility that he is in the hands of religious charlatans. This suggestion runs right alongside the compelling invocation of the saving goddess and becomes especially insistent toward the end of the book as Lucius finds his financial and emotional resources exhausted by the repeated demands of cult officials for more initiations and more payments. It is not enough that Lucius is required to spend a considerable sum on supplies and garments for his first (and, he thinks at the time, only) initiation at Corinth where he was converted (22–23). Twice after he settles in Rome at the behest of the goddess, he is astonished to learn that he must be initiated again, with all the concomitant expense, this time into the rites of Osiris (26–30).

These demands seem so unreasonable to Lucius that his faith is rattled and he has serious doubts that grow with each new injunction imposed on him.[27] For each fresh initiation, he is forced to spend

---

26. For further discussion of conversion from an interactionist perspective, see Rambo 1993, chapters 5 through 8 and notes.

27. When the second initiation is demanded, Lucius begins feeling "conscientious scruples" [*religiosum scrupulum*] and senses a "cloud of doubt" [*ambiguitatis caligo*] hanging over him (27). With the third demand, he is so tormented by doubt that it appears for a moment that he might resist: "I was troubled by serious concern and I didn't know what to think. . . . and, by Hercules, I even began to have misgivings about the good faith of the priests" [*nec levi cura sollicitus, sed oppido suspensus animi. . . . et hercules iam de fide quoque eorum opinari coeptabam sequius*] (29). In both cases, however, Lucius' doubts are dispelled and he goes through with the ceremony.

beyond his means; for the second one he is reduced to selling his clothes to raise the necessary funds after being badgered repeatedly by the god (28). Yet each time, an opportunely materializing vision or a convoluted clerical explanation smooths over Lucius' cognitive dissonance; he rationalizes the cult's demands because he *wants* to believe. The critical commentary of the author that is implicit in these scenes functions much as the detached observation of a twentieth-century social scientist identifying the convert's "redhot" phase. The skeptical voice expresses itself further in the strain of venality that runs through the later chapters of the Isisbook. It is not only the priests of Isis and Osiris who seem to have one eye to profit. Before his first initiation, Lucius himself has a dream about recovering his lost wealth (20) and after his move to Rome appears to embark on a successful legal career in addition to serving Isis and Osiris. None of this is consistent with the ascetic features of the cult that seem to assert themselves at other points in the book; an Isiac convert, it would appear, can "have it all." The skeptical undercurrents of the Isisbook give the reader more than a taste of a satirical treatment of religious credulity in the manner of Lucian.

Winkler has explained the dissonance of voices in Book 11 in a way that is compatible with my reading, and there is no need to reiterate his discussion at length. He sees that in the final book Lucius the *actor* can be read as both an honestly redeemed Isiac and as a dupe, and that neither role is authorized by Apuleius. Instead of the "surcease of doubts" that we would expect at the end of a narrative of conversion, we get, to our dismay, an "escalation of provocative uncertainty" that replicates Lucius' uncertainty but, unlike his, is not relieved. What is missing, furthermore, is any expression of the narrator Lucius' *present* authority as a confirmed convert. The narrative circle, as Winkler puts it, is never closed; the *actor* and the *auctor* never merge; the past never catches up with the present. Neither the author Apuleius nor the narrator Lucius endorses the solution of Lucius the *actor* (1985, 216–24). The *Metamorphoses,* Winkler writes, "manages in Book 11 to *approach* a simple model that *would* integrate its own diversity as a single narrator's discourse (the confession), but signally refuses to make that announcement" (241). And so the suppression of any integrating narrator's voice that we have noticed in Books 1 through 10 persists up to the very end of the narrative.

In chapter 4, section 2, I discussed the gap between the present narrator and the past experiencing self as a device enlisted by the author to reproduce the experience of sudden conversion. And so it is, up to the moment of Lucius' conversion; but the failure of the two egos to be united after that point suggests that the function of the device has undergone a transformation. It now becomes a tool with which to tease the reader with the possibility of a closure that never comes. All of this, according to Winkler, is part of a much larger "oscillation in reference frame of the narrative," which has three dimensions of volatility and shows slippage along three axes: that of tone (between the serious and the comic), that of unity (from integrated to episodic and disjointed), and that of authority (from suggestions of an author-endorsed "message" to the complete absence of a center of authority). The *Metamorphoses* is, as Winkler understands, a very unstable text in every sense of the term. I too think that the ultimate point of this instability is to illustrate the character of religious knowledge: any belief in a religious system as a closed, definitive, fixed, and integrated structure of meaning is subjective, arbitrary, and nonauthorized, as is any belief in a particular signification of the text of the *Metamorphoses* itself.[28]

The *Metamorphoses* is, of course, not *exactly* like the conversion narratives of Tolstoy, Dante, or Augustine, in spite of the parallels that I have drawn. Unlike these confessional narratives, and unexpectedly like the confessional fiction of Sartre, the Latin novel is simultaneously an invocation and a critique of religious experience; this dual identity alone can account for its seriocomic tone. But the path of the narrative that I have followed—the *actor*'s path, the invocation—has very much in common with those later sober narratives of conversion. I have sought to direct attention back to this aspect of the novel because it seems to me that the power of the invocation has been overshadowed in recent years by a critical preoccupation with the playful, if not the aporetic, features of the Apuleian text. Such brilliance in representation need not imply autobiography. It is not necessary that an empathetic and imaginative artist who is alert to the nuances of earlier oral and written narratives actually have an experience himself in order to be

---

28. For Winkler's discussion of the narrator's failure to impose any structure of meaning on the events of Books 1 through 10, see especially 1985, 140–53. On the three major areas of "oscillation" in the narrative's frame of reference, see especially 153–79. On how these features of the text relate to the question of the nature of religious knowledge, see, e.g., 125; 131–32; 179; 226–27; 316–20, passim.

able to invoke it with vividness and intimacy. In spite of the critique of religious experience that is built into the narrative, the same narrative's invocation of such experience remains, in the final analysis, an extremely sympathetic one. Thus Apuleius is perhaps the first in a long line of intellectuals who have understood the pull exerted by the divine but who have not been able themselves to make the leap.

References

Adler, H., and V. Hammett. 1973. "Crisis, Conversion, and Cult Formation: An Examination of a Common Psychosocial Sequence." *American Journal of Psychiatry* 130:861–64.

Allison, J. 1968. "Adaptive Regression and Intense Religious Experiences." *Journal of Nervous and Mental Disease* 145:452–63.

———. 1969. "Religious Conversion: Regression and Progression in an Adolescent Experience." *Journal for the Scientific Study of Religion* 8:23–38.

Anderson, G. 1982. *Eros Sophistes: Ancient Novelists at Play.* American Classical Studies 9. Chico, Calif.

———. 1984. *Ancient Fiction: The Novel in the Greco-Roman World.* London and Sydney.

Aubin, P. 1963. *Le problème de la 'conversion.' Étude sur un terme commun à l'hellenisme et au christianisme des trois premiers siècles.* Paris.

Auerbach, E. 1959. *Mimesis: Dargestellte Wirklichkeit in der abendländischen Literatur.* 2d ed. Berlin.

Augustinus. 1981. *Confessiones.* Ed. M. Skutella. Stuttgart.

Austin, R. 1977. "Empirical Adequacy of Lofland's Conversion Model." *Review of Religious Research* 18:282–87.

Babcock, W. 1985–86. "MacMullen on Conversion: A Response." *The Second Century* 5:82–89.

Barrett, W. 1962. *Irrational Man: A Study in Existential Philosophy.* Garden City, N.Y.

Bartalucci, A. 1988. "Considerazioni sulla festa del *deus Risus* nelle *Metamorfosi* di Apuleio." *Civiltà classica e cristiana* 9:51–65.

Batson, C.D., P. Schoenrade, and W.L. Ventis. 1993. *Religion and the Individual: A Social-Psychological Perspective.* Oxford.

Batson, C.D., and W.L. Ventis. 1982. *The Religious Experience: A Social-Psychological Perspective.* Oxford.

Beaujeu, J. 1975. "Sérieux et frivolité au IIe siècle de notre ère: Apulée." *Bull. de l'assoc. Guillaume Budé* 4:83–97.

Beckford, J. 1978. "Accounting for Conversion." *British Journal of Sociology* 29:249–62.

Beit-Hallahmi, B. 1974. "Psychology of Religion, 1880–1930: The Rise and Fall of a Psychological Movement." *Journal of the History of the Behavioral Sciences* 10:84–90.

Bellah, R. 1964. "Religious Evolution." *American Sociological Review* 29:358–74.

Berger, P. 1967. *The Sacred Canopy: Elements of a Sociological Theory of Religion.* Garden City, N.Y.

Berger, P., and T. Luckmann. 1966. *The Social Construction of Reality: A Treatise on the Sociology of Knowledge.* Garden City, N.Y.

Bernhard, M. 1927. *Der Stil des Apuleius von Madaura.* Stuttgart.

Bertocci, P. 1958. *Religion as Creative Insecurity.* New York.

Boisen, A. 1936. *The Exploration of the Inner World: A Study of Mental Disorder and Religious Experience.* New York.

Bowie, E. 1985. "The Greek Novel." In *The Cambridge History of Classical Literature,* vol. 1 (Greek), ed. P. Easterling and B. Knox, 683–99. Cambridge.

Bowie, E., and S.J. Harrison. 1993. "The Romance of the Novel." *Journal of Roman Studies* 83:159–78.

Braun, M. 1938. *History and Romance in Greco-Oriental Literature.* Oxford.

Brosman, C. 1983. *Jean-Paul Sartre.* Boston.

Brotherton, B. 1934. "The Introduction of Characters by Name in the *Metamorphoses* of Apuleius." *Classical Philology* 29:36–52.

Brown, P. 1967. *Augustine of Hippo.* Berkeley.

Burkert, W. 1987. *Ancient Mystery Cults.* Cambridge, Mass.

Carr, L., and W. Hauser. 1976. "Anomie and Religiosity: An Empirical Reexamination." *Journal for the Scientific Study of Religion* 15:69–74.

Clark, E. 1929. *The Psychology of Religious Awakening.* New York.

Clark, W.H. 1958. *The Psychology of Religion.* New York.

Coe, G. 1916. *The Psychology of Religion.* Chicago.

Cooper, G. 1980. "Sexual and Ethical Reversal in Apuleius: The *Metamorphoses* as Anti-Epic." In *Studies in Latin Literature and Roman History,* vol. 2, ed. C. Deroux, 436–66. Brussels.

Courcelle, P. 1963. *Les* Confessions *de Saint Augustin dans la tradition litteraire: antécédents et postérité.* Paris.

Dabrowski, K. 1964. *Positive Disintegration.* Boston.

Dante Alighieri. 1961. *The Divine Comedy.* 3 vols. Trans. J. Sinclair. New York.

Dean, D. 1968. "Anomie, Powerlessness, and Religious Participation." *Journal for the Scientific Study of Religion* 7:252–54.

DeFilippo, J. 1990. "*Curiositas* and the Platonism of Apuleius' *Golden Ass.*" *American Journal of Philology* 111:471–92.

Derchain, P., and J. Hubaux. 1958. "L'affaire du marché d'Hypata dans les *Métamorphoses* d'Apulée." *L'antiquité classique* 27:100–104.

Dewey, J. 1929. *The Quest for Certainty.* New York.

Dillon, J. 1977. *The Middle Platonists.* Ithaca, N.Y.

Dodds, E.R. 1965. *Pagan and Christian in an Age of Anxiety.* Cambridge.

Donini, P. 1979. "Apuleio e il platonismo medio." In *Apuleio: letterato, filosofo, mago,* ed. A. Pennacini, P. Donini, T. Alimonti, and A. Monteduro Roccavini, 103–11. Bologna.

Dowden, K. 1982. "Apuleius and the Art of Narration." *Classical Quarterly* 32:419–36.

———. 1993. "The Unity of Apuleius' Eighth Book and the Danger of Beasts."

In *Groningen Colloquia on the Novel*, vol. 5, ed. H. Hofmann, 91–109. Groningen.

Durkheim, E. 1915. *The Elementary Forms of the Religious Life*. London.

Ebel, H. 1970. "Apuleius and the Present Time." *Arethusa* 3:155–76.

Elkind, D. 1970. "The Origins of Religion in the Child." *Review of Religious Research* 12:35–42.

Elsom, H. 1988. Review of Gianotti (1986) and P. James (1987). *Journal of Roman Studies* 78:248–49.

Festugière, A.-J. 1954. *Personal Religion among the Greeks*. Berkeley.

Finkelpearl, E. 1986. The Metamorphosis of Language in Apuleius' *Metamorphoses*. Ph.D. diss., Harvard.

————. 1991. "The Judgment of Lucius: Apuleius, *Metamorphoses* 10.29–34." *Classical Antiquity* 10:221–36.

Fisher, H. 1973. "Conversion Reconsidered: Some Historical Aspects of Religious Conversion in Black Africa." *Africa* 43:27–40.

Flakoll, D. 1976. "A History of Method in the Psychology of Religion (1900–1960)." *Journal of Psychology and Theology* 4:51–62.

Forbes, C. 1943–44. "Charite and Dido." *Classical World* 37:39–40.

Frankl, V. 1963. *Man's Search for Meaning*. New York.

Freccero, J. 1986. *Dante: The Poetics of Conversion*. Cambridge, Mass.

Fredriksen, P. 1986. "Paul and Augustine: Conversion Narratives, Orthodox Traditions, and the Retrospective Self." *Journal of Theological Studies* 37:3–34.

Freud, S. 1961. "The Future of an Illusion." In *The Standard Edition of the Complete Psychological Works of Sigmund Freud*, vol. 21, ed. J. Strachey. London. First published in German (1927).

Gallagher, E. 1990. *Expectation and Experience: Explaining Religious Conversion*. Atlanta, Ga.

Gaselee, S., ed. 1977. *Apuleius: The Golden Ass*. Trans. W. Adlington. Loeb Classical Library. Cambridge, Mass.

Geertz, C. 1973. *The Interpretation of Cultures*. New York.

Giangrande, L. 1972. *The Use of Spoudaiogeloion in Greek and Roman Literature*. The Hague.

Gianotti, G. 1986. *"Romanzo" e ideologia. Studi sulle* Metamorfosi *di Apuleio*. Forme materiali e ideologie del mondo antico 26. Naples.

Goodman, M. 1994. *Mission and Conversion: Proselytizing in the Religious History of the Roman Empire*. Oxford.

Gorlow, L., and H. Schroeder. 1968. "Motives for Participating in the Religious Experience." *Journal for the Scientific Study of Religion* 7:241–51.

Greil, A. 1977. "Previous Disposition and Conversion to Perspectives of Social and Religious Movements." *Sociological Analysis* 38:115–25.

Griffiths, J.G. 1978. "Isis in the *Metamorphoses* of Apuleius." In *Aspects of Apuleius' Golden Ass*, ed. B. Hijmans and R. van der Paardt, 141–66. Groningen.

————, ed. 1970. *Plutarch's de Iside et Osiride*. Cardiff.

————, ed. and trans. 1975. *Apuleius of Madauros: The Isis-book (Metamorphoses, Book XI)*. Leiden.

Grimal, P. 1972. "La fête du rire dans les *Métamorphoses* d'Apulée." In *Studi classici in honore di Quintino Cataudella*, 457–65. Catania.

———, ed. 1963. *Apulei Metamorphoseis 4.28–6.24: le conte d'Amour et Psyche.* Paris.

Habinek, T. 1990. "Lucius' Rite of Passage." *Materiali e discussioni per l'analisi dei testi classici* 25:49–69.

Hadot, P. 1981. *Exercises spirituels et philosophie antique.* Paris.

Hägg, T. 1983. *The Novel in Antiquity.* Oxford.

Haight, E. 1943. *Essays on the Greek Romances.* New York.

Hall, G. 1904. *Adolescence.* 2 vols. New York.

Hanson, J.A., trans. 1989. *Apuleius, Metamorphoses.* Loeb Classical Library. Cambridge, Mass.

Harmon, A.M., trans. 1927. *Lucian.* Vol. 1. Loeb Classical Library. Cambridge, Mass.

Harrison, S.J. 1990. "The Speaking Book: The Prologue to Apuleius' *Metamorphoses.*" *Classical Quarterly* 40:507–13.

Hawkins, A. 1985. *Archetypes of Conversion: The Autobiographies of Augustine, Bunyan, and Merton.* Lewisburg, Pa.

Heine, R. 1962. *Untersuchungen zur Romanform des Apuleius von Madaura.* Ph.D. diss., Göttingen.

Heirich, M. 1977. "Change of Heart: A Test of Some Widely Held Theories about Religious Conversion." *American Journal of Sociology* 83:653–80.

Heiserman, A. 1977. *The Novel before the Novel.* Chicago.

Heller, S. 1983. "Apuleius, Platonic Dualism, and Eleven." *American Journal of Philology* 104:321–39.

Helm, R., ed. 1992. *Apuleius I: Metamorphoseon Libri xi.* Leipzig.

———, trans. 1961. *Metamorphosen oder Der goldene Esel.* 5th ed. Shriften und Quellen der alten Welt. Berlin.

Hermann, L. 1951. "Le fragment obscène de *l'Ane d'or.*" *Latomus* 10:329–32.

Hijmans, B. 1987. "Apuleius, Philosophus Platonicus." *Aufstieg und Niedergang der römischen Welt* II.36.1:395–475.

Hijmans, B., and R. van der Paardt, eds. 1978. *Aspects of Apuleius' Golden Ass.* Groningen.

Hijmans, B., R. van der Paardt, E. Smits, R. Westendorp Boerma, and A. Westerbrink, eds. 1977. *Apuleius Madaurensis, Metamorphoses Book IV. 1–27.* Groningen.

Hildebrand, G., ed. 1842. *Apulei Opera Omnia I: Metamorphoses.* Leipzig.

Hooker, W. 1955. "Apuleius' Cupid and Psyche as a Platonic Myth." *Bucknell Review* 5:24–38.

James, P. 1987. *Unity in Diversity: A Study of Apuleius' Metamorphoses.* Altertumswissenschaftliche Texte und Studien 16. Hildesheim.

James, W. 1958. *The Varieties of Religious Experience.* 1902. Reprint, New York.

Johnson, W.R. 1976. *Darkness Visible: A Study of Virgil's Aeneid.* Berkeley.

Joly, R. 1961. "Curiositas." *L'antiquité classique* 30:33–44.

———. 1966. "Notes sur la conversion d'Augustin." *L'antiquité classique* 35:217–21.

Jones, C.P. 1978. *The Roman World of Dio Chrysostom*. Cambridge, Mass.

———. 1986. *Culture and Society in Lucian*. Cambridge, Mass.

Jones, R. 1977. "Some Epistemological Considerations of Paradigm Shifts: Basic Steps towards a Formulated Model of Alternation." *Sociological Review* 25:253–71.

———. 1978. "Paradigm Shifts and Identity Theory: Alternation as a Form of Identity Management." In *Identity and Religion*, ed. H. Mol, 59–82. Beverly Hills, Calif.

de Jonge, B.J. 1941. "Ad Apulei Madaurensis *Metamorphoseon* Librum Secundum Commentarius Exegeticus."Ph.D. diss., Groningen.

Jordan, M. 1985–86. "Philosophic 'Conversion' and Christian Conversion: A Gloss on Professor MacMullen." *The Second Century* 5:90–96.

Journoud, S. 1965. "Apulée conteur: quelques réflexions sur l'épisode de l'âne et de la Corinthienne." *Acta classica Universitatis Scientiarum Debreceniensis* 1:33–37.

Jules-Rosette, B. 1975. "The Conversion Experience: The Apostles of John Maranke." *Journal of Religion in Africa* 7:132–64.

———. 1975. *African Apostles: Ritual and Conversion in the Church of John Maranke*. Ithaca, N.Y.

Junghanns, P. 1932. *Die Erzählungstechnik von Apuleius Metamorphosen und ihrer Vorlage*. *Philologus* suppl. 24:1. Leipzig.

Kenney, E.J. 1990a. *Apuleius: Cupid and Psyche*. Cambridge.

———. 1990b. "Psyche and Her Mysterious Husband." In *Antonine Literature*, ed. D.A. Russell, 175–98. Oxford.

Kenny, B. 1974. "The Reader's Role in *The Golden Ass*." *Arethusa* 7:187–209.

Kilbourne, B., and J. Richardson. 1988. "Paradigm Conflict, Types of Conversion, and Conversion Theories." *Sociological Analysis* 50:1–21.

Kim, B.-S. 1979. "Religious Deprogramming and Subjective Reality." *Sociological Analysis* 40:197–207.

Knudten, R. 1968. Review of Berger (1967). *Journal for the Scientific Study of Religion* 7:292–94.

Koester, H. 1982. *Introduction to the New Testament*. Vol. 2, *History and Literature of Early Christianity*. Philadelphia.

Koestler, A. 1951. *The God That Failed*. London.

Kuch, H. 1985. "Gattungstheoretische Überlegungen zum antiken Roman." *Philologus* 129:3–19.

———. 1992. "Zur Gattungsgeschichte und Gattungstheorie des antiken Romans." *Eikasmos* 3:223–33.

Kuhn, T. 1962. *The Structure of Scientific Revolutions*. Chicago.

Labhardt, A. 1960. "*Curiositas*: Notes sur l'histoire d'un mot et d'une notion." *Museum Helveticum* 17:206–24.

Lancel, S. 1961. "*Curiositas* et préoccupations spirituelles chez Apulée." *Revue de l'histoire des religions* 160:25–46.

Laski, M. 1967. *Ecstasy: A Study of Some Secular and Religious Experiences*. Bloomington, Ind.

Leites, N. 1953. "Trends in Affectlessness." In *Personality in Nature, Society, and Culture,* 2d ed, ed. C. Kluckhohn and H. Murray, 620–22. New York.

Leuba, J. 1896. "Studies in the Psychology of Religious Phenomena." *American Journal of Psychology* 7:309–85.

Levin, D. 1977. "To Whom Did the Ancient Novelists Address Themselves?" *Rivista di studi classici* 25:18–29.

Loder, J.E. 1966. *Religious Pathology and Christian Faith.* Philadelphia.

Lofland, J. 1977. " 'Becoming a World Saver' Revisited." *American Behavioral Scientist* 20:805–18.

Lofland, J., and N. Skonovd. 1981. "Conversion Motifs." *Journal for the Scientific Study of Religion* 20:373–85.

Lofland, J., and R. Stark. 1965. "Becoming a World Saver: A Theory of Conversion to a Deviant Perspective." *American Sociological Review* 30:862–75.

Louth, A. 1983. *The Origins of the Christian Mystical Tradition from Plato to Denys.* Oxford.

McHugh, P. 1966. "Social Disintegration as a Requisite of Resocialization." *Social Forces* 44:355–63.

MacKay, L. 1965. "The Sin of *The Golden Ass.*" *Arion* 4:474–80.

MacMullen, R. 1981. *Paganism in the Roman Empire.* New Haven, Conn.

———. 1983. "Two Types of Conversion to Early Christianity." *Vigiliae Christianae* 37:174–92.

———. 1984. *Christianizing the Roman Empire, A.D. 100–400.* New Haven, Conn.

———. 1985–86. "Conversion: A Historian's View." *The Second Century* 5:67–96.

Malherbe, A. 1987. *Paul and the Thessalonians: The Philosophic Tradition of Pastoral Care.* Philadelphia.

Maslow, A. 1954. *Motivation and Personality.* New York.

———. 1964. *Religions, Values, and Peak-Experiences.* Columbus, Ohio.

Mason, H.J. 1971. "Lucius at Corinth." *Phoenix* 25:160–65.

———. 1978. "*Fabula Graecanica.* Apuleius and His Greek Sources." In *Aspects of Apuleius' Golden Ass,* ed. B. Hijmans and R. van der Paardt, 1–15. Groningen.

———. 1983. "The Distinction of Lucius in Apuleius' *Metamorphoses.*" *Phoenix* 37:135–43.

Maude, A. 1987. *The Life of Tolstoy.* 1929. Reprint, Oxford.

May, R. 1975. *The Courage to Create.* New York.

Mayrhofer, C.M. 1975. "On Two Stories in Apuleius." *Antichthon* 9:68–80.

Melchert, N. 1977. "Mystical Experience and Ontological Claims." *Philosophy and Phenomenological Research* 37:445–63.

Merkelbach, R. 1962. *Roman und Mysterium in der Antike.* Munich.

Mette, H. 1956. "Curiositas." In *Festschrift Bruno Snell,* ed. H. Erbse, 227–35. Munich.

Misch, G. 1951. *A History of Autobiography in Antiquity.* 2 vols. Trans. E.W. Dickes. Cambridge, Mass.

Mitchell, B. 1973. *The Justification of Religious Belief.* London.

Moles, J. 1978. "The Career and Conversion of Dio Chrysostom." *Journal of Hellenic Studies* 98:79–100.

Molt, M. 1938. Ad Apulei Madaurensis *Metamorphoseon* Librum Primum Commentarius Exegeticus. Ph.D. diss., Groningen.

Moreschini, C. 1965. "La demonologia medio-platonica e le *Metamorfosi* di Apuleio." *Maia* 17:30–46.

———. 1978. *Apuleio e il Platonismo*. Florence.

Morrison, K. 1992. *Conversion and Text*. Companion volume to *Understanding Conversion*. Charlottesville, Va.

Mortley, R. 1972. "Apuleius and Platonic Theology." *American Journal of Philology* 93:584–90.

Nethercut, W. 1969. "Apuleius' *Metamorphoses*: The Journey." *Agon* 3:97–134.

Nock, A.D. 1933. *Conversion: The Old and the New in Religion from Alexander to Augustine of Hippo*. Oxford.

———. 1986a. "Conversion and Adolescence." In *Arthur Darby Nock: Essays on Religion and the Ancient World*. Vol. 1, ed. Z. Stewart, 469–80. Oxford.

———. 1986b. "The Milieu of Gnosticism." In *Arthur Darby Nock: Essays on Religion and the Ancient World*. Vol. 1, ed. Z. Stewart, 444–51. Oxford.

Nock, A.D., ed., and A. Festugière, trans. 1945–54. *Corpus Hermeticum*. 4 vols. Paris.

O'Connell, R. 1969. *St. Augustine's* Confessions: *The Odyssey of Soul*. Cambridge, Mass.

O'Donnell, J., ed. 1992. *Augustine, Confessions: Text and Commentary*. 3 vols. Oxford.

O'Meara, J. 1954. *The Young Augustine*. London.

Otto, R. 1923. *The Idea of the Holy*. Oxford.

Paardt, R.T. van der, ed. 1971. *The Metamorphoses III*. Amsterdam.

Paloutzian, R. 1983. *Invitation to the Psychology of Religion*. Glenview, Ill.

Penwill, J. 1975. "Slavish Pleasures and Profitless Curiosity: Fall and Redemption in Apuleius' *Metamorphoses*." *Ramus* 4:49–82.

———. 1990. "*Ambages Reciprocae*. Reviewing Apuleius' *Metamorphoses*." *Ramus* 19:1–25.

Perry, B.E. 1920. The *Metamorphoses* Ascribed to Lucius of Patrae. Ph.D. diss., Princeton University.

———. 1925. "On Apuleius *Met*. 2.31–3.20." *American Journal of Philology* 46:253–62.

———. 1929. "On Apuleius *Met*. 1.14–17." *Classical Philology* 24:394–400.

———. 1929. "The Story of Thelyphron in Apuleius." *Classical Philology* 24:231–38.

———. 1948. Review of the Robertson/Vallette Budé edition of the *Metamorphoses* (1940–45). *Classical Philology* 43:192–99.

———. 1967. *The Ancient Romances: A Literary-Historical Account of Their Origins*. Berkeley.

Peters, G. 1993. *The Mutilating God: Authorship and Authority in the Narrative of Conversion*. Amherst, Mass.

Polanyi, M., and H. Prosch. 1975. *Meaning*. Chicago.

Portogalli, B. 1963. "Sulle fonti della concezione teologica e demonologica di Apuleio." *Studi classici e orientali* 12:227–41.

Pottle, D. 1978. The Platonic Elements in the *Metamorphoses* of Apuleius. Ph.D. diss., Tufts University.

Pratt, J.B. 1920. *The Religious Consciousness*. New York.

Proudfoot, W. 1985. *Religious Experience*. Berkeley.

Pruyser, P. 1968. *A Dynamic Psychology of Religion*. New York.

Rambo, L. 1982. "Current Research on Religious Conversion." *Religious Studies Review* 8:146–59.

———. 1993. *Understanding Religious Conversion*. New Haven, Conn.

Reardon, B. 1991. *The Form of Greek Romance*. Princeton.

———, ed. 1989. *Collected Ancient Greek Novels*. Berkeley.

Remus, H. 1984. "Sociology of Knowledge and the Study of Early Christianity." In *Religion and the Sociology of Knowledge: Modernization and Pluralism in Christian Thought and Structure*, ed. B. Hargrove, 99–121. New York.

Richardson, J., M. Stewart, and R. Simmonds. 1979. *Organized Miracles: A Study of a Contemporary, Youth, Communal, Fundamentalist Organization*. New Brunswick, N.J.

Riefstahl, H. 1938. *Der Roman des Apuleius: Beitrag zur Romantheorie*. Frankfurt am Main.

Robertson, D.S. 1919. "A Greek Carnival." *Journal of Hellenic Studies* 39:110–15.

———, ed. 1969–72. *Apulée: Les Métamorphoses*. 3 vols. Trans. P. Vallette. Paris.

Rogers, W.R. 1968. "Order and Chaos in Psychopathology and Ontology: A Challenge to Traditional Correlations of Order to Mental Health and Ultimate Reality, and of Chaos to Mental Illness and Alienation." In *The Dialogue between Theology and Psychology*, ed. P. Homans, 249–62. Chicago.

Rüdiger, H., ed. 1960. "Nachwort." In *Der Goldene Esel*. Trans. A. Rode, 517–59. Zurich.

Rugg, H. 1963. *Imagination*. New York.

Salzman, L. 1953. "The Psychology of Religious and Ideological Conversion." *Psychiatry* 16:177–87.

Sandy, G. 1971. "Knowledge and Curiosity in Apuleius' *Metamorphoses*." *Latomus* 31:179–83.

———. 1972–73. "Foreshadowing and Suspense in Apuleius' *Metamorphoses*." *Classical Journal* 68:323–35.

———. 1974. "*Serviles Voluptates* in Apuleius' *Metamorphoses*." *Phoenix* 28:234–44.

———. 1978. "Book 11: Ballast or Anchor?" In *Aspects of Apuleius'* Golden Ass, ed. B. Hijmans and R. van der Paardt, 123–40. Groningen.

Sarbin, T., and N. Adler. 1970. "Self-Reconstitution Processes: A Preliminary Report." *Psychoanalytic Review* 57:599–616.

Sargant, W. 1961. *The Battle for the Mind: A Physiology of Conversion and Brainwashing*. Baltimore.

Sartre, J.-P. 1938. *La nausée*. Paris.

———. 1964. *Nausea*. Trans. L. Alexander. New York.

Schein, E. 1971. *Coercive Persuasion.* New York.

Schlam, C. 1968a. "The Structure of the *Metamorphoses* of Apuleius." Ph.D. diss., Columbia University.

———. 1968b. "The Curiosity of *The Golden Ass.*" *Classical Journal* 64:120–25.

———. 1970. "Platonica in the *Metamorphoses* of Apuleius." *Transactions of the American Philological Association* 101:477–87.

———. 1971. "The Scholarship on Apuleius since 1938." *Classical World* 64:285–309.

———. 1978. "Sex and Sanctity: The Relationship of Male and Female in the *Metamorphoses.*" In *Aspects of Apuleius'* Golden Ass, ed. B. Hijmans and R. van der Paardt, 95–105. Groningen.

———. 1992. *The* Metamorphoses *of Apuleius. On Making an Ass of Oneself.* Chapel Hill, N.C.

Schweiker, W. 1969. "Religion as a Superordinate Meaning System and Socio-Psychological Integration." *Journal for the Scientific Study of Religion* 8:300–307.

Scobie, A. 1969. *Aspects of the Ancient Romance and Its Heritage.* Beiträge zur klassischen Philologie 30. Meisenheim am Glan.

———. 1973. *More Essays on the Ancient Romance and Its Heritage.* Beiträge zur klassischen Philologie 46. Meisenheim am Glan.

———. 1975. *Apuleius'* Metamorphoses *(Asinus Aureus) Book 1: A Commentary.* Beiträge zur klassischen Philologie 54. Meisenheim am Glan.

Scobie, G. 1975. *Psychology of Religion.* New York.

Segal, A. 1990. *Paul the Convert.* New Haven, Conn.

Seggar, J., and P. Kunz. 1972. "Conversion: Evaluation of a Step-like Process for Problem-Solving." *Review of Religious Research* 13:178–84.

Shupe, A.D., Jr., R. Spielman, and S. Stigall. 1977. "Deprogramming." *American Behavioral Scientist* 20:941–56.

Singleton, N. 1977. Venus in the *Metamorphoses* of Apuleius. Ph.D. diss., Ohio State University.

Skulsky, H. 1981. *Metamorphosis: The Mind in Exile.* Cambridge, Mass.

Smart, N. 1973. *The Science of Religion and the Sociology of Knowledge.* Princeton.

Smith, W.S. 1989. Apuleius' Miserly Host and the Transformation of Satire. Paper delivered at the Second International Conference on the Ancient Novel, Dartmouth College, Hanover, N.H., July 23–29.

Snow, D., and R. Machalek. 1983. "The Convert as a Social Type." In *Sociological Theory,* ed. R. Collins, 259–89. San Francisco.

———. 1984. "The Sociology of Conversion." *Annual Review of Sociology* 10:167–90.

Snow, D., and C. Phillips. 1980. "The Lofland-Stark Conversion Model: A Critical Reassessment." *Social Problems* 27:430–47.

Solmsen, F. 1979. *Isis among the Greeks and Romans.* Cambridge, Mass.

Spilka, B., R. Hood Jr., and R. Gorsuch. 1985. *The Psychology of Religion: An Empirical Approach.* Englewood Cliffs, N.J.

Stace, W. 1960. *Mysticism and Philosophy.* New York.

Starbuck, E. 1901. *The Psychology of Religion.* 2d edition. 1899. London.

Straus, R. 1976. "Changing Oneself: Seekers and the Creative Transformation of Life Experience." In *Doing Social Life*, ed. J. Lofland, 252–72. New York.

Strickland, F. 1924. *The Psychology of Religious Experience*. New York.

Tatum, J. 1969. "Thematic Aspects of the Tales in Apuleius' *Metamorphoses*." Ph.D. diss., Princeton University.

———. 1969. "The Tales in Apuleius' *Metamorphoses*." *Transactions of the American Philological Association* 100:487–527.

———. 1972. "Apuleius and Metamorphosis." *American Journal of Philology* 93:306–13.

———. 1979. *Apuleius and* The Golden Ass. Ithaca, N.Y.

———, ed. 1994. *The Search for the Ancient Novel*. Baltimore.

Thibau, R. 1965. "Les *Métamorphoses* d'Apulée et la théorie platonicienne de l'Erôs." *Studia Philosophica Gandensia* 3:89–144.

Thiel, H. van. 1971–72. *Der Eselsroman*. 2 vols. *Zetemata* Heft 54. Munich.

Tolstoy, L. 1966. *War and Peace*. Trans. A. Maude. Ed. G. Gibian. New York.

———. 1983. *Confession*. Trans. D. Patterson. New York.

Troyat, H. 1965. *Tolstoi*. Paris.

Turcan, R. 1963. Review of Merkelbach (1962). *Revue de l'histoire des religions* 163:149.

Ullman, C. 1982. "Cognitive and Emotional Antecedents of Religious Conversion." *Journal of Personality and Social Psychology* 43:183–92.

———. 1989. *The Transformed Self: The Psychology of Religious Conversion*. New York.

Vallette, P. 1969–72. Introduction to *Les Métamorphoses*, 3 vols., ed. D.R. Robertson, vi–xxxvii. Paris.

Versnel, H., ed. 1981. *Faith, Hope, and Worship: Aspects of Religious Mentality in the Ancient World*. Leiden.

Wainwright, W. 1981. *Mysticism: A Study of Its Nature, Cognitive Value, and Moral Implications*. Madison, Wis.

Wallas, G. 1926. *The Art of Thought*. New York.

Walsh, P.G. 1970. *The Roman Novel*. Cambridge.

———. 1982. "Apuleius." In *The Cambridge History of Classical Literature*, vol. 2 (Latin), ed. E.J. Kenney and W. Clausen, 774–86. Cambridge.

———. 1988. "The Rights and Wrongs of Curiosity." *Greece and Rome* 35:73–85.

Weber, M. 1922. *The Sociology of Religion*. Boston.

Weil, S. 1973. *Waiting for God*. Trans. E. Craufurd, intro. L. Fiedler. New York.

Wesseling, B. 1988. "The Audience of the Ancient Novel." In *Groningen Colloquium on the Novel*, vol. 1, ed. H. Hofmann, 67–79. Groningen.

Wilson, A.N. 1988. *Tolstoy: A Biography*. New York.

Winkler, J.J. 1985. *Auctor and Actor: A Narratological Reading of Apuleius's* The Golden Ass. Berkeley.

Wittgenstein, L. 1953. *Philosophical Investigations*. Oxford.

Wright, C.S. 1963. "No Art at All: A Note on the Proemium of Apuleius' *Metamorphoses*." *Classical Philology* 68:217–19.

Index

Actaeon *ecphrasis*, 67–71, 130n
Actor, 226, 303–4
  in Apuleian *Metamorphoses*, 14,
    35–37, 182, 227–29, 239, 310; epis-
    temological bearings ruptured,
    105, 261; in the Isisbook,
    320–21n, 326; perspective, 44–45
  in Augustine's *Confessions*, 139,
    209–10, 211
  in *Nausea*, 272, 278n, 310
Adler, H., 192–94, 322
Adler, N., 199–200, 323–24
Adlington, W., 12
Aeneid (Virgil), 62n.13, 111, 115–16,
  261
Affect. *See* Emotions
Alienation, 158, 163, 194–95, 199, 239,
  286
  felt by *Nausea* protagonist, 273;
    forced in rehabilitation, 189–90
  of the object of laughter, 83, 86, 87
  See also Anomy
Allegory, 12–13, 252n, 268–69
  Platonic, 10, 259–60
Allison, J., 195n
Alternation
  as noncreative cognitive change,
    176
  as term for conversion, 186–88
Ammianus Marcellinus, 62n.13
Ancient Romances, The (Perry), 3n
Angst, 153n, 161n
Anhedonia, 148, 156, 203
  Tolstoy's, 151–53, 169, 203, 223n,
    224
Animals. *See* Beasts

Anomy, 169–72, 174n.18, 203, 213,
  287, 289
  of *actor* in *Nausea*, 272, 279
  portrayal of in Apuleian *Metamor-
    phoses*, 172, 237, 252, 279, 318
  in rehabilitation, 189–90
  of Tolstoy's perspective, 157–58,
    162, 169, 237
  transcendent realm as shield
    against, 172, 292–93, 318
  See also Alienation
Antinomianism, 113–14
Aporia, 151–54, 243
  in Apuleian *Metamorphoses*, 161,
    223–24n, 327; authorial, 55n, 132,
    137
Apostles of John Maranke, conversion to, 189n, 296n
Appearance, 51, 55n, 129, 273, 314
  relationship to reality, 93–94, 276n,
    281
  shifts in during preconversion
    experience, 60–61, 152
  unreliability of, 56, 91, 92n.1
Apuleian criticism, 1–6, 9–10, 147,
  252n, 326–28
  on nature of Lucius' sin, 147, 216
  use of Bunyan model of conver-
    sion, 165
  See also individual authors and topics
Apuleius, 4, 31, 43, 62n.13, 321n, 326
  Platonism and, 260–61
  on statues in Carthage, 68n
  use of inherited material, 98, 103–4,
    128–33
Aristides, Aelius, 27, 28n, 31

Aristomenes' tale, 45–48, 51, 63–65, 216, 238–39, 243, 267
   Kafkaesque pattern in, 86–87
   missing from Lucianic *Onos*, 130n
   Perry's analysis of attempted suicide and, 72–74
   as programmatic sequence, 131–32
Art
   digressive descriptions of, 8
   treatment in Greek novel genre, 129
Asceticism, religious, 12, 326
Attitude change, 21–22, 189, 322–24
   parallels in Apuleian *Metamorphoses*, 195–96
   secular conversion as, 185–87, 188nn. 30, 31
   See also Forced conversion
Aubin, P., 30n
Auctor (Author; Narrator), 10, 14, 43, 243, 326–27
   in Apuleian *Metamorphoses*, 14, 43, 53–54, 93n, 182; Apuleius and Lucius as, 228–29; in the Isis-book, 320–21n, 326; voice of, 310, 326
   Augustine as, 33, 39, 210–11, 226–28, 273
   voice of in *Nausea*, 272–73, 310
Auerbach, E., 62n.13, 75n.23
Augustine, St., 5n, 147, 155n, 255n, 261–62, 327
   conversion experience, 228n, 230–31, 299–304, 319; as model, 146–47, 149–50, 152–53, 174n.20, 179
   as narrator, 33, 39, 210–11, 226–28, 273
   See also *Confessions* (Augustine)
Aulus Gellius, 9
Author. *See* Auctor
Autobiography, 19–20, 213–14
   narratives of conversion, 27, 38, 143–65; Augustinian *Confessions* as, 202–15, 226–28; narrator as

commentator and interpreter, 226–28, 239

Batson, C.D., 142, 174–75, 178–82, 232–33, 294
Beasts (Animals)
   as motif in Apuleian *Metamorphoses*, 65–67, 88, 117–19
   metaphorical transformation of humans into, 107–13, 116–17, 123, 131
Beckford, J., 165
Beecher, Henry Ward, 296
Belief, 48, 52, 93
   problems of in Aristomenes' tale, 46–47, 132
Bellah, R., 25n, 294, 315n
Berger, Peter, 122–23, 167–74, 291–93, 315n, 324
   use of term anomy, 203, 213
Boisen, A., 194n
Bourgeois values, rejected by *Nausea* protagonist, 275–77, 310
Brainwashing. *See* Forced conversion
Brosman, C., 308n
Buddha, the (Siddhartha), 174n.20, 179
Bunyan, John, 146–47, 163, 165
Burkert, W., 21n, 29

Camus, Albert, 180
Categories, 55n, 62–66, 117, 277, 278–79, 281
   ontological, 62–67, 91, 107, 129, 205, 215
Chaos, 171, 172
   for Rogers, 194
Charite episodes. *See* Thrasyllus
Christianity
   conversion to, 23n, 33n, 140, 174n.20; in antiquity, 24–30
   early studies based on, 164–65; of pre-Columbian Incas, 173
   and novel genre, 8–9
   See also Protestantism; Roman Catholicism

Cicero, 4–5, 31

Clark, E., 164

Cleaver, Eldridge, 311–12n.19

Coerced conversion. *See* Forced conversion

Cognition, 2, 138, 176, 231, 233, 248
aspects of in religious experience, 182–84, 293
conversion in Apuleian *Metamorphoses* rooted in, 14–15, 37, 248, 312–13, 317n, 326
dissonance, 162, 326
language's relationship to, 307n.17
role in conversion experience, 26, 37–38, 189n, 199, 294; disintegration and reconstruction central to, 14–15, 105, 138, 173, 192–96
structures of, 22, 38, 49, 180–81, 281, 289; alienation from, 201–2, 251; place in creativity of, 175–77, 233; reorientation and, 191–92
See also Epistemology; Paradigm shifts

Comic, the, 44, 75n.23, 88, 89, 95, 103n
interpenetration of the serious and, 9–10, 119, 327
in Thelyphron's tale and Risus festival episode, 82–84

Communism, conversion to, 188, 295n

Confession (Tolstoy), 149–50, 152–55, 157–58, 179, 273
parallels in Tagore's account, 164–65

Confessions (Augustine), 202–15, 226–29, 262, 300–304
hints of in *Nausea*, 274–75, 278, 280
parallels in Apuleian *Metamorphoses*, 202–6, 209n, 211n, 212–14, 216–19, 223–24, 236–49
parallels in *The Divine Comedy*, 264–65, 269, 270

Consciousness, 168, 170, 187, 270

Convention(s), 119, 125, 157, 198, 237
disillusionment with, 149–56, 158, 201–2, 224
reality under surface of, 156–57n
See also Morality; Social conventions

Conversion experience, 18–30, 34, 37–38, 49, 138–40, 285–99
in American and British Protestant tradition, 18, 164–65, 174n.28, 295–96
analogies with dynamics of paradigm shifts, 177–78
Batson and Ventis' model of, 174–75, 178–82, 233
to Christianity (*see* Christianity, conversion to)
counter-conversion, 162–63, 180, 232n
forced (*see* Forced conversion)
generic nature of, 21–22, 22–23n, 162–63, 188
pagan (*see* Paganism)
philosophical (*see* Philosophy)
Platonic concepts of, 259–61
role of relationship between social contacts and attitudes and, 322–24
secular, 185–87, 188nn. 30, 31 (*see also* Psychotherapy)
sense of renewal and rebirth in, 315
stages of (*see* Crisis phase of conversion experience; Preconversion experience)
sudden (*see* Sudden conversion)
See also Augustine; Dante; James, William; Religious experience; Tolstoy

Conversion experience in Apuleian *Metamorphoses*, 9, 14–15, 62n.13, 139–41, 210–28, 261
compared with secular conversion, 195–96
as example of sudden conversion, 227, 228
as generic model, 15, 21, 22, 37, 167

Conversion experience (*continued*)
  parallels with Tolstoy's experience,
    150–51, 152–63, 165
  related to James' discussion, 143,
    145, 149
  See also Isisbook
Conversion narrative(s), 14–22,
    52–53, 63, 138n, 156, 327
  epistemic structures of in terms of
    values, 318–19
  Hellenistic type of, 31–34
  Platonism and, 261–62
  preconversion pattern of, 14–15, 38,
    105
  search for transcendent center rep-
    resented in, 201–2
  use of in studies of religious expe-
    rience, 182n
  See also *Confession* (Tolstoy); *Con-
    fessions* (Augustine); *Divine Com-
    edy, The; Nausea*
Conversion narrative, Apuleian
    Metamorphoses as a, 1, 11, 15–17,
    20–21, 33–35, 61, 139, 327–28
  epistemic structures in terms of
    values, 318–19
  Nock's attempt to explain, 25–26
  parallels with Augustinian *Confes-
    sions*, 202–6, 209n, 211n, 212–14,
    216–19, 223–24, 236–49
  Platonic patterns and motifs in,
    259–62, 281
  as prototype of quest type, 214–15
  psychological depth and complex-
    ity of, 24
Corinthian matron, liaison between
    the ass and, 119, 124–28, 131, 195
  place in Greek source, 129
Cosmic order, 172–73
  dualistic, 22, 315n
  represented by Isis, 172, 261, 313,
    318, 321–22
  See also World view
Counter-conversion, 162–63, 180,
    232n
Creativity, analogies with religious

experience, 37, 175–78, 232–33,
    271
Credulity (*Credulitas*), 47, 49, 51–53,
    56, 93, 101, 325–26
Crisis phase of conversion experi-
    ence, 38, 139, 203, 229, 286–87,
    295
  in Apuleian *Metamorphoses*, 37, 180,
    197–99, 237, 313; parallels with
    Tolstoy's experience, 150–51,
    152–63, 165
  for Augustine, 213, 248, 300
  disintegration of cognitive struc-
    tures in, 14–15, 105, 138, 195–96
  portrayed in *Nausea*, 272–82
  resolution of for James, 141, 162
  schematizing studies of, 196–99,
    234–35
  social interactionist perspective on,
    166, 183–84, 193
  Tolstoy as exemplar, 149–63, 241
  at unconscious level, 235
  See also Preconversion experience
Cult(s), 29, 140n, 191–92, 193n, 196,
    197n.39, 234
  representation in Apuleian *Meta-
    morphoses*, 11, 191, 312n.19,
    322, 325–26; Lucius' initiations
    into, 197, 318, 320, 323–24,
    325–26
  social dynamics of, 322–25
Culture, 17, 167–68, 281, 296n, 298n
  discourse, 18–20, 307, 316
  as framework for conversion expe-
    rience, 22, 146–47, 165
Cupid and Psyche, tale of, 36–37, 48,
    251–59, 261, 262, 319
  happiness at end of, 225n
  missing from Lucianic *Onos*, 130n;
    Platonic overtones, 5, 10, 259,
    271
Curiosity (*Curiositas*), 154, 243n, 253,
    267–68, 303
  in Augustinian *Confessions*, 202,
    217–20, 222, 224, 243–48
  as theme in Apuleian *Metamor-*

phoses, 154, 246–47n, 255–57, 267, 320

Dabrowski, K., 194n
Dante, 33, 39, 247n, 255n, 315, 319, 327
  The Divine Comedy, 262–71, 276, 303–7, 317
  within Platonic tradition, 261–62
Death (Mortality), 62–64, 178, 185, 253, 277, 293
  integration of in religious world views, 287, 293
  as preconversion concern, 38, 139, 201, 215
  problem of mitigated by assignment to Elysian fields, 314, 318
  as ultimate marginal situation, 170–73
Death and rebirth theme, 199, 287–88, 315, 318
Deceit (Deception; *Fallacia*), 208, 257
  as a major theme in Augustinian *Confessions*, 203–4, 206–7, 210
  as theme of Books 7–10's major sequences, 96–104, 106, 131, 221n.14, 238
  See also Mendacity
Delusion, 205, 212, 240–42, 267
Deprogramming. *See* Forced conversion
Desiderium dei (Longing for God), 205, 231, 242–44, 254, 300n.11
  description if in *The Divine Comedy*, 264, 270–71
  search for meaning rooted in, 155, 287
Desire, 203, 226, 277, 304, 324
  in Apuleian *Metamorphoses*, 198, 203–4, 215–24, 231, 252–59, 319–21
  displaced/misguided, 215, 251, 263–67, 271, 275
  divine realm identified as "true" object of, 287–88
  as a major concern in Augustinian

Confessions, 203–11, 215–21, 223–24, 300
  shift in, 215–19, 300, 304–7, 319
  See also *Desiderium dei*; Sexual desire
Dialogue with Trypho (Justin Martyr), 33n
Dido, in the *Aeneid*, 133
Dio Chrysostom, 24, 31–34
Diophanes, Milo's tale of, 48, 54, 130n, 132
Discourse, 21–22, 226
  cultural, 18–20, 307, 316
  of dualism, 22, 34, 146, 221
  religious, 15, 38, 180, 291–93, 297
  social, 118n
Disillusionment, 180, 212, 280
  with conventions, 141, 149–56, 158, 161, 163, 201–2, 224, 289
  Tolstoy's, 149–56, 158–59, 163
Diversion, 210, 235, 244–45, 247
  of attention from problem of meaning, 154–55
  from existential questions, 198
  search for: in Apuleian *Metamorphoses*, 220–24, 227, 240–41, 256; in Augustinian *Confessions*, 240–41; by characters in *Nausea*, 276–78; by Dante the pilgrim, 267–69
Divine Comedy, The (Dante), 262–71, 276, 303–7
  parallels with Apuleian *Metamorphoses*, 262–71, 317
Divinity(ies), 15, 39, 50, 53, 231
  intervention, 8, 9, 48
  power, 27–29
  role in tale of Cupid and Psyche, 252–53
  See also God; Isis; Transcendent deity/divinity; Transcendent realm
Dogmatism, 51–52, 181
Dream(s), 64–65, 97–98, 110, 170, 311
  state of in *Nausea*, 276

Dualism, 34, 144–45, 160
  discourse of, 22, 34, 146, 226
  ontological, 205, 215
  Platonic, 276n, 281
Dualism, religious, 25n, 54–55, 93n, 257, 302, 315n
  in Egyptian paganism, 30, 315n
  as framework for religious world views, 38, 145–46, 172, 288
  opposition between worlds of Isis and Fortuna, 316–17
Dumas, G., 160–61n

Ebel, H., 56, 92n.1, 201
Ecphrasis
  in Apuleian Metamorphoses, 67–71, 130n
  in Greek novel genre, 129
Edwards, Jonathan, 18, 295–96, 316
Ego-self. See Self
Elsom, H., 6n
Emotions (Affect; Feelings), 26, 162, 194
  aspects of in religious experience, 181–84, 185n.27, 199, 235
  role in cult recruitment, 323–24
Entertainment, 8–9, 56, 244–45
  Apuleian Metamorphoses seen as written for, 3–4, 7–8, 71
  as object of misguided desire for Augustine, 205–6, 218–19, 220–21, 223–24
  as object of spurious desire in Apuleian Metamorphoses, 206, 218–24
Ephesian Tale (Xenophon of Ephesus), 9
Epicureanism, 154
Epistemology, 2, 18n, 169, 202, 226
  aporia in, represented by magic, 223–24n
  breakdown and disorientation of, portrayed in Nausea, 272–75, 278–80
  expressed in terms of values in narratives of conversion, 318–19

  place in Augustine's conversion experience, 205, 213, 215, 236–37, 300, 301–3
  place in religious crisis and conversion, 14–15, 138–39
  sin a problem of, in The Divine Comedy, 263, 270
  stability provided by religious world view, 286–88
  See also Knowledge; Paradigm shifts
Epistemology, treatment in Apuleian Metamorphoses, 6n, 43–45, 92–93n.2, 222, 318
  breakdown of, 102–3, 131–32, 137, 203, 236–37, 261
  conversion rooted in, 34, 37, 147
  importance demonstrated in Aristomenes' tale, 45–48, 132
  as nature of Lucius' failing, 13, 216
Epistrophe, use of term, 30n, 31
Eros (Erotic, the), 8, 12–13, 111n, 113
  energy transformed and redirected, 300n.111, 319–21
  as a mode for conversion experience, 146–47, 297, 304
Estrangement. See Alienation
Étranger, L' (Camus), 180
Eunuch priests, episode of, 103–4, 105n.7, 118–20, 126, 129, 131
Exile, 239, 267, 323
Existential crisis, 142, 181, 198, 235
  experienced at an unconscious level, 179, 180, 236n
  as first stage in religious experience, 178–79, 182n
Existentialism, 153n, 157n, 161n, 180
  Sartre's Nausea as novel of, 271–82
Experience, 47, 49, 168, 192, 298n
  reality-transforming, 175–78
  relationship to narrative, 16–17, 19, 214–15
  relationship to religious experience, 52–53, 165, 175, 182n
  structure imposed on, 122–23, 226

treatment of in Apuleian *Metamor-
phoses*, 16, 36, 44–47, 218,
220
Ulysses' search for in *The Divine
Comedy*, 267
See also Religious experience

Fallacia. See Deceit
Falsehood. *See* Mendacity
Feelings. *See* Emotions
Festugière, A.-J., 12, 147n
Fiction(s), 20, 38, 44, 94, 106
in Apuleian *Metamorphoses*, 53–54,
92
chain reaction of, 97–98; play with
issues of, 54, 129
See also Deceit; Mendacity
Fides (Trust) as motif, 96–98, 117,
222n.17
breakdown of principle of, 87–90,
106–7, 116–17, 131
Finney, G.C., 232n
Fisher, H., 23n
Fish-stomping episode, 74–75,
130n
Forced (coerced) conversion, 37,
138n, 167, 193n, 199
deprogramming of cult members,
191–92
drug treatment and prison programs as, 187, 189–90
of whole cultures, 173
Fortuna (Tuche), 8, 211n.5, 254, 315n,
316–17
instability represented by, 225–26,
238, 314
Fotis, tryst of Lucius and, 51, 216–17,
219, 223, 239–40
Frankl, V., 194n
Freccero, J., 263n
Furies, the, 115–16, 258
Furor. See Madness

Geertz, Clifford, 294
Gender boundaries, transgression of,
129

Genre
of Apuleian *Metamorphoses*, 6–15,
35, 134, 260–62
of comic romance, 2–4, 7, 39, 260
differences between Augustinian
Confessions and Apuleian *Metamorphoses*, 226–29
Greek novel as, 8–9, 128, 129–33
and representations of conversion,
19–20
See also Conversion narrative(s);
Conversion narrative, Apuleian
Metamorphoses as a
God
Augustine the convert's love of,
300–302
as center of unity for Dante the
convert, 306
music invested with attributes of in
Nausea, 308–9
sleep and stupor as metaphor for
life without, 255n
See also *Desiderium dei;*
Divinity(ies); Transcendent deity
Gorsuch, R., 293–94, 298–99
Grace, 121, 229, 256n, 261, 271
Greek novel (Greek romance
[genre]), 8–9, 128, 129–33. See
also *Onos*
Greil, A., 189n
Griffiths, J.G., 312n.19, 319n
Guilt, 86–87, 146–47, 165, 240

Habinek, T., 21n
Habit, as force hampering the actor,
248–49, 270, 280
in Apuleian *Metamorphoses*, 231,
248–49, 254, 255–56
"Haemus" episode, 48–49, 51–52,
130n, 132
Hammett, V., 192–94, 322
Happiness
cycle of expectations of in
Apuleian *Metamorphoses*, 224–26
rejection of learning as source of,
207–8, 210–11, 213n

Happiness (*continued*)
  true: Augustine's search for, 209,
    211–12, 224–25, 300, 320;
    bestowed by divinity, 225n,
    226n; found by convert, 226, 288,
    297, 320–21n
  See also Joy
Hawkins, Anne, 140n, 146–47, 214,
  235–36n
Healthy-minded, the (the "Once-
  born"), for James, 141–45
Heirich, M., 182n, 183–86, 294
Hermeneutics, 226
  games of, 43–44n, 48n, 52n, 55n
Hildebrand, G., 89n
Hindu tradition, conversion in,
  164–65
Homer, 128, 266–67
  transformation in the *Odyssey*, 65,
    66n
Hood, R., Jr., 293–94, 298–99
Horace, 9
Hospitality, 87–88, 120–21
Humanism, 18, 118n, 188n.30, 275–76
  Platonic modes, 281–82
Humanity, 167–72
  qualities retained by Lucius the
    ass, 117–28

Identity
  for postmodernism, 118n
  sense of lost in separation from
    social world, 169
  in tales of transformation, 65–66,
    118
Iliad (Homer), 128
Illusion(s), 70, 92, 94, 96, 204
Inebriation (Intoxication)
  images of in Tolstoy's account of
    pre-conversion life, 213n
  life devoted to conventional values
    equated with, 212–13
  as result of dealing with problem
    of meaning, 154–55
Insight, 177, 180, 181
Intellect, 47, 162, 199

Augustine's disdain for accomplishments, 207–8, 210–11
complacency as a source of false
  opinions, 96, 103n
retained by Lucius in ass form,
  65–66, 118–19, 122
use in quest, 146–47, 150–51,
  153–54
Irony
  in Apuleian *Metamorphoses*, 5, 49,
    116–19, 126, 249; in presentation
    of Lucius' conversion, 182, 321n;
    in tale of Cupid and Psyche, 256
  in Dante's *Divine Comedy*, 267
  in *Nausea*, 272, 277, 280, 310
Isis, 9
  portrayal in Apuleian *Metamor-
    phoses*, 10–11, 23, 50, 126–28, 195,
    259; role in Lucius' redemption,
    12, 147, 180, 310–22, 325; as sav-
    ing divinity, 9, 30, 157, 262;
    supernatural powers, 27–28,
    261
Isisbook (Book 11), 3–4, 11, 150, 193,
  222, 310–28
  dual attitudes toward Lucius' con-
    version, 181–82
  Lucius' speech regained, 123, 316
  missing from Lucianic *Onos*, 130n
  Nock's discussion based on, 26
  seen as example of hermeneutic
    game, 44n
Islam, 23n, 174n.20

James, P., 81n
James, William, 15, 18, 33, 37, 223n,
  249
  model of conversion experience,
    141–46, 148–66, 201, 213, 295–99,
    316; emergence in modern stud-
    ies of conversion, 166–67;
    emphasis on cognitive aspects,
    289–91; on fundamental shift in
    world view, 28n; influence on
    Nock, 23n, 24; reliance on "con-
    fessions," 27; on subconscious

incubation and sudden conversion, 229–32, 235
on noetic quality of mystical experience, 288, 298
study of religious psychology,
140–41
Johnson, W.R., 62n.13, 116
Jones, R., 185–88
Jouffroy, Theodore, 162–63, 180, 232n
Journoud, S., 126–27n.16
Joy, 300–301, 305, 309; felt by Lucius,
315, 320–21n. *See also* Happiness
Judaism
nature of conversion in, 22–23n, 25,
27, 174n.20
novel genre, 8–9
Judgment
errors of, made by Lucius the ass,
119
prudentia, 246–47n; suspension of,
47–48, 51–52
unfair or corrupted, 92, 96, 132
Jules-Rosette, B., 189n, 296n

Kafka, Franz, 86–87, 134n
Kim, B.-S., 191–92
Knowledge, 33, 49, 53, 158, 243n, 264
arrived at through mystical experience, 298–99
for Ovid, 58–60
treatment of in Apuleian *Metamorphoses,* 2, 43, 48–49, 54–55, 92,
246–47n; arbitrary nature of,
13–14, 91, 95
See also Cognition; Epistemology;
Paradigm shifts
Knudten, R., 167n
Koestler, Arthur, 188, 295n
Kuhn, Thomas, 17, 177, 185–87. *See
also* Paradigm shifts

Landlord, episode of, 111–13, 117,
242
Language, 57, 307n.17
as ordering mechanism, 122–23,
168, 278–79, 316

See also Discourse; Muteness
Latin literature, influence on
Apuleius, 110–11n, 132–33. *See
also* Ovid; Virgil
Laughter, 82–86, 87
Lewis, C.S., 261
Lies. *See* Mendacity
Limbo, portrayal in *The Divine Com-
edy,* 264, 266
Lofland, J., 196–99, 322, 323, 324
Logic, Perry on lapses in, 71–81
Longing for God. See *Desiderium dei*
Love
attempt by *Nausea* protagonist to
retain as a value, 280
distinction between "natural" and
"intellectual" in the *The Divine
Comedy,* 263–64
portrayal in Latin love elegy, 111n
Lucian, 6–7, 7nn. 6, 7, 57–58, 65
Nigrinus, 24, 31–34
See also *Onos*
Lucius of Patrae, 6, 7nn. 6, 7, 57, 129.
See also *Onos*
Lucius or the Ass (Lucian). See *Onos*
Lucretius, 236n
Lust. *See* Sexual desire

MacMullen, Ramsay, 24, 27–30
Macrobius, 4–5
Madness, 111n, 240–42, 270
as a theme in Apuleian *Metamorphoses,* 112–13, 240–42, 257–58
See also Mental illness
Magic, 49–50, 74, 128–29, 244
in Apuleian *Metamorphoses,* 12–13,
36, 55–56, 60–61, 128–30, 197
belief in, as subject of Aristomenes'
tale, 47
as object of curiosity, 244–45,
247
as object of false desire, 216–18,
222, 223
See also Transformation
Marxism, 188n.30, 291n
Mason, H.J., 130n, 150

Material (Physical) world, 167–68
    characterized by fluidity and trans-
        formation, 56, 59–62, 91, 92n.1,
        107, 137
    disintegration of linked with disin-
        tegration of social world, 132–33,
        161–62, 189n
    distortion of experienced in *Nau-
        sea*, 273–74, 278–79, 309
    as seen by the dysfunctionally
        melancholy, 159–60
    transformed perceptions of,
        186–87, 296
McHugh, P., 189–91
Meaning, 138, 175–76, 180, 189n,
        234–35, 248
    construction of, 140n, 171–72
    crisis in portrayed in *Nausea*,
        272–82, 307–10
    provided by religion, psychology
        on, 293–94
    quest for, 214–15, 230, 290–93, 295
    role in Tolstoy's conversion experi-
        ence, 150–54, 158
    treatment in Apuleian *Metamor-
        phoses*, 2, 63n, 161, 203, 226, 229
Meaning, structures of, 193, 304, 310,
        316, 322, 327
    anomy as result of collapse, 237
    challenge to in conversion, 37–38,
        138–39, 251, 285
    discovery by narrator in autobiog-
        raphy, 226
    failure of in Lucius' world, 161, 203
    reliance on as force of habit, 231
    role in preconversion experience,
        50, 137, 145–46, 156–57, 166, 202,
        285
    superstructure of, 226, 286–87, 300
Meaninglessness, 169, 171, 194–95
Melancholy (Soul-sickness), 33,
        141–46, 148–49, 158–60, 160–61n,
        289–90
Mendacity (Falsehoods; Lies), 55n,
        95–104, 132, 221n.14, 257. *See also*
        Deceit

Mental illness, 158–60, 160–61n,
        163–64, 194–95. *See also* Madness
Merkelbach, R., 11, 21n
Metamorphosis. *See* Transformation
Metamorphoses (Lucius of Patrae), 6,
        7nn.6, 7, 57. See also *Onos*
Metamorphoses (Ovid), 56–57, 58–60,
        66, 132–33
Metamorphosis, The (Kafka), 86
Metaphor, 129
    for life without God, 255n, 270
    use of in Apuleian *Metamorphoses*,
        56, 129, 132–33, 241, 254; trans-
        formation of humans into beasts
        as, 107–13, 116–17, 123, 131
    use of in *The Divine Comedy*, 268,
        269–71
Metaphysics, 66, 138–39, 261, 264
    centering of world in, 286–87, 295,
        300
    Isis as anchor and center, 312–14,
        321–22
    longing of *Nausea* protagonist,
        281–82, 308
    as nature of preconversion con-
        cerns for James, 145–46, 151,
        289–90
Methodology, 140–41, 165–66
Milesian tales, 4, 8
Millenarian movement, study of,
        196–99
Mitchell, B., 188n.30
Modernism, presence in *Nausea*,
        278n, 279, 307
Monism, 315n
Monotheism, attack on, 105n
Moralism, in some religious readings
        of Apuleian *Metamorphoses*,
        12–13
Morality, 26, 59
    Augustine's crisis in terms of,
        212–13, 215, 227–28, 300
    treatment of in Apuleian *Metamor-
        phoses*, 3, 51–52, 102, 131, 147,
        222; absence of indication of
        growth in, 121, 227–28, 256n;

breakdown of, 105; defense of conventional by Lucius the ass, 88, 119–21, 123; found in the society of outlaws, 89–90; sexual, violation of, 50–52, 119–20, 121, 147

Mortality. *See* Death

Multivocality, 56, 228, 310, 326–27

Music
 pleasure of as object of Augustine's suspicion, 210
 seen as transcendent in *Nausea*, 272, 308–10

Muteness, of Lucius, 122–23, 129, 130–31, 168, 307n.17, 316

Mystery religions, 11, 26, 29

Mysticism and mystical experience, 58, 162, 233n.25, 278, 307n
 elements of in Apuleian *Metamorphoses*, 297–98, 311
 nature of *desiderium dei* in, 264
 place in conversion experience, 199, 288, 297–99, 299–300n.10, 303–7

Narrative, 8–9, 16–17, 19–20, 165
 strategy, 126–27
 technique, 226–29, 236
 See also Conversion narrative(s)

Narrator. *See* Auctor

Nausea (Sartre), 262–63, 271–82

Necromancy, 62–63, 129, 221–22

Nigrinus (Lucian), 24, 31–34

Nock, Arthur, 11, 23n, 24–30, 33n, 315n

Nothingness, place in *Nausea*, 273, 278

Odysseus (Ulysses), 246–47n
 portrayal of in *The Divine Comedy*, 266–67

"Once-born," the (the Healthy-minded), James on, 141–45

Onos (Lucius or the Ass) (Lucian), 6–7, 57–58, 65
 and motifs and episodes of

Apuleian *Metamorphoses*, 98, 103–4, 128–33

Ontological categories, 62–67, 91, 107, 129, 205, 215

Opinion
 elevated to status of knowledge, 102–3
 false, 43, 92–93, 95–96, 100, 103–4

Ordering (regulating) mechanisms/principles
 disruption of, 66, 127–28
 Isis as, 50, 312, 313
 language as, 122–23, 168
 place in mental health, 194–95
 See also Cosmic order; Social order

Osiris, 321; rite of, 325

Other, the, as role model for cult converts, 323–24

Outlaws, society of, 66–67, 88–90, 112–13

Ovid
 influence on Apuleius, 132–33
 Metamorphoses, 56–57, 58–60, 66

Paardt, R.T. van der, 53, 68n

Paganism (Primitive [traditional] religion), 21n, 105n, 325
 conversion phenomena in, 23, 29–30, 139–40, 147, 188, 202, 260
 distinction between prophetic religion and, 25, 315n
 Egyptian, 30
 Greco-Roman, 11, 23–24, 30, 314–15n

Paradigm shifts, 17, 37–38, 177–78, 185–88
 in Apuleian *Metamorphoses*, 236–37, 252
 in Augustinian *Confessions*, 205, 215, 236–37
 coerced or directed, 189–96
 in *The Divine Comedy*, 270–71, 303–7
 James' concept of conversion as, 289–91
 in *Nausea*, 280

Paradigm shifts (*continued*)
  in religious conversion, 285–86,
    289, 296, 303–4
  role in preconversion experience,
    139, 201–3, 251, 262, 285–86
  See also Epistemology; Knowledge
Paradoxography
  as generic framework for Apuleian
    Metamorphoses, 3, 7–8, 128–29,
    260
  magic as standard subject of, 56
  as nature of the Greek source for
    Apuleian *Metamorphoses*, 128–29,
    133
Parody, 5, 158
  in Lucian's *Metamorphoses*, 7
  Lucian's *Nigrinus* as, 24, 32
  in *Nausea*, 272, 278
Paul, St., 23n, 174n.20, 235–36n
Perception, 47, 79, 288
  of reality, 86–87, 316; changes in
    portrayed in *The Divine Comedy*,
    270, 306–7; in *Nausea* as dis-
    torted, 272–75, 281, 309; para-
    digm shifts in, 186–87, 251; place
    in James' discussion of conver-
    sion experience, 144–45, 156–60;
    in *War and Peace*, 158–59n
  See also Vision
Perry, B.E., 3–4, 8, 71–81
  on Greek sources, 7nn. 6, 7
Phaedrus (Plato), 10, 259, 271
Philosophy, 175n, 210, 255n
  Apuleian *Metamorphoses* read in
    terms of, 2–3, 10, 30, 34, 58
  conversion to, 16, 24–25, 30–34, 188
  Tolstoy's struggle over values,
    143–44
Photius, 6–7, 57
Physical world. *See* Material world
Pietas (Piety), breakdown of institu-
  tion of, 106–7, 116
Plato, 10, 31, 31–34, 259, 271
Platonism, 228, 276n, 281–82, 315n
  Augustine and Dante within tradi-
    tion of, 261–62, 271

dualism, 160, 205
  influence on Apuleius and the
    Metamorphoses, 10–11, 30, 121,
    160, 260–62, 281
  in depiction of Isiac religion, 10, 23,
    315n, 319n
  in tale of Cupid and Psyche, 259
Pleasure *(Voluptas)*, 215, 218, 275
  felt by characters in *Nausea*, 277
  role in conversion experience, 201,
    226, 235, 288, 297, 319
  treatment in Apuleian *Metamor-
    phoses*, 198, 203–4, 245, 251, 317n;
    change in source of during con-
    version experience, 319–21;
    derivation of in tale of Cupid
    and Psyche, 252–59; misbegot-
    ten, 215, 219–21, 241, 243
  treatment in Augustinian *Confes-
    sions*, 206–7, 209–12, 304; follow-
    ing conversion, 301; involvement
    of false values, 203–4, 251,
    300–301; misbegotten, 215,
    219–21, 241, 243
  treatment in *The Divine Comedy*,
    265–66, 304–7
Pliny, 105n
Plutarch, 10, 315n
Postmodernism, 118n, 137, 138,
  278n
Poststructuralism, 18, 138, 157n, 286,
  303
  Platonism vilified by, 276n, 281
  in Winkler's criticism, 2, 14, 55n
Pratt, J.B., 164–65
Preconversion experience, 38, 49–52,
  162–63, 201–14, 251
  changes in cognitive structure dur-
    ing, 49–52, 285–86
  disintegration of ontological cate-
    gories, 62–66, 107
  portrayal in Apuleian *Metamor-
    phoses*, 237, 261; absence of con-
    scious progress in Lucius,
    121–22, 227, 228, 256n; *Confes-
    sions* of St. Augustine compared

with, 202–4, 205–6, 209n, 211n,
     212, 213–14
portrayal in Dante's *Divine Comedy*,
     262–71
schematizing studies of, 196,
     234–35, 322–23
Tolstoy's state of mind, 203, 223n,
     224, 241
transformations as part of, 60–71
See also Conversion experience;
     Crisis phase of conversion expe-
     rience
Professional ambitions, rejection of
by Augustine, 207–8, 210, 275
by *Nausea* protagonist, 275, 277
Protestantism, American and British,
     conversion experiences in, 18,
     164–65, 174n.28, 196–99, 295–96
Proudfoot, W., 19
Psyche, tale of. *See* Cupid and Psy-
     che, tale of
Psychiatry and psychoanalysis. *See*
     Psychotherapy
Psychodynamic factors, in conver-
     sion, 185n.27, 233
Psychology, 91, 140n, 163–65
approach to Apuleian *Metamor-
     phoses*, 15, 34, 132–33, 252n
developmental, 175n, 293–94
as factor in conversion to Chris-
     tianity in antiquity, 24–27, 29, 30
verisimilitude principle, 228
See also Psychology of religion;
     Social psychology
Psychology of religion, 18, 37, 121,
     140–41, 293–94
for Batson and Ventis, 175
discussion of conversion crisis in
     terms of psychopathology,
     142–45, 148
early history, 150, 163–66
views on conversion, 150, 183, 186
See also Conversion experience;
     James, William; Social psychol-
     ogy
Psychotherapy, 199

analogies to conversion, 37, 167,
     178n.23, 187, 192–95
psychiatric tradition: assumptions
     about religion, 185n.27; conver-
     sion experience from perspective
     of, 197n.39, 234
psychoanalytic thought on conver-
     sion, 183, 193, 195n
Purgatory, portrayal in *The Divine
     Comedy*, 264, 268–69
Puritan theology, as Bunyan's cul-
     tural framework, 146–47

Quest, 7, 128, 255
metaphysical, 151, 153–54, 163
as paradigm for Apuleian *Meta-
     morphoses*, 147
as paradigm for Augustinian *Con-
     fessions*, 214–15
place in conversion experience,
     146–47, 163, 199, 201, 230
for pleasurable spectacles in
     Apuleian *Metamorphoses*, 220–24

Rambo, L., 140n, 311–12n.19
Reality, 38, 59, 112, 168, 293–94, 322
construction of, 100, 169–73,
     174–77; within ontological dual-
     ism, 205, 215; perpetuation of
     conventional, 52, 248
empirical, 189n, 193
as motif in Apuleian *Metamor-
     phoses*, 35–36, 37, 56, 137–38, 161,
     179–80, 238–39; instability of, 66,
     74–75, 118, 128; for Lucius fol-
     lowing conversion, 182, 317n; in
     Lucius' preconversion world
     view, 62; mistaken for a dream,
     64–65; ontological dualism as
     nature of, 205, 215; transforma-
     tion of, 60–61
negative transformation of Tol-
     stoy's, 157–58
perception of (*see* Perception)
place in conversion experience,
     189n, 196–97, 262, 288–94, 297;

Reality (*continued*)
disengagement from conventional definitions of, 49–50; for James, 144–45, 156–60; as process of grounding for Heirich, 184–85; transformation of, 174–75, 181, 315–16
relationship to appearance, 93–94, 276n, 281
relationship to representation, 16–17, 20, 75n.24, 79
religious deprogramming as social construction of, 191–92
system for ordering, 39, 226; disruption of, 166, 213, 285
use of term, 20, 55n
Rebirth. *See* Death and rebirth theme
Redemption, in Apuleian *Metamorphoses* as moral allegory, 12–13
Regulating structures. *See* Ordering mechanisms/principles
Religion, 138n, 226
conversion away from as form of resolution, 162–63
conversion experience (*see* Conversion experience)
deprogramming, 191–92
distinction between "primitive" and "historical," 25, 105n, 315n (*see also* Paganism)
meaning provided by, 293–94, 300
paradigm shift in terms of, 202
prophetic, 24–25, 315n (*see also* Christianity; Judaism)
psychology of (*see* Psychology of religion; Social psychology)
readings of Apuleian *Metamorphoses* in terms of, 2–3, 10–15, 138
relationship to the social world for Berger, 171–73
See also Discourse, religious; World view, religious
Religious experience, 17–18n, 23, 26–29, 229, 262, 286–99

association with mental illness, 142–45, 148n, 158–62, 194–95
cognitive aspects, 182–84, 293
culture's role in, 18–19
emotional aspects, 181, 182–83, 185n.27
exploration in *The Divine Comedy*, 262–71
portrayal in Apuleian *Metamorphoses*, 1, 7, 45, 104, 261, 327–28; James' analysis of sudden conversion applied to, 229–30, 231–32, 233, 234–35; place of Isisbook in discussions of, 3–4, 11; subjective character of for Winkler, 13–14
studies of, 21; Batson and Ventis' model, 174–75, 177–82, 233; by Heirich, 183–85; by James, 140–46, 148n, 158–60, 163–65; sociological approach, 166–74 (*see also* Psychology of religion)
terminology of used by *Nausea* protagonist, 278
See also Conversion experience
Representation, 18, 84, 86–87, 134n
relationship to reality, 16–17, 20, 75n.24, 79
Resocialization
in Adler and Hammett's model of conversion, 193
in drug treatment programs, 187–88
of members of prison populations, 187, 189–91
Resurrection, in the Zatchlas scene, 62–63
Rhetoric, field of, as a "false" pleasure for Augustine, 207–8, 210
Richardson, J., 197–98, 234–35, 322–23
Risus festival, 82–88, 120, 158, 222n.16, 245n, 274
lack of logic in criticized by Perry, 76–77, 79–81

Latin literature's influence on, 133
missing from Lucianic *Onos*, 130n
theatricality in Lucius' performance at, 53–54
transformations during, 61–63, 64n
Ritual(s), 25, 324
portrayal of in Apuleian *Metamorphoses*, 86, 104, 195, 253; Lucius'
initiations, 197, 318, 320, 323–26
Rogers, W.R., 193–95
Roman Catholicism, conversion to,
232n
Pentecostal movement, 183–84
Romance (genre), 2–4, 7, 39, 260
Greek, 8–9, 128, 129–33
Roman Empire, transformation by
conversions to Christianity,
27–30

Sacred Canopy, The (Berger), 167–74
Sacred Tales (Aristides), 27, 28n
Salvation, 256n, 259, 282, 314
Sarbin, T., 199, 323–24
Sartre, Jean-Paul, 39, 157n, 255n,
327
Nausea, 262–63, 271–82, 307–10
Satire, 7, 128, 133, 150n
in Apuleian *Metamorphoses*, 7–8, 51,
103–4, 119–21, 126, 326
Schadenfreude, 82–83
Scheintode, 63–64, 129, 255
Schlam, C., 125n, 131–32n
Science, 17, 177, 233
paradigm shifts in, 185, 186
Scobie, A., 54, 75n.23
Sculptures, transformation of, 67–71
Segal, A., 22–23n, 28n, 140n
Self (Ego-self), 39, 62n.12, 146–47,
178n.23, 196, 293–94
construction of, 315n
surrender of, 26, 179–80, 230
transformation of, 59, 62, 66n, 199,
301–2, 316
Self-awareness, Lucius' level of, 277
Self-consciousness, as mark of Greek
novel genre, 129

Self-deception, Augustine on, 206,
208
Self-referentiality, in Apuleian *Metamorphoses*, 54–55
Sensuality, Augustine on, 206–7
Serious, the, 10
interpenetration of the comic and,
9–10, 119, 327
Sex
treatment of, in Apuleian *Metamorphoses*, 12–13, 258
treatment of, in Augustinian *Confessions*, 240, 254
union of the ass and the Corinthian
matron, 119, 124–28, 131,
195
place in the Greek source,
129
violation of morality, 50–52,
119–20, 121, 147
Sexual desire, 241, 297
condemned by Augustine, 204–5,
210
treatment of in Apuleian *Metamorphoses*, 102, 115–16; and in
Augustinian *Confessions*, 216–17,
219, 223, 240; in scenes of bestiality, 110, 113; seen by critics as
the sin in, 147, 216
Siddhartha (the Buddha), 174n.20,
179
Sin, 248
concern with in conversion experience, 146–47, 163, 165
in reading of Apuleian *Metamorphoses* as moral allegory, 12–13,
147, 216
treatment of in *The Divine Comedy*,
263, 269–70
Sinclair, J., 263n
Siren, the, portrayal in *The Divine
Comedy*, 266
Skepticism, 162–63, 310
in Apuleian *Metamorphoses*, 13–14,
36, 43–49, 52, 56, 326
Skonovd, N., 198, 324

Skulsky, H., 92, 118n, 126n.15,
221n.15
study of metamorphosis as literary
motif, 58–60, 63, 66
Smart, Ninian, 14n
Smith, W.S., 86–87, 134n
Social codes, 117
transgression of, 96–102, 131
Social contract, 105–6, 112, 168
Social conventions and institutions,
106–7, 118n, 276, 300
in Apuleian *Metamorphoses*, 96–102,
117–18
breakdown of, 82–84, 107–13,
116–17, 119–23, 132–33
seen by Ovid as arbitrary, 59
Tolstoy's disillusionment with,
150n
Social interaction (Socialization),
191–92, 322–24
perspective on conversion experience, 166, 183–84, 193
perspective on cult formation and
adherence, 196, 324–25
Social order, 91, 137, 166–74
alienation from, 189–90, 239
disintegration of, 161–62
portrayal of in Apuleian *Metamorphoses*, 56, 132–33, 150;
alienation from, 168–71, 172–74,
239; disintegration in, 82–84,
105–6, 161–62
transformed perceptions of, 186–87
use of religion to support or to
threaten, 291–93
Social psychology, 2, 140n, 141, 166
as approach to Apuleian *Metamorphoses*, 15, 138
conversion experience studied by,
20, 142
Social sciences, 16–17, 20, 165, 183,
324. *See also* Psychology; Social
psychology; Sociology
Sociology, 140n, 141, 166, 167–74,
291–93
Socrates, 32, 61

Solmsen, F., 36
Somnium Scipionis (Cicero), 4–5
Soul
ascent to transcendent realm,
259
in Dante's *Divine Comedy*, 263
Soul-sickness. *See* Melancholy
Spectacles, 220–24, 244–45, 253, 268.
See also Diversion; Entertainment
Speech
power of regained by Lucius, 123,
316
See also Language; Muteness
Spilka, B., 293–94, 298–99
Spoudaiogeloion, 9–10. *See also* Comic,
the; Serious, the
Starbuck, E., 163–64
Stark, R., 197, 322, 323
Stepmother, tale of wicked, 49,
98–101, 106, 114–15, 117
sexual desire as obsessive and
destructive in, 216, 218, 241
Stranger, The (Camus), 180
Straus, R., 324
Stress, emotional, role in conversion
experience, 183–84, 199, 235
Structure/structuring mechanisms.
See Cognition, structures; Mean-
ing, structures of; Ordering
mechanisms
Stupefaction, 154–55, 213n, 223–24,
268–69, 276–77, 321n
Subconscious (Subliminal) incuba-
tion, 177, 178n.22, 229–35, 261.
See also Unconscious, the
Subjectivity, 17, 313
in Apuleian *Metamorphoses*, 34,
84
Sudden conversion, 227, 228, 235–
36n
counter-conversion as, 232n
and subconscious incubation,
229–35
Suicide, 72–74, 98
Surrealism, 74
Symposium (Plato), 10, 259

Tagore, Devendranath, 164–65
Tatum, J., 5, 9, 12, 31, 137, 254n
  on use and translation of term
    metamorphosis, 57, 58n
Temperament, role in conversion
  experience, 141–46, 148–49
Theatrical allusions and images
  in Apuleian *Metamorphoses,* 53–54,
    104, 129, 150n
  in Greek novel genre, 129
  in Tolstoy's *War and Peace,* 150n,
    158
Thelyphron
  exile of, 239
  tale of, 62–64, 81–82, 84–85, 86–87,
    130n, 217
  lack of logic in, criticized by Perry,
    77–79, 81
Thrasyleon episode, 66–67, 88–90,
  130n
Thrasyllus, tale of, 96–98, 106–10,
  130n, 133, 216
  Charite's role, 96–98, 104, 110, 115,
    118, 131
Tlepolemus episode. *See* Thrasyllus,
  tale of
Tolstoy, Leo, 163–65, 166, 191, 255n,
  273, 327
  preconversion experience, 143–46,
    148–63, 203, 223n, 224, 251,
    290–91; anomy of perspective,
    157–58, 162, 169, 237, 318; anxi-
    ety about death, 201, 215; exis-
    tential crisis cited by Batson and
    Ventis, 179
Transcendence, 93n, 153, 287, 316
  search for, 201–2, 264
Transcendent deity/divinity, 262,
  290;
  in historic religions, 25n, 315n
  Isis' self-representation as, 313–14,
    314–15n
  See also God
Transcendent realm, 39, 226, 231,
  287–88, 291–93
  Augustine on, 300–303

Isis and Osiris as central points in,
  311, 314, 321
  for *Nausea* protagonist, 281–82,
    307–10
  in tale of Cupid and Psyche,
    258–59
Transformation (Metamorphosis)
  in Apuleian *Metamorphoses,* 55–58,
    60–71, 74, 92n.1, 128–29, 216;
    cited by Augustine, 5n; during
    conversion experience, 316, 319;
    Ovid's influence on, 132–33; of
    Pamphile into a bird, 223, 241;
    psychological, 57, 107–13
  as a literary motif, 58–60, 128–29
  of material world in *Nausea,*
    273–74, 278–79
  in religious experience, 33–34,
    181–82, 288, 296; for Augustine,
    299–300n.10, 300n.11; of vision
    of reality, 315–16
  in secular conversion experience,
    187–88
  See also Conversion experience
Trial, The (Kafka), 86–87
Truth, 44n, 47, 53, 55n, 101, 125
  Augustine's concern with, 205, 240,
    248
  Dante's vision of, 306
  false judgments held as, 92, 94
  principle of psychological
    verisimilitude, 228
  revealed as nothingness in *Nausea,*
    278
  search for in conversion experi-
    ence, 33, 44, 144
  source in dualistic religious dis-
    course, 302
  world of opened up by mystical
    experience, 298
Truth, treatment of in Apuleian *Metamorphoses,* 43–44n, 48, 52, 80, 101
  conflicting versions in Aris-
    tomenes' tale, 47, 48n
  fluidity, 93n, 102, 105
Tuche. *See* Fortuna

"Twice-born," the, James on, 141–46, 148–49. *See also* Melancholy

Ullman, C., 182n, 185n.27
Ulysses (Odysseus), 246–47n
  portrayal in *The Divine Comedy*, 266–67
Unconscious, the, 154, 179, 198
  subliminal incubation, 177, 178n.22, 229–35, 261
Urteil, Das (Kafka), 86–87

Value(s), 53, 167–68, 180, 318–19
  breakdown of used in resocialization, 189–91
  conflict over, 33, 37, 38, 169, 264–65; in Augustinian *Confessions*, 202–16, 236; portrayed in *Nausea*, 272, 274–80, 307–10
  paradigm shift from "false" to "true," 156, 191, 202–3, 251, 262, 297; in Augustinian *Confessions*, 203–5, 224–26, 236–39, 243, 300–303; in *The Divine Comedy*, 265, 303–4; in religious world views, 287–88
  role in conversion experience, 52, 138, 196–97, 251, 262, 292, 297; disillusionment as step in, 141, 289; disintegration of old systems of, 201–2, 285–86; Tolstoy's philosophical struggle over, 143–44, 151–56, 158, 163
  treatment in Apuleian *Metamorphoses*, 51, 113, 254, 257, 317n; abandonment of, 105–6; crisis of, 202–16, 236, 252; Lucius' disillusionment with, 161, 180; paradigm shift from "false" to "true," 203–5, 224–26, 236–39, 243, 252–53, 321, 323; retained by Lucius the ass, 119–21
Varieties of Religious Experience, The (James), 140–46
Ventis, W.L., 142, 174–75, 178–82, 232–33, 294

Venus, 313, 319; role in tale of Cupid and Psyche, 253–55, 258, 259, 319
Verwandlung, Die (Kafka), 86
Virgil, 133, 258n.6; *Aeneid*, 62n.13, 111n, 115–16, 262
  portrayal in Dante's *Divine Comedy*, 247n, 263–64, 266, 268–69
Virtue, 31, 88–90, 121, 267
Vision, 253, 254, 288, 311
  in mystical experience, 298–99, 306–7
  of reality, 158–59n, 288, 309
  transformation of in conversion experience, 296–97, 317
Voluptas. See Pleasure

Walsh, P.G., 12
War and Peace (Tolstoy), 150n, 152n, 154n, 158–59n
Weil, Simone, 312n.20
Wicked (Evil) women, Book 10 tales of, 98–102, 113, 130n
  stepmother tale, 49, 98–101, 106, 114–15
Will, role in conversion, 177, 230–31
Winkler, John, 66n, 130n, 134n
  Apuleian criticism, 1–2, 7, 10, 84, 95–96, 138, 222n.17; on Aristomenes' tale, 48n; on the denouement, 133n, 320–21n; on episode of the eunuch priests, 103n; on fish-stomping episode, 75n.23; on inserted tales, 43–44n; on liaison between the ass and the Corinthian matron, 127n.17; on Lucius' skepticism, 52n; on Lucius' transformation, 66; on multivocality, 43, 55n, 137, 228, 229, 326–27; religious reading, 13–14, 261; on statue of Actaeon, 70–71
Witches, 55–56, 62, 63, 82
  role in Aristomenes' tale, 46, 216; role in Thelyphron's tale, 78–79, 81

World view, 28n, 62n.13, 166, 285–86
  in Apuleian *Metamorphoses*, 26–27,
    28n, 47, 62n.13, 317–18; disinte-
    gration of, 72, 74; transformation
    of, 60–71, 312
  for Augustine following conver-
    sion, 301–3
  changes in during psychothera-
    peutic process, 187–88, 192,
    194
  connection between language and,
    307n.17
  of the "healthy-minded" and the
    melancholy, 142, 144–45, 148,
    157–60
  Ovid's, 59
  place in conversion experience,
    166, 186–88, 189n, 323; collapse
    of structures of meaning sur-
    rounding, 50, 139, 251; for James,
    141, 156–57
  postmodern, 138
  religious, 25, 174, 243, 286–99;
    acquisition of, 141, 173–74, 248;
    dualism as framework for, 38,
    144–45; integration of death in,
    287, 293
  Tolstoy's aporetic, 151–52
Wulff, on psychology of religion
  methodology, 140n

Xenophon of Ephesus, 9

Zatchlas scene, 62–63, 217